ENGLAND'S MISTRESS

The Infamous Life of Emma Hamilton

Kate Williams fell in love with the eighteenth century whilst studying for her BA at the University of Oxford. She has an MA from Queen Mary, University of London and a DPhil from the University of Oxford. Her articles and essays have been published in a wide range of books and journals and she has appeared on BBC and Channel 4 programmes to discuss her work. She lives in London. For further information visit her website www.kate-williams.com

Praise for *England's Mistress*

'The first self-made superstar, the first manipulative media celebrity, dazzling Europe with her style and beauty as muse to artists and mistress to Nelson . . . Emma famously gets her comeuppance, and her headlong flight to romantic destruction is told with novelistic dash.'
The Times, Books of the Year

'Of all the rags to riches to rags tales in our island story, Emma Hamilton's is one of the most affecting . . . Sparkling like Emma's pawned diamonds, this biography, drawing on quantities of unmined material, finally makes us understand why Nelson needed to be prised out of Emma's embrace to fight Napoleon, and why Sir William (by no means an old fool) happily accepted his ménage à trois.'
Daily Mail

'Kate Williams has done a wonderful job recreating the life of the woman she wants us to relate to . . . This is an immensely colourful, readable portrait that revels in Emma's resilience and her ability to surmount what look to us now to be unimaginable odds. Williams resists psychological speculation on Emma's motives in order to concentrate on the facts of her life and its context without relinquishing a sense of who Emma was; not an easy trick to pull off.'
Independent on Sunday

'It is the thoroughness of the research and attention to detail that make Kate Williams' new biography of Emma Hamilton so interesting. The iconic Emma has been continuously reimagined since her lover Nelson's death, but Williams offers a new portrait. In dogged archival work, the author discovered letters by Hamilton unused by other biographers; she also got behind the heavily edited Victorian edition of Emma's known letters . . . Refreshingly, Williams avoids the usual prurient treatment of famous women with murky pasts . . . This is a sympathetic portrait: a contemporary take on Emma Hamilton as an ambitious, self-promoting, media-savvy celebrity, who came to life only with male attention and the public spotlight.'
Independent

'In *England's Mistress* [Williams] has created a readable and often surprising portrait of [Hamilton] and the age that created her. In recounting Emma's dramatic life, Kate Williams has done a thorough job in researching and presenting her subject's historical context. She knows what servant girls ate and how they were treated, what political cross-currents swept across Europe in the wake of the French Revolution, how London society behaved in the late 18th century. And she has plumbed the documentary records that exist, from Emma's and Nelson's correspondence (Nelson, unfortunately, burnt most of her letters to him) to Emma's account books . . . *England's Mistress* divertingly and instructively illuminates a time and culture both

far away and intriguingly like our own, and resurrects a woman whose mingled vulnerability and resilience - to say nothing of her glamour - still have the power to fascinate.'
Washington Post, Book World

'Williams illustrates how Emma's beauty - immortalised in paintings and later in fashion magazines - captured the public imagination in much the same way as modern-day style icons . . . Gripping.' *Metro*

'Reworks Emma's life for the Noughties Generation.'
Mail on Sunday

'Enjoyable reading.' *Sunday Times*

'Every intricate detail is laid out, and Kate Williams' writing is so immediate, you feel all but transported back 200 years. From the vivid descriptions of the brothels of St James' to the court of Naples, both of which Emma frequented, the author brings both the places and people to life. Even with her heroine, for whom Williams obviously feels an enormous sympathy, we see the real woman: needy, insecure, beautiful, the eternal reinventor, desperately trying to escape her sordid past but forever a product of it . . . Her story, which opens a window onto all sections of society, deserves far more than today's 15 minutes of fame, and this fascinating book should ensure that.'
Birmingham Post

'The skill of *England's Mistress* rests . . . on the way Williams plays with the resemblance between Hamilton's story and the casualties of our own culture, which increasingly produces and promotes this type of fleeting celebrity.'
Times Literary Supplement

'This rich and bouncy biography of a driven woman - mad for fashion, mad on passion - makes Posh look like a novice.'
Good Housekeeping

KATE WILLIAMS

ENGLAND'S
MISTRESS

arrow books

First published in Great Britain in 2006 by
Hutchinson

Arrow Books
Random House, 20 Vauxhall Bridge Road,
London SW1V 2SA

www.rbooks.co.uk

Addresses for companies within The Random House Group Limited can be found at:
www.randomhouse.co.uk/offices.htm

The Random House Group Limited Reg. No. 954009

A CIP catalogue record for this book
is available from the British Library

ISBN 9780099451839

The Random House Group Limited supports The Forest Stewardship
Council (FSC), the leading international forest certification organisation. All
our titles that are printed on Greenpeace approved FSC certified paper carry
the FSC logo. Our paper procurement policy can be found at:
www.rbooks.co.uk/environment

Typeset in Bembo by Palimpsest Book Production Limited,
Grangemouth, Stirlingshire
Printed in the UK by CPI Bookmarque, Croydon, CR0 4TD

Contents

List of Illustrations

Section 1

Lady Hamilton as Circe by George Romney, c.1782 © Tate, London 2006

Waltzing! Or a Peep into the Royal Brothel, Spring Gardens by I R Cruikshank, c. 1816 © Guildhall / Heritage-Images

Cupid Unfastening the Girdle of Venus by Sir Joshua Reynolds, 1788 © Hermitage, St. Petersburg, Russia/ The Bridgeman Art Library

*Lady H *******'s Attitudes* by Thomas Rowlandson, c.1797 © Copyright The Trustees of The British Museum

The Honourable Charles Greville, William Hayley, George Romney and Emma Hart (in Romney's studio) by George Romney, c.1784 © Copyright The Trustees of The British Museum

Lady Hamilton (as a Bacchante) by Charles Knight after George Romney, 1797 © Copyright The Trustees of The British Museum

Mrs Cadogan (Mother of Emma, Lady Hamilton) by Norsti, c.1800 © Royal Naval Museum

Portrait of the Hon. Charles Francis Greville by George Romney / Private Collection © Christie's Images / The Bridgeman Art Library

The Spinstress: Lady Hamilton at the Spinning Wheel by George Romney, c.1797 © English Heritage Photo Library / Kenwood: Iveagh Bequest

Lady Hamilton as Nature by George Romney, 1782 © Francis G. Mayer / Corbis

A View of the Bay of Naples, Looking Southwest from the Pizzofalcone towards Capo di Posilippo by Giovanni Battista Lusieri, 1791 (watercolour, gouache, graphite, and pen and ink on six sheets of paper)
Size: Unframed: 101.8 x 271.9 cm (40 1/16 x 107 1/16 in.) Framed: 120 x 290.2 x 7.3 cm (47 1/4 x 114 1/4 x 2 7/8 in.) © The J Paul Getty Museum, Los Angeles

Lady Hamilton as Miranda by George Romney, 1785–6 © The Philadelphia Museum of Art / Corbis

Sir William Hamilton by David Allan, 1775 © The National Portrait Gallery, London

Section 2

Emma Hamilton as a Bacchante by Elisabeth Vigée le Brun, c.1790–2 © Lady Lever Art Gallery, National Museums Liverpool

The Attitudes of Lady Hamilton by Pietro Antonio Novelli, date unknown © National Gallery of Art, Washington, Ailsa Mellon Bruce Fund

Emma Hamilton as a Bacchante from *Drawings faithfully copied from Nature at Naples and with permission dedicated to the right honourable Sir William Hamilton* by Tommaso Piroli after Frederick Rehberg, 1794 © National Maritime Museum, London

Emma, Lady Hamilton, Dancing the Tarantella by Mariano Bovi after William Lock, 1796 © Copyright The Trustees of The British Museum

Le Signorine Napoletane; or *Una Casa di Tolleranza nella Napoli del 1945* © Archivio Carbone / Prima Pagina

Lady Hamilton as a Bacchante, after Elisabeth Vigée le Brun by Henry Bone, c.1803 © Wallace Collection, London, UK/ The Bridgeman Art Library

Autograph letter of Lady Hamilton, 1798 © British Library

Tête à Tête: The Consular Artist and the Venus de Medicis published in 1790 by *Town and Country Magazine* © British Library

Detail from *Portrait of the Family of Ferdinand IV* by Angelica Kauffman, 1783 © Museo di Capodimonte, Naples / Scala Archives

Rear Admiral Sir Horatio Nelson by Lemuel Francis Abbott, c.1798 © National Maritime Museum, London / Greenwich Hospital Collection

Admiral Nelson Recreating with his Brave Tars after the Glorious Battle of the Nile by Thomas Rowlandson, c.1800 © National Maritime Museum, London

Frances, Lady Nelson by Henry Edridge, c.1807 © Royal Naval Museum, Portsmouth

A Cognocenti Contemplating ye Beauties of ye Antique (Emma, Lady Hamilton; Horatio Nelson, Viscount Nelson; Sir William Hamilton) by James Gillray, published by Hannah Humphrey, 11 February 1801 © National Portrait Gallery, London

Section 3

A Mansion House Treat; or *Smoking Attitudes!* by I R Cruikshank, 1800 © Copyright The Trustees of The British Museum

Dido, in Despair! (Emma, Lady Hamilton) by James Gillray, published by Hannah Humphrey, 6 February 1801 © National Portrait Gallery, London

Six Patch Boxes & Anchor Necklace © National Maritime Museum, London

Three Gold Vinaigrettes © National Maritime Museum, London

Fan celebrating the Battle of the Nile, 1798 © National Maritime Museum, London

Dresses a la Nile Respectfully Dedicated to the Fashion Mongers of the Day by Anonymous, published by W Holland, 24 October 1798 © National Maritime Museum, London

Baron Nelson of the Nile Ribbon © National Maritime Museum, London

Dress Flounce – Nelson Bronte, c.1799 © National Maritime Museum, London

A Commemorative Silver Pair-cased Verge Pocket Watch with 'Nelson' Movement © Christie's Images Ltd. 2005

A Rare Derby Large Cylindrical Mug Showing 'Britannia' Holding a Picture of Nelson © Sotheby's, London

Merton Place, Surrey © The Nelson Museum, Monmouth

Horatia Nelson after Henry Bone, c.1806 © National Maritime Museum, London

Modern Antiques by Thomas Rowlandson, 1806 © Copyright The Trustees of The British Museum

Silk Picture in a Frame (Embroidery by Emma Hamilton) © National Maritime Museum, London

L'Assemblee Nationale; or *Grand Co-operative Meeting at St Ann's Hill* by James Gillray, published by Hannah Humphrey, 18 June 1804 © Copyright The Trustees of The British Museum

The Death of Admiral Lord Nelson – in the Moment of Victory by James Gillray, published 28 December 1805 © National Maritime Museum, London

Moral Maxims from the Wisdom of Jesus (book) inscribed by Emma Hamilton in 1809 © Sotheby's, London

Lady Hamilton at Prayer by George Romney, c.1782–6 © English Heritage Photo Library / Kenwood: Iveagh Bequest

King's Bench Prison by Thomas Rowlandson, and Augustus Charles Pugin, aquatinted by Joseph Constantine Stadler, published by Rudolph Ackermann on 1 December 1808 © National Portrait Gallery, London

Lady Hamilton as Circe by George Romney, 1782 © The National Trust, Waddesdon, The Rothschild Collection (Rothschild Family Trust) Photographer: Mike Fear

Acknowledgements

I first stumbled upon a letter by Emma Hamilton in the British Library. The discovery quite literally changed my life. I was a graduate student, looking in the archive for letters by women to flesh out my PhD on seduction in the eighteenth century. After weeks of reading dreary, decorous letters by Georgian women, I was about to give up. Then I picked up Emma's letter; I could not believe what I was reading. A torrent of emotion streamed off the page, strikingly naked in its honesty. Emma, it seemed to me, really was writing from the heart. I had to read on.

As I called up more letters, I was surprised by how the woman in the letters differed from that usually portrayed. The edition of letters that was published by Alfred Morrison in 1893–4 has been crucial to scholarship on both Nelson and Emma. But Morrison, I found, had altered and cut many of the letters to please the prurient, conservative values of the period. Reading the letters in the original suggested a very different Emma from the woman we thought we knew. She was far more than some sexual siren or silly woman caught up in politics she did not understand, or a soft-hearted girl who somehow found herself at the top of the tree; Emma was a shrewd, determined woman who let nothing prevent her from attaining her dreams. But she was also driven by a desire for passion – for which she was willing to sacrifice anything.

Little did I know in those early days how far the journey to find Emma would lead me. I have visited every place that she lived in England and overseas, and I followed the route of her journey to Naples in 1786 and back through Vienna and Eastern Europe in 1800, as well as tracing her cruise to Malta. I have been lucky enough to spend much time in the truly inspiring city of Naples and in Sicily. In England, I followed her journey to London in 1777, her visits around the country in 1791 and her Tour with

Nelson in 1802. When I was not in an archive, I was on a train or in a car hunting for Emma.

I have been fortunate enough during my four years of research to find hundreds of new documents in archives across the world. Much of this research would not have been possible without the assistance of the many archivists and librarians upon whom I prevailed. I'm grateful to all the libraries and individuals who have allowed me permission to reproduce quotations from manuscripts in their possession. I thank the following museums and archives: the British Library, the National Maritime Museum, the Royal Maritime Museum, London Metropolitan Archives, the Monmouth Nelson museum and local history centre, the Beinecke Rare Book and Manuscript Library, the Houghton Rare Book and Manuscript Library, the Huntington Library, California, the Victoria and Albert Museum, and record offices across the country.

I am indebted to the collectors of Nelson documents, many of whom prefer to remain anonymous. Clive Richards has been very generous indeed, with both time and hospitality. Anna Tribe, Nelson's great, great, great grand-daughter, kindly accommodated me at her home and showed me her Nelson documents. Many others have helped me in terms of advice and introductions, including David Constantine, Flora Fraser, Claire Harman, Alex Kidson, Tom Pocock, Michael Nash, Nick Slope and Peter Warwick and Colin White, and for other assistance, I'm grateful to Janet Norton and Emma Hayward. Martyn Downer has been my vital support: reading my drafts, passing on introductions and references to documents and always being full of supportive comments. Jennie Batchelor, Sam Gilpin, Emma Jay and Matt Kelly carefully read drafts for me. Most stalwart of all has been James Miller who has read this biography many times, listened to my talks on Emma interminable times and can now spot a Romney at 500 paces.

My agent, John Saddler, has worked tirelessly on my behalf since I first began to work on the book, and I'm indebted to him for his commitment, attention and boundless interest in the book. At Random House, Tess Callaway has patiently guided me through the publishing process, and she, along with Faye Brewster, Mary Chamberlain, Cecília Durães, Kate Elton, Anne Kragelund, Emma Mitchell, Claire Round, Patricia Slattery and Christina Usher have gone way beyond the call of duty. I'm particularly indebted to Gail Rebuck for her kindness and enthusiasm for the book, as well as providing a truly wonderful place to work in Rome. My editor, Paul Sidey, has been my constant support, full of zeal for Emma from the beginning and always ready with friendly words as the project developed. His wisdom and sharp eye for detail have been invaluable. These and many other people helped to make *England's Mistress* possible – thank you all!

I love him, I adore him, my mind and soul is now transported with the thought of that blessed ecstatic moment when I shall see him, embrace him . . .

I must sin on and love him more than ever. It is a crime worth going to Hell for.

Emma Hamilton on Nelson, 1804

Prologue

*M*odel, courtesan, dancer, fashion icon, actress, double agent, political hostess, mother, ambassadress and hero's mistress, Emma Hamilton performed many roles in her astonishing rise from poverty to wealth and fame. None would have greater consequence for her than the part she played in Naples on 22 September 1798. She had joined the welcome party for Rear Admiral Horatio Nelson as his fleet anchored off the Bay of Naples. Nelson had come to protect Naples from the advancing French, and the Neapolitans were determined to give him a welcome fit for a hero. Rehearsals had been going on for weeks, but no one had been practising as carefully as Emma Hamilton. Ravishingly beautiful and still only thirty-three, she knew that Nelson's arrival was her great chance.

Her life would never be the same again.

Five years earlier, on Nelson's first visit to the city, Emma had hardly noticed the unprepossessing naval captain. By 1798, after his amazing success at the Battle of the Nile had made him the one man who seemed able to save Europe from Napoleon, she saw his arrival as an opportunity to propel herself on to a bigger stage. Nelson was exhausted after weeks of fighting the French and in pain from his shot eye and the wound where his right arm had been amputated. As soon as the great man boarded the welcome boat, Emma threw herself upon him, weeping with happiness. To the sounds of cheers and cannon fire resounding across the bay, she gathered Nelson into her arms and, leaving the dumbfounded royal entourage and her husband, Sir William Hamilton, in her wake, supported the triumphant but exhausted hero into the ship's cabin. The man fêted as England's bravest man had collapsed on to the bosom of Europe's female star. Emma Hamilton was already legendary as the girl from nowhere who had catapulted herself into high society. Her consummate piece of stage management on that July day marked the start of her passionate affair with Nelson – and the beginning of her ascent to a level of fame we would find breathtaking, even today.

How did Emma, a girl born into terrible poverty and exploitation reach the position where she was able to seduce and charm England's most famous man? What did she have to do to get there?

If it were fiction, the tale of Emma's life would be dismissed as improbable. Following her takes us through the grand sweeps of eighteenth-century history, to reveal all the glory and horror of her age. To understand how Emma turned herself into the most famous woman of her time, we must go back thirty years and more than a thousand miles, from the glittering Neapolitan court and the duties of an ambassador's wife to her poverty-stricken birth in the slums of north-west England.

I. Battle to Escape

1

Harsh Beginnings

*E*mma Hamilton was born Amy Lyon on Friday 26 April 1765 into squalid poverty. Ness was a ramshackle huddle of thirty or so miners' hovels set in scrubby, stony, infertile land. Moored on the Wirral peninsula in Cheshire, just over twelve miles from Liverpool, the village now gleams with luxurious houses for commuters, but for a girl child in the eighteenth century, it was a one-way ticket to misery. The Stanley family, the owners of the area around Ness, reclined in elegant splendour at nearby Hooton Hall, ignoring the miners and the few fishermen scraping out a miserable living by the bleak shore. Ness was at the forefront of the burgeoning industrial revolution, and Amy was destined for a cruel and meagre life: back-breaking labour by the age of ten, a hard marriage and an early death.

Baby Amy owed her very existence to coal – the black gold of the eighteenth century. For the first half of the century, the factories, sweatshops and businesses in nearby Chester and the surrounding area had been powered by coal shipped in from North Wales along the connecting Dee estuary, but the waterway was silting up and Welsh coal was growing very expensive. When reserves were discovered in 1750 at nearby Denhall, the landscape of Ness changed forever from an area only sparsely populated by fishermen and the odd farmer to a mini Wild West town: teeming with investors and get-rich-quick merchants. After the Stanleys finally opened their mine to huge excitement in the late 1750s, cartloads of brawny young colliers arrived from Lancashire, Staffordshire and North Wales. Others trekked over from Ireland to build a quay for exporting the coal, and labourers came to build the Stanleys' new mansion on the banks of the River Dee. Ness was designated as the

3

village to house them, and quickly built, cheap cottages mushroomed on the stony fields. In this brand new village, much of it still a building site, twenty-one-year-old Mary Kidd arrived in 1764. Since there were five men to every woman in Ness, she was guaranteed to be popular.

Ness's men were hardened by dangerous work. Conditions at the Denhall mine were notoriously poor, and they had to crouch in muddy, icy water and hack at the sides of the flooded tunnels. Mice and cockroaches scampered into their pockets to eat their food, especially if they worked near the areas where the pit ponies were stabled. Once extracted, the coal was loaded into boats roped together in sets of four or five on the underground canals. Miners lay on the boats and 'walked' their feet along the ceilings of the tunnels to push the boats to the bottom of the shaft, where the coal was hoisted up. Men of twenty were bent and crabbed within a few years of beginning work and others were dead: poisoned by pockets of methane gas or killed by rock falls.

Emma's mother had travelled from Hawarden, a small village just outside Chester across the Dee. She was in Ness for a holiday of sorts. William Kidd, Mary's elder brother, had moved to Ness and was working as a miner. Banns were published for his marriage to Mary Foulkes, a Chester girl, in January 1763, and their first son, Samuel, was born in the spring of 1764 and christened on 15 April. In the eighteenth century, every available female relative was roped in to help with a new baby, and so Mary travelled to Ness around the time of Samuel's birth to be an unpaid nursemaid, cleaner and cook to her brother and a sister-in-law she hardly knew. On the ferry across the Dee between Flint, near Hawarden, and Parkgate, and then the walk to her brother's home, Mary was excited, buoyant with holiday spirit. Ness was the first place she had seen other than her dead-end home town – and she was determined to make the most of it. Having escaped her other siblings, dreary cottage and angry, resentful mother, she was intent on enjoying herself.

Mary was slim, lively and fond of fun, and men competed for her attention. She was the new belle of the village (although there was hardly much competition). Frantic to escape Hawarden and the iron grip of her mother, Mary flung herself at Henry Lyon, the blacksmith at the mine. Emma later implied her father was from Lancashire, and he was possibly from Skelmersdale or Ormskirk where his surname is most common in the parish registers. In order to have reached the position of a blacksmith, he would have to have been in his late twenties and so was probably born around 1737. Judging from Emma's stature and appearance, Henry was tall, broad, handsome and dark. To impoverished Mary, he would have appeared impossibly wealthy and independent. Henry's courtship was swift, perhaps rough. By 27 May, perhaps less than two months after Mary's arrival, the banns were published for their wedding.

Emma's parents were married on 11 June 1764 in Great Neston church. As the wedding was held on a Monday, it is unlikely that any relative, even William Kidd or his wife, attended. Like many working men, Henry was illiterate and signed the register with an X, and Mary also signed with a cross. Henry probably had to return to the smithy soon after the ceremony. Even though working-class weddings were low-key affairs, Mary's seems hurried. Most women were married in their late twenties – the average age was twenty-six – after their fiancés had set aside sufficient money to set up a home. Mary, however, was unusually young. Pregnancy may have made marriage a necessity.

First babies were often conceived outside of wedlock and, indeed, many communities encouraged it to preclude the disaster of marriage to an infertile wife. As there is no birth certificate, we must assume that Emma claimed her birthday on the day her mother told her to do so. Henry and Mary were not religious and there is no reason why Emma should have been any different from most of the first children born in Ness. Emma's fondness for celebrating a birthday on 26 April and stressing 1765 as the year of her birth suggests she was concerned to emphasise her legitimacy. Only Mary and her brother William knew the actual date of Emma's birth, but the possibility that Mary's pregnancy had forced the marriage might explain the couple's unhappiness. Mary came to Ness looking for a life more exciting than the one that she left behind, only to find herself trapped in poverty and despair in a part of England far harsher than Hawarden.

Mary's new home was a miner's cottage near the road to Denhall, rented from the mine authorities. A low-built house, connected to two others, it was one of hundreds of similar workers' cottages in the area. Sandstone steps skittered up to the low door. Now it is a pretty cottage and the subsidence gives it a picturesque appeal; but then it was a rackety, dirty, cramped place to live. At twenty-one, Mary was a drudge in a dirty hovel, her day consumed by domestic chores, in a village populated by people who were in the 1850s, according to visitors, 'as primitive as their village was secluded'.[1] At four, she awoke to fetch water, light the fire and prepare Henry's breakfast. After he left at five, she began her daily battle against the dirt that silted up the windows and covered every surface with a grimy film. Outside her window lay a treeless expanse of scrub scarred by heaps of coal waste and cheap stone cottages blackened by sooty rain. She knew that soon after she gave birth, she would be expected to work in the mine with the other women. There was little to look forward to and not much to enjoy. Henry returned in the late afternoon, exhausted by a day of labouring in hot and dangerous conditions, and like most men in Ness, he drank and probably beat his wife.

Birth for the poor was painful. Helped only by neighbours, women drank gin to dull the pain or pulled on a knotted rag. Mary called the child Amy, her sister's name and a Kidd family favourite. Perhaps Henry was not particularly interested in his daughter's name. Many communities held a form of party for new mothers, twenty-eight days after the birth, a version of the older 'churching' ceremony, which was an attempt to combat post-natal depression and to celebrate the mother's survival, but it appears that Mary had no such party. No relations came to assist her and, because there were so few women in the village, she had little companionship. Lonely and overwhelmed, the young Mrs Lyon struggled not to vent her frustration on the child. She might have had a closer immediate bond to a son, but Amy was a burden and a seemingly inescapable tie to Ness. Mary's life stretched out drearily before her: a monotony of children, domestic labour and poverty.

Emma was baptised on 12 May. On the register, her name looks like 'Emy', but Emma herself always claimed it was Amy, a common name in the Kidd family. It is likely that the registrar simply misspelt it: parents were at the mercy of the registrar's choice of orthography, particularly if, like Henry and Mary, they could not read. One in three children like Emma died within infancy, but she was born in the best season for survival: disease was more virulent from June to September and babies died of cold from November to February. There was hard work ahead for the infants who lived. Denhall employed most children over nine or ten as cheap labour. All the girls born in Ness were, by the age of ten, pulling baskets to the surface every day, covered in dirt and regularly harassed by the men. At the end of the day, they returned to home to cook and clean for their family.

The grim cycle of Emma's life seemed preordained. But then – suddenly – two months after her baptism, Henry died. By 21 June 1765 he was buried. Mary and Emma were free.

Emma never discussed her father, and her mother did not disclose any details. Research into death in the eighteenth century gives us some clues about the cause of Henry's demise and his daughter's refusal to discuss him. Emma and her mother might have been covering a scandal.

Men who worked in or near a mine had a short life expectancy but their deaths from respiratory diseases were lengthy and painfully protracted. If Henry had been tubercular, he would no longer have been working. He would have been visibly sick and Mary would have been unlikely to marry him. There are no records of any pit disasters or smallpox epidemics in the summer of 1765. No cause of death is recorded and in the yard of Great Neston church, there is no marker for his grave. Mary did not receive a pension or payout from the mine, which was usually awarded if the employee died on site. She had no contact with her husband's family following Henry's death. Instead, she fled back to Hawarden. If she had expected a pension, or if there had been help forthcoming from the local community, she would have stayed.

Only Mary knew the whole truth about what happened on that hot night in June. It is very likely that alcohol was involved. Alcohol killed more men than tuberculosis or smallpox, and caused most accidental deaths. The gin sold in Ness was much cheaper and stronger than what we drink today and a few pennies bought immediate oblivion. Nowadays, the majority of deaths from alcohol or other substance abuse occur in the first half of the month, after people have received their pay. Over two hundred and fifty years ago, Henry was probably following a familiar pattern: he received his wages and drank them away.

It is possible that Henry killed himself in a fit of drunken despair. If he had simply knocked himself out on the way home from the pub or fought with another man, Mary would have had less reason to flee in shame. Nowadays, suicides peak in the months of May and early June, and it is unlikely the eighteenth century was different, although suicide was hardly ever recorded as the cause of death. Many more men committed suicide than women (and the women who did so were generally driven to it by extreme poverty or unwanted pregnancy). Ness was an alienating place, Henry's job was exhausting, life with his wife was difficult, and the sleepless nights with a new baby perhaps tipped him over the edge. Suicide was common, but it was considered a disgrace and a sin, and unless the local rector was particularly sympathetic, Henry would have been denied a funeral and a grave in the churchyard, incentive enough for Mary and Emma never to mention him.

Alternatively, Henry's death may have been the consequence of an argument. Exhausted and irritable after a day with the baby, Mary may have begun a bitter argument when her husband strolled in, squandered wages reeking on his breath. After a struggle, Henry might have fallen so violently that he died. There was no local police force or constable, so the law in Ness depended on the justice of the peace, presumably Lord Stanley at Hooton Hall. As the local landowner, he would have been most interested in protecting his property. In the eighteenth century, justice was dominated by the propertied classes, and an offence as trivial as stealing a handkerchief was punishable by hanging. Men like Stanley dismissed fights between poor workers as the feuds of the lower classes. Death from a drunken fall was common enough and, without the medical science that exists today, the exact cause of death would have been impossible to determine.

Henry's death was one of the greatest mysteries in Emma's life. It seems most likely that he and Mary fought, but we will never know the truth about whether the cause of death was accident, suicide, ill-health or murder. Whatever the reason, the consequence was the same: Mary was a widow and Emma was fatherless. At the time, eighty per cent of those accused of witchcraft were older women or widows. No longer controlled by their fathers and without husbands, they were objects of intense suspicion and hatred. A widow at twenty-two, Mrs Lyon was not going to be popular.

Mary was a determined girl but within fifteen years she was working for free as Emma's housekeeper. She remained submissive to her daughter's every desire until she died. Her devotion was self-sacrificing by any standard, but particularly when most children made their own way through life, and moreover mother and daughter were very distant in Emma's childhood and teenage years. Perhaps Mary's willingness to cater to Emma's every need and whim, like a servant rather than a mother, stemmed from guilt. In the eighteenth century, widows habitually bolstered their shaky respectability by wearing black dresses and veils, weeping over lockets of their spouse and persistently recalling the days of their marriage in conversation, but nobody reports that Mary ever mentioned her husband. Emma never spoke of her father and when she holidayed near Ness she did not visit. Once she was Lady Hamilton, Emma was praised for her reluctance to sponsor stories that she was the secret daughter of the gentry. But perhaps she knew it would be foolish to talk too much about her father, in case it reminded a few old miners about an unexplained death in June and a flighty wife who ran away.

In later years, Mary's brother William repeatedly demanded money from Emma and her mother. He always received it, perhaps because he threatened to tell scandal-mongering journalists the truth about Henry's death.

Emma never returned to Ness but its legacy remained. She inherited her mother's impetuousness and her father's forceful personality. The poor daughter of a young bride whose husband had died in shady circumstances, little Amy Lyon was in the same class as thousands of other children who grew up to supply England with its beggars, criminals and prostitutes.

2

Liquor and Honey

*L*ittle Amy had to toughen up quickly. In her new home, money was sparse and the struggling Kidds resented Mary. Sarah Kidd took pity on her little granddaughter, seemingly so unlucky from birth, but few others did so. Emma always identified herself as a girl from the north of England, despite the fact that she had hardly lived there. Her twelve years in Hawarden was a period she tried hard to forget.

Hawarden (pronounced Harden) is now a prosperous village seven miles west of Chester, with a church, a family pub and a post office. In the 1760s, however, the area was among the country's most impoverished. Hawarden served the estate and mine of Broad Lane Hall (now called Hawarden Castle), owned by Sir John Glynne, whose father had inherited Hawarden in 1721. About 3,500 villagers lived in stone cottages and mud hovels crammed around a dirt road about half a mile long. A church, a few shops, three or so public houses and a makeshift gaol or village lock-up constituted their services. Sir John Glynne employed most villagers in his mine, dairy, fields and farm or took on the lucky ones as house servants. The others scrabbled out a living as hired labour.

Britain was gripped by an agricultural depression caused by the industrialisation of farm practices (reducing the need for workers) and a series of poor harvests in the 1750s. As the country became more dependent on grain imports, prices soared. It was impossible – as many commentators showed in careful sums – for even a skilled labourer to feed and clothe himself, a wife and two children, and most men had at least four children. Families ran up debts they could never repay. The press whipped up hysteria about the spiralling cost of wheat, investors put their money into anything but land or farming, and the poor went hungry. Young men escaped to the mines or joined the army, leaving villages like Hawarden inhabited by the unemployable, the sick and women struggling to subsist. Households without a man in employment were the most destitute. Languishing at the bottom of the rural economy, Emma's new family had no food or money to spare and little room in their ramshackle cottage for a disruptive newborn baby and her wild-eyed mother.

Accounts of Emma's background have been promoted that the surviving records reveal as quite wrong. Most far-fetched of all is the notion that Henry Lyon gave up his life as an aristocrat to marry Mary. No member of the gentry would have worked as a smith or signed his marriage certificate with an 'X', the mark of an illiterate. The Kidds have also been misrepresented: Emma's mother was not seventeen when she gave birth but twenty-two. Her grandfather was not a drunken shepherd but a collier, and he was dead by the time Mary left for Ness. The family was poor because Sarah was widowed, not because her husband was feckless.

The parish registers in the period give an impression of Hawarden as a close-knit society: the same surnames and even first names recur. But Emma's grandparents, Thomas and Mary (later Sarah) Kidd, were outsiders. The first Kidds in the registers, they arrived in the nearby village of Shotton, part of Hawarden parish, at some point before 1743. The family came from another part of England – perhaps the area around Manchester where the surname Kidd is common – and Thomas began work in one of the area's many mines. They already had at least one child, William, and a girl who died in 1745. Twenty-eight-year-old Sarah gave birth to a succession of children in Shotton, and then Ewloe, where they moved in about 1746.* Mary was born in late 1742 or early 1743 and christened in 1743. She soon became stand-in mother to Anne, Sarah, Amy, Thomas and John, two, six, eight, eleven and fourteen years her junior respectively. Some of them learned the basics of reading and writing, perhaps at a church school in Shotton. William Kidd could sign his name, although Anne and Mary signed with an 'X'. Men (and sometimes women) who could sign their names were called upon to witness weddings, and Thomas junior did so in 1780.

---

* Mary was christened on 19 May 1743, Anne followed in 1745, and a girl, Amy, was christened in 1748, but she died soon after and was buried in the same year. Sarah was christened in 1749; Thomas was baptised in 1750 and died soon after. Amy was christened in 1751, Thomas in 1754, and John in 1757.

All those who met the adult Emma remarked on her strong Lancashire accent. Although she had lived near Chester since she was a baby, she did not have a Chester accent. It was an age when rural accents and dialects were almost incomprehensible to outsiders, but Emma's speech was seemingly untouched by the place in which she grew up. Her anomalous speech suggests that her family was not native to the area but originally from northern England and that she had little contact with the villagers around her.

By 1771, Hawarden had become more salubrious. A travelling journalist, Nathaniel Spencer, declared it:

> a very considerable village, situated on the road leading to Chester, near the river Dee, and has still the ruins of a strong castle, although it does not appear by whom it was built. The village has some good inns, with three annual fairs, viz on the eighth of May, the first of October, and the twenty-fourth of December, all for cattle. The air of this county is very cold, but it is also healthy. There are lots of sheep on the mountains and the black cattle are fed in the valleys. There are great crops of rye, oats and barley, and although they have not much wheat, yet it is esteemed exceedingly good . . . They prepare a sort of liquor from honey, called Metheglin, which was used by the ancient Britons.[2]

The Kidd family moved to Hawarden from Ewloe sometime in the 1750s, presumably because Thomas had work in John Glynne's mine. No doubt they soon became very fond of metheglin. Their cottage, now demolished, stood on the main road, near the church and the Fox and Grapes pub. When her husband died in 1761, marked in the register as 'collier', forty-six-year-old Sarah had to support her family. William was sent to work in Ness, Mary followed to assist with his baby in 1764, and the rest had to find the money to live. By the time Mary returned, Thomas junior may have been working as a shepherd, guarding his neighbours' sheep on Saltney Marshes. But even his peppercorn salary was under threat. Glynne, like every landowner, was keen to fence off common land for his own use. Thanks to his efforts, fewer villagers bought sheep every year.

The family depended on the little money Sarah Kidd earned from toiling as the village carter. Three or four times a week, she drove a cart to Chester carrying coal, agricultural produce and sometimes people. She probably stabled her horses at the Fox and Grapes. Chester had two markets a week, on Wednesdays and Saturdays, and fairs in February, July and October. Chester was a wealthy city, with a population of about 20,000, complete with a handsome Theatre Royal and elegant assembly rooms for balls and parties. Any traveller wishing to enjoy such graceful bourgeois charms had to battle terrible roads. Robbers and highwaymen so menaced the routes into Chester that the frequency of attacks was a subject of national concern. The roads were also treacherously pitted, and Sir John Glynne devoted himself at Parliament to agitating for their improvement. Armed with a whip and perhaps a gun, Sarah regularly dragged elderly horses over the mud in the pouring rain and returned to argue with the customers who refused to pay for their orders. In her mid-forties, she must have cherished hopes of working less. The sudden arrival of Mary and Amy quashed such plans.

The Kidds hardly had the money for candles, boots or clothes. Sarah was disappointed in Mary for burdening them with yet another hungry mouth. Even if Henry Lyon had died of natural causes, there would have been gossip about the demise of a man so soon after marriage. News travelled fast across the Dee, and if the Hawarden villagers picked up rumours that his death had been suspicious, they would have ostracised Emma and her mother. Emma claimed that her grandmother brought her up but Sarah had a full-time job and a large family. It is more likely Emma was farmed out to neighbours and a cheap wet-nurse, then later bundled in the back of Sarah's cart and quieted with sugared milk and a little gin. The aristocrats Emma later charmed were raised by armies of nannies, governesses and tutors, but she had no one to stimulate her senses, structure her play, or teach her reading or sewing, and there was no institution to educate her. Fatherless children were usually the targets of bullies, and Emma probably struggled to make friends. She grew up hungry to be the centre of attention.

Parents often control their children by telling them to behave or not behave like someone they know. 'You'll turn out like your mother' rang in Emma's ears throughout her childhood. A daughter in Mary's position had to be a patient servant and accept insult, for many families would not allow a widow to return. Emma would have seen the Kidds and their neighbours humiliate and disparage her mother, and it would have been difficult for her not to align herself with them against Mary.

William Kidd left Ness for Hawarden not long after his troubled sister and niece. Never one to take responsibility for his actions, he probably claimed that gossip about Mary had driven him away. Initially, he and his one-year-old son, Samuel, crammed into the cottage, along with Mary and her baby and the other Kidd children, Anne, Sarah, Amy, Thomas and John. William's first wife had died – possibly giving birth to another baby – and he married a Mary Pova in Hawarden in 1769, giving his profession as labourer. He had a daughter in the same year, and then Mary in 1771 and Thomas in 1773. Anne married one Richard Reynold in 1774. Until William and then Anne moved out, the house was full to bursting. It is possible that Sarah had to look after William's children after he married. Perhaps remembering the strain, the adult Emma kept in touch with some of her aunts' families but tried to avoid most of her other relations, particularly feckless William.

Full names were only infrequently used, as children were often called nicknames or a combination of their own and their father's names, as in Sarah o' John. Amy o' Lyon could soon become 'Emily', the name that she seems to have used as a young adult. From the very first, she was made aware that she was a Lyon in a family of Kidds.

3

Growing up Poor

*E*mma later claimed that she had lived in 'very rough lodgings' in her youth. She was right: her home in Hawarden was a country slum, just like the hundreds of thousands that dotted Britain's struggling rural districts. Constructed from bricks made of mud mixed with straw, her new house was covered in damp thatch. Like the other cottages, it would have comprised two rooms, a living room and kitchen and a sleeping room. Windows were stuffed with rags or closed with cheap shutters. Sarah Kidd had no time to beautify the house, and they relied on the few bits of furniture her husband had made them years before: a few wooden chairs, a table and a couple of trunks.

In the sleeping room, Emma and her mother shared a bed, or possibly a straw pallet on the floor. Mary found herself back where she slept as a child and a teenager, listening to the spluttering coughs and sniffs of her siblings.

The men breakfasted at four in summer and five in winter. Sarah and Mary were up half an hour or so before to fetch water for cooking, supplementing the rainwater they gathered in a barrel. Men's work began and ended at set hours and gave them time for leisure. Women's chores were never finished. At least twice a day, Sarah or Mary walked through the rain or cold to stand in the long queue at the pump. If it was functioning, they worked the stiff handle until there was a gallon or so in the bucket and then carried it back. They also had to find fuel for the fire. Sarah probably did not risk pocketing more than a few pieces of coal from the sacks she carried to Chester for if her neighbours spotted a different type of smoke from the chimney, they could report her. Wood was not an option, for Glynne and other landowners

owned the surrounding forests. Most poor families used gorse, sticks or
furze, but Sarah had no time to scour the hills. Luckily, however, she
had privileged access to one of the most efficient domestic fuels: horse
dung. Sarah, like most carters, would have collected the hods of manure
in a bucket, mixed them with pieces of straw, kneaded them into lumps
and left them in the sun to dry (or inside if the weather was stormy)
before storing them in a bucket by the fire. The Kidd cottage was filled
with horse dung in various stages of assemblage and the hods released
an acrid meaty smell as they burned. As it was necessary for heat, light,
cooking, water heating and rubbish disposal, the fire would be continually lit when the family was awake. Emma grew up in a house so
dependent on dung that her clothes, hair and even skin carried the
stench of manure.

In the eighteenth century, a house was considered hygienic if there
were no lice or insects visible in its eating and sleeping areas. People
washed their bodies infrequently and then usually only in the milder
summer months. Even the genteel rarely bathed more than their faces
and hands. There was no toilet, and new-fangled inventions like piped
water were a novelty for the adventurous urban rich. At night, the
family used an indoor chamber pot, usually kept in the kitchen area
(which it was Mary's task, as the family's domestic worker, to empty).
Otherwise, they may have used a rudimentary privy – a hole in a
wooden bench over the ground shared between three or four houses
– or relieved themselves behind hedges or in fields. They ate and drank
off wooden trenchers and basins and it was the woman's job to wash
the dirty dishes with grit in the local stream, along with the family's
clothes and linen. As the stream was the main place for bathing, and
an occasional toilet for the village, as well as the animals grazing upstream,
typhoid and diphtheria were rampant, inevitably killing the weakest
children.

Everything Emma ate was cold or boiled. Meat, potatoes and even
puddings were dropped into a smoky iron pot suspended over the fire.
Her staple diet consisted of bread, lard and potatoes (which were cheaper
than bread), eked out with the water in which meat had been cooked,
and varied with a little oatcake or porridge. When the family felt rich
she might enjoy a breakfast of oat bread and Cheshire cheese, bacon
and potatoes for lunch, and a Sunday meal of beef and stewing vegetables followed by a dumpling or boiled roly-poly pudding. Ovens were
the preserves of the wealthy, and the Kidds could not afford to pay the
baker the few pennies he charged to cook pies or meat. In times of

real hardship, every meal might be cold potatoes and dripping and some country families sank to eating horse bran or even straw. Rural poverty was so terrible that young people ran away to the city, hoping to find more food by foraging in the busy alleyways or in the piles of waste from the great houses. The only way to supplement a diet was to grow vegetables or rear a pig. In the days before freezers, it was customary to retain about half the meat and share out the rest among the neighbours, who would do the same in return when they killed their animal. But the Kidds were too chaotic to rear a pig.

Although Sarah was the earner, meat would be given first to the men and then the boys. As the most expendable member of the family, the youngest girl was last in line for food. As hostilities with Spain and America increased the price of wheat, Emma, like thousands of little girls across Britain, would have felt the pinch. One third of girls died by the age of five, and the more siblings a young girl had, the more likely she was to die. Malnourished from childhood, only one in seven girls who survived until five reached twenty-five, and these rates were worse in poor villages. If Emma had playmates, they probably changed from summer to summer as the other girls weakened and died.

Emma was not the dying kind. Her spirit was irrepressible. In a rare reference to her childhood later in life she described herself as 'wild and thoughtless' as a little girl. She was so incompetent as a servant that it seems unlikely that she grew up habituated to domestic work. The dilapidated, insecure life of the Kidds left Emma comparatively unburdened by hours of cleaning, carrying, washing and cooking, free to dream of a different life.

There is an apocryphal tale of the young Emma, at about the age of nine or ten, selling coal by the side of the Chester road. It would have been very dangerous if she had done so. Any woman standing beside the road – particularly a young one – would be considered a prostitute. Women sold their goods at market or in the village and never walked alone. Moreover, Sarah was not authorised to sell coal, only deliver it to middlemen. If the story is true, Emma had stolen the coal and was endangering herself. It is more likely that she simply liked to stand by the road in the village to watch the glamorous coaches calling at Broad Lane Hall. Hardly old enough to go out alone, she was already intent on escape.

The only highlights in her year were the three annual fairs. After the morning sale of livestock, the fields were taken over by stalls selling trinkets, posies, wine and gingerbread for a few pennies, as well as puppet plays, musicians and performers of all kinds. Every feast ended in dancing and drinking and many young couples crept behind hedges (the records show most women fell pregnant on a holiday). There was a week of celebration for St. Deniol's Day, the Saint's day of the local church. The May Fair crowned a queen, who was carried around the village in a cart decorated with ribbons, and a different girl was adorned with corn dollies and chosen to be Harvest Queen.

Festivals and fairs were scant consolation for Mary, miserable at being seemingly stuck in Hawarden for good. Her neighbours relished the opportunity to gloat, and the young widow was lonely. She was pretty but no young man wanted a wife without a dowry who was the subject of salacious gossip and saddled with a child. Despite this, circumstances suggest Mary found a protector – and a powerful one.

Stories abound that Mary was mistress to Sir John Glynne or even grand Lord Halifax at nearby Stansted Hall. This is romantic fiction: Halifax would never have pursued a long affair with such a low-born woman. Although Mary might have caught John Glynne's eye in between the death of his first wife in 1769 and his marriage to his daughters' governess in 1772, it seems unlikely. The records show that Glynne attended Parliament less punctiliously after 1764, even though he had previously been conscientious about showing his face and volunteering for committees. He was flirting with the governess, not Mary. Notions that Mary was a mistress to Glynne betray a misunderstanding of rural life: the squire and his sons spent summers hosting hunting parties and passed their winters in town. They ignored their tenants, and Mary could not have met Sir John unless she worked as an upper servant for him (and she was never a lady's maid). As we may see from Sir John's letters and diaries now in the Hawarden record office and the National Library of Wales, he paid scant attention to the dull minutiae of land rents, yields and the wages of footmen.[3] In Hawarden, the real controllers of patronage, favour and money were the squire's steward or land agent, who managed Glynne's estate, his workers and also the servants at the hall. If Mary was having an affair with a wealthy man, it was most likely with a senior servant at Broad Lane Hall or assistant steward of Glynne's estate, who would have slipped her extra food and money.

Mary was surely lover to a man with money for a sustained period of time, perhaps throughout Emma's childhood. It is unlikely that Emma survived on the potatoes and old cheese that made up the diet of her neighbours. Like all country people, Hawarden villagers were stunted and sunken-eyed through malnutrition. They suffered from rickets, and their hair, teeth and skin betrayed their lack of protein. Emma grew tall, strong and beautiful with a thick mane of hair and strong white teeth. She had sparkling eyes, clear skin, voluptuous good health and bounding energy. In the late 1760s and 1770s, England was wracked with famines, a smallpox epidemic, and sweeping influenza, but Emma appears to have suffered no severe childhood illnesses. Thomas Pettigrew, one of Lord Nelson's early biographers, who knew Emma's London employer, Dr Budd, noted that when she worked as a servant she had no 'means to cultivate her intellectual faculties', so she must have learned to read, write and do simple addition as a child. Somehow, Mary found money that protected Emma from the worst of village hardship and helped her grow into a beauty.

It seems likely that Mary's lover was connected to Broad Lane Hall. Emma's fortunes appear to have been in some degree dependent on Glynne's. Soon after Sir John's death on 1 June 1777, her childhood came to an abrupt end. Mary travelled to London, maybe to follow her lover, and Sarah, at nearly sixty, decided to rid herself of her hungry granddaughter. Emma began work for Dr Honoratus Leigh Thomas, a Chester surgeon. He lived in Hawarden because his much younger wife, Marie, was sister to Glynne's land agent, Boydell. Her choice of employers is a clue that Mary's protector may have been an assistant to Boydell who perhaps lost his position on his master's death. However she came by the position, Emma was now on her own. She was, after all, twelve, the average age for girls to begin in service.

Emma's poverty-stricken youth left her desperate for love, dogged by terrible insecurity and determined to steal the limelight. Resentful of her treatment and dissatisfied with Hawarden, she so dreaded the future of a labourer's wife that she would do anything to escape. Emma was ambitious and she craved sensation. She was not the type of girl to become a meek and deferential domestic servant.

4

Scrubbing the Stairs

Twelve years old and already beautiful, Emma began work for Dr and Mrs Thomas. With her mother in London and her grandmother's interest in her at an end, Emma might have felt sufficiently worried to devote herself to work. Instead, she hated her new job and tried her hardest to fail.

As a maid of all work, Emma was at the very bottom of a household of seven or so servants. Forty-eight-year-old Dr Thomas was an important man: he had had the honour of witnessing Glynne's marriage to his children's governess, Augusta, in 1772.⁴ Emma's contact with such a distinguished family would have been minimal: her orders came from the cook and the housemaids. As an adult, she romanticised her early life by claiming that she was a nursemaid, and biographers have continued to perpetrate the myth, but there was no such division of labour in the lower ranks of an eighteenth-century household. Moreover, the parish registers show that there were no babies in the house: Josiah Thomas was born in 1773, and no more children appeared until Sophia in 1780, after Emma had left. Like many thousands of girls across Britain between the ages of about eleven and sixteen, Emma was an unpaid child labourer carrying out the most physically demanding work in the household. Since female servants under sixteen were unsalaried and paid only with bed and board, families employed as many young maids as possible to cut costs. By the age of twenty-one, most had fallen ill from the round of heavy manual labour, become pregnant, married, or turned to prostitution. A tax had been introduced on male servants in 1767 and so in all but the richest families, girls like Emma took on the jobs that we would consider the preserve of men: hauling coal, moving furniture, carrying and splitting firewood and caring for the family's pigs.

When the twelve-year-old Emma was not carrying fuel, she was scrubbing or fetching water. The newest servant was given the most detested tasks such as scouring pans, dealing with the slops and cleaning the chamber pots. Having grown up with the Kidds, anything else was probably beyond her. As one mistress complained, young girls could wash up, carry buckets and scour floors but were incapable of dusting or washing delicate clothes and tea things, and they were hopeless at ironing. Most mistresses gave their servants negligible training because they expected to lose them within a year and Mrs Thomas was probably no different. She probably resented having to employ a wild, untrained young girl as a favour to her brother.

Emma's bed would have been a few blankets and a pillow in a cupboard or shared room, but most probably on the landing or kitchen floor, where she was vulnerable to the attentions of other servants, visitors or family members. Servants were expected to sleep wherever they could, even with the family pigs or in the coal-hole. Junior servants tended to curl up by the hearth, partly for warmth and also because their job was to stoke the fires in the morning. Wherever she slept, Emma would have been up before dawn. As there was probably no running water (even if there was, it would be cold, restricted to the scullery and available only for a few hours a day), her first job was to fetch water at the pump and heat it for washing and cooking. Within a few months, the hands of most young maids were scarred with burns, and the most common cause of death for eighteenth-century girls was burns or scalds. Emma would have broken for her main meal at around eleven, eaten supper at four or five, and spent her evenings scraping the pots or perhaps carrying out basic mending.

Keeping a house clean was an enormous undertaking. Families like the Thomases burned over a ton of coal every six weeks and the walls, floors, ceilings and furniture needed regular scrubbing to remove the black dust. It could take a whole day to clean a room properly. The open range in the kitchen needed scouring daily, and one of Emma's least pleasant tasks would have been scraping off its grease and grime. The chimney needed to be swept as far as she could reach twice a week. Laundry consumed three or four days every fortnight. City maids commonly emptied commodes down the sides of buildings, but a country maid had to carry the chamber pot down the steep back stairs and throw the contents into the garden.

There was an impassable gulf between the upper and lower servants. Ladies' maids and companions were middle-class girls who could embroider, write neatly, play music and often speak French. A very hard-working and lucky maid of all work in a miserly family might possibly be trained as a cook but the others could look forward only to a future of the most tedious domestic labour. Worst of all, like all girls in her position, Emma had to feign servility and respectful admiration for her employers. One author of a manual for servants declared that since a maid's life was 'one continued round of activity', 'no girl ought to undertake, or can be qualified for such a situation, who had not been thus bred up'. A servant should be from a 'sober, well disposed family' and 'of a tractable disposition'.[5] Emma was nothing of the kind.

Masters saw their young servants as easy prey. Since most, like Emma, spent much of their day cleaning isolated rooms alone, they were easy to trap and grope. At night, there was even more opportunity for they slept in unlocked rooms or on the floor. The master usually beat the servants (women were not legally permitted to punish them), and often backed up his physical violence with harassment – thinking it a good way to keep the girls in check. Despite the harsh treatment meted out to them, girls often fell in love with their masters. The best-selling novel of the age was Samuel Richardson's *Pamela* in which a pretty, clever servant resisted her master's advances and then charmed him into marrying her. Bored and overworked, servants longed to be the fine lady wife, or even the kept mistress living in luxury. However, it tended to be only the elderly widowers who married their staff. The typical eighteenth-century man simply seduced his servants and fired them when he was bored of them.

Emma had been working for the Thomas family for only a few months before she found herself unemployed again. Mrs Thomas probably dismissed her, no doubt weary of the inefficient, untidy, party-mad twelve-year-old she had taken on as a favour.[6] Although Emma was aggrieved to be dismissed, her head was stuffed with romantic dreams and she was, as she later said, 'wild and thoughtless when a little girl'. She wanted to move to a place where she could be a new person: free from the stigma of the scandal of her parents' marriage, her father's strange death and the disgrace of being a Kidd. As the *Carlton House Magazine* noted, 'What lass, in the rural village, that hears the name of London, but wishes to be there?'[7] In the autumn of 1777, Emma joined the hundreds of girls from across the country heading to London each year to seek money and sensation.

5

Travelling to London

*E*mma's journey to London by coach would have been the most daunting experience of her young life. She left no record of her feelings about it, so we can only piece together her experiences from the reports of other coach travellers of the time. Wearing her best dress to save it from thieves, carrying a few belongings and some cheese and bread, she set off early in the morning for an inn on the outskirts of Chester. Unable to afford the stagecoach, she probably took the stage wagon, a goods vehicle that took poorer passengers. Parked at the back of the yard, behind the crowds of hawkers, passengers and beggars, the stage wagon was a twelve-foot-long frame over four thick wooden wheels, covered only by a torn, dirty sheet. It would be pulled along the 180-mile journey south to London by six or eight horses in pairs. Old and worn out from years of dragging other carriages, they were less than half a year away from the slaughterhouse.

Twenty or so women, children and elderly men (younger men travelled on horseback) bundled themselves into the wagon around bags of vegetables and crates of chickens. Children took the most uncomfortable spots over the wheels or at the very back. Then they had to hold tight to their money. A passenger couldn't pay until he or she left the wagon and anyone who failed to cough up would be arrested. Emma's journey cost around six shillings, with extra money needed for food and lodging along the way – over two months of Sarah's wages. If Mary had not been mistress to a man of means, Emma would have been unable to afford the fare.

The journey from Chester to London usually took just over five days, but could last seven, or even nine, depending on the traffic, the state of the roads, and the frequency of stops. Travelling south through Nantwich to Lichfield, then Birmingham and Northampton, the passengers were usually too uncomfortable to marvel at the unfamiliar towns. Battered by the wind and the rain, they felt every clatter as the wagon bumped over unkempt, pitted roads littered with rubbish and the detritus of broken carts, the wheels splashing into the deep streams of mud. Post-chaises swept past (so fast that their horses had a life span of only two years) at about ten miles per hour and aristocratic carriages overtook as swiftly as their coachmen could whip. The horses drawing Emma's wagon would never move faster than a walk. On many journeys a horse collapsed and the passengers had to wait while the carter hunted for another. Every time the wagon halted to load and unload goods, the travellers had to disembark, sometimes for hours, passing time perhaps by swapping tales about drunken carters and robbers, before battling for a place back on board.

At night, the wagon stopped and the passengers slept where they had been sitting all day. If they were lucky, a landlord at an inn might, for the price of six- or ninepence, give them a supper of cold boiled beef and bread in the kitchen followed by a bed in the straw of the stables. Hardened travelling salesmen, soldiers and sailors stalked the inns on the lookout for easy prey and many girls never reached their destination.

The town of Barnet was the main coaching centre for passengers arriving in London from the north. Like any eighteenth-century coaching inn, the courtyard under the rooms was covered by a large wooden roof (the only remaining example is the George, on London's Borough High Street). Passengers had to leave their original wagon and push through crowds of sightseers, prostitutes touting for clients, horse-keepers, waiters, and hawkers selling cheap ribbons, papers, jewels and pencils, to find a cart to take them into the city. To country ears, like Emma's, the London accent sounded entirely unfamiliar.

Finally crammed into a coach bound for the city, they joined the long queues waiting for hours to enter the Great North Road. Sometimes up to one hundred and thirty a day rattled through the gate, along with horses, wagons and herds of cows and sheep from as far away as Wales. Emma's wagon would have taken the route through Finchley Common, seven miles of thick undergrowth colonised by robbers. Not long before her arrival, eleven carriages were ransacked there in a single night. One unfortunate man was even mugged on his way into London and accosted by the same highwayman on the way out. Closer to the city, market gardens and nurseries flourished. In glasshouses, exotic fruits such as melons and pears grew under human manure brought every morning from the town by the night-soil men. Nearby were the holes in the ground where the bodies of the poor were thrown. The hogs destined to become London's bacon roamed freely, and smoking kilns towered over the piles of warm bricks, under which the workers ate their food and slept.

Further along the Great North Road lay the rural villages of Highgate and Islington, home to pleasure gardens busy with Londoners at the weekend enjoying wine, tea, cakes and music. Looming over Angel was every poor traveller's greatest fear: the holding prison for migrants. With hundreds of new people from the provinces arriving in London every day and the population complaining about overcrowding and crime, immigration was a controversial political issue. Since factories, sweat-shops, and building sites depended on low paid labour from out of town, the government could not ban immigrants. Instead, ministers attempted to assuage the fears of the public by claiming to get tough on the criminals and work-dodgers – which meant locking up large numbers of innocents. Officers scanned the new arrivals from Barnet and arrested those they thought looked drunk, work-shy or even slightly untidy.

The Chester coaches arrived at the Golden Cross Inn on London's busy Strand. On the southern end of the area that would later be a square named Trafalgar, the Golden Cross was a gambling hut and a museum of freaks. Apparently, a live human centaur had been displayed there only a few years before Emma's arrival. Procuresses for brothels prowled the inns that received coaches from the provinces, looking to recruit young girls fresh from the country by feigning motherly concern and promising honest work. Emma managed to avoid the bawds and find a position as a maid for a Mrs Richard Budd.

The Budds were probably the first or second couple to make Emma an offer. Every girl knew that the standard of proposals would decrease as she waited. They all craved positions in aristocratic homes, where the work was less arduous because the family were often away and it was easy to pick up dresses, candles and tips, but they hoped in vain. Aristocrats recruited servants by personal recommendation. Girls arriving from the country were crammed into the homes of the middling classes. Doctors, tradesmen and merchants considered country girls less corrupt and more willing to accept low pay than Londoners. They and their wives met the wagons when they arrived in the inns to pick their own servant and to avoid paying commission to an employment agency. Emma was young, healthy and had worked as a maid before, and the Budds had no teenage sons, so perhaps they did not mind employing such a pretty girl. They packed Emma into their carriage and headed for their newly built home in Chatham Place, Blackfriars.

After passing through Temple Bar, one of the two remaining gateways to the City (until four years previously, the heads of traitors were pinned up on the gates), Emma saw her first sight of her new home: the City. The Budds' cart bumped past shops, slaughterhouses, slums and vertiginous, toppling houses flanked by great stacks of refuse. Wagons, coaches and rubbish carts jostled to overtake herds of animals driven by farmers toward the market at Smithfield or the abattoir at Tower Hill. Errand boys wove through swarms of shoppers and servants. Tradesmen headed through for the markets: Billingsgate for fish and coal; Mark Lane, Bear Quay and Queenhithe for grain; the Borough for hay; Blackwell Hall for cloth; and Leadenall for leather and poultry. The air hung heavy with the stickily astringent smell of the sugar-processing plants and coal fumes from factories working from dawn to dusk to make the luxury goods that adorned the West End and were exported all over the world. Bricklayers and labourers were everywhere, carrying materials, clambering over rubble and foundations and assembling in groups to be recruited for work. Thousands of houses were built in London between 1762 and 1779. Many more were abandoned when the money ran out, to be looted for timber by children. Crowded into the slums or 'rookeries' in the alleyways were the workers who built houses for the wealthy and wove the material for their clothes.

Although London was the world's largest city, it was small by modern standards.[8] Even by the 1760s, a lady could have traversed it on foot in half a day. Knightsbridge marked one limit, Bloomsbury the other. Aristocrats hunted in the surrounding areas, and stray hounds and deer hurtled through the areas now occupied by Harrods and the British Library. Kensington was market gardens, Belgravia was mostly rural, while families visited the pretty village of Paddington on summer evenings to watch farmers bringing in the hay. The compact nature of the city created particular concentration within certain limits: shops in Cheapside and the Strand, brothels and theatres in Covent Garden, palaces in St James, wealth in Mayfair, and poverty in St Giles. Visitors marvelled at the difference between gracious west London with its elegant, newly-built stucco mansions and straight open streets, and the narrow dark streets, overhung by signs, in the eastern part of the city.

One eighth of the British population, 850,000 men, women and children, lived crowded into the seven square miles of land that marked London's main environs. One in six inhabitants of Great Britain had lived in the capital at some point, when only one in forty French citizens lived in Paris. Thanks to immigration, London doubled in population from nearly 700,000 in 1700 to 1,300,000 in 1820. In the 1770s, hundreds of souls like Emma arrived in London daily from the provinces, searching for work. The population swelled when the aristocracy arrived in carriages from the country to houses in Mayfair for the social season and the sessions of Parliament in spring. Trooping in their wake came all those who lived off the rich: servants, robbers, sellers and prostitutes. Foreign tourists and investors crammed the city along with spies and diplomats monitoring the activities of Lord North, the Prime Minister, and King George III. Dubbed the 'farmer king' for his love of blunt speech, plump George was already struggling with the mental strain that would later become a devastating mental illness.

London was the biggest, most profitable and dirtiest city in the world. Visitors complained that the buildings were coated in grime and declared the sky totally obscured by smog. Many of the roads were blocked with rubbish and awash with mud four inches deep. Even in the most beautiful part of the Strand, near St Clement's church, the thick mud from the street splashed those who forgot to shut their coach windows. Pedestrians tried to protect themselves from dirt by putting down large stones and hopping between them, blocking the route for carriages and animals. Since there were thousands of wooden houses with open fires but no public fire brigade (private fire-fighters could be secured for a huge subscription), the sky was red with flames most nights, and the ensuing messes of debris, molten lead and ash flowed into the mud in the roads. Apprentices, unsurprisingly, spent most of their time cleaning silt off their masters' houses.

London was the envy of Europe for its superior and glamorous shops. As one German tourist commented, 'everything one can think of is neatly, attractively displayed, in such abundance of choice, as almost to make one greedy'.[9] All those who visited Cheapside were dazzled by the huge glass windows bursting with brilliant and varied luxury goods from far-flung countries. On one point visitors and inhabitants agreed: London was the most expensive city in the world. There were rich rewards on offer for those able to tap its voracious hunger for luxury and glamour.

6

The School of Corruption

*E*mma's new home was a sparklingly new townhouse near Blackfriars Bridge over the Thames. Although it bordered the Fleet prison and was not far from the seedy, notorious docks, the genteel square of Chatham Place epitomised bourgeois living. Merchants' wives in fine day dress embarked on the trip to town, stepping into their waiting sedan chairs, chairs supported on poles carried by two footmen. Milkmaids and butchers' boys hurried past them, eager to hawk their wares to the housekeepers.

Built in the 1760s, the elegantly spaced red-brick houses were let for high sums of between £60 and £100 a year and sold for thousands. The businessmen and merchants who occupied them were inordinately proud of the street sign and house numbers, modern innovations rare in the 1770s. Chatham Place houses had the latest trappings: new roofs sealed with lead to guard against leaks and state-of-the-art security with thick cast-iron railings around the front and heavy doors that bolted with chains. Convinced that crime was on the increase (a terrifying ten houses were burgled every month), Londoners expected their houses to be heavily protected. They were also a little nervous: it was only very recently, after Blackfriars Bridge was built, that the area had been gentrified, and shiny new townhouses arranged in squares had sprung up over patches that had been the dens of thieves.

Houses like the Budds' still remain in central London, particularly in the City and Bloomsbury area. Above the vaults, cellar and kitchen in the basement were three or four storeys of elegant, high-ceilinged living quarters lit by large sash windows. New houses no longer included space for the occupant to carry on his trade downstairs, for they were built for the growing class of people who commuted to separate work-places. The dining room, library, parlour and perhaps two or three reception rooms were on the ground and upper floors, and the domestics slept in the attic or down by the kitchen. The design of the Georgian townhouse suited families like the Budds, who wanted to avoid seeing their servants.

No researcher on Emma has explored her life as a maid with the Budds, but her experiences of service in London were crucial in forming the woman she became. Although Emma never spoke about working for the Budds, we know she was in service because she later recognised the actress Jane Powell as her old friend from domestic work. Pettigrew, an early biographer of Nelson, confirmed with Budd that he had been her employer. It makes sense that Emma worked for a middle-class family, and Jane Powell's biographers assert that she worked as a maid in Chatham Place. We can piece together Emma's life with the Budds by delving into the history of the Blackfriars area and by collating all the sources on the life of a maid in a townhouse from contemporary servants' manuals, diaries kept by mistresses and handbooks for housewives. Emma's disillusioning experiences of domestic service fuelled her ambitions to be famous.

On arrival, Emma would have been taken to meet the cook, who organised the maids. Cook gave Emma her duties and instructed her in the house rules. She was forbidden to entertain visitors, have boyfriends, drink, gamble or speak to the men of the house or to visitors unless necessary. She may even have been given a new name: few mistresses had the energy to learn names, and instead called a new girl the same name as her predecessor. After lunch in the kitchen and an hour to arrange her few belongings in the small bed she shared, probably with Jane Powell and another maid, Emma was set to work. Country girls, with no immunity to London germs, were renowned for falling ill as soon as they arrived in the metropolis, and a mistress had to extract her money's worth. Even one as robust as Emma would have struggled with initial bouts of coughing, flu or stomach complaints. The summer of 1778 was the first of four very hot summers, and diseases spread fast. From 1779 to 1782, the 'Epidemic Ague', a disease of fever, delirium and quick death, swept through the damp, windowless, airless slums of London, killing thousands, becoming one of the most devastating diseases of the century.

In 1775, one journalist estimated that one in eight of those living in London were servants, which would imply an astonishing 80,000 domestics. Many, like Emma, had come from the country, and commentators believed they were drawn by the 'pleasures to be enjoyed in the capital'.[10] Female servants in London had more freedom than their country counterparts. In addition to the usual Christmas, Whitsun and Easter, most London maids were allowed to take eight days off per year (ostensibly to view the public hangings at Tyburn). Over half of the population of girls between fifteen and twenty in London were domestic servants, and a veritable teenage culture sprang up to cater for them – shops, cafés, fairs and cut-price early nightclubs, perhaps a band and a beer supply under an awning in the city centre. Commentators grumbled about the 'excessive' sums 'expended in these Temples of Idleness' by maids, apprentices and labourers.[11] Otherwise, they hung around street corners and outside shops. Horace Walpole claimed that he had twice been about to 'stop my coach in Piccadilly, thinking there was a mob, and it was only nymphs and swains sauntering or trudging'. Female servants did not have to wear livery, unlike male servants, and many wore good silk dresses cast off by their mistresses. They spent their wages on cheap entertainment.

We can reconstruct the life of the Budds by reading the accounts of similar families. Chatham Place was convenient for Dr Budd's work at St Bartholomew's hospital in Smithfield, on the edge of London's East End. Attachment to a hospital was a high-prestige position awarded only to the most esteemed doctors. After breakfast, Dr Budd would take a sedan chair to his usual coffee shop to read the papers and drink thick coffee from a pot that had been simmering for hours over the fire. At about ten o'clock, he took his chair to St Bartholomew's, a hospital newly rebuilt and completed in 1770. Four buildings around a courtyard, it probably held about 200 of the sick and the infirm. More than 7,000 patients were treated there in 1748, a statistic that suggests they died soon after they arrived. All were poor. The comfortably off were treated at home.

Nurses cared for the patients from day to day, and there were only three surgeons who set broken bones, treated wounds, drained boils, bled patients, gave enemas and pulled teeth. The leading surgeon was Percival Pott, an inspiring doctor who had the power to attract and appoint excellent staff. Budd's name does not appear on the registers of the hospital as a physician or surgeon, and so he was probably an associate physician and consultant. His job was more genteel, administration in the offices near to the Great Hall and then ward rounds or talks with rich visitors whose purses funded the hospital. Such contact earned him private commissions and the finances to run his expensive Chatham Place household. Budd lunched at his coffee house or at home on pies, stews or delicacies such as sheeps' trotters, pig's ears and brains. On some days, he waited all day at his coffee shop for an apothecary to attend and communicate to him the symptoms of the sick. It was probably just as well not to linger in London's third biggest hospital – the beds were bug-ridden, the nurses were untrained, and infection was rife.

In the morning, like most ladies of her class, Mrs Budd busied herself with accounts, writing letters, planning menus or attending to the children. At about half past ten, she took her carriage to buy cloth and paper in the City or fancy goods in Covent Garden and the Strand. She usually returned at midday to dress for dinner and then spent the afternoon making or receiving calls and administering accounts.

Emma was probably unpaid because she was under sixteen. Budd's income was not high, perhaps £200 a year, and even if she did receive a salary, it would not have been more than £1 a year. She would have had to work harder than in Hawarden for her keep. Most houses had to be washed twice a week from top to bottom, and staircases and entrances had to be scrubbed daily. The maids shared the jobs of housemaid, scullion and kitchen maid. They needed an almost continuous supply of water to keep the Budds' house clean. Many times a day, Emma and Jane staggered with buckets from one of the pumps by the Thames. Luckily, the river was thought to have the healthiest air in London and a visit there was a pleasant trip and a chance to socialise by the fountain.

At five o'clock every morning, Emma would light the kitchen fire, clean the hearth and prepare the utensils for the cook to make breakfast. She scrubbed, swept and dusted the breakfast parlour and then, after the family woke, she lit their bedroom fires, emptied their chamber pots, and brought them hot water with which to wash. While the family breakfasted at around eight on bread and meat or porridge, Emma and the other maids made the beds, put back the shutters, swept the rooms, cleaned the grates, dusted and took the washstand water downstairs. After breakfast, she had to clean the plates and dishes, scour the pans with a mix of sand and soap and then start scraping at the fireplaces. Her hands were perpetually plunged in soapy water for her job was to scrub: furniture, utensils, stonework, floor and hearths. The streets were so muddy that clothes often needed to be washed daily. A French visitor decided that an ideal lower servant was a 'fat Welsh girl, who was just come out of the country, scarce understood a word of English, was capable of nothing but washing, scowering, and sweeping the rooms, and had no inclination to learn anything more'.[12] Emma, however, knew exactly what she was missing.

Short biographies of Emma's fellow maid Jane Powell were published after she became an actress and all claim her work in Chatham Place was harsh. The Budds, like most employers, no doubt expected their servants to work like drones, show meek obedience whenever they encountered a member of the family, and accept punishment submissively. Servants were beaten for laziness, insolence, untidiness, slowness, carelessness and often if the master was simply irritated. One girl who became a maid of all work at the age of ten claimed she was regularly hit with sticks. Maids strove to avoid their mistresses and were always ready to go to the pump or buy provisions at the market. Although the cook dealt with the tradesmen (a sought-after task, as it gave the opportunity for taking bribes), maids were allowed to buy milk from the cows led by milkmaids through the squares. Emma's lunch break came at around half past eleven, and then she resumed her laundry, polishing and sweeping. After her supper at four she would assist with the preparation of the Budds' meal. A typical supper for middle-class families was pea soup, stewed carp or tripe, rabbit or veal, vegetables and then a jam or fruit tart, usually taken at about five. Emma had to work longer in summer because of the light, but in winter, unless the Budds entertained at home, she was free by seven, after all the pans had been scrubbed and replaced and the bedrooms prepared for their occupants.

Mrs Budd would have given Emma one of the many best-selling servants' manuals. Rather than assisting the servant to live on a tiny salary and cope with homesickness, a spiteful mistress, the sexual advances of a master and the petty cruelties of the household's children, such books dwelt on how servants could be corrupted by dissolute behaviour and drink. The authors preached that the 'Town proves a school of corruption' and the streets 'swarm with these servants of Iniquity, who are continually carrying on a trade of sin' and 'subsist by the price of slaughtered souls'.[13] Like most servants, Emma and Jane paid no attention to such instructions. In their room upstairs after work, they tried to beautify themselves, then ventured out to the city.

Neither girl had any desire to stay in domestic service and work her way up to becoming a cook. If Emma already suffered from the psori-asis that later plagued her, she would have tried to avoid putting her hands in soapy water whenever possible.[14] Everywhere she saw women in fine clothes she could not afford. As one of the magazines that she might have read when she was in Chatham Place declared, 'luxury was never at so great a height as at present'.[15] Indignant with envy, she scrubbed the hearth, cherishing hopes of a better life.

7

Temptations to Voluptuousness

After seven o'clock, genteel families such as the Budds drank tea behind thick curtains that shut out the street. Elsewhere, the owners of gin palaces and taverns brushed the straw over the floor and set up tables for gambling as prostitutes began their toilette. The novelist Henry Fielding described the alleys of the City as 'a vast wood or forest in which a Thief may harbour with as great security as wild beasts do in the Desarts of *Africa* or *Arabia*'.[16] The backstreets of London were no place for a young girl fresh from the country. Emma was lucky to have Jane as her guide.

Jane Powell was Emma's first close female friend. She had a crucial influence on her new fellow maid, little Miss Lyon, fresh from the Welsh hills. Jane's contemporaries described her as restless, fond of pleasure and ambitious from childhood to perform on the London stage. As she told the new maid at Chatham Place, she was desperate to be an actress. The darlings of the newspapers, actresses wore fabulous clothes, enjoyed the adulation of the public and the adoring advances of famous men and – if they wanted – could marry into the aristocracy. Acting was essentially the only occupation open to women that paid a reasonable salary. Electrified by Jane's effusive descriptions, Emma shed her old self, the unsophisticated country girl, and became a sharp city maid, hungry for stardom in the theatre.

We can reconstruct Jane's life by reading contemporary accounts of the theatre, playbills, newspaper gossip and the collections of biographies of the stars of the Drury Lane, Haymarket and Covent Garden theatres, *Authentic Memoirs of the Green Room* and *Secret History of the Green Room*. The authors of these early gossip magazines were usually struggling playwrights who knew the theatre well, and, since their sources were the actors, their friends and agents, or even the theatre management, the pieces were fairly reliable. The *Green Room* books were reprinted frequently, and Jane never changed her entry, which suggests that she was reasonably satisfied with the contents.

According to her biographers, Jane's father was an army sergeant. After her mother died in childbirth, Jane, her siblings and the new baby moved from their home in Kent to his London barracks in Blackfriars. By the age of eleven or so, she had become the toast of the company, no doubt by acting in camp plays. Her father cut short her fun by sending her to work for Dr Budd at Chatham Place, probably, like Emma, at the age of twelve or thirteen. Of 'a romantic turn', Jane detested her work. As the writer puts it:

> We find her in a menial capacity with a family in the vicinity of Chatham-square, an enthusiastic Spouter, and unable to attend her business, from a desire of seeing Plays, and studying Speeches. The confinement and slavery of her place did not agree with her temper.

Emma surely joined her in rehearsing tragic parts while they scrubbed the floor, 'spouting' Ophelia when the cook was out of earshot. It seems as if Emma was dismissed first and Jane, perhaps finding the job unbearably dreary without her, 'decamped her servitude', as her biographer put it, and fled the Budds' house with a soldier called Farmer to Coxheath Camp. Private Farmer soon decided to be rid of her. Vainly pretending to herself that he had loved her, Jane called herself Mrs Farmer, but soon fell into 'every distress and disgrace that can befall her sex'. She first became the company laundress, and then a serial mistress-cum-prostitute or 'conspicuous Character in the Camp'. Finally, 'despising a subaltern when she could charm his Commander, she eloped with the Captain to London, where they lived together in a style she had not been used to'. When he deserted her, she was left at the age of fourteen to 'forage for herself'. She could not return to domestic service, for 'she was now unfit, as well as from the habits she had lately been used to, as from a want of character [i.e. a reference], so necessary to persons of that description'. No support came from her family and Jane found herself bereft of 'present subsistence, or even of a favourable prospect'. She had no choice but to work as a street-walker, probably in the Covent Garden area. As her biographer put it, 'we need not wonder at or explain the remedy she adopted to relieve her from embarrassment; – a remedy which, when embraced from necessity, deserves forgiveness, but when embraced from inclination deserves the severest reproach'.

Jane never lost her ambition to act. She raved about plays and the theatre so enthusiastically with her clients that she was 'distinguished from others of the frail sisterhood by the appellation of the Spouter'. Her fortunes improved when she gained an influential client, presumably a rich aristocrat with theatrical connections. After she left her profession to be his exclusive mistress, he pulled strings, negotiated with the theatre management and paid money for her to appear on stage and also bought her costumes.[17] Jane, as Mrs Farmer, made her debut in 1787 at the Haymarket as Alixia, a tragic heroine in Nicholas Rowe's *Jane Shore*. Having worked as a prostitute for eight years, Jane was ready to play mature roles at twenty-two.

As the theatre record books show, Jane had steady work in minor roles, often in tragedies and Shakespeare's history plays. She married William Powell, a prompter and minor actor at Drury Lane. Her advantages were her height (it helped her to be seen on the stage) and her expressiveness, but her face was not beautiful.[18] She spent a long time working in secondary roles, striving after the popular fame so crucial to stardom. In the season of 1789–90, for example, her weekly salary was one of the lowest at £3, considering that Miss Farren earned £17 a week and Dorothy Jordan took home £10 a night. Gradually, however, Jane grew more popular.[19] By 1800, in her mid-thirties, she was seen as the second tragedienne after Sarah Siddons, and she was earning a decent salary of £8 a week. She appeared on stage for the last time in 1829 before dying in London five years later.

Emma and Jane would renew their friendship when they were in their thirties. In 1777, however, stardom was a dream. They were intent only on finding fun. The lamps attached to the Budds' door cast a light that reached no farther than the middle of the street, and once they left Chatham Place, they were in the dark. In the absence of a police force, with only decrepit old watchmen as guards, the local area around Chick Lane and Field Lane to Turnmill Street and Cowcross (around modern-day Farringdon tube stop, just north of the City, about half a mile from St Paul's Cathedral), was one of London's most dangerous places and a playground for criminal gangs.[20] Soldiers discharged from the war, labourers and aristocrats used the cover of darkness to prey on maids. Dressed in makeshift finery and already a little drunk on snatched gin, the girls had to walk quickly toward the centre of town. High above them, in rooms poorly lit by tallow candles, younger girls worked late, five to a room, sewing shirts, while children in other garrets counterfeited coins in bowls of green acid.

Young servants tended to mill around Covent Garden, watching the cock-fighting and magicians, buying hot meat sandwiches from the all-night food shops and looking for young men, labourers and servants like themselves. James Parry, later a friend of Emma's, claimed he met her and Jane when they were teenage maids, giggling on the streets.

Maids loved attending fairs. Henry Fielding thundered, 'What greater Temptation can there be to Voluptuousness than a Place where every Sense and Appetite of which it is compounded, are fed and delighted', and where the lowliest might dress up and pretend to be rich gentlefolk.[21] One visitor decided that girls moved to London simply to attend the Lord Mayor's Procession in early November, others complained that fairs left the young 'debauch'd and corrupted'. There were hundreds of fairs. On May Day, dairymaids hired garlands of white damask decorated with ribbons and flowers and topped with a silver tankard to walk their cows around London. There were bonfires on Guy Fawkes Day and Oak Apple Day, which celebrated Charles II's escape from the Parliamentarians. She was probably allowed a day or so for Bartholomew Fair, which took place in Smithfield Market, very near to Chatham Place. In the last week of August and the first week of September, the area was overrun with sideshows and stalls selling sweets. The year before Emma arrived, an edict to close the fair after three days caused riots. At Bartholomew Fair, there were wild men captured in Scotland, female wrestlers, fortune-tellers, singers, early versions of fairground rides and tents showing short plays of familiar stories from romance or legend. In one year, the most popular attraction was an elephant able to fire a gun. Emma and Jane hoped that they might be discovered. Everybody knew that the libertine Earl of Rochester had found a young Elizabeth Barry declaiming tragedy between food stalls at Bartholomew and transformed her into the most successful actress of her generation.

Young people grew up fast. Emma's path through life was so far very typical and we might hazard that, like most girls of her age and position, she lost her virginity at twelve (there was no legal age of consent), most likely during the holiday periods of Christmas, Easter, Whitsun or the Bartholomew fortnight. Fairs were an opportunity for the young to enjoy themselves, and pregnancy was often the consequence. Emma was enjoying herself, but Mrs Budd was growing increasingly concerned about her behaviour. The final straw came when Jane and Emma stayed out all night. Since it appears to have been in early autumn, they had probably been at Bartholomew Fair, enjoying the quacks, laughing at the puppet shows, and flirting with apprentices. When they returned, Mrs Budd was waiting for them. What she had to say was short. Emma was fired. Something must have made the doctor's wife very angry, for she didn't dismiss Jane, and Emma, although not very industrious, was young, strong and cheap. Mistresses had a perennial dilemma: if they gave notice to one girl, would the next be any better? Emma may have answered back or perhaps Mrs Budd suspected a pregnancy. Either way, her mind was made up, and Emma was turned out and sent straight to the streets.

Nearly a quarter of servants in Emma's time left their position within a week to three months. Servants could be sacked for the slightest mistake or sign of illness, or simply because the family needed to save money or were leaving town. One magistrate estimated that, around the time of Emma's arrival in the capital, there were more than 10,000 domestic servants without a position. There was no redundancy pay and even if she had been a good worker, there was no guarantee of a reference. Without a recommendation or the money to return home, the single female servant had no choice but to head for the areas where the poor lived and try to avoid falling into prostitution or crime.

Thirteen-year-old Emma already had the energy, beauty and self-confidence that would carry her far, but such qualities had a darker underside – an addiction to glamour, a hot temper, and a desire to please by winning attention. There was no way that her life of drudgery could continue: she was too pretty and ambitious. On leaving the Budds, equipped only with a few dresses and one or two trinkets from admirers, Emma headed straight for Drury Lane Theatre in Covent Garden, the most sensational spectacle in London.

8

Powder and Paint

*E*mma, as a squire later described her, was 'designed by Dame Nature for the Stage'.[22] First, however, she had to find somewhere to live. She fled to her mother, who was living in the St Giles area, near modern-day Oxford Street.[23] Paying up to threepence a night, London's new workers slept sometimes twenty to a room and between three and eight to a bed in windowless, rat-infested cellars and garrets. Every draughty crevice was stuffed with paper or rags and the rooms were pitch dark, even at midday. Going out was as risky as staying inside, for ragged, cunning humans waited in every dark corner, looking for something to steal, and even a clean dress on a woman would do. Dozens died every week, too poor to do anything more than buy a few drops of gin and sprinkle them on a rag to suck, while stray dogs and rats picked at the sewage around them. Emma was lodging in squalor, gathering flea bites on her shins, and she had no plans to hang around. She was soon trying for a job at the oldest and most prestigious theatre in London.

Her chances of becoming an actress were slim. Hundreds of girls queued at the stage door every month, but few were allowed to audition. Many actresses came from theatrical families and most began on the provincial stage or as dancers. Quick, clear and sweet speech was more important than beauty and Emma's voice was raw and untrained. She had no patron to smooth the way by bribing theatre owners or supplying her with contacts and clothes. Most aspiring actresses ended up working as waitresses, barmaids or prostitutes. Emma did have one advantage over the others: she could read. She also had spirit, vital in the rough and competitive world of the theatre, as well as sturdy health, experience in service, freedom from parental control (no concerned mother would allow a thirteen-year-old to serve as an actress's assistant), and youth (her salary would be very low). Emma was probably removed from the audition line and put to work as maid to Mrs Linley, the wardrobe mistress.

Drury Lane, on the site of the modern-day theatre of the same name, was big business. Only one other theatre – Covent Garden – could stage full plays, and, since London had only one opera house and no other regular theatre for ballet, comedy, musicals, or indeed any type of entertainment, over two thousand eager patrons crammed into Drury Lane every night. In the season of 1778–9, when Emma arrived, her new home employed forty-six actors, thirty-two actresses, thirteen dancers and six singers, as well as a full orchestra, and about one hundred and fifty support staff: seamstresses, hairdressers, carpenters, painters, animal handlers, chorus masters and choreographers, along with temporary painters and workmen when needed. The yearly profits often hit over £6,000, once the costs of around £40,000 had been paid. The architect Robert Adam had renovated the building in the 1770s by adding a graceful classical façade and decorating the walls in sumptuous gold leaf, while improving the stage lighting. Beneath the graceful, gilded ceilings were terrible rivalries and factions. Emma had arrived at a theatre in crisis.

In 1776, Richard Brinsley Sheridan, at the age of twenty-five, bought a half share in the theatre from its actor-manager, David Garrick. A brilliant playwright, Sheridan was an incompetent manager. Playwrights claimed he never answered their letters and he forgot to pay his employees. Most of the time, as the actress Kitty Clive wrote, 'everyone is raving against Mr. Sheridan'. He appointed his family to the plum positions. His pompous father became artistic director, and he made his father-in-law, Thomas Linley, musical director, putting his mother-in-law, Mary Linley, in charge of costumes and props. Infuriated by their autocratic and inexperienced new managers, performers defected to Covent Garden and provincial theatres. The servants also left, and so, as Emma found, there were new jobs on offer.

Mary Linley was forty-three. Four of her twelve children had died in infancy, and her husband, Thomas, set the remaining eight to work singing at public recitals. Crowds admired their eldest daughter, beautiful, talented Eliza, while they mocked her greedy parents. In his hit play of 1771, *The Maid of Bath*, Samuel Foote poked fun at how Mary had tried to force seventeen-year-old Eliza to marry a widower of sixty, a disaster averted only when Sheridan whisked the teenager to France and later married her. Initially, Mary flourished as her son-in-law's wardrobe mistress. By the time Emma arrived, she was wilting, mourning Thomas, her eldest son and favourite musician, who had drowned in a boating accident in August. She was also concerned over her daughter. Now retired from singing, Eliza was only twenty-one but weak from bouts of tuberculosis and a series of miscarriages. Her father told her husband that, if he touched her, it was a 'nail in her coffin' and Sheridan left her to pine in their house in Great Queen Street. By the time Emma arrived, he was besotted with the beautiful actress Mary Robinson, known as Perdita. Grieving for Thomas and angry to see her daughter humiliated by her husband's infidelities, Mrs Linley was embittered and almost impossible to please.

No needlewoman, Emma was Mary's errand girl. Since the stock dresses were shabby, there was vicious competition for the good costumes. Even the most talented actress struggled onstage without a gorgeous dress in velvet or silk and jewels for attracting light to the face. As one actress complained, a performer 'may as well be dead as not in the fashion'.[24] Mary had the difficult job of implementing Sheridan's wardrobe cutbacks. He wrote in his notebook, 'New Performers and old ones on new salaries to provide their own white silk stockings'. Players often tore their stockings on the splintered scenery and had to replace them at the cost of a shilling per pair, as well as buying their own gloves, all out of a salary that could be as low as £1 a week. The performers were livid about Sheridan's cutbacks and blamed Mary, declaring her so mean that she would cut off the 'flowing robe of a tragic performer to gain for herself the covering of a footstool, or the materials for a velvet pincushion'.[25] As Mary's messenger, Emma would have taken the heat of their anger.

Emma's contact with the actresses was an education. As one theatre biographer gossiped, the stage employed 'many Ladies and Gentlemen respectable now, whose previous situations in life would have precluded them the possibility of mixing in virtuous society'.[26] Few actresses led perfectly virtuous lives. Many became the mistresses of wealthy men in return for money, clothes and patronage, and the rest tended to have affairs with other actors. Although Mrs Frances Abington had been a courtesan for the celebrated madam Charlotte Hayes, 'more indebted to her vivacity than to her beauty', by 1778, she had become the theatre's lead comedienne.[27] Thanks to her famed sense of style on and off the stage, she was also employed as a fashion consultant, called in by the social elite for emergency fashion disasters and panics before balls and weddings. Margaret Cuyler, another comedienne, was dubbed one of the 'Most Fashionable Votaries of Venus' (i.e. a courtesan) by the *Rambler's Magazine* of 1783, but maintained a successful career. The third leading actress, Elizabeth Farren, only three years older than Emma, was acting on provincial stages before the age of ten (she was so poor that the other actresses lent her clothes to wear onstage) and she made her debut at Drury Lane at about the same time as Emma arrived. After a glittering career, she married the Earl of Derby, and was even selected to walk in the procession of the Princess Royal at her wedding. Mary Robinson capitalised on her connection to the aristocracy in a different way: she began an affair with the Prince of Wales when he saw her play Perdita in *A Winter's Tale*, and then extracted a substantial pension from him. Emma learnt an important lesson from her new mistresses: a dubious background did not prevent a woman from entering the most eminent society.

As Emma watched from the wings, she realised that acting was more difficult than she had thought. Players had to work hard, accept low pay, and battle against other actors trying to undermine them or seize their position. Only the stars were paid if absent through illness or if the theatre closed (after the death of a royal, they were shut for two weeks). New plays were rehearsed in only a fortnight, and casts had to rehearse several plays at the same time. One actress might have up to forty different parts in a season of 150 nights and many also worked as singers and dancers. They needed excellent memories for it was difficult to hear the prompter. Forgetting a line was not only ridiculed by the crowd but heavily fined by the management. The competitive environment bred venomous jealousy, and some even attacked or, like Peg Woffington, stabbed their rivals onstage. They all wanted to outdo each other with fine clothes – and they besieged maids like Emma with demands and threats.

In the morning, the theatre's maids were kept busy running errands or helping the other servants with cleaning or watering the trees in front of the stage. Rehearsals of up to four pieces began on the main stage at ten, while the musicians and dancers also practised. Wearing coats and boots because the theatre was unheated, the actors read their lines by the dim light from the upper windows. At two, stagehands began preparing the stage for the performance. The actors devoted the afternoon to fitting costumes, learning lines, drinking, gossiping and

42

complaining about their wages, before dining at four. Throughout it all, Emma and the other maids sorted costumes and parried the actors' teasing and the actresses' commands to fetch, carry or help with an alteration.

The backstage area that maids had to negotiate was much larger than the area devoted to the front of house. Behind the maze of ladders, stairs, dingy corridors and ramps used by animals and carriages, there were offices, areas for sewing and painting scenery and, because play-bills always advertised new scenes and dresses, two dozen or so storage rooms overflowing with backdrops and props. The hundreds of wax candles for the chandeliers were stuffed into the cellar. There were twenty dressing rooms and those who could afford it had their own personal dresser and maid. The rest used and bullied girls like Emma.

The actresses' dressing rooms were chaotic. Chalk lines divided the women from each other, and each had a candle and a small mirror. In air thick with carmine, powder, stain removers, gin and perfume, women undressed while others rehearsed their lines. Aristocrats came backstage to meet the stars and actors wandered in to practise. Linley and his minions arrived to explain last-minute changes to the set or casting. Some women petted lapdogs or nursed their babies and the newest were sick from nerves. Amid all the confusion, maids repaired torn bodices or unravelled hems and shooed away unwanted admirers or playwrights.

No fine lady could dress herself, and much of Emma's job was to assist the dresser by pulling corset laces tight and buttoning hooks. Actresses piled their tresses high to be in the fashion and to be better seen by the crowd. Their foot-high confections of powdered and deco-rated hair required daily maintenance, and Emma would have tied up stray strands, repowdered sections, refreshed flowers and picked out the dirt. Her own hair was unpowdered, luxuriant chestnut but unfash-ionably naked. After a frantic round of dressing in the airless heat, the actresses sauntered to the green room. The maids remained, trying to tidy the tangle of dresses before they returned.

A different play was acted every night of the week except Sundays when the theatres were closed. There was dancing and singing in between acts and the evening would usually finish with a vaudeville performance or a knockabout farce. When Emma arrived, the theatre had been open since 17 September and a big hit was the bubbly musical *The Camp*, about a young woman who disguised herself in male dress to follow her soldier lover to war. Since the most sexually enticing part of a woman's body was considered to be her lower leg, dramas in which an actress wore male breeches and stockings were inordinately popular, and the crowd-pleasing *The Camp* treated the audience to the vision of Robinson, Farren and Cuyler onstage together in breeches. Emma would have seen or at least heard Sheridan's hit, *The School for Scandal*, as well as William Congreve's *The Way of the World*, in which Abington took the role of the sparkling heroine, Millamant, *Romeo and Juliet*, *Hamlet* and *The Tempest*, *The Beggar's Opera* and *Jane Shore*.

Only the boxes could be booked in advance. The doors into the theatre opened at five-fifteen. Servants held seats for the aristocracy while ticket holders scrambled for the best places, or employed a man to reserve a seat. Fifteen people were killed in a stampede at the Haymarket Opera House in 1794. An average playgoer might wait an hour in the street, half an hour inside the theatre before the doors to the auditorium were opened and another hour in his seat before the curtain rose. To fill the time, he might read the leaflets on sale at the door that detailed which luminaries occupied each box. At ten to seven (six-fifteen in winter), a bell rang to instruct the orchestra to stop and the performance began. There was no heating and little space between seats, so people wore their coats throughout the performance, which could last up to five hours, growing increasingly uncomfortable on the hard wooden benches.

As the play proceeded, Emma would have hurried around the theatre carrying water, props, soap and drapes. She may even have ventured on to the stage. In his diaries, Sheridan instructed that, in order to save money, servants and assistants should be used on busy nights in processions and crowd scenes. The future Lady Hamilton may have first appeared to the public as a vagrant in *The Beggar's Opera* or as a peasant in one of Shakespeare's crowd scenes. Backstage staff marvelled at the stamina of the performers. An actress strove to compel the attention of thousands who shrieked insults and compliments as well as suggestions on delivery, movement, and even dress. If she was popular, they might clap through her entire performance.[28] When the theatres were rebuilt in the 1790s, they appear to have contained water closets but, in Emma's time, those in boxes used chamber pots while everyone else had to dash outside. Sellers touted fruit in the gallery and prostitutes cruised for customers. Scene shifters added to the chaos, along with the stream of people arriving at the end of the third act for half price. Many performers resorted to outrageous overacting to keep the attention of the audience. Foreign visitors gaped as English actors feigned death by staggering back and forth across the stage while bellowing loud groans. Any actress who succeeded in conveying believable emotion was truly worth her salary.

After the show was over, Emma took Mary her tea and then began to sort the company's clothes to go to the washerwomen: the richest dresses were brushed and aired, then the silk dresses and stockings had to be sorted into a separate pile from the cotton shirts and dresses. Only much later was she allowed to drag herself back to her lodgings, aching from carrying, her head ringing with the sound of the theatre. It was a struggle to remain a maid, surrounded by beautiful women paid to behave as they pleased.

In December, tragedy struck. The Linleys' second (now eldest) son, fourteen-year-old Samuel, was sent home from his ship with cholera. He was buried on 6 December. Eighteen-year-old fencing master and socialite, Henry Angelo, a pallbearer at the funeral and a friend of the Linleys, claimed that Emma left Mary's employ because she was so distressed by his death.[29] Angelo was making excuses for his friends: no maid would voluntarily leave a position that she liked in December. Emma was probably the victim of a cost-cutting drive. Families always fired maids if money was tight for it was so easy to find a replacement later. Perhaps Mrs Linley wished to get rid of Emma before the January slump or suspected her of getting above her station. Mistresses often took against maids – especially pretty ones – and in the days before employment rights, no one thought to concern themselves as to why. Emma was not given a reference, but one would not have done her much good anyway. Few families wanted a girl who had been employed in a theatre.

Emma had managed to keep clear of prostitution for nearly eighteen months. It was not a bad achievement, as many new arrivals to London succumbed within three months or less. A girl sacked without references had little alternative after she had sold the few clothes she owned. Within a few days, Henry Angelo spotted Emma on the streets, hungry, but in a prime position for a man looking for a girl: standing against a post on the corner of New Compton Street in Soho.

9

The Square of Venus

*C*ovent Garden was the biggest and most flamboyant street spectacle in Europe. Rakes and pickpockets swarmed across the piazza, and the streets and alleys nearby teemed with prostitutes. Visitors were pop-eyed with excitement. 'Covent Garden is the great Square of Venus', reported one, 'and its purlieus are crowded with the practitioners of this Goddess.'[30] There were, he decided, 'lewd Women in sufficient numbers to people a mighty Colony'. Among the new arrivals was thirteen-year-old Emma Lyon, the latest attraction in a Drury Lane tavern.

Henry Angelo saw Emma in Soho, but she was soon working nearby in the area around Drury Lane.[31] Emma probably began as a barmaid and a tavern waitress and then became a prostitute. Either way, it was only a temporary job for a few months, common for girls of her class, and it never deserved the stress put on it by her detractors and most Nelson scholars and biographers since. One in eight of all London's adult females worked as prostitutes in the late eighteenth century. Reliable commentators put the number at well upward of 50,000 out of a population of around 850,000. Such estimates didn't count the kept mistresses nor the many maidservants and wives who supplemented their income with casual sex work. Sailors, builders, soldiers, workmen and students thronged the city, as well as visiting merchants, travellers and businessmen, most of whom were single or far from their wives. A contemporary wrote that 'there are few men who in some period of their lives have not dealt in mercenary sex'. Since well-bred girls waited until marriage or at least evidence of a long-term commitment, most men chose to pay for sex.

Nearly all of London's prostitutes were, like Emma, single teenage girls without male relations, recent migrants to the city. Around a third had been domestic servants who turned to the streets when they were fired. Most were under eighteen, some hardly older than twelve, and nearly all had lost their virginity, usually about one or two years before beginning work. Many had been pregnant at least once.

Girls like Emma had few options. They needed money to be apprenticed, and they usually lacked the skills to become a seamstress or a milliner. Work in the soap factories or brick kilns meant a twelve-hour day in steaming conditions, risking acid burn and injury. Many women believed prostitution less dangerous than factory work and more bearable than domestic service: there were no early starts, back-breaking scrubbing, lascivious masters who considered their maids fair game, or need to be perpetually servile. A prostitute was her own mistress, and to mistreated servants, weary of obeying, any independence was alluring. We might think nowadays that we would rather steal or beg. Beggars, however, were usually attacked and crimes against property were so stringently punished that a girl who stole a handkerchief could be executed or deported. While the authorities prosecuted theft with vigour, they let off those they found soliciting for sex – particularly the younger girls – with a caution. Society turned a blind eye to prostitutes for it was thought that without them, men would resort to sodomy or to assaulting respectable 'innocent' girls. It was also thought to have economic benefits: if men paid for sex, they would be less anxious to marry and thus spare employers the burden of paying out the larger wages due to married men.

Young girls took to the streets without understanding the dangers. Many prostitutes were addicted to gin within months of starting work, and nearly all had been viciously beaten (clients were usually acquitted for any crime on a prostitute) or had suffered from botched abortions. Since many men in large cities had syphilis or gonorrhoea, nearly all prostitutes were infected within a year of walking the streets. Some caught pneumonia and all lived hand to mouth, pawning their clothes to buy drink. Only those who stole from their clients broke even. Some girls did marry or progress to different employment, but many died within five years from disease, abortion or assault by a client.

Attractive girls attached themselves to a tavern. Only the old and diseased women operated solely on the streets, often resorting to dark corners or colonising one of the many deserted, crumbling houses.

The tavern owner charged clients for the use of a room and took a cut of the girl's wages, but he could drum up custom if the night was slow, and his house was a form of protection for her. Taverns were gambling clubs, betting shops and drinking dens and, because no respectable woman would visit such establishments in the evening, tavern owners depended on prostitutes and barmaids to add a little feminine allure.

More than thirty thousand of London's prostitutes operated in Covent Garden and the streets in the boundaries marked by St Martin's Lane, Longacre, Drury Lane and the Strand. 'Drury Lane ague' was the slang term for syphilis and 'Drury Lane vestal' a prostitute. The area depended on a constant influx of girls like Emma. Newly built after much of it burned down in 1769, Covent Garden was a playground for the young. Resplendent in silk dresses of garnet, violet and rouge pink, beribboned and bejewelled, prostitutes mingled with the fashionable crowds around the theatre and the poorer Londoners enjoying the sideshows and sword swallowers, girls selling oranges or garish hothouse blooms. One Frenchman claimed that the 'women of the town' were 'more numerous than at Paris, and have more liberty than at Rome'. The street echoed to lewd invitations, and in backstreets the women waited almost naked. Male prostitutes, ornate in elaborate costume jewellery, loitered on corners. Procuresses and their bouncers or bullies shadowed girls to ensure they did not run away. Aristocrats came from miles around to watch the show, or, like biographer James Boswell, only a few years before, to seek young actresses and *demi-mondaines*. Even if she was only a barmaid, Emma had become a part of London's biggest and most popular tourist spectacle.

Covent Garden even had a guidebook. From 1765, *Harris's List of Covent Garden Ladies* was published every year, the work of a variety of hacks. *Harris's List* detailed the prostitutes' appearance, their lodgings, and their particular talents. Up to eight thousand copies were apparently sold every year by tavern keepers or from the kiosks around the piazza that also sold contraceptives, tobacco, sweets, pornography, and pills for venereal disease. The book often indicated the clients they preferred, such as 'Miss G — N', who was 'particularly fond of sailors'. All used stage names (even a young lady who dubbed herself Sarah Siddons, after the most famous actress of the day) so we would be unable to identify Emma, even if the *Harris's List* from 1777–8 had not been lost. In 1788, after Emma had long left the city, an enterprising lady in Queen Street adopted the name of 'Miss H-m-lt-n' and claimed to be 'very fond of dancing'. By 1788, Emma's fame had spread so far that prostitutes were imitating her.

Emma had been turned away from the Linleys' just in time to catch the Christmas trade. London was packed with gentlemen, workmen and servants. 'Every house from Cellar to Garrett is inhabited by Nymphs of different orders, so that Persons of every Rank can be accommodated,' declared one commentator. There were girls costing thousands of pounds in today's money, and girls for a few pennies. Emma now understood the true profession of the fine ladies who sauntered around Drury Lane. Without warm underwear, she was heated only by gin. Lead-based white paint and beauty spots coated her face, her lips gleamed red with cochineal and her hair was piled high on her head. Her dress was brightly coloured but the style was two or three seasons out of fashion. Once spun on looms by children in the sweatshops of Spitalfields and sold to fine ladies by Cheapside drapers, gowns cut for ladies who never walked outside came to Emma after they had been worn out and passed to maids who sold them to the second-hand clothes markets in Monmouth Street or Rag Fair. She would have owned only two dresses at most, but the small wardrobe was an advantage: it helped men to recognise her.

The room of a tavern barmaid or prostitute bore the traces of the hundreds who had passed through: the dirty floorboards were worn down by boots and the walls were permeated with the stench of beer from downstairs. Purse under her skirts to hide it from pickpockets, she grabbed some breakfast of a fatty meat pie or a piece of bread from a cookshop. Barmaids began their day of cleaning in the morning, and prostitutes started work in the afternoon, between two and four, earlier if the previous night had been quiet. A few tricks a day was usually enough, and in winter it was hard to find more for even the drunks would not linger long on the streets. She had to work her patch: finding a man who looked neither diseased nor deranged, being careful not to stray too near other women, who might attack her, evading those she knew were rivals, potential thieves or simply insane.

Prostitutes caught at men's sleeves or elbows and demanded they buy them wine, attempting to encourage them back to the snug at the rear of the tavern, where waitresses served them wine or 'purl', hot beer mixed with gin, through a slit in the wall. A more flash sailor or a tourist afraid of being robbed in her rooms might attempt to take her to a bagnio, a type of hotel where rooms were generally hired by the hour. The client first had to pay the man who sat at the bottom of the stairs for the use of the room, and then he was taken upstairs. Sex with prostitutes was often routine. Anal sex was considered to be a shocking crime, and threesomes, group sex and flagellation were generally confined to the more expensive brothels. Men risked being robbed if more than two women attended to them. Some customers at the tavern were high on new wages, others simply craved a moment's release from their dreary lives.

A client would often want to stay the night, as the room was nearly always more spacious than the overcrowded slum lodging that was his home, and the prostitute would have to hurry him away before rinsing herself to stave off the pox if she wasn't too drunk or tired. Most women had their own special preventative: some used urine, others whatever might be at hand: gin, brandy, beer or punch. Warm water was thought to have greater disinfecting properties, so they warmed it by holding it in their mouths. If a woman had managed to persuade a client to use it, she washed out her condom – a reusable item made from sheep's gut tied with a ribbon. But condoms cost money. Most trusted the folk belief that if a woman had been with many men, their sperm was mixed in her womb and so she would not conceive. The greater the number of clients, the safer she believed herself to be from venereal disease and pregnancy.

A common activity for the tavern prostitute or barmaid was striking lewd postures, performing a striptease while imitating the poses that could be bought in a cheap print from the nearby stalls. In the brothels of Covent Garden, Emma saw and perhaps performed an act she would later transform into a beautiful art that would make her famous.

The tavern customers were men from her own class: labourers, servants, apprentices, builders and traders. They spent their winter wages on drink and then girls who, if often no younger and no healthier than their wives, gave, for ten minutes, the appearance of being happy. The girls were fondest of sailors. With their tanned faces, tattoos, earrings, distinctive and often dandyish clothes, bellowing voices, rolling gait, incomprehensible nautical jargon and strange stories about monsters, they were like a different species. The girls loved them for their presents of trinkets and because they tended to be kinder than soldiers or labourers. One sailor, Captain Jack Willet Payne, later a friend of the Prince of Wales, claimed to have had an affair with Emma when she was on the streets. A young Horatio Nelson might even have passed her as he wandered through Covent Garden with his fellow sailors. For a man just offshore after a dangerous voyage, flush with cash and lonely after months or even years of all-male company, the alehouse and the prostitute were the first ports of call. Tough, independent Emma would have made an ideal sailor's mistress. But she was already trying to escape the tavern by becoming an artist's model.

Many painters lived and worked in the garrets of Covent Garden and all – even the most distinguished – scoured the area's brothels and taverns for potential models. Emma was just the type of girl to catch a painter's eye. Tall, curvaceous and creamy skinned, with glossy chestnut hair and an oval face, she was the English ideal of beauty. After adopting the name of Emily to seem a little more classy, she was snatched up by the two greatest portrait painters of the time: bitter rivals George Romney and Joshua Reynolds. Sir Joshua, foremost portrait painter of the age and president of the Royal Academy from 1786, was well known for hunting in the brothels of Covent Garden for models, and it seems that he found Emma, perhaps before Romney. His *Cupid Untying the Belt of Venus* shows a dark-haired, pale-skinned model who looks very like Emma, her bosom exposed, wearing an almost transparent dress, languishing in bed while Cupid unties her blue sash. Prince Potemkin, adviser to Catherine the Great of Russia, requested a copy to adorn the Hermitage, where it still hangs. Another painting which features a model that looks very like Emma is Reynolds's *Death of Dido* in which a statuesque dark-haired beauty lies collapsed over a rock, a painting later bought by the Prince of Wales.

Emma also appears to have modelled for one of Reynolds's greatest paintings, *Thais*, now resplendent in the drawing room of Waddesdon Manor, Buckinghamshire. Thais, mistress of Alexander the Great, emerges from the darkness, draped in white, hair flowing behind her, holding a torch to encourage Alexander to set fire to the Temple of Persepolis. When the painting was shown at the Royal Academy in 1781, it caused a sensation. The public demanded to know the identity of the model. She was known only as 'Miss Emily' and was thought to have worked as a courtesan for the celebrated madam, Charlotte Hayes. Journalists described her as a 'woman of the town' and called her variously Miss Emily Potts, Warren, Coventry and Bertie.[32] It was also suggested that she had modelled for Romney and later commentators declared she had been the mistress of Charles Greville.[33] The evidence all indicates that the model was Emma Lyon – by the time the portrait was exhibited, she had worked for Hayes, used the name of Emily, modelled for Romney, and been mistress to Greville. Greville acquired the painting for a costly £157 (although letters show he still had not paid by 1786).

The novelist Fanny Burney praised the 'Thais, for which a Miss Emily, a celebrated courtesan sat, at the desire of the Hon Charles Greville'.[34] Emily was neither a common name nor a generic name for a prostitute. Greville referred to the model for *Thais* as 'Miss Emily', the same name as he called Emma.[35] Most important of all, the woman in the painting looks exactly like Emma.

Newspaper reports, caricatures and first-hand accounts suggest Emma also modelled for the Royal Academy of Art in London.[36] She must have been either desperate for money or, in contrast to the other Covent Garden girls, interested in the work of artists. Unlike male models, who lined up in designated London streets, competing to be chosen for their rugged physique by flexing their muscles, few women wanted to model. Those who did were usually elderly courtesans from Drury Lane and St Giles brought by their madams because they were past the age of entrancing clients. James Northcote, artist and assistant to Joshua Reynolds, was horrified by the 'battered courtesan' he saw modelling for his master's painting of Iphigenia.[37] Their work was exhausting. Models had to stand on a raised dais, in the bright light of the top floor rooms of the Royal Academy until four in winter and six in summer, with short breaks every two hours, attempting to maintain a pose with the help of a staff or a rope hanging from the ceiling. A furious St Giles madam once broke in and tried to attack an artist for forcing one of her girls to stand nearly naked for a whole day, without giving her even a crust of bread. Few madams allowed their best girls to carry out such poorly paid work, and the prostitutes found it a hateful and shameful, even unnatural way to make money. In an effort to recruit them, the Academy agreed not to record their names.

Emma perhaps preferred to model outside of the Academy. She certainly seems to have posed for Romney. His paintings of the time show models who have resemblances to Emma. One early biographer claimed Emma worked from the same Covent Garden tavern as a Miss Arabel, who had modelled for George Romney, and introduced him to Emma. Gossip columnists and her friend, Elisabeth Vigée le Brun, claimed Romney met her in her youth. A letter Emma wrote to him in 1791, begging him not to divulge details about her early life, indicates that she knew him before she became Greville's mistress. 'You was the first dear friend I open'd my heart to . . . you have seen and discoursed with me in my poorer days, you have known me in my poverty . . . I own through distress my virtue was vanquished.'[38] Poverty, distress and vanquished virtue are extreme words to describe her restrained life as Greville's 'fair tea maker' in a Paddington village. Emma surely refers to the period in the 1770s when her 'virtue' was actually threatened. Aged only fourteen, it seems, Emma was a favourite model for both Reynolds and Romney. As a caricature of her drawn in 1798–9 later implied, she may also have met Henry Fuseli, friend of Reynolds, whose *Nightmare* shows a dark-haired model who looks very like Emma, lying in a faint across a bed.

Emma's work as a model provided vital experience for her next position. In early 1779, Emma left Covent Garden and her brief flirtation with tavern nightlife for good. London's most celebrated quack doctor, James Graham, had been searching the taverns of Covent Garden, and he had picked Emma to star in his absurd, exotic Temple of Health.

10

Celestial Goddess

*I*n 1778, James Graham, entrepreneur, sex therapist and showman, burst on to London society. He hired a townhouse in the fashionable area of the Adelphi, off the Strand, called it a 'Temple of Health', and gave nightly lectures about sexual matters and the power of electricity, as harnessed by him, to cure all ills. Graham was a supreme showman and his lectures were extravaganzas featuring explosions, smoke, fireworks, music, and, to London's utter delight, a phalanx of glamour girls posing in flimsy white dresses. In an adjoining room was the 'Electrical Throne', which dispensed electric shocks to clients. Next door lay his prized Celestial Bed, which, he claimed, guaranteed 'perfect Babies even to the Barren'. Dubbed the 'Emperor of the Quacks', the handsome thirty-five-year-old with a genius for self-promotion became London's first celebrity guru, and the girls on the stage were his stars.

Emma never discussed her early life, but she seems to have told friends that she modelled in the temple, and she later sponsored stories in the newspapers that referred to her as a Goddess of Health. Dubious as the Temple was, to be an assistant to Graham was a much less scandalous occupation than being a tavern girl and it was a job Emma felt she could acknowledge. Her early life as Graham's model was often central to newspaper reports about her — even thirty years later — and Emma never denied it, although she refuted other assertions. Somehow she managed to make the leap from lowly tavern girl to mistress to the aristocracy, and it is most likely she attained this promotion through dancing at the Temple.

It seems as if Emma began work in early January. Graham combed

Covent Garden looking for girls with confidence, natural grace, beauty and the appearance of good health. He also advertised in the newspapers for a 'young woman' who was 'personally agreeable, blooming, healthy and sweet-tempered . . . She is to live in the Physician's family, to be daily dressed in white silk robes with a rich rose coloured girdle. If she can sing, play on the harpsichord or speak French, greater wages will be given. Enquire Dr Graham, Adelphi Temple.' His readers knew what kind of a girl he was advertising for, under the flowery description – one willing to live with a man in the Strand, like a mistress. Since Emma was still under sixteen, she was, like maids of her age, paid in board and the odd penny of pocket money.

Fanning the flames of London's interest in new shows with effusive promotion, Graham declared the Temple an 'enchanting Elysian Palace!' where love, beauty and 'all that can ravish the senses, will hold their court'. An Aladdin's cave, stuffed with rented glitz, the lecture theatre sparkled with gold decorations, silver statues of Venus, and expensive mirrors. Oriental drapes and paintings of medieval knights adorned the walls and chandeliers and crystals glittered down from the ceiling. Graham had even affixed coloured panes to the original sash windows so they resembled stained-glass windows. Huge glass tubes bubbled with gold liquid (Graham claimed it was electricity). On the stage was the 'Temple of Apollo', a cupola on pillars almost eight feet high, topped with flaming lamps.

The great Celestial Bed occupied the adjoining bedroom. Graham claimed that the Bed was worth the preposterous sum of £100,000 (around £6 million). The Bed was available for hire at £50 a night (nearly £3,500). The Goddesses danced around the bed to advertise it to customers and then repeated the performance once the clients were under the sheets. The Celestial Bed was a king-size concoction of brass, purple satin and crystal pillars, raised three feet off the ground, topped with a dome filled with 'Arabian' perfumes in the 'style of those in the Seraglio of the Grand Turk', and a statue of Hymen holding a cage containing two live doves. Like a bed in a high-class brothel, the underside of the canopy was decked with mirrors, the panels were carved with erotic scenes, and the frame could be tipped forward, back or sideways. While the couple used the bed, music played around them and, according to Graham, 'streams of light' whooshed up the pillars. Then the so-called electricity bubbling in the tubes apparently connected with the 500 magnets inside the bed to create an explosion of, in Graham's words, 'exhilarating force of electrical fire'. The 'fire', Graham promised, caused the users to be 'powerfully agitated in the delights of love'. Such 'superior ecstasy' would apparently produce a conception and guarantee a child. The divine illusion of the Bed was probably maintained by the Goddesses playing the secret music behind the wall, wafting perfumes around the room, and pulling levers that jolted the bed to give the clients what they believed were 'electrical shocks'.

Graham's promise of a child was a sure-fire winner with aristocrats desperate for an heir. Women were soon queuing in their carriages outside the Temple in the hope of being 'cured' of their infertility. Graham's rhetoric harmonised with the widespread belief that conception occurred only when the woman had an orgasm, which caused her to ovulate spontaneously. It was not until 1845 that scientists discovered that dogs ovulated in regular cycles and began to suggest that the same principle might apply to humans. Although a belief in the need for ovulation encouraged an interest in female sexuality, medical books did not encourage men to try to please their wives. Authors placed the responsibility firmly on the woman to greet her husband's efforts with 'equal ardour'. Infertility was always seen as the fault of the woman: she was weak, undersexed or simply lazy.

As a Goddess on the stage and performing around the bed, Emma was the luminous star of Graham's light and sound spectacular. As the artist Elisabeth Vigée le Brun claimed, Emma, as Graham's Hygeia or Goddess of Health, 'attracted the curious and the idle in droves; artists were particularly charmed by her'.[39] Emma became a symbol of beauty to the capital's most fashionable citizens. 'Daily he attracted overflowing audiences,' claimed a neighbour, and Henry Angelo described 'carriages drawing up next to the door of this modern Paphos, with crowds of gaping sparks on each side, to discover who were the visitors, but the ladies faces were covered, all going incog'. Famous customers included John Wilkes, the rabble-rousing former Lord Mayor of London, and also tabloid-courting MP Charles James Fox. The Prince of Wales also enjoyed its 'superior ecstasy', probably with his mistress, the actress Mary Robinson (who never guessed that the Goddess dancing around her bed had recently been one of her dressers at Drury Lane). Following behind Fox and the rebellious prince trailed the fashionable Whig set, the main political opposition who grouped around the heir to the throne. Graham ensured their attention by criticising the Tory government and the war with America. The Bed, he declared, would create 'Beings rational, and far stronger and more beautiful' than the present 'puny' race that 'crawl and fret, and politely play at cutting one another's throats for nothing at all'.

The daily work of a Goddess began with menial domestic tasks: dusting and cleaning the 'Temple', running errands, and even slopping out the basement (all the houses in the Adelphi flooded when the Thames overflowed). Throughout the day, patients arrived to receive the curing vibrations of the magnetic Celestial Throne, electric shocks in milk baths or friction rubs and pulses of electric current. By half past four, the patients had returned home and the Goddesses began dressing for the evening's work in white dresses and pink sashes.

The heavy doors creaked open at five. For two guineas, London's socialites secured seats while 'harmonious sounds . . . breathed forth from the altar of the great electrical temple'. At seven, an explosion of fireworks stunned the audience into silence and Graham emerged from a trapdoor in the floor, swathed in satin and encircled by his parading goddesses who wore, as one visitor noted, 'no more clothing than Venus when she rose from the sea'. He then delivered his 'libidinous lecture' on the 'celestial brilliancy of that universal resplendent and tremendous fire' in his medicines and bizarre apparatus and their power to cure sexual ills and general debility. Quacks at the humblest fair put on a show, but none had ever fused the theatrical with the 'medical' with such verve. Bursting with self-promotion, sexual titillation and semi-mystic promise, Graham held his audience spellbound. All the while, the Goddesses sang ethereal airs while dancing and posing to show off their radiant health or demonstrate the exercises he recommended. Candles blazed, fireworks exploded, electricity bubbled and the more louche guests lit pipes – surprisingly, none of the hyped-up doctor's performances ever sparked a serious fire.

Graham promised to tell the secrets of 'rendering permanent the Joys of the Marriage Bed; of preserving and heightening personal Beauty and Loveliness' and how to maintain the 'deep – full – LONG toned juvenile virility' that 'ensures female admiration'. Although his argument that pleasurable sexual activity was important to a marriage was revolutionary in an age when men married wives to breed children and maintain their home and kept mistresses for sex, the lectures revealed more about male ideas of female sexuality than conjugal equality. In a torrent of suggestive rhetoric, verbal pyrotechnics and explicit description, he trumpeted the 'balmy – spirituous – vivifying' properties of the male emission. 'Without a full and genial tide of this rich, vivifying luminous principle', he claimed, 'continually circulating in every part', no 'man or woman can enjoy health'. Graham successfully exploited widespread ignorance about sex, fears of infertility, and fashionable obsessions with electricity, recently discovered and barely understood. Preposterous as his breathless panegyrics were, they were the nearest most had to sex education. At the close of the show, the audience received electric shocks by means of conductors hidden under their cushions. As a finale, a spirit apparently emerged from under the floor and handed the doctor a bottle of Electrical Aether. Then, the windows fell dark, the room was suddenly illuminated and a Goddess appeared. She began to worship the Aether.

> Hail! Wondrous Combination!!! – but chief – THOU FIRE ELECTRIC!
> Celestial Renovator! – Thou Life of all Things – Hail!
> – In Majesty and Mystery combin'd!
> Enthron'd – unveil'd – in this tremendous – this most genial Temple!

To the teenage Goddesses, the Temple was a hilarious joke. Behind the glitz was a chaotic mass of hired clutter, and Graham was always trying to seduce young girls (Mary Robinson later gave up acting to write novels and ridiculed him in *Walsingham* as a lecherous fraud). And yet it was surely hard not to be affected by the pathos of the desires of many of those who gazed upon them: youthful health, happiness in love and children. When Graham stopped ranting about electricity, his advice to the infertile was genuinely useful. Borrowing his point from Dr George Cheyne's influential *English Malady* that plain living was the cure for society's debilitating addiction to fashion and luxury, Graham declared that moderate consumption of rich food and alcohol, fresh air and exercise, along with regular sex, could encourage conception. To cure overindulgence, he recommended a diet of vegetables, plain meat and barley, a striking precursor to modern wheat-free and dairy-free diets. Rather less beneficial was his extreme detoxifying diet composed of apples and half a roast potato a day.

The Goddesses had to sell Graham's 'cures'. He wrote hundreds of pamphlets and books claiming that his potions of electrical fire could remedy every possible ill, including 'excessive gaiety', consumption, blindness and infertility, as well as preserving beauty through 'exciting the electrical fire in the body and limbs'. Graham made preposterous claims for his special potions, probably a collation of salts and water, if not arsenic or worse. Electrical Aether rallied the impotent 'exhausted by inordinate and excessive sacrifices to Venus and Bacchus' and Imperial

Pills cured venereal disease. Nervous Aetherial Balsam induced an abortion, or as Graham put it, abolished 'every menstrual obstruction in the world – however complicated, or however confirmed'.

Many declared the Temple no better than a brothel.* Although Graham claimed that the Bed was reserved for married couples, many men followed the example of the Prince of Wales and took their mistresses. It was said that the Goddesses were available for hire on the bed. A rake living nearby joked that one of Graham's beautiful employees had caught a fatal chill after spending too much time in 'the damp sheets of the Celestial Bed'. Lucrative as the Temple appears to have been, Graham soon moved on. By 1781, he had given up on electricity in favour of the restorative qualities of mud bathing in a cheaper house off Pall Mall. He was later arrested for debt and for allowing gambling and immoral activities. After his release, he toured the provinces selling pills but was imprisoned again for debt and in 1794, just short of fifty, he died, in penury and allegedly insane.

Gossip columnists in Emma's later years could never resist commenting on her short period of work at the Temple, and caricaturists nearly always depicted her on the Celestial Bed. When she married, the newspapers tittered that her husband fell in love with her after he saw her modelling for him in a show. Twenty years later, they still burbled about how her perfect figure ensured her job at the Temple and recalled Graham's description of Goddesses as 'veined with alabaster and streaked with celestial hue'. Despite its preposterous side, the Temple taught Emma useful lessons about dance, posture and performance. Shows she performed later would seem spontaneous when in fact they had been carefully planned, and like Graham, she exploited lighting and music to add to the effect of a pose and build up an atmosphere around her performance.

Emma soon left the Temple. The wages were poor and Graham was unreliable. She probably left because she was offered a better job, perhaps after being spotted by one of the silver-tongued ex-soldiers who worked as scouts for the bawdy-houses. By late spring, she had a position in Madam Kelly's, one of the most exclusive brothels in London.

---

* One commentator described it as an 'abandon'd place' where 'modesty must hide her face' in which 'Damsels who use unnumber'd names' cruised the audience for customers. Many 'cures' were dubious: Graham boasted that he recommended that a lonely middle-aged woman hire a beautiful young female prostitute.

11

Santa Carlotta's Nunnery

All of London's powerful men knew the address of Madam Kelly's glamorous brothel on Arlington Street off Piccadilly, next to the modern-day Ritz hotel. Aspiring actresses competed for a place at Kelly's for many stars of the eighteenth-century London stage, including Mrs Abington and Clara Hayward, had learnt posture and dance at Arlington Street. Emma prepared to sing and dance for Madam Kelly's visiting aristocrats and royal Princes. One tourist wrote, the 'admission into these houses is so exorbitant, that, the mob are entirely excluded: there are only a few people who can aspire to the favours of such venal divinities'. Emma, however, did not plan to stay long. Dancing at Kelly's was her route to gaining a high-status protector.

Kelly's house was so notorious that she advertised the arrival of new staff. The *Town and Country Magazine* published a picture of 'Miss Lyon' who looked identical to Emma, reporting that the beautiful Miss Lyon had been recently set up in the finest brothel buildings by her 'Martial Lover'. The magazine looked forward to seeing 'Miss L– flourish as one of the most celebrated demi-reps of the ton', or the most fashionable London set.[40] Kelly capitalised on Emma's celebrity as a Goddess of Health by parading her around St James's Park. There, Henry Angelo caught a tantalising glimpse of a girl now too expensive for his purse. After her brief stint as a walking advertisement, fourteen-year-old Emma settled to work in her new home.

Research by previous historians into Emma's life has failed to ascertain Madam Kelly's identity. However, if we follow the trail in letters, periodicals and newspapers it becomes clear that she was the celebrated Charlotte Hayes. Born in a London slum in around 1725, Hayes became a prostitute at the age of ten or eleven. In about 1750, she was gaoled for debt and met Dennis O'Kelly, an Irish con man. After she was released, she continued to work and in 1761, a client lent her the capital to open her own brothel in Berwick Street. By the early 1770s, she was running a string of 'Nunneries' around the St James area of Piccadilly. She married Dennis in 1770 and, like many attempting to seem genteel, called herself only Mrs Kelly. By 1784, under the names of Mrs Hayes and Mrs Kelly, she had a monopoly on the sex trade in the St James area, and newspapers and caricaturists acknowledged her as being at the top of her profession. Famed for gratifying every possible 'caprice which Flesh is heir to' for men such as the Duc d'Orléans and the Duke of Cumberland, youngest brother of the King, Kelly achieved success by matching her clients' peculiar desires to the skills of her staff.

The *Town and Country Magazine* dubbed Kelly's brothel 'Santa Carlotta's Nunnery' and advertised how it 'administers absolution in the most desperate Cases'. The joke about the link between brothels and nunneries was an old one, but by the 1780s, the name was a skit on the notion that the girls were virgins when they arrived (so their keepers claimed) and then kept virtual prisoners. Kelly's employees struggled under the strict discipline. It was, as they discovered, impossible to leave until they became old and the madam sold them to a cheaper brothel, unless they were lucky enough to find a client who would buy them out.

St James was the centre of high-class prostitution and its brothels became known as the *Bordels du Roi* (the Royal Brothels) after the riotous Prince of Wales, who was in the process of moving out of his parents' home, Buckingham House, and into his own residence, Carlton House, on Pall Mall. Only three years older than Emma, the Prince spent wildly in anticipation of an income of around £100,000 per year after his twenty-first birthday (around £6 million) and Mrs Kelly and the other madams of St James were the beneficiaries. Within five years of living at Carlton House, he had run up debts of nearly £300,000. The prince's sprees turned an already fashionable area into a playground for the rich. In the daytime, families roamed the waist-high grass of St James's Park, queued up to buy fresh milk from one of the cows, and vied for a sight of the elephant from the royal menagerie on its daily promenade. At night, men looked for cheap prostitutes in the park and expensive girls in the nearby houses. St James was a man's world and no respectable woman, even if she were accompanied by an army of male chaperones, would venture into the streets near the Park. By the 1830s, there were over 900 brothels and 850 similar smaller establishments crammed into the half square mile of St James. Gold showered through their doors – one Dutchman declared that the money dissipated in the brothels in a single night would maintain his home country for six months. Emma had taken up employment in the most expensive sex resort in the world.

Kelly was fifty-five and at the top of her profession. She had no mercy for anyone: madams in debt, girls desperate to be set free and grovelling men begging not to be exposed to their colleagues or wives. She charged her guests eye-popping prices for food, drink and medicaments, and kept her staff hopelessly in her debt. As soon as a new girl arrived, Kelly took her clothes and loaned her expensive jewels, dresses and a gold watch. A timepiece was the crucial sign of a Georgian courtesan, since genteel ladies never wore watches but courtesans had to time their clients. She rented dresses and watches to her staff so that if one escaped (in her finery, for she had nothing else), she would issue a warrant for the girl's arrest for theft. Kelly took a large cut of her employees' earnings and billed them for bed, board and laundry, as well as obliging them to buy expensive silk underwear, costume jewellery, make-up and contraceptives. She tried to increase their indebtedness to her by slyly offering them pastries, sweet wine, hairstyling and trinkets, and forced them to hand over any gifts from clients. She punished attempts to freelance outside the brothel and imposed fines for infringements of her complicated rules. Rather than renting out rooms for seductions (the authorities vigorously prosecuted any brothel involved in the seduction of an innocent girl), Kelly preferred to increase her profits by hiring out her staff to other brothels, social events and country parties. She refused to take married women – husbands tended to demand big shares of their wives' wages, to which, legally, they had a right – but she boarded children for a fee.

Charlotte's establishment in Arlington Street had exquisite carriages, servants in livery, and furniture worthy of a palace. The girls received their customers in an opulently decorated parlour. No more than six to eight employees worked there at any one time, most between fourteen and twenty-four. Only the very beautiful or very skilled worked into their late twenties. Unlike the Covent Garden prostitutes, they didn't wear the same dress, and often changed their look or name, since clients loved novelty. Others sought to please by dressing as famous actresses such as Sarah Siddons and Mrs Abington or society leaders like Georgiana, Duchess of Devonshire.

'The ladies of pleasure in London', wrote one client, 'give us an idea of the celebrated Grecian courtesans, who charmed the heroes of Athens.' An Arlington Street training had some notable advantages over the typical education of a genteel fourteen-year-old girl, who learnt needlework and music from her governess and spoke to few men other than her father and servants. Kelly invited tutors to teach her employees music, dancing and languages and her girls learnt other equally useful skills: to feign interest in men's complaints about their wives and monologues about hunting, and to please by being cheerful and willing to flatter.

A courtesan needed elaborate, high hair so a new Kelly girl had to pay an early visit to a hairdresser. Hair salons were everywhere in London and specialist stylists, such as David Ritchie, author of *Treatise of Hair* in 1770, had waiting lists that were months long. The construction of such confections of coiffure took over three hours of skilled work with pins, braids and curling tongs and further hours to decorate. Pupils paid a shilling to practise on life-size models in the back of the shop, and at the front, two hairdressers put pads made of horsehair on the client's head and then stacked the hair on top in a curving tower of three feet or higher. They looped hair in curls to ornament the style and then added a string of fake pearls, a few long feathers, dyed blue, pink or yellow (a style fit only for prostitutes, according to Queen Marie Antoinette's mother), or even flowers, fruit, or models of houses or boats. The writer Hester Thrale jibed that two fashionable ladies whom she met had the equivalent of two gardens on their heads, 'an acre and a half of shrubbery besides slopes, grass plants, tulip beds . . . and greenhouses'. Such hairstyles made hats impossible, so the hair was usually wrapped in a length of gauze for outdoor excursions. The style would remain in place for about three months, and was then reset and, in order not to crush it in the interim, the woman had to sleep on a special head support. As hair could not be washed or brushed after styling, many coiffures were infested with insects and lice, sometimes even mice. The fashion for high hair began around 1765 and by the early 1780s it was at its most excessive (becoming less popular after a tax on powder was introduced in 1786 and virtually dying out after a law was passed in 1795 that hairdressers had to take out an expensive annual licence for powdering). Although commentators mocked it, the style added height, slimmed the face and emphasised a lovely neck.

Kelly girls were ornately styled and carefully groomed. Emma's dress was a highly fashionable imitation of French court dress: stiff wide skirts of embroidery and brocade worn over heavy corsets, finished off with a heavy train. At Kelly's, however, the bodices were cut much lower. Charlotte's girls looked like impressive brocaded ships and had to turn sideways to pass through a door. Courtesans usually wore pink – peach, coral, sugar pink and rose – which suited Emma's creamy complexion perfectly. A tightly laced bodice opened over a piece of different coloured material called a 'stomacher', and a rigid skirt that resembled a jewelled lampshade was worn over a colourful underskirt. Dresses were padded with false hips and bottoms made from cork, fake breasts were fashioned from porcelain or cloth and sometimes even a fake stomach bulge was added. Magazines made ribald jokes about the cork rump, showing men finding that their lover was 'corked'. The overall impression was of an impossibly curvy woman squeezed into a silk dress two sizes too small. Stays were pointed and boned down the front in a way that prevented the wearer from bending forward and made crossing the legs while sitting impossibly uncomfortable. Anyone wearing them always had to sit very upright and moving from sitting to a standing position was usually rather painful.

Thick make-up was also very much in vogue, so much so that in 1770, the government passed a law allowing a man to divorce his wife if he could prove that she had fooled him into marrying her by using make-up to hide her ugly looks or even her true age. Courtesans were the most heavily painted women of all. A Kelly girl first applied a base of cold cream and then smoothed a thick layer of white lead paint over her face. Her eyebrows were shaved off and replaced by false ones made from mouse skin and darkened with black lead. Cheeks were ornamented with beauty spots cut from silk and glued on. She coated her mouth with a dilution of red plaster of Paris, painted blue cream on her eyelids, rouged her cheeks brightly and sometimes whitened her teeth with lead or chalk. Despite all this ornamentation, nail polish was not used and we would find ladies' hands surprisingly bare, in contrast to their ornate make-up and hairstyles. Rose or orange water was used as a perfume. Under the light of flattering candles, sumptuously dressed and loaded with jewellery, Emma was a beautiful piece of art.

In the morning, the Kelly girls had to don plain clothes to scrub the rooms (somewhat difficult with their three-foot hairdos) and wash the linen, an interminable task in a brothel. While most hygienic Londoners changed their sheets three times a year, one attraction of Kelly's was the cleanliness of both the sheets and the staff – one writer claimed that men went to prostitutes because they were cleaner than their wives. In the afternoon, Kelly girls retired to the parlour. No fire was lit until a client arrived, so they huddled with blankets over their opulent dresses, whiling away the hours gossiping and playing cards. Arguments broke out over men, clothes and their positions in the hierarchy, and sometimes descended into fights before the brothel bouncer or 'bully man' broke it up. They all waited until the sound of a bell signalled the arrival of a gentleman.

Some clients were nervous first-timers escorted by friends, or drunken men on a spending spree. Others were jaded regulars or dissolute debauchees. St James was still buzzing about the recent death of Mr Damer, the privileged only son of Lord Milton. Damer visited a bagnio and commanded twelve of the most handsome women of the town to be brought to him. He locked the door, and, and, apparently, 'made them undress one another, and, when naked, requested them to amuse him with the most voluptuous attitudes. About an hour afterwards, he dismissed them and then, drawing a pistol from his pocket, immediately put an end to his existence.'[41]

In the receiving room, Kelly discussed prices and requirements and the gentleman either took a girl immediately or a servant led him through to the salon. Candles were lit, the fire quickly kindled, and the girls stuffed their blankets and cards under the sofas and arranged themselves beguilingly. Buzzing with ideas borrowed from erotic novels such as John Cleland's *Fanny Hill*, the men settled down as the girls served them wine and fine meats while others like Emma danced and sang. Arlington Street also entertained rich, independent women, who came to watch the show. The evening usually began with civilised chatter, music and flirting but it could turn rowdy: one army captain and his men broke china and mirrors there seven nights in a row.

Emma had a chance to refine her natural grace as she danced, sang and perhaps played the guitar. 'Lewd Posture', a form of erotic dance, was the most popular form of entertainment. The performer wore a light dance dress or less and drew shawls across herself as she performed twirls, extended her leg behind her, and bent and stretched while others played a guitar or sang. Sometimes the women danced in twos or even groups. The employees also staged impromptu plays or recited speeches, often tales of seduced women that filled the pages of bawdy contemporary books such as *Nocturnal Revels* which allowed them to pretend to be ruined girls remembering their seduction while kneeling to beg for forgiveness. Emma's job was to dance while the other girls took men upstairs, sometimes up to three a night. One contemporary book instructed, 'You must not forget to use the natural accents of dying persons . . . You must add to these ejaculations, aspirations, sighs, intermissions of words, and such like gallantries, whereby you may give your Mate to believe you are melted, dissolved and wholly consumed in pleasure, though Ladies of large business are generally no more moved by an embrace, than if they were made of Wood or Stone.'[42] The women had to stay awake and, as one visitor noted, 'sit up every Morning until Five o'clock to drink with any straggling *Buck* who may reel in the early Morning and bear with whatever behaviour these drunken Visitants are pleased to use'.

Sometimes Emma had only to be a pleasant companion for dinner, drinks and cards, talking of horses and hunting with the aristocrats, stocks and shares with the businessmen, and politics with everybody, as it looked increasingly likely that England would lose the American War of Independence. When attempting to take refuge in a brothel from the English obsession with politics, Lord Tyrconnel was so infuriated by the zeal of the 'nymphs' for politics that he 'left them in a passion and the next day returned to France'.[43] Those who ruled the country came to Arlington Street and many claimed that St James courtesans bartered their favours for votes.

Kelly often paraded her staff around the Ranelagh and Vauxhall pleasure gardens and took them to the theatre or opera. Clients sometimes hired them simply as escorts for parties or days out. One rake, William Hickey, took three Kelly girls in a coach to Turnham Green, 'to drink tea at the Pack Horse, and treat the misses to a swing'. On fine days, Emma perhaps visited the tea gardens at Sadlers Wells and Highbury or concerts in Hanover Square.

Emma was beginning to make friends and she soon found a protector. Sir Harry Fetherstonhaugh, a spoiled young squire, was characterised by gossip columns as the brothel regular 'Sir Harry Flagellum' and 'The Sporting Lover'. Kelly listed him as Baron Harry Flagellum in a day book for another of her brothels. He had become interested in Emma and asked to take her for long-term hire at his house, Uppark, to entertain him and his friends. He would have had to shell out a lot of cash to Kelly to cover Emma's 'debts' and the madam's loss of earnings, and he had to agree to buy her clothes. Many girls, after being rented out, became kept mistresses. Kelly expected to be able to extract an even larger amount when Fetherstonhaugh demanded Emma's ultimate release.

Emma hoped Sir Harry Fetherstonhaugh might be her escape. In her year or so at Kelly's, Emma had found out about glamour and the kind of tricks to tempt a man's passion, and she had also learnt to rely on herself and hide her emotional needs. Her hard, brilliant exterior hid a secret longing for a man to cherish her, who she could believe loved her for herself.

12

Life in the Country

*E*mma was on long-term hire to a stag party set to last the entire summer. Uppark is a graceful Queen Anne style country house, situated in a rich agricultural estate on the South Downs. Almost as soon as Sir Harry inherited Uppark, he turned his new home into a venue for wild drinking and hunting parties. Fifteen-year-old Miss Lyon was hired to entertain the host and his guests, serve at dinner, dance and smile. She meant to work hard, confident that she would persuade Sir Harry to take her as his long-term mistress.

Emma had her own suite of apartments in the house and was dispatched to a cottage in the grounds only when Sir Harry's mother visited or respectable guests arrived.[44] The *Morning Post* noted that the 'little Bird of Paradise, whose amorous indiscretions have been so often held up to the public view in a light rather too serious to be entertaining, is about to produce fresh matter of envy, admiration, or ridicule . . . by a connection that does not seem even to be dreamed of by the most *knowing*' – perhaps his long-suffering mother.[45] Charles Greville later accused Emma of behaving at Uppark with 'giddiness and dissipation', but, proud at being chosen out of all the other Kelly girls and anxious to prove herself worth the high price Sir Harry had paid, she was striving to be the life and soul of the party.

Sir Harry, in the words of one contemporary, was 'not a man to control any Inclination that he can gratify'. Twenty-six, tall and athletic, he had a thin face, sandy hair, blue eyes and a typically English complexion, made more florid by heavy drinking. An only child, he soaked up attention from his friends as he had from his doting parents. Buried in boxes of Uppark papers is his teenaged exercise book.

Beautifully inscribed with signatures in large looping script, the work is sporadic and soon tails off: he begins to write out some Anglo-Saxon history in French and manages to list all the counties of England, but gives up on a mathematics diagram and then discards the book altogether.[46] Sir Harry was lazy, unreliable and selfish but he was tremendous fun, with a voracious appetite for late-night drinking, dogs and gambling, and bags of charisma to charm the ladies. He expected to be forgiven his bad behaviour – and he always was. While visiting Naples as part of his grand tour, he tempted the young Duke of Hamilton into a debauched spree. A genteel woman fell pregnant and Sir Harry fled, leaving Sir William Hamilton, English ambassador to Naples and the Duke's distant relation, to pay off the woman with £300, a 'loan' Sir Harry would never repay.[47] The duke's disgruntled tutor described Sir Harry as 'good natured, formal, effeminate, and obliging, without violent Passions or Ambition, a negative character who will rather be acted upon than act for himself'. Solely motivated by the love of an easy life, fluffheaded Sir Harry avoided anyone who might challenge him in any way.

Despite being preoccupied chiefly with hunting and drinking, Sir Harry was MP for Portsmouth, a nearby town on the south coast, and the surrounding area. Like many of the younger MPs, he allied himself with the Whig set (against the Tory incumbents), a group who advocated wider representation in Parliament. He supported Charles James Fox, the de facto leader of the group. Most of the guests at Uppark were Fox's supporters. Despite his jowly, slovenly appearance and aversion to baths, gadabout party boy Fox was wildly charismatic, with the appeal of a young Bill Clinton, and he commanded fervent loyalty from his followers. So spoiled as a child that he was allowed to paddle in bowls of cream, as an adult he was addicted to gambling and fun. Fox and his friends focused their hopes on the accession to the throne of the Prince of Wales for he supported them and promised to further their goals when King.[48] To his exhilarated supporters, Fox was the young, vibrant leader of a radical Whig faction, the harbinger of a new social order based on ambition and riches rather than birth and blood.

In London, Emma could hardly see the sky for smog, but the Uppark windows surveyed the radiant South Downs. Deer, foxes and rabbits thrived on the 900 acres of land, and thousands of sheep grazed the sloping grounds. The house recently suffered a severe fire, but it has been restored and it is still possible to appreciate how it would have appeared to Emma. Uppark was initially built by Ford Grey, Earl of

Tankerville, notorious for seducing his young sister-in-law in 1682, a scandal exploited by Aphra Behn's *Love Letters Between a Nobleman and His Sister*. The libertine earl dedicated his old age to home improvements, demolishing the original Tudor structure of the house and rebuilding it in a Queen Anne style.

Sir Harry's grandfather became rich through trade and marriage to a merchant's daughter and he instructed his son, Matthew, to buy a grand house and a baronetcy. When Matthew bought Uppark from the Tankervilles in 1747, he used the money earned from factories and warehouses to create aristocratic splendour, then travelled to Italy to buy matching furniture. Sir Harry inherited Uppark on the death of his father in 1775, but he had just recently returned from Europe to enjoy his prize. Only three years before Emma arrived, Sir Harry's mother found he had spent more than £3,000 in three months, the equivalent of well over £160,000. Their stately home in Northumberland was sold the following year, possibly to fund Harry's debts. Unrepentant, he continued to live beyond his means. In Europe, he bought beautiful antiques, artifacts and paintings, including many of himself by the (expensive) artist Pompeo Batoni. Uppark gave young Miss Lyon her first experience of real Italian art.

An establishment on such a scale was new to her. Behind the graceful façade, armies of workers, controlled and disciplined by Sir Harry's powerful steward and housekeeper, slaved to keep up appearances. Over fifteen footmen and upper servants waited on Sir Harry, and thirty or so below them did the dirtier work. Housemaids scrubbed floors, laid fires, cleaned rooms and made the beds. Scullery maids scoured the hearth and washed the dishes, and cooks feathered and skinned the catches for dinner, while laundresses dealt with the piles of hunting outfits, sheets and linens. In the lower rooms, valets scrubbed boots and specialist servants cleaned and prepared guns below stairs. At times, over one hundred servants were employed in the house. Outside, grooms and stable hands tended to Sir Harry's horses and dog handlers cared for his hounds.

Uppark had its own large and efficient dairy as well as a smithy, which Sir Harry and his friends called on frequently to shoe their horses, and it probably had a brewery, granary, carpenter's and candlemaker's. An additional fifty men came in from the village to work in the grounds as herdsmen, shepherds, labourers, carters and wheelwrights. Only ships and army platoons had so many employees. In the years when Sir Harry was travelling and only his mother occupied the house, the servants' wages came to over £20,000 in today's money, even though most of the staff were unpaid. Their uniforms and livery alone cost thousands.[49] Sir Harry's return from Europe combined with the visits of his friends and their packs of servants trebled the expenses. Emma's clothes added to Sir Harry's costs, for on many days she would have been expected to change her outfit four times a day: a breakfast gown, a riding habit, a tea dress and an evening dress. An employee of Sir Harry's but able to command the servants like any visiting lady, Emma's position in the household was ambiguous. Sir Harry probably hired her a lady's maid, but his servants would have had ways of making their resentment known toward the impostor by 'forgetting' to bring up her water or lay her fire.

Emma spent over a year at Uppark. Every day followed a similar pattern. Sir Harry and his friends rose at around eight, two or three hours after their servants, and breakfasted together from nine. As they ate, servants polished saddles and bits, brushed, fed and exercised the horses. Soon after breakfast, the party of perhaps up to thirty men, now changed into riding habits, accompanied by servants, grooms and their horses, set out over the estate with packs of hunting dogs in search of some of the 800 deer that roamed free. Occasionally they charged off to other estates. At around noon, the servants arrived bearing crockery and a fortifying meal of meat and wine. The housekeeper and her maids had to stay alert: if the hunting proved poor, or if it rained heavily, Sir Harry and his friends would return to the house, expecting a hearty lunch. For Sir Harry, the country was a place of pure pleasure, created to fit his needs.

Emma had never ridden before, but fear irritated Sir Harry and she made a determined effort to learn. She soon became an expert equestrienne, riding side saddle as all women did in the eighteenth century. When the hunt set off, she followed behind on a smaller lady's mount (to hunt required specific male servants and they would not work for a woman). Accompanying the hunt conferred high status. Sir Harry would allow his steward to dine with him on occasion but never to hunt. Emma delighted in wearing a fashionable riding habit, and she was eager to ride out with the men because this made it clear to everyone that she was a guest and not a servant.

When she did not accompany the hunting parties, Emma ambled around Uppark's beautiful grounds and then prepared herself for the evening's work. Her maid could brush and air her dresses, but she had to supervise the laundresses as they grudgingly washed her stockings, shifts and dancing costumes. Then she had to put on her make-up in preparation for the long, boozy dinner to come. By early evening, Uppark's graceful dining room was a riot of drunken men, rowdily using the chamber pots, which were out on display, and shouting for more wine. Stuffed with fine venison and beef, they gambled at cards and watched Sir Harry's beautiful mistress dance and sing. In the candle-light, their eyes glinted with pleasure − and desire. Emma smiled gaily, but she was far less delighted to have them catch at her dress than she seemed. She was going through the motions, well aware that her job was to keep up the pretence that the guests were attending a wild society soirée, rather than a mundane gathering of hunting-obsessed men. Her life at Uppark was one long theatrical performance.

She was lucky to be out of London. In early June 1780, a protest about giving Catholics the vote blew up into the biggest riot the capital had ever seen. King's Bench prison was burned down, the distilleries at Holborn burst into flames and escaping gin turned the water supply alcoholic. For four nights, the London sky blazed as houses were torched; 450 people died and swathes of the city lay in ruins. Sir Harry and his MP friends stayed well away, and kept on hunting.

Surrounded by other people's possessions, and portraits of the Fetherstonhaugh family and their horses, Emma grew lonely. She had food, handsome rooms, clothes, a good allowance and endless compliments, but she felt neglected by Sir Harry. He and his friends fêted her, but they implied she could be passed between them and joked about her. In Sir Harry's view, he had paid for her services, and she should reward his investment by being always engaging and enthusi-astic. Low spirits and headaches annoyed him. Increasingly, Emma was sent off to the house in the grounds because he had visitors he did not wish her to meet. Always shy of emotional commitment, Sir Harry was too busy having fun in the 1780s to worry about a needy teenage mistress.

In search of sympathy, Emma began to strike up a friendship with a man she had previously overlooked: Charles Greville, second son of the Earl of Warwick and MP for Warwick, in the Midlands. Older and much poorer than Sir Harry's friends, he hated hunting and had very little in common with his brash host, other than an enthusiasm for Italy and faith in Charles James Fox. Neither rich nor good-looking, he was thirty-two, still unmarried and excluded from circles of power at Westminster and the London social set. Greville was a forgettable type of man − the wallpaper of a party rather than its life and soul. Sir Harry and his young blades laughed him off as an oddball and ignored him outright when he talked about his collections of minerals, and they were utterly baffled by his hatred of hunting. Once Greville thought lovely Miss Lyon might pay him some attention, he made every effort to spend time with her, lagging behind the hunt with her and no doubt staying back at the house when she did. Excited by the idea of a secret intimacy, he was soon in love with Sir Harry's glamorous mistress.

Emma began to look forward to spending time with this shy, serious man whom the others shunned. In London he socialised with painters and art collectors and, after her work as a model, Emma wanted to know more about art. As Sir Harry's interest in her began to wane a little, she welcomed Greville's attention and flirted terribly with him, singing for him, begging his opinion and hanging on his every word. He called her Emily, and when Sir Harry sent her away from the house for a particularly long period, she even travelled up to London to visit him. Soon, however, her thoughts about any kind of new relationship were superseded by a more serious worry. By the summer of 1781, Emma was beginning to suspect that she might be pregnant.

13

Desperate Letters

*E*mma's child with Sir Harry was conceived in late June or early July. She could have purchased contraceptives by post from Madam Kelly or when she and Harry visited London, but perhaps she had not used them. Men hated uncomfortable, ill-fitting condoms and complained that contraceptive sponges felt as big as apples. They also found the ritual of douching unromantic. Emma was not in a position to make any demands of Sir Harry. But perhaps – since she was careful never to fall pregnant again until she met Nelson – Emma had, even if only subconsciously, hoped that a child might encourage Sir Harry to formalise their arrangement, perhaps even to marry her. More eminent men than him had wed *demi-mondaines*. Sir Harry's reactions, however, could be hard to predict. Initially, Emma kept her suspicions about her condition a secret.

In the autumn of 1781, Sir Harry made plans to return to London for the season and to attend Parliament. Feeling vulnerable, Emma probably promised to be sweet and uncomplaining and in return Harry decided to make her his permanent mistress and to set her up in lodgings in London, presumably after paying a large release fee to Madam Kelly. Emma's efforts had been rewarded. She would never have to return to St James. The Uppark records show that Fetherstonhaugh's estate included a number of large houses in the Strand, which were rented for between £20 and 60 per half year.[50] He may well have allocated Emma an apartment in one of these. There she would have to wait, looking out on to the bustling street that had been her first sight of London only a few years ago. Emma yearned for the city, but, now she was a kept mistress, she was permitted to see it only with Sir Harry or an elderly female chaperone.

Harry threw himself into his parliamentary social life and London nightlife and his visits to her dwindled. Emma did not know it, but he was in deep financial trouble. His mother, Lady Fetherstonhaugh, and the Uppark steward had recorded his refusal to disclose the extent of his debts in the accounts, and they were now demanding that he confess what he owed. He had failed to pay back a £3,000 loan to his mother for so long that she was charging him interest and he had to stave her off with £90.⁵¹ Entirely unaware, Emma waited for him every evening, dressed in the new outfits he had bought her, perfumed and carefully made-up, despondent when he failed to appear. She relied on his visits to give her the money she needed for washing, food, clothes and rent. Frustrated by her situation and in terrified denial about her pregnancy, she began to creep out to see Charles Greville and, it would seem from his letters, other old flames too.

When Sir Harry did visit, Emma's clinginess lashed him to fury. Her pregnancy, now in its third month, made her tearful and panicky about his behaviour. In September or October, she confessed the truth. Sir Harry was furious. It was not the first time he had been in trouble (it was rumoured that he was sent to Naples after getting a village girl pregnant). He accused Emma of having affairs and trying to trap him. But the baby was his. Even if she had had other lovers, she would have used protection and a woman tends to conceive with the man with whom she has intercourse most often. Refusing to listen to reason, Sir Harry reacted like a spoiled child. He saw her behaviour as treachery: he'd paid out to release her from Kelly's and this was how she had rewarded him. Only sixteen, Emma was too frightened to pretend to be apologetic or humble, the only way to prompt his sympathy. Angrily, he told her that their relationship was over. She was to leave the lodgings and he never wanted to see her again.

After she had sold the trinkets and some of the dresses Sir Harry had given her, Emma was once more nearly destitute. She knew that Kelly would not take her back for Fetherstonhaugh was a valued customer. She could have returned to Dr Graham in 1781 in his new Temple at Pall Mall, where he was promoting the therapeutic benefits of mud bathing. However, she needed more money than Graham could pay her and it seems more likely that she set up as an independent companion for men, contacting old friends and visiting parties. She hoped that Sir Harry might change his mind. The money required to keep her child for a year was a trifle for a man of his wealth, no more than the cost of an evening's gambling. Eighteenth-century society looked forgivingly on the offspring of aristocratic men. Many supported their children or persuaded their wives to bring them up along with the legitimate offspring. Sir Harry was less amenable. He was horrified at the thought of a baby and disgusted at Emma for having fallen pregnant.

Sir Harry ignored Emma all winter and left London to join a hunting party in Leicestershire. Once there, he refused to answer any of her letters. She begged Charles Greville for help but he encouraged her to keep writing to Sir Harry. Many girls in her position used an abortionist, such as the Fleet Street doctor advertising as a 'gentleman of eminence in the profession whose honour and secrecy may be depended on', able to ensure that 'every vestige of pregnancy is obliterated'.[52] But Emma wanted to keep her child.

By early January, she was six months' pregnant and very afraid. Sir Harry was showing no sign of relenting. She travelled to Chester to stay with some friends of her grandmother. All the while, she corresponded with Greville, who was considering taking her as a mistress. He had asked to see her birth certificate in December (Kelly had presumably instructed her to knock a few years off her age and pretend she was under sixteen). Few men arranged to take on a mistress when she was swollen with another man's child, and Greville exploited his powerful position. Emma, he knew, would have to make all the promises. He did not have to make the contract typical in such negotiations, in which the man offered to supply the woman he chose as a mistress with money, accommodation, clothes and a carriage. Rather than offer his protection immediately, he waited. In January, she wrote him a desperate begging letter:

> O G what Shall I Dow, what Shall I Dow . . . O G that I was in your Possession, as I was in Sir H. What a happy Girl would I have been, girl indead, or what else am I but a Girl in Distress, in Reall Distress, for God's sake G. write the Minet you get this and only tell me what I ham to Dow, derect me some way, I am almost Mad. O for Gods sake tell me what is to become of me.[53]

Emma's letter expresses her heartfelt distress but it is not entirely naive. She borrows her hysterical language from plays about tragic heroines, and also the tales of seduced girls the courtesans acted out in Kelly's parlour. By repeating 'what shall I do', she succeeded in communicating her distress without promising that she would not return to Sir Harry or indeed seek another man. Greville seized his moment. He puffed himself up and pronounced, 'Nothing but your letter & your distress could incline me to alter my system.' Gratified to see the glamour girl of Uppark plead, he was determined never again to see her choose other men over him. On the day he received her letter, he sent a money order and a set of stipulations.

He admonished her that 'it was your duty to deserve good treatment' from Sir Harry and criticised her for being 'imprudent' the 'first time you came to G. (i.e. Greville) from the country', and complained that 'the same conduct was repeated when you was last in town'. We can deduce that she came to see him from Uppark, but then refused to sleep with him or perhaps met with another gentleman friend. Enjoying his revenge, he hectored, 'to prove to you that I do not accuse you falsly I only mention 5 guineas, & half a guinea for coach'. He had given her money to visit him, and she had not behaved as he wished. Greville pressed home his point:

> As you seem quite miserable now, I do not mean to cause you uneasiness, but comfort, & tell you that I will forget your faults & bad conduct to Sir H. & to myself & will not repent my good humour, if I shall find that you have learnt by experience to value yourself & endeavour to preserve your Friends by good conduct & affection.

Greville explained to Emma how he expected her to 'preserve' him. She must give up Harry, and her other lovers, and see only him. 'I would not be troubled with your connexions (excepting your mother) and with Sir H.'s friends for the universe.' If she pursued Sir Harry again, or chose to 'hunt after a new connexion, or try to regain the old ones you gave up as lost', then the deal would be off for 'it would be ridiculous in me to take care of his girl'. However, he added, if 'you mean to have my protection, I must *first* know from you that you are clear of *every connexion, & that you will never take them again without my consent*'. Emma would have to sever all contacts, not only with Sir Harry and old paramours, but also with friends, fellow courtesans, and her entire family, other than her mother. She should come to town, 'free from all engagements' and 'live very retired'. Even her maid Sophy had to go (he promised the girl money and a 'good many kisses' goodbye – not much of a recompense). Presumably a Londoner, poor Sophy was stranded in Chester because Greville could not bear Emma to have a servant who had worked for her when she was companion to many men. Emma was not even allowed to keep her old name. 'You should part with your maid and take another name. I will get you a new set of acquaintance, & by keeping your own secret, & nobody about you having it in their power to betray you, I may expect to see you respected and admired.'⁵⁴ She had no choice but to accept his terms. The bargain was agreed.

Deeply relieved to have a protector, Emma spent the following days staying with friends and then family in the Chester area, who were all smiles now that Greville was sending her money. Then, she set off back to London, in a little more comfort than she had experienced when she was twelve. Greville had warned her to ensure that she should not 'be on the road without some money to spare, in case you should be fatigued and wish to take your time', so she was able to take perhaps a week, allowing herself to stop at inns and eat properly. When she arrived, exhausted and disoriented, Greville was not there to meet her (escorting on journeys was usually the job of a servant, and, moreover, Greville was paranoid that anyone might see him with the famous Miss Lyon, mistress of Sir Harry). Instead, his servant took her to a lying-in house for the final weeks of her pregnancy, probably in the City or East End where they were most common. There, attended by the landlady and an occasional midwife (doctors were expensive and called only in emergencies), she waited to give birth. Greville probably did not visit, for he would have been nervous about his coach being spotted outside a lying-in house. In her January letter to Greville begging for help, Emma added, 'Don't tell my mother what distress I am in' (he must have met Mary in the previous summer when he entertained Emma in London), but it seems as if he did tell her, and perhaps Mary visited Emma at the lying-in house.

As many as one in ten eighteenth-century women died in childbirth, or within a few days of delivery, and even mature matrons dreaded giving birth. Many wrote letters to their unborn child in case they died. Only seventeen, Emma was terrified. She was weakened by bloodletting, a practice fashionable in lying-in houses. When the time came, she would have lain on her left side, with the knees bent up and drawn to the abdomen, a position recommended in lying-in houses because it allowing the patient to preserve her modesty and avoid looking at the doctor if he was needed. Wearing a shift, tucked up under the arms, she gave birth to her baby. There was no anaesthesia and caesareans were carried out only if the mother died in labour, and the child was still alive. Emma had no drugs or alcohol to dull the pain (lying-in houses tended to forbid them). She had to give birth by herself for the alternatives were terrible. If a woman could not eject the baby then she died undelivered (the option for poor women), or the doctor began a horrific operation in which the baby was killed with a blunt hook poked into the vagina, and then cut and removed in pieces. But Emma was young and strong, and gave birth relatively easily to a daughter whom she named Emma. The baby was taken from her arms almost immediately.

After birth, well-off women relaxed in their rooms, cosseted by the servants, showing off the new arrival to visitors while languidly sipping gruel, tea and a special hot spiced wine mixture called 'caudle'. Emma had to return to Greville. Her daughter was boarded with a wet-nurse, probably near the lying-in house. Greville aimed to ensure she would have few opportunities to journey into town and visit her child. He sent little Emma off to her great-grandmother in Hawarden as soon as possible. Emma knew what was expected of her: she had to pretend that her pregnancy had never happened. Within a week or so, she was travelling in a coach to a new home in Paddington. There, she began to reinvent herself. Amy Lyon, the flamboyant would-be actress and extrovert girl about town, became Mrs Emma Hart, just arrived from Chester, Charles Greville's quiet and terribly shy new mistress.

14

Charles Greville's Penitent

*G*reville rented Emma a small house on the rural outskirts of London. Surrounded by market gardens, the village of Paddington Green was a cluster of houses around an inn, a church and a large hay barn. Londoners travelled over on summer evenings to enjoy the fresh air and watch the peasants at work. Emma's new home was truly 'very retired'.

When Emma arrived from the lying-in house, Greville would not have been there to meet her (when a man took a mistress, he left her to settle into her new home alone). Her mother, however, was already ensconced, eager to welcome her. Every kept mistress needed a chaperone, and Greville spared himself the expense of hiring one, as well as a housekeeper, by bringing in Mary. Emma's feelings as her coach drew up outside the house were mixed. After her rackety life with Fetherstonhaugh, she hoped to be able to settle into happy security as Greville's loving mistress. She was painfully aware, however, that she had not seen him for over six months, and she fretted she was too much changed by pregnancy to attract him. When he arrived later that evening, she flung herself at him, promising love, obedience and anything else he wanted. Greville had to content himself with her caresses for even by eighteenth-century standards, a few days after labour was too early for sex. Instead, he listened to her promises with pleasure. He intended to test her.

As Greville had instructed her, she had changed her name to Mrs Emma Hart, perhaps a pun on 'heart', of which Greville tended to think Emma had too much. But, from the outset, he made ever more demanding rules that she struggled to obey. First of all, her daughter had to stay in the north. Greville wanted to head off any chance of Emma trying to show Sir Harry the child when he was in London, in the hope that he might be softened by the sight of his daughter. Although all genteel women boarded their babies out of the home with a wet-nurse (apart from aristocrats who hired a nurse in), most used a local woman, and few had to endure being on the other side of the country from their child. Had little Emma been male, both Greville and Harry might have been more amenable toward offering support or assuming the responsibility of a father. As a girl, she was unwanted.

Emma's mother also had a new name. Mary Lyon was now Mrs Cadogan. The name sounds a little like Kidd, or even a blend of Kidd and Lyon, but it was usual for a woman to take the name of the man with whom she cohabited (as Emma's old friend, Jane Powell, had done when she called herself Mrs Farmer) and Mary had perhaps been friendly with a man of the same name, though the registers contain no record of Mary's marriage.[55] However, it is serendipitous that Cadogan is a rare surname. A John Cadogan was living in the Paddington area in 1773. He witnessed the marriage of his sister, Judith, to a Robert Lynn, at St Marylebone (where Emma would later marry). When nearly every bride and groom on the same register could sign their names, Judith signed X, which indicates that the Cadogans were poor.[56] Perhaps Mary left St Giles to live with Cadogan in Paddington around 1775. After the relationship ended, she remained in the area and Greville decided it would be an ideal place to keep Emma. Greville encouraged her to retain the name of Cadogan, to pursue his project of keeping the old Miss Lyon secret, quiet and retired, hidden from her old friends and lovers.

Mary, only in her late thirties, was hardly older than Greville, but he relegated her to the position of unpaid housekeeper. Perhaps she felt guilty for abandoning Emma in her childhood or maybe she simply saw that Emma was successful and wanted to hitch herself to her daughter's star. Although he was almost twice Emma's age and lacked Harry's looks, charisma and wealth, Greville was still the second son of the Earl of Warwick. Emma had secured the protection of a scion of one of the country's most influential aristocratic families.

Charles Greville was born in May 1749 (on the same date Emma was christened, sixteen years later). His father, Lord Brooke, was made Earl of Warwick in 1759 when Greville was ten. His mother, Elizabeth Hamilton, was the daughter of Lord Archibald and Lady Jane Hamilton, and the elder sister of Sir William Hamilton. After a stormy marriage,

his parents divorced. Shy and awkward, Greville delighted in his collection of rare minerals and jewels and, like most men of his class, lived
beyond his means, spending his money on expensive girls of the town.
When he visited Naples, his interest in the local courtesans astonished
his host, his uncle, Sir William Hamilton, himself a renowned hedonist.
Greville had secured a cheap deal in Emma: the toast of the Temple of
Health, Kelly's and Uppark, his own beautiful courtesan, without having
to foot a pay-off to Madam Kelly.

Greville needed to hunt down bargains. In 1773, his father died
and left him merely £100. His elder brother gave him nothing, the
allowance from his father of £200 a year ceased and he had to subsist
on only £500 a year, an inheritance from his mother. He took the
seat for Warwick in the House of Commons and assumed his brother's
position at the Board of Trade. Not a natural politician, he failed to
join a faction in the Commons or network other positions or kick-
backs at the Board and, consequently, his income remained insuffi-
cient. Sir William Hamilton advised him to seek a rich wife, and
Greville attempted to present himself as a man of substance to the
papas of rich young women by building an expensive house in the
new and fashionable Portman Square (a strategy so common that
Tobias Smollett satirised it in his novel *Peregrine Pickle*). Greville
required a wife who could bring in around £20,000 per annum. But
hundreds of younger and richer gentlemen were similarly ambitious.
His passion for keeping mistresses did not enamour him to the fathers
of genteel girls, many of whom had raised their daughters to expect
love and companionship, rather than the typically distant aristocratic
marriage, in which a man gained children and social respectability
from his wife, but took a mistress for sexual gratification and affection.

By the time Greville met Emma, he had burnt fingers. An impoverished second son for over ten years, he had failed to find a wife or
a lucrative position at Court, and had wasted his money on women of
the town. In 1780, he had gained a job with the Admiralty, which
brought a rent-free house in King's Mews (now covered by Trafalgar
Square), where he lived. The house at Portman Square still unsold, he
rented a small house for Emma on a discreet side road off Edgware
Row, the main street running through Paddington Green. Since he had
Mrs Cadogan to carry out the domestic drudgery, he only needed to
appoint a few extra maids. Trapped in the country, Emma would not
require clothes or a hairdresser, and he would ensure she spent the

minimum on food, wine, travel and candles – beeswax was one of the greatest household expenses at the time.

Greville wished to keep Emma all to himself. As he threatened, 'I will never give up my peace, nor continue my connnexion one moment after my confidence is again betray'd.'[57] But he desired more than her fidelity. As his letters to her and Sir William show, he tried to school the self-confessed 'gay wild Emily' to be a completely new woman: submissive and penitent for her earlier hectic life. Every aspect of her existence was to be different: her occupation, dress, food, friends, hobbies and even speech. A spendthrift with a wandering eye, he wanted Emma to behave like a mouse.

In styling his mistress as his pupil, Greville was at the forefront of fashion. After the publication of Jean-Jacques Rousseau's *La Nouvelle Hélöise*, which pivoted on the sexualised relationship between the heroine and her teacher, novelists, playwrights and artists were keen to show how a relationship in which a man taught a woman to behave correctly could be gratifying for both parties. Jane Austen joined the craze in *Northanger Abbey*, probably written in the 1780s, in which giddy Catherine Morland falls in love with Henry Tilney as he schools her in proper judgment. One man even took two poor washer maids and devoted himself to training them to be modest, intending to marry the one he preferred – he was somewhat piqued when both rebelled and ran away. In France at about the same time as 'Mrs Hart' was practising her deportment in Edgware Row, the husband of the sixteen-year-old future Josephine Bonaparte was haranguing her to improve her writing, education, carriage and behaviour. Emma, always desperate to please, tried very much harder than Josephine. More was asked of her than simply writing good letters. Greville had a role in mind for her.

The Magdalen hospital for penitent prostitutes was established in 1758. Girls who showed a desire to reform were taught to eschew vanity and love of finery and to embrace meek behaviour. Dressed in uniforms of thick brown cloth (men thought that women turned to vice because they loved fine clothes), the inmates or 'Magdalens' ate plain fare and passed the day in sewing. They soon became national obsessions and featured in magazines, plays and novels. So many wanted to sit in the public gallery overlooking the ranks of girls at chapel on Sunday mornings that the authorities had to issue tickets. Greville was titillated by the idea of his own Magdalen and he fell hook line and sinker for the myth: regulation, sober dress and diet, industry and housework could make a flighty girl virtuous and submissive.

At Edgware Row, Emma had to live in 'a line of prudence and plainness', as Greville reported to friends. Later, he declared he had reformed her 'pride and vanity' and taught her to be 'totally clear from all the society & habits of kept women', so she did 'not wish for much society' and 'has avoided every appearance of giddiness, and prides herself on the neatness of her person & of the good order of her house'. Greville visited daily and often stayed there, supervising every aspect of his mistress's life. Emma dressed in new modest outfits in subdued colours, while wearing less make-up and styling her hair plainly. George Romney's son claimed that she dressed always in her penitential maid's outfit while with Greville and when Henry Angelo happened to see her, he declared she was dressed so drearily that she might as well have been a nun. Instead of her Uppark feasts of game and sugary puddings, she ate small portions of meat, bread and vegetables. Her diet was very similar to those Graham had recommended and his praise of apples as the ideal slimming food may have remained in Emma's mind for the receipts show she bought plenty of apples, even in January. Greville also trained her to enunciate more elegantly. She worried when she saw her child again that little Emma 'speaks countryfied', but she promised her lover 'she will forget it'.[58]

Emma spent her days playing at being a modest young lady in settled, pedestrian domesticity. Greville left her at home while he attended dinners and receptions and forbade her to go to the pleasure gardens or even to a local concert. Obsessed with order and cleanliness, he hectored her to improve her messy ways. Soon, he was able to declare 'there is not in the parish a house as tidy as ours'. Otherwise, he encouraged her to occupy herself with improving reading and with practising singing and the guitar. He wanted to ensure his Magdalen could amuse him in the evening. Women were educated to sing and play because there was no other way of enjoying music at home unless someone in the family – usually the wife – could perform.

The new Magdalen made little headway with Greville's recommended books, so addicted was she to women's magazines, such as the popular *Lady's Magazine*, a mix of puzzles, stories, songs, embroidery patterns, and a little news. She did, however, enjoy *The Triumph of Temper*, William Hayley's long narrative poem that instructed women to be meek and good by showing the heroine, Serena, retaining a sweet temper and a 'wish to please' throughout various obstacles. When Emma was separated from Greville, she wrote that parting with him made her so unhappy that she failed to keep up the stoic temper of Serena or, as she put it, 'I forget the Book'.[59] In July 1782, the 'Man Milliner' gossip column of the *European Magazine*, a magazine to which Greville subscribed and sometimes contributed, offered a tantalising titbit of information about Emma while joking about the hobbies of fashionable ladies. Most of them cared only for 'Admiration', but Greville's mistress, 'Mrs Greville', was apparently solely interested in 'Poetry'.[60]

In the evenings, she entertained Greville with little anecdotes about her docile days. They may have sung together or were perhaps joined by a maid, for it seems that Mrs Cadogan had no gift for music. Pleased by her progress, Greville began to invite some of his friends over to meet her. He knew not to make the same mistake as Sir Harry by leaving his lover alone, bored and desperate for male attention. Emma's new admirers included William Hayley and the playwright Richard Cumberland, as well as the painter Gavin Hamilton (no relation to Greville) and various minor aristocrats. More cultured than the loutish Uppark set, they flirted with her in a friendly, respectable way. Emma flourished under their attention, delighted that her new admirers seemed to be as interested in her opinions as her beauty.

Emma threw herself into the role of the penitent prostitute. Courtesans were fascinated by the Magdalen hospital and many pretended to have been inmates in order to enhance their earning power. The 'Magdalen' look was in fashion. The *European Magazine* noted that the essential hat for the stylish lady at the Ranelagh pleasure gardens was 'the Religieuse or Nun's cap'. A light hat of 'Italian gauze, crimped to a point, before coming down at the sides', it was hugely popular.[61] Emma perhaps was wearing such a cap when she attended Ranelagh with Greville on one of the few occasions she went out in the evening. Excited by the illuminations and the music, she burst into song. The crowd loved it, but a furious Greville hauled her back to Paddington Green in disgrace. At home, she hurried to change into a plainer dress and knelt, begging him to retain her as his penitent or abandon her out into the street. Mollified, Greville agreed to retain her and continue his course of instruction.

Emma did not seem to resent her lover inspecting her expenses, checking her dress, and searching for evidence of vanity and giddiness. Like any good pupil, she found gratification in excelling at her examinations. She showed him stringent accounts for even the most inconsequential expenses: apples, coal, eggs, stockings, cotton and needles. In this, she was sharper than Greville who was stupid about the cost of provisions. The prices charged for the commodities are high, particularly for a small household consisting of Emma, her mother, a cook and only one or two maids. Like clerks in counting houses across the City, she inflated the prices slightly and siphoned off a little for herself.

After the debacle at Ranelagh, she found her way around the rules but was careful never to break them. Greville was supporting Emma, her daughter and her mother, he had rented her a sweet little house and he was kind to her, as long as she obeyed him. Few canny girls would demur to dress up as a nun and feign the mien of a fashionably penitent prostitute in exchange for such security. But most of all she followed Greville's rules because she had fallen in love with him after a few months as his mistress. More engaging and good-natured than he seems in his pompous letters, Greville's standoffish exterior hid a warm sense of humour. He was a reflective man, with a shyness and vulnerability that melted Emma's heart. Believing her lover's boasts that he was Sir William Hamilton's heir and so would soon be rich, she hoped she might be established as his permanent mistress.

Although Greville was uninterested in the Warwick landowners that he represented, he was involved in London politics, particularly, like all Whigs, in the fight between Charles James Fox and Sir Charles Wray for the seat of Westminster in the elections of 1784. Fox had been a minister but a row over a bill that concerned the East India Company so incensed the King that he dissolved Parliament and appointed the twenty-four-year-old William Pitt as Prime Minister. In the elections that followed, voting for Fox was, to a certain extent, a vote against the King. Fox's many female supporters wore a special uniform, blue dress and yellow petticoat (after the colours of George Washington's armies in the American War of Independence), blue hat with yellow lining, and 'elegant balloon ear-rings of three drops, blue and gold, together with elegant gauze sleeves and tippets, with wreaths of laurel, having gilt letters on the leaves inscribed 'Fox, Liberty, Freedom, and Constitution'.[62] As her letters reveal, Emma certainly owned many blue dresses and hats while living at Edgware Row and perhaps Greville encouraged her to dress as a supporter of Fox – in vain, as it happened, for Wray won the seat.[63]

Greville was pleased with his experiment. His little Magdalen was turning out excellently. As he wrote, she 'avoided every appearance of giddiness, and prides herself on the neatness of her person and the good order of her house . . . She has vanity and likes admiration but she connects it so much with her desire of appearing prudent that *she is more pleas'd with accidental admiration than that of crowds which now distress her.'* Apparently, she would rather have Greville's measured praise for buying meat at a bargain price than a crowd of men applauding one of her sensuous dances. As she put it in a letter to him later, 'You have made me good.'

Emma preserved her newfound security by appearing to be happily acquiescent to her lover's will. She channelled her energy into singing, dancing and sticking to her strict low-sugar diet. The raw, blowsy girl was slowly transformed into an elegant performer and decorous hostess. Greville's attitude toward Emma was complex: he wanted the real girl docile, retired and utterly under his control, but he was ambitious that images of her should be admired. Most of all, he wanted to make money out of her. A number of aristocrats had attempted to turn a poor girl to profit through training her to go on the stage but, although Emma was the spitting image of Sarah Siddons, the great tragedienne who was driving Drury Lane wild, Greville had other plans. She would model for paintings and he would receive a cut of the sale. Emma seized the opportunity to exploit her dramatic talent. As prime muse and model for George Romney, she would become famous.

II. Mistress of Fame

15

London's Muse

On a bleak, rainy Friday morning in March 1782, wrapped up so no one could recognise her, Emma clambered into a discreet carriage and set off for Mayfair. Still sore from giving birth, she wanted desperately to stay at home. Already, the evenings of fussing around Greville, pretending she had not given birth while coddling his every need, were proving tiring. But she did not have time to rest. She was on her way to sit for George Romney, painter to the stars. Although only seventeen, she wanted to be famous – and she knew this was her chance.

At his magnificent studio house in Mayfair, 32 Cavendish Square, fifty-year-old George Romney readied his paints for 'Mrs Hart's' arrival and tried to calm his nerves. He set out various possible backgrounds and drapes and stoked the fire. For years he had been looking for his muse, for the woman who could embody modern beauty in a classical form. He had met Emma before but she had been young, raw and flippant. Charles Greville, his friend and intermittent patron for over ten years, had promised him that she was now hard-working and reliable. Romney hoped so, but he was more concerned that she was still beautiful. Despite his success, he still felt excluded from the artistic establishment, and he needed a model whose looks could transform his art. His career depended on it.

When Emma arrived, she followed Romney's servant through galleries crammed with paintings and then the sitters' waiting room, the books of engravings of possible poses still open on the couch. In back rooms, disgruntled apprentices filled in backgrounds and cleaned paint pots. At the far end of the apartment was Romney's large painting room, lit through the long windows by the pale morning sun. As his servant opened the door, she felt a surge of heat. Artists usually kept their studios warm to dry the paintings and to keep their models warm, but Romney's was stifling, for he was convinced that heat relieved his pain from varicose veins. He kept the windows shut and the fires blazing all day. Some of his sitters complained, but he ignored them, knowing the heat encouraged women to remove more of their clothes. The fire was burning high for Emma's visit.

The painting room was chaotic, strewn with large mirrors and candles, unsold portraits, canvases whitewashed and ready for use and piles of brushes and paints. Painted backgrounds of the countryside and sea views were propped along the walls, along with books and sticks for gentlemen to hold while posing, and harps, books and pieces of needle-work for their wives. Romney gently distracted Emma's attention from the pretty instruments and books – they were for the squire's wife who wanted to parade her virtue. He wanted his new visitor to pose as something far more daring.

Wearing her best crimson dress with white gauze around the neck-line, Emma sat on a chair raised from the floor, a couple of feet above Romney. As in the Royal Academy, she would use a rope hanging from the ceiling if standing, but all she could do on that Friday morning at eleven o'clock was sit and smile. He could not paint her figure, but Greville had promised him that she would soon be slim once more, thanks to her strict diet at Edgware Row. In his painting studio, shy Romney was transformed into an actor on a stage, flamboyant and overexcited. He painted best when he felt he was performing, and alter-nated between frenetic energy and languor, rushing up close to gaze at Emma's face and then dashing backward to take in the general effect. He sketched her a little, encouraged her to smile, tried to have her talk, but the icebreaker was his spoiled studio dog. When she spotted the little spaniel, like so many of his lady sitters, she cuddled it to her and soon broke out into a real, unforced smile.

The sitting was a success. After two hours, with a break for tea or a little light wine and pauses for mixing paints, Emma was allowed to go home for lunch, exhausted but pleased by her day's work. Most people only modelled once or twice for the same painting, but within a week she was back. On 20 March, she sat again. The outcome was the gorgeous *Sensibility*, now on show as *Lady Hamilton as Nature* in the Frick Collection in New York. Half-turned to the viewer in her lovely red dress, Emma cuddles Romney's dog so it covers her still rounded waist.

Loosely pulled back from her face with a gauze band, her thick chestnut hair streams over her shoulders. The rich rose of the gown sets off her delicately pink cheeks, creamy neck and décolletage. Emma's sparkling smile is infectious.

Aristocratic female sitters typically look away from the viewer, to the side or modestly downward, but Emma's eyes glitter mockingly up at us, locking us in her irresistible gaze. Romney captures a luminous sensuality entirely absent from more grandly remote society portraits. The representation, *Sensibility*, is borrowed from Emma's favourite poem, *The Triumph of Temper* by William Hayley, about the heroine's 'wish to please', and it is possible that she suggested the subject. In *Sensibility*, Emma's pose reflects her familiarity with the subject: she radiates youthful sensitivity and innocence. If she was suggesting that she would try to please both Greville and Romney, it was a promise she would keep.

Almost as soon as it was finished, *Sensibility* became the most popular portrait in Romney's gallery. Many of his visitors wanted to buy it but Greville preferred to keep it and bought it for £20.[64] The painting was soon reproduced as a print and became inordinately popular, displayed in shops across London, sold to hundreds of ordinary people who wanted it on their walls. As Emma's figure returned, she became a regular.

Emma's frequent journeys to Romney's studio in Cavendish Square began a determined entrepreneurial endeavour to disseminate her image across England. Greville's plan to make money by selling portraits of Emma was clever, but he underestimated just how famous it would make her.

Emma met the nervous, obsessive painter when he was ascending fast. George Romney had been born into a Cumbrian farming family in 1734. Although he came late to portraiture, he was already a successful London painter by the age of thirty-three. In 1773, restless and discontent, he sold his business and travelled to Italy for creative fulfilment. In Rome, he socialised with other artists and their models, met the great artist, Henry Fuseli, hired a female model to practise nudes, filled sketchbooks with plans and impressions and found new inspiration. He imagined a new type of painting, a fusion of classical lines with a contemporary idea of female allure.

On his return to London, Romney had one ambition: to find the model able to bring his ideas to life. He set up a studio at Cavendish Square, previously occupied by the society painter, Francis Cotes, and began once more on what he complained was the 'cursed drudgery of portrait painting', thirteen hours a day, every day. Sufficiently spacious to entertain crowds and opulent enough to convince anyone that he was a fashionable painter, his Cavendish Square apartment was ideal for a man with big ambitions. He soon became London's second portrait painter, after Joshua Reynolds, president of the Royal Academy. By the early 1780s, determined to steal Reynolds's fame and clientele, Romney increased his prices to eighteen or sometimes twenty guineas for a quarter length, approaching Reynolds's price of thirty. He no doubt hired a splendid carriage to rival Reynolds's lavish vehicle, famous across London. The Academy, through its association with the Court, controlled the upper echelons of the portrait industry and had excluded Romney in his youth because he had not trained in life drawing. Once he was better established, they invited him to exhibit but he declined, still smarting from their earlier disdain. William Hayley, who quickly became his most trusted confidant after they met in 1776, encouraged him to remain aloof from the Academy and pushed him to paint more sensual and imaginative canvases.

By the eighteenth century, portraits had replaced tapestry as the most popular wall covering. In a time without photographs, any important event was commemorated with a portrait: election to a club, inheriting an estate, the birth of a child and acquiring a mistress. Relatives and friends commissioned portraits of each other and gave away copies of their portraits as presents. After a painting was completed, Romney sent it to a printmaker who engraved an imitation on a copper plate and then made hundreds, perhaps thousands of black-and-white impressions for those who could not afford the real thing. Artists competed fiercely to satisfy public demand. James Northcote, assistant to Reynolds, estimated that there were about 800 painters in London, but he concluded that there was only work for eight, of all types, including history and landscape. A portrait painter needed smooth social skills: he had to be a gentleman and a host, a self-promoter and an entertainer, all the while alert to the subtlest differences in the social status of his clientele. Romney had perfected his act and the crowds flocked to his studio.

Despite his success, Romney was still searching for the model who could bring to life the ideas inspired by his tour of Italy. Ordinary tavern girls did not have the sophistication and famous actresses and beauties like Harriet Mellon and Kitty Bannister, although electrifying onstage, could be stiff in portraiture, determined to appear more virtuous in their portraits than they did onstage. And no respectable woman would model as a goddess – they wished only to be painted as themselves. Romney wanted a model to try to imitate the spirit of his classical models. He also wanted her to pose in a way that implied she was dancing or running, but squires' wives and actresses would only sit, or at their most daring lean on a post. Melancholic Romney could not rival Reynolds's suave social poise or his cosy relationship with high society. He needed to present himself quite differently.

At the same time as Romney was dreaming of showing modern beauty in classical form, the British public was newly avid for pictures of glamorous young women and ideas for styles in dress. France had glittery Marie Antoinette and her court of fashion plate female courtiers, but in England, the Hanoverian Queen and Princesses were plain and stolid, and most aristocratic women simply dull. A new breed of female celebrity evolved. Actresses, courtesans and models fed the public hunger for glamour and ideas for styles in dress. Paintings of them were the top attractions at exhibitions and artists' studios, their prints were plastered across shop windows and the newspapers discussed their love lives in salacious detail, with the stories often planted by the women themselves. The name of a virtuous lady would be read only twice, in the announcement of her marriage and in her obituary, and so those women who were willing to pass up their chances of respectability had a free run to exploit the hunger of London's sixty or so newspapers for scandal, style, and high glamour. Any girl hungry for fame needed to be painted often – and Emma was determined. She sat for Romney twice in June, nine times in July, four times in August, and four more in December. The day books show 118 sittings between 1782 and 1784, and, since the record for 1785 is lost, she probably posed for him more than 200 times in total.

Thanks to her early training in dance and posture, Emma excelled in Romney's studio. As a fellow artist declared, she had honed her skills modelling as Graham's Goddess of Health, so when she met Romney, he hardly needed to instruct her: 'he asked her to adopt a thousand graceful attitudes, which he then painted'. With him, she 'developed a new talent which was later to make her famous'. Emma had an unparalleled ability to move and express moods, as well as a flair for dress, which allowed her to drape and arrange her clothes to transform her look. Her acute awareness of the effect of her own image gave her an instinctive understanding of Romney's ambitions. She used her skills as a model to reinvent herself as other characters, turning her raw beauty into the embodiment of sensuality and grace. Delighted by her

93

versatility, Romney challenged her to move between roles, from the seductress Circe, to a playful young girl or a tragic heroine, retaining all the while her essential beauty. As William Hayley later wrote to her, 'you were not only his Model but his Inspirer', extravagantly declaring that Romney admitted 'he ow'd a great part of his Felicity as a painter' to the 'Intelligence with which you used to animate his diffident & tremulous spirit to the grandest efforts of art'.[65]

She had to work hard to create the look her new friend wanted. He knew little about fashion, and his vague commands to women to wear white satin dresses (which sent one client, Lady Hester Newdigate, into a panic of borrowing and dieting) never created the portrait he had in mind. He reviled powdered mountains of hair, corsets and stays, wide upholstered skirts and heavy jewellery, and wished women to wear dresses that followed the line of the body. Since the costume worn in the portrait was always the responsibility of the sitter, Emma set her mother to work altering old outfits, and buying new material. Once she had regained her figure, Romney discouraged her from stays and pushed her to wear fewer clothes, maintaining the blazing temperatures. She arrived in full dress, every inch the modest eighteenth-century lady, and then transformed herself into a nymph, an audaciously modern version of classical beauty, by loosening her hair and draping satin and muslin so it flowed gracefully around her body.

At the studio, Emma talked and sang as Romney tried to capture her face, first testing the colours on the top or the sides of the portrait, then swathing them on with thick bristle brushes, some of them up to three feet long, before filling in the details with shorter, more delicate sable brushes. Sometimes he simply sketched her or made studies, other times he worked on detailed portraits. Emma experimented with a few poses in front of Hayley – he never forgot 'the wonderfully expressive features of my friend Emma, as she used to display them in a variety of characters to me and our beloved Romney' – but modelled for the majority of her pictures alone.[66] Although artists encouraged sitters to invite their friends to entertain them (guests also paid the artist if they attended), Greville had forbidden her to see her friends. Without an audience, model and artist quickly came to rely on each other. As Emma came to trust Romney, she began to dance and move in the spirit of the characters and the great portraits were born.

Romney produced hundreds of canvases of Emma and about sixty finished portraits, as well as cartoons and sketches. His work with Emma was a real artistic experiment and a relief from turning out similar portraits of stolid squires. The portraits of her are a new type of spontaneous and emotional portraiture, expressive, adventurous, and far removed from routine and safe society work.

Emma appeared to best advantage as either a half figure, usually showing her waist, or in full length, and Romney's most beautiful portraits show her in such a pose. *Circe*, Romney's second finished portrait of Emma, is one of his most impressive. Depicted full-length, she is tall and graceful, dressed in a flowing pink and white robe that shows off her ivory skin. Hair cascading lavishly around her shoulders, she steps forth from the darkness, eyes aflame, as compelling as Circe herself, her striking beauty turning men into grovelling pigs. Like *Sensibility*, *Circe* is one of the few portraits in which Emma gazes directly at the viewer, challenging her audience head on.

Romney's studio was essentially a shop, and Emma had to ensure that she was not seen by the customers, who would be outraged to encounter any outré women, however much they might admire their portraits. Like all actresses and courtesans, she came between nine and twelve and never later than one-thirty unless it was a Saturday, when the fashionable set was often out of town.[67] On weekday afternoons, 32 Cavendish Square was a social whirl, the galleries, according to a friend of Romney's, 'filled from Top to Bottom, his Painting and Drawing room crowded with Pictures of People of the First Fashion and Fortune'. Squires and their wives came to search for suitable poses amongst the engravings of previous portraits and valets brought dogs to be sketched quickly and then removed before they ran riot. In the absence of art galleries (the British Museum had a few dusty rooms of archaeological treasures, usually open by appointment), artists' studios functioned as exhibitions: people went to learn about art, meet friends and while away an afternoon looking at paintings. Lovers arranged to bump into each other, fallen women contrived to meet their more respectable friends, and rakes prowled for new mistresses.

Romney's customers clamoured to know more about his beautiful new model. He began to exploit their curiosity by painting her in modern dress and by dropping hints about her past. *Emma Hart in Morning Dress*, one of her personal favourites, shows her in a stylish black velvet dress with a large pink silk petticoat, a white scarf and a luscious velvet bow around her neck. Her chestnut curls are topped with a huge-brimmed black hat that flatters her translucent skin and deep dark eyes. In *Emma Hart Reading the Newspaper*, she wears a similarly fashionable outfit and her eyes are glued to a gripping story.

Respectable ladies did not officially read newspapers and certainly not the eye-popping scandal rags. The joke was clear: the young star reads about herself. In *Emma Hart in a Straw Hat*, she peeps coyly from under her floppy sunhat. In these portraits, the viewer's position is slightly above her, and unlike *Circe* or *Sensibility*, she looks up at her viewers, beseeching and submissive. Romney also painted her with elegant simplicity as *Ariadne*, in a turban, in a low-cut gypsy outfit and as Thetis, slave girl lover of Achilles.

The *World* newspaper praised Romney for his 'tender, bewitching touch' in his portraits of Emma and declared them 'full of captivation'. Romney's work expresses his profound feelings for Emma, his fascination with her beauty and his delight in her unpretentious personality. Unlike the frail women Thomas Gainsborough captured with feathery delicacy, Romney's sturdily energetic Emma is full of life and eager to laugh, even at herself. Increasingly, the paintings were private jokes on wild Amy Lyon's endeavours to play the virtuous housewife of Paddington Green. *Emma Hart as a Magdalen* is the definitive satire on Greville's assiduous efforts to form her into a penitent prostitute: swathed in Magdalen robes, she kneels in praying position, her covered head upturned for forgiveness. No other painter had Romney's gift for humour. His rival, Reynolds, knew how to commit gravitas to canvas but struggled to communicate *joie de vivre*. Ultimately, the president of the Royal Academy preferred the ideal to the real, and Emma was simply too earthy for him: a sexy, down-to-earth girl with a wicked sense of humour.

The Spinstress is Romney's most teasing version of her, now on show at Kenwood House, Hampstead. Once more positioned below the viewer's line of vision Emma slyly peeps over her shoulder. Her white dress is skin-tight, enticingly pulled around her bosom. Emma's beguiling smile hints at the absurdity of her pose, dangling a suggestively shaped spindle while a white hen pecks around her feet. It is all a joke: the costume is much too impractical for work and she is far too exotic to be a mundane farm girl. Francis Cotes, the previous artist at number 32, had painted ladies with a spinning wheel as the epitome of sedate virtue.[68] Romney took the same motif and turned it into a satire on Greville's attempt to keep his sexy mistress in bucolic retirement. He continued the joke by sketching her modelling for the portrait while Greville, Sir William Hamilton and William Hayley look on. Just as Marie Antoinette dressed as a shepherdess, here the kept mistress plays at being a humble domestic drudge. Duchesses, actresses and courtesans were battling for the role of famous muse but Emma was suddenly more famous than any of them. The image of the girl from nowhere was all over London.

Romney made *Sensibility* and *Circe* the focus of his gallery and Emma became the star attraction. Her presence was everywhere, in the extravagant portraits in the gallery, the half-finished canvases in the studio and the engravings in the book. Visitors were titillated by the idea of being in the same room as her. People jostled to see her portraits, some even hoped to catch a glimpse of her in the morning. Men asked if they could take her as a mistress. Women demanded to be painted in a similar fashion, hoping that they might appear as gorgeous as she did. The pictures sold quickly. A Mr Crawford bought *Emma Hart in a Straw Hat*, and Admiral Vernon paid sixty guineas for *Alope Exposed with her Child*. A head of a *Bacchante* was bought by Sir John Leicester, and Mr John Christian Curwen, one of Romney's best patrons, snapped up another *Bacchante*, a version of *Serena*, as well as the *Spinstress* when Greville was unable to pay the price. To satisfy demand, Romney painted copies of his originals. Charles Greville was surprised, and not pleased with his mistress's new-found popularity. Never imagining that Emma (and her past) would become the point of interest, he was dismayed that people craved to see her.

As engravings filled print shops, Emma's flowing shifts, which followed the line of the body, and the way she wore her hair loose and without powder, encouraged English women to question their stiff brocaded suits and coiffures. At the same time, pictures of the looser dress fashionable in Paris were circulating and the press began to denounce encumbering hoops, corsets and rigid petticoats, blaming them for heart attacks, miscarriages, short breath and hysteria.[69] Fashion magazines contained few pictures and so prints of Romney's portraits of Emma in her figure-hugging drapery became a primary source of fashion ideas for genteel and upper-class women across England.[70] The trend took time to spread. In 1786, a German visitor to London was surprised, after seeing portraits by English painters like Reynolds and Romney, to find women still attired in rigid dresses and wearing their hair in powder.[71] But as the most stylish women took to wearing shifts, drapery and simple muslin gowns and as fashion plates appeared of Marie Antoinette resplendent in similar outfits, and later Empress Josephine (who, it was said, dampened her muslin so it would cling to her curves), the brocaded look fell out of favour. Women welcomed the autonomy of movement allowed by the draped style, delighted to be able to sit down, bend over and even walk quickly.

Everybody gossiped that Romney and Emma were lovers. They were half-right: shy, emotional Romney was infatuated with his model and she dominated his private thoughts as well as his public gallery. Emma had been schooled in encouraging men to talk about themselves, and he responded to her breathless interest in him. He liked to think that she, who comprehended his creative aims so well, might also understand him as a man. After twenty years living apart from his wife, he was lonely but still too conscious of his humble roots to flirt with the smart women he painted. However, unlike Sir Harry Fetherstonhaugh, he did not believe women existed only for his own pleasure, and he restrained himself, knowing that any attempt to seduce her would wreck her new-found security. He poured out his passion in agitated notes to Hayley. Emma, in her turn, felt affectionate toward him and was deeply grateful for his interest in her. But the edgy workaholic painter was not her type and she was well aware that her relationship with Greville and his willingness to care for her mother and child was conditional on her absolute fidelity. Her relationship with Romney was an unrequited passion, predicated on her unavailability and his restraint: she was a natural exhibitionist and he was something of a voyeur. She was learning how to keep a man's attentions by resisting him.

Romney's obsession with Emma pervaded his paintings for the rest of his life. He filled dozens of sketchbooks with pictures of her nude, clothed and in various poses. Even when he painted other women, he made them look like her: dark hair, pale skin, pink cheeks, full mouth, oval face, tall and long-legged. He showed both her exuberant, sensual personality and her pleasure in life, and he never equalled the vibrancy and grace of his portraits of her in his other work. As he complimented her, 'I have had a great number of ladies of figure siting to me since you left England but they all fall short of The Spinstress, indeed, it is the sun of my hemisphere and they are but twinkling stars.'

Many portraits were destroyed. Some rotted away in the damp rooms of his Hampstead home, where he moved in 1798, and others have been destroyed. Lost are paintings of Emma as *Iphigenia, Joan of Arc,* a Pythian princess, and a picture of how he guessed she was in childhood. Hundreds more canvases of Emma were begun than ever completed.

As a result of Romney's devotion, Emma became the most painted woman ever in Europe, and there are more portraits of her than of

Queen Victoria or any English or European actress or aristocrat. Thanks to Romney's interest, other painters began to demand a sitting from her, including Joshua Reynolds, Thomas Lawrence, Alexander Day, Guy Head and Gavin Hamilton, as well as European artists like Angelica Kauffman, Elisabeth Vigée le Brun, Johannes Schmidt and Wilhelm Tischbein. If he had not painted her so often and with such skill, they would not have been so eager to capture her likeness. Even those who caricatured her borrow their vision from Romney by reworking the poses he used.

While paintings of Emma hung on the walls of expensive stately homes, cheap prints of the same portraits soon adorned poorer homes across the country. She became a commodity and versions of portraits of her began to appear on consumer goods: cups, fans, screens and sometimes even items of clothing. Like frequently photographed women today, her image was seared on to the public consciousness. She became a fantasy figure for thousands of men and a fashion leader for women. Even if she had never become as celebrated as she did, the loveliness of her portraits would have ensured her lasting fame. By 1783, Emma had become the most wanted model in London. She had no idea of the storm clouds gathering behind her.

Charles Greville detested his new role as the lover of an icon. He was making plans to be rid of her.

16

Entertaining the Envoy

*I*t was the summer of 1783 and Greville was jumpy. His uncle, the wealthy, newly widowed Sir William Hamilton, was about to arrive in England for the first time in over five years. Greville was intent on grabbing money from his uncle and Emma flurried around him, promising to use her every wile to charm her middle-aged visitor, confident that she would soon have him eating out of her hand. Dressing herself in her prettiest outfit and arranging herself in the parlour at Edgware Row, she rehearsed topics of conversation suitable for a deeply depressed old man. When handsome, fashionable Sir William sprang into her home, full of jokes, eager to touch her hand and give it a long, lingering kiss, she was surprised – and excited.

Fifty-five-year-old Sir William had arrived to organise his late wife's estates and earn himself a few pounds by selling off his most precious vase from his collection, as well as catching up with his dozens of friends. The fourth and youngest son of Lord Archibald Hamilton, Sir William became a diplomat after a stint in the army. Since 1764 he had been Envoy Plenipotentiary to Naples, fulfilling the role of an ambassador but denied the name and the salary, because the British government considered the kingdom irrelevant to English trading and military interests, dismissing it as a close ally of Spain. He devoted himself to childish King Ferdinand and demanding Queen Maria Carolina in order to aggrandise his own position by developing closer ties between England and Naples. A natural hedonist, he flourished in the Neapolitan Court, where decisions were made on the hunting field and in the ballroom. The only way to infiltrate the inner circle was by spending huge amounts of cash, and so it was fortunate that he had married a splendidly wealthy

Welsh heiress, Catherine Barlow. Thanks to the peasants planting wheat on her Pembrokeshire estates, he spent unrestrainedly on sumptuous horses and carriages, hosted lavish dinners and ordered fittingly grand outfits of gold, silver and silk.[72] As the fashion for the Grand Tour expanded, the English flocked to Naples, attracted by its party-mad reputation, and Sir William expended vast sums on their accommodation and entertainment. Since the recent discovery of the ruined classical city of Pompeii, he had also earned a reputation as one of the biggest collectors in Italy, spending thousands of Catherine's pounds on statues, vases and art.

Emma's new friend had grown up in the Royal Court, with the future King George III. His mother, Lady Jane Hamilton, had been the mistress of Frederick, Prince of Wales from about 1736 until 1745. Frederick appointed her his wife's Lady of the Bedchamber. Then, dizzy with lust, he also made her the Queen's Mistress of the Robes – not even the poor Queen's clothes were free from her rival's claws. Lady Jane possessed the highest position open to a woman in the Royal Household, and held absolute sway over Frederick and his family throughout her son's early life. Sir William called King George his foster brother, boasting that 'my Mother reared us and the same Nurse suckled us'.[73] With this, he hinted what many suspected: he was Frederick, Prince of Wales's son. Archibald Hamilton, fifty-eight at his birth, was neglected by Jane, and, according to the wickedly accurate Lord Hervey, long reduced to the 'passive character his wife and the Prince had graciously allotted him'.[74] It may have been that Lady Jane achieved such spectacular influence over Frederick because William was his child.

Sir William socialised with the highest aristocrats in England and some of London's most colourful men. He was a focal member of the Society of Dilettanti, a circle of genteel libertines fascinated by foreign sexual cults, led by Richard Payne Knight, a sensualist masquerading as a scholar. A more level-headed friend was Sir Joseph Banks, celebrated naturalist and President of the Royal Society of Science. Sir William was attracted to wealthy eccentrics and one of his closest friends was his second cousin, William Beckford, novelist, collector and the richest man in England, famous for his sybaritic lifestyle and profligate spending. Greville fitted in well with his uncle's raffish, cultured set. When he had visited Naples at the age of twenty, Sir William had been pleasantly surprised to find he was a man after his own heart, interested in both art and *demi-mondaines*. They were immediately friends and Greville was soon asking for money and favours.

Although he made extravagant use of her wealth, Sir William neglected Catherine. Quiet and accomplished, she reviled the shallow Neapolitans, along with their boorish King and hypocritical Queen. Sir William admired his wife's musical talents and prized her spotless reputation, but he found her company insipid and was irritated by her frequent bouts of low spirits and illness. Dejected by Hamilton's boundless enthusiasm for everything but her, Catherine found comfort in a Neapolitan orphan she adopted as a daughter. After the child's death, probably from malaria, in 1775, she suffered further depression and her health deteriorated. In May 1782, Sir William realised that the city he loved had wrecked 'Lady H's tatter'd constitution'. Catherine was dying. In his Villa Portici, at the foot of Vesuvius, she lingered painfully until August. She left him a letter chiding him for his 'dissipated life', writing that 'you never have known half the tender affection I have borne you', and that she loved him 'beyond the love of Woman'.

After indulging in his guilt among Catherine's belongings, Sir William set off for England on his first visit since 1777. He hoped to release the money from Catherine's estate and sell his best vase to the Duchess of Portland, a woman celebrated for being, like him, intoxicated only by empty vases. He owed £4,000 to antique dealers and he needed money. When he arrived, he stayed in the newly built and fashionable Nerot's Hotel, close to the St James shops and dealers, the Palace and the King's Place brothels, and far too expensive for him. London welcomed him back: the April edition of the *European Magazine* began the fanfare early by opening with a full-page engraving of him and an admiring biographical sketch.[75] The King teased him about remarrying, but William was in no hurry to scour London's eligible aristocrats for a suitable wife.

Sir William was immediately enchanted by Emma and began visiting her almost daily, putting off his visit to his late wife's estates in Wales and procrastinating about meeting the Duchess of Portland. Emma received him joyfully: she had plenty of free time and had never had such an engaging guest. Tall, thin and very fit from trekking up Mount Vesuvius, Sir William had a sharp nose and bright inquisitive eyes, but those who met him were most often struck by his clothes. A famously stylish dresser, he set off his good looks with sumptuous suits of pink, blue and red silks, and handsome shoes with large silver buckles. Intellectual and cultured, he had a charismatic personality and a true gift for friendship. The perfect diplomat, he shied away from saying anything that might offend or annoy, peppering his conversation with hilarious anecdotes about King Ferdinand and juicy morsels of gossip about the Neapolitan Court.

Emma, cooped up in the country and pining for the gossip and glamour of high society, devoured Sir William's stories and begged him for more. She was very lonely. Early in 1783, Greville had gained the position of Treasurer to the Royal Household and he was often away from Edgware Row. She threw her energies into pleasing Sir William and he, in turn, was utterly bowled over by his nephew's alluring, witty mistress. Still bruised by the death of his wife, he craved female attention, and here was a gorgeous young woman with seemingly nothing to do but entertain him and serve him tea and cakes. Soon, they were giggling together in corners, flirting incessantly and teasing each other robustly. Emma could be as bold as she pleased, for Sir William was much less easily offended than Greville. He even snatched her away for spontaneous visits to town. She dubbed him 'Pliny', after the Roman scholar and vulcanologist. He called her the 'Fair Tea Maker of Edgware Row'.

Emma told herself that her friendliness toward him was a dutiful effort to further the connection between her lover and his uncle. But she found herself looking forward to Sir William's visits, hugging herself with pride about his admiration for her. Only a few years ago, she thought, she had been hopelessly poor, and now a wealthy envoy came all the way to Paddington simply to sing with her and listen to her jokes.

Sir William's favourite niece, vibrant Mary Hamilton, had been looking forward to his visit, expecting to be spoilt rotten. Twenty-seven-year-old Mary had only just left her position at Court as third companion to the Princesses. After six years of deadly dull embroidery and early nights in threadbare Windsor Castle, only alleviated when the Prince of Wales (six years her junior) had fallen passionately in love with her when she was twenty-three, she was excited to be living with friends in Piccadilly. Not rich, she was hoping that she might be able to charm Sir William into giving her a big present towards a dowry. She was acutely annoyed to find she had a rival – and a woman of dubious reputation at that. She teased her uncle mercilessly about his fascination with 'Greville's mistress'. When he began to enquire about having his own portrait of Emma made to adorn his Naples home, it was the last straw. Her uncle, she declared, was neglecting his friends in London in his frenzy to put the city's artists into competition, 'painting this Woman's picture for him to take to Naples'.[76] Sir William foisted on her the job of negotiating the sale of his vase to the Duchess. To her credit, she successfully sold the vase (now in the British Museum). Hopefully her uncle rewarded her with a present for her efforts.

Forgetting his debts, Sir William commissioned Joshua Reynolds to paint Emma as a *Bacchante*, hoping that the great artist would produce a portrait that outshone Romney's. Sir Joshua's *Bacchante* was, however, a failure. Although he captured some of her infectious gaiety and replicated the exquisite detail of her gold-trimmed cashmere shawl, the fussy drapery and hair confused the lines, the face was too wide, and the finger in the mouth – a familiar erotic posture used for courtesans and actresses like Frances Abington – made her look simpering. Sir William paid the price of thirty guineas and then, in the spring of 1784, commissioned Romney to paint her as another *Bacchante*, a more daring full-length image in which the viewer gains a side view of Emma's bosom. She wears a peach-pink dress that sets off her complexion, and he captures her from the same side as *Sensibility*, but she is running with a dog. Slim and vibrant, she smiles with delight at the viewer, her hair and dress streaming behind her. Bacchantes, according to a contemporary best-seller on music history, participated at orgies nearly naked, dancing wildly, their hair dishevelled.[77] No respectable woman would consent to be portrayed as a nymph in the throes of desire. Emma allowed Sir William to commission a painting of her in the most scandalous pose because she desperately desired his good opinion.

Sir William was utterly infatuated with Emma, but he considered his flirtation with her to be no more than a fun interlude, a mere holiday romance. Predicting that Greville would soon grow bored and cast her off, he did not expect to see her again after he left England.

'If I was the greatest laidy in the world I should not be happy from you,' Emma wrote to Greville in 1784. Although they were often bickering, she blamed the strains in the relationship on his job at the Treasury and his uncertainty about Sir William's plans. Finally, after delaying it for a year, Sir William and Greville set off to survey the Welsh estates. Greville did not trust Emma alone in London and he dispatched her to Cheshire with her mother to collect little Emma and then travel on to spend the summer by the sea at Abergele.

Emma met up with her daughter, now aged one, at her grandmother's house in Hawarden. Mother and daughter began to build a relationship. She decided Abergele was too far away and 'uncumfortable' and set off instead for the glamorous sea resort of Parkgate, on the west coast. Only a few miles from her birthplace, Parkgate was a world away from grimy Ness. Visitors admired the handsome promenade of white and red houses and flocked to the elegant entertainments. Over thirty hotels graced the long sea front and small alleys were named after roads such as Drury Lane in London to attract the urban rich. Perched on the promenade were a theatre, a billiard room, several coffee shops and restaurants, a racecourse, and assembly rooms for dancing, tea drinking and card parties. Since it was the main port for passenger boats to Ireland, most of the actors and aristocrats travelling there spent a couple of days in the town. England's elite partied in Parkgate, most recently Mrs Fitzherbert, new wife of the Prince of Wales. The visit of sweet-natured Maria, a quiet Catholic widow and the most controversial woman in England after the secret marriage that had so infuriated the King that he swore she would never be Princess of Wales, meant one thing: the hoteliers put up their prices.

Emma claimed she had found a cheap apartment at Mrs Darnwood's boarding house, now Dover House, 16 Station Road, but its pleasant position right by the sea came at a cost. Little Emma played with Mrs Cadogan by the sea, while her mother embarked on a stringent detoxifying and beautifying regime that was, as she confessed, a 'great expense': 'a shilling a day for the bathing horse and whoman and twopence a day for the dress'. Bathing machines were liberally advertised in the local papers: a carriage driven by a liveried man and a horse which had at the back a long covered tunnel, so that the lady could bathe in (dark) privacy.[78] It seems as if Emma had developed eczema at Edgware Row, and it was particularly painful on her knees and elbows. Greville had been repulsed by her peeling skin, so she was anxious to prove it was improving, declaring she washed her knees and elbows at least twice a day in seawater and massaged them with moisturising cream, as well as hiring a maid to slather seaweed all over her before she went to bed.

She missed him deeply. 'I am allmost broken hearted at being from you', she pined.

you don't know how much I love you & your behavier to me wen we parted was so kind, Greville, I don't know what to do, but I will make you amends by your kind behaiveir to you for I have grattude and I will show it you all as I can, so don't think of my faults Greville think of all my good & blot out all my bad, for it is all gone & berried never to come again.

When he did not reply, she stepped up her promises, pledging to become a new woman, the epitome of 'evenness of temper and stea-dyness of mind', thanking him for his 'angel like goodness'.[79] She begged him not to 'think on my past follies' and declared that the 'wild unthinking Emma' was no more.

> Am I not happy abbove any of my sex, at least in my situation, does not Greville love me, or at least like me, does not he protect me, does not he provide for me, is he not a father to my child . . . To think of your goodness is too much.[80]

When she finally received a letter from him, she replied in a tumble of gratitude, rhapsodising how little Emma 'hopes you will give her an opportunity of thanking you personally for your goodness'. She had fallen in love with her small daughter and had begun to cherish hopes that the little girl might charm her lover. Greville read the letter angrily, suspecting her of trying to wheedle a place for little Emma at Edgware Row. He dashed off a furious reply, making it clear that he would decide when he would meet the toddler, if at all.

Hurt, she replied that 'you have mad me unhappy by scolding me; how can you' and promised he could decide her child's future: 'I will give her up to you intirely . . . put her there where you propose'. In her next letter, she regretted she never had the 'luck & prospect' of an education like her daughter's. 'All my happiness now is Greville, & to think that he loves me makes a recompense for all.' She promised she would be 'gentle & affectionate & everything you wish me to do I will do' and declared 'I shall think myself happy to be under the seam roof with Greville.' She was trying hard to be as tender, obedient and grateful as *The Triumph of Temper* instructed, but her effusive prom-ises no longer had the same effect on her lover. After ten weeks away from her, Greville was no longer titillated by games of punishment and forgiveness. He was as weary of her as any collector who tires of a piece he owns.

Greville returned from Wales determined to hook an heiress. He faced a lot of competition. Contemporary newspapers were full of advertisements for 'a Girl of moderate fortune, who hath the good sense and generosity to prefer a good husband to a rich one' from a 'young man of liberal education' using an address at a coffeehouse for corre-spondence.[81] As a minor aristocrat with only £500 a year and onerous debts, famous only for having a gorgeous mistress displayed in sexy poses in galleries and print shops across town, Greville was not much of a catch. Only if Sir William confirmed him as his heir could he attract the interest of wealthy women. As he wrote to his uncle, 'suppose a lady of 30,000 was to marry me, the interest of her fortune would not prove equal to her pretentions' unless 'your goodness should ensure me at a future period an estate which would come hereafter'. Everything depended on him winning Sir William to his cause. If he wanted to grab an heiress, he would have to do it before his amorous uncle found a new wife.

17

Negotiations

'The thought of your coming home so soon makes me so happy, I don't know what to do,' Emma gushed to her lover from Parkgate in August 1784. When she returned from the seaside, Greville allowed her to bring her daughter to live with her while he searched for another establishment for the child. Sir William left a month or so later to return to Naples before the weather turned too harsh to travel, and she waved him off, still buoyant and happy. He nodded and smiled indulgently when she told him how much she was looking forward to seeing him again. Greville, he knew, was about to cast her off.

After turning Emma into the epitome of the virtuous housewife, Greville was no longer attracted to her. In fact, he had begun on a secret double life (so secret that it has never been noted). He was having an affair with Elizabeth, Lady Craven, a playwright and daring socialite who was separated from her husband. Lady Craven gave no precise dates for the affair but boasted that when Greville left his position as Treasurer to the Royal Household, which he did in late 1783, his leisure 'was bestowed on me'.[82] He spent as much of his time with her as he could, leaving Emma to pose for Romney, entertain Sir William, and play with her daughter.

Although Greville was falling out of love with Emma, he continued to feel responsible for her. He did not want to simply abandon her as Sir Harry had done but he could not afford to pension her off and he knew she would make violent scenes when he rejected her. By December, he was bored of little Emma, and he found a Mr and Mrs Blackburn in Manchester who would raise her with their daughters and send her to school, guaranteeing discretion for a high fee. When their maid came to collect the child in the second week of the month, Emma was devastated and Greville found her distress infuriating, hardening his resolve to dispose of her, even though he had no idea how to do it. At the same time, he heard that his uncle had proposed to a cultured young widow, Lady Clarges, whom Sir William thought 'would suit me well'.[83] She turned him down, but Greville knew he might not be so lucky next time.

Christmas gave Greville time to think. By the beginning of 1785, he had developed an audacious plan: to send Emma to Sir William as his mistress. In one fell swoop, he would put someone else into the Palazzo Sessa to discourage canny widows and foist on his uncle the responsibility of giving Emma a pension. He prepared his mistress to obey him, pressing her to read the flurry of moralising tales recommending obedience in a woman that suddenly appeared in the *European Magazine*. Since his friends wrote for the magazine, it is perhaps no coincidence that at the moment when he wanted to dispose of Emma, it began to publish tales about how 'Cleora' was ruined because she was too fond of her own way while 'Louisa' was obsessed with praise and 'vainly imagines that those that admire her are always her adorers'.[84]

Greville wrote to Sir William from his King's Mews house, keeping Emma ignorant about his plans. He started by grumbling about his debts, averring he had been cutting himself down to the barest necessities, 'reducing every expence to enable me to have enough to exist on, and pay the interest on my debt'. At the same time, he praised Emma, extolling how she was 'much improved' now she has 'none of the bad habits which giddiness and inexperience encouraged, and which bad choice of company introduced'. Now, he boasted, she 'is naturally elegant, & fits herself easily to any situation'. He declared her the type of woman to stick to one man, and he was 'sure she is attached to me or she would not have refused the offers which I know have been great'.

Emma may have guessed that he was considering marriage, but she would not have expected it to alter her position, since many men retained their mistresses after tying the knot. Still unhappy about her separation from her daughter, she threw herself into working with Romney and sat for him fourteen times from early January to the beginning of March 1786. She posed as a bacchante, as Leda loving her swan, and as allegorical embodiments of 'Nature', all typical poses of a mistress. Romney had an inkling of Greville's plans to dispose of her, and he rushed to make as many studies of her as possible. When he made a copy of the *Bacchante* for himself, he removed the gauze from the bosom so her breast is partly exposed. It became one of his most popular paintings and when it finally left for Naples, there was a clamour of complaint that it had not been engraved.

Despite Greville's efforts, Sir William seemed to be oblivious to what he wanted. In March, Greville began to lay it on with a trowel. 'I wish the tea-maker of Edgware Row was yours,' he wrote, outrageously, promising that Sir William would find this perfect 'modern piece of virtù . . . tolerable and even comforting'. He assured his uncle that he could dispense with her whenever he wished. If Emma thought herself a burden to him, she would 'give up the connexion' and not 'even accept a farthing for future assistance'. He even told Sir William a 'clean and comfortable woman' would suit him, adding, shockingly, that the most sensible thing for a man of his advanced age 'would be to buy Love ready made'. Greville added a dash of emotional blackmail by claiming that he was so poor he would probably 'be unable to provide for her at all', leaving her destitute, conjuring the ludicrous scenario of Emma in a convent. Determined to convince his uncle, he posted a torrent of pleas, promises and emotional blackmail. In letter after letter, he griped about his debts, implied that his uncle would not find anyone else, appealed to his pity for Emma, and boasted he had reformed her into the perfect mistress, cheap, loyal and sexually compliant. Never once did he mention Emma's feelings or suggest she might miss her daughter.

Sir William considered himself young and handsome and he took exception to his nephew's characterisation of him as too old to find a new wife. But, long in the habit of not saying what he meant, he shied away from an outright refusal. 'I wou'd take her most readily,' he replied, adding, 'I really love her and think better of her than of any one in her situation.' However, although 'her exquisite beauty had frequently its effects on me', he thought, 'there is a great difference between her being with you or me, for she really loves you when she cou'd only esteem and suffer me – I see so many difficulties in her coming here'. English ladies and the Royal Family would be offended by her presence and 'it would be fine fun for the young English Travellers to endeavour to cuckold the old Gentleman their Ambassador'. He suggested that Emma should be sent to the country, where he would provide for her until his nephew could take over again after his marriage.[85] Greville refused: if Emma was in England, she would harass him with requests, embarrass him with showy behaviour in public places and probably continue posing for Romney.

Realising the extent of his uncle's resistance, Greville embarked on a different approach. He declared he wished Sir William to take Emma for a only few months. He promised he only needed a little time, more money and freedom from his 'incumbrances' to obtain the hand of a pretty, eighteen-year-old heiress, Henrietta Willoughby. Believing Greville's luck was about to change, Sir William gave him a letter to show to Henrietta's father in which he named his nephew as his heir. Once he believed the marriage was on the cards, he was amenable to the idea of taking Emma for a short period of time. English lady visitors had not proved as open to his advances as he had hoped and he was lonely. He wrote sadly to his niece, 'what is a home without a bosom friend & companion? My Books, pictures, musick, prospect are certainly something, but the Soul to all is wanting.'

Greville sensed his advantage and pushed it home. He promised Emma wanted only 'a refined & confined life' and 'would conform to your ideas'. Always obedient, 'she has natural gentility & quickness to suit herself to anything, & takes easily any hint that is given with good humour'. Unlike most mistresses, 'her expenses are trifling', she did not mind when she was visited, and she occupied herself maintaining 'the neatness of her person & on the good order of her house'. Greville claimed she would happily live in a remote villa and that she was so easy to please that she would prefer a 'new gown or hat' to male admiration, and 'if you will only let her learn music or drawing, or anything to keep her in order, she will be as happy as if you gave her every change of dissipation'. He stressed the temporary nature of the 'trial'. 'You will be able to have an experiment without any risque' for if it did not turn out well, she would 'have improved herself and may come home'.

Greville's calculating behaviour was callous but not unreasonable by eighteenth-century standards. He was not abandoning her. The only lover Lord Byron attempted to pass on to a friend was his dearest long-term companion, Teresa Guiccioli. What was cowardly and cruel about Greville's plan was his failure to explain it to Emma. He knew that if he did so, she would refuse to go to Naples.

In the summer of 1785, Mrs Cadogan suffered a stroke, at the age of only forty-one. Her recovery was slow and Greville claimed he could not add to Emma's grief by ending their relationship. Instead, in December, he lied that he had to travel on business to Scotland and he instructed her to ask Sir William if she could holiday with him for six months while he was away. Eager to help her lover, Emma obeyed. Her careful expression suggests Greville helped her with the letter to Sir William. 'As Greville is oblidged to be absent in the sumer, he has out of kindness to me offer'd, if you are agreable, for me to go to Naples for 6 or 8 months, and he will at the end of that time fetch me home.' She promised, 'I shall always keep to my own room when you are better engaged or go out, and at other times I hope to have the pleasure of your company and conversation, which will be more agreeable to me than any thing in Italy.'

Greville enclosed Emma's appeal with a letter reminding Sir William how cheap she was to keep, asking his uncle to pay for the journey and emphasising that when he married, his 'first concern will be to provide for her, whether she is with you or not'. Emma believed she would be staying with William as a guest but Greville portrayed her as a sex object, describing her in a way that would be more suitable to an advertisement for a prostitute in *Harris's List*; 'a cleanlier, sweeter bedfellow does not exist'.

William sent £50 for the journey and a welcoming letter to Emma. Since the roads were impassable in winter, March was the earliest she could travel. Excited by the success of his plan, Greville was happy to humour Emma throughout Christmas and New Year. She busied herself packing dresses for spring and summer, warm outfits for the journey and guidebooks. Her winter dresses and hats remained in the wardrobe for when she returned. Greville's friend, the painter Gavin Hamilton, kindly offered to escort mother and daughter to Rome. Everything was falling into place. Greville wrote happily that he had 'cleared Emma and myself of everything connected to our establishment'. It had taken him two years, but Emma was finally off his hands.

Emma was nearly twenty-one and the passions and demons that would drive her far were firmly in place. Her childhood had made her ambitious, hungry for the limelight and afraid of rejection, driven by a desire to please and win praise. Greville's strictures kept her on edge, aware that her position depended on correct behaviour. Energy, kindness and enthusiasm were her best features, an egomania born of insecurity the worst. When Emma later summarised her friend, Lord Bristol, as 'very entertaining & dashes at every thing, nor does he mind King or Queen when he is inclined to show his talents', she described herself. Like many energetic, attention-seeking and gregarious party-lovers, she could be unreliable, tardy and thoughtless, and she had great self-confidence but little self-knowledge. Emma was a terrible judge of character, which made her generous but always vulnerable to exploitation. Often slightly tense, she was exciting but never relaxing company and she threw herself into frenetic social activity to escape the low spirits that engulfed her when she felt alone.

Sir William was taking (in Greville's words) the 'prettiest woman in London', already famous for her beauty and her scandalous past. In her absence, prints of her as Magdalens, bacchantes, and goddesses circulated and the legends about her grew. Everyone knew she was leaving. As the *World* newspaper tittered at the time of her departure, any of the 'dozen portraits' of Emma by Romney 'might have gone abroad with Sir W. Hamilton and answered his purposes full as well as the piece he has taken with him, a piece more cumbrous and changeable than any of the foregoing'.

18

Torn by Different Passions

*A*fter wishing a tearful goodbye to Greville, Emma set off for Naples with her mother and Gavin Hamilton on 13 March 1786. The trio travelled in a south-easterly direction through France, attempting to avoid the unrest that was beginning to overtake the country. As they scrimped along in hired coaches to eke out Sir William's gift of fifty pounds, English aristocrats swished past them in glossy, brand-new carriages equipped with maids, doctors, cartloads of furniture and hampers of food and drink. Emma's party had only minimal comforts and they feared the ordeal of crossing the Alps. Carriages had to be dismantled and carried over in pieces, while their inhabitants were bumped over the peaks in an 'Alp Machine' a sedan chair attached by ropes to poles carried by two to four porters. Worried about her mother's weak state of health, Emma probably paid to travel by boat from Marseille to Geneva. Once they reached Switzerland, they could relax. Sir William's servant was waiting for them at Geneva, ready to whisk them into one of his master's most stylish carriages, equipped with a full purse to take care of their needs.

Eighteenth-century travellers dreaded southern Italy. James Boswell declared his bones almost broken by the roads. Henry Ellis, famous for attempting the North-West Passage, grumbled he would rather circumnavigate the globe than travel from Rome to Naples. Horrified by the grubby hotels, most English rode straight from Rome, stopping only to change horses, a drive that took about twenty-five hours, arriving in Naples in the middle of the night. Hopefully, Emma also did so, sparing her mother the grimy hostels where, according to one traveller, the room shuddered to draughts while the windows were covered only with splintered, broken shutters, and rain spattered on to the beds.[86] Unlike all the aristocrats, however, Emma had lived in slums and was used to rough lodging. After Geneva, she was able to devote her attention to the most important matter: making herself look beautiful for Sir William.

'You have sent me to a strange place,' Emma lamented to Greville. She arrived in Naples on her twenty-first birthday. Perhaps she first saw the city early in the morning as her carriage bounced through the streets, past the poor sleeping on the steps. To a girl used to London fog, the sky would have seemed inordinately bright: she could see not only the stars, but also the red sparks exploding out of Vesuvius and the twinkle of the sea in the bay. Passing dilapidated Renaissance palazzos, baroque churches and glossy shop windows, they turned into a quiet side street, Santa Maria a Cappella Vecchia. The coach slipped through the gate, and Emma and Mrs Cadogan found themselves in the courtyard of their new home. In the dark, the Palazzo Sessa looked like a ramshackle ruin.

Emma struggled to appear composed. Sick and disoriented after six weeks on the road, she was unhappy to find no letter from Greville awaiting her.

You don't know how glad I was to arrive hear the day I did, as it was my Birthday & I was very low spirited. Oh God, that day that you used to smile on me & stay at home & be kind to me, then that day I should be at such a distance, but my comfort is I shall rely on your promise & september or October I shall see you.

Despite her homesickness, she was excited to see her old friend and admirer again and was won over by his gracious welcome. Ignoring Greville's instructions to stow Emma in a suburban villa, he had prepared the splendid suite on the ground floor reserved for his most distinguished guests. Mother and daughter were shown to their lovely quarters: a sitting room painted white with gold stars on the ceiling, two more rooms, and a luxurious bedroom with a fireplace. One window faced the Chiaia, the main promenade, and from the other they could see the sweep of bay all the way to Vesuvius.

Emma prepared for bed with her eye trained tremulously on the volcano. Everyone expected it to erupt within a few months. In recent years, six major eruptions had killed hundreds and devastated the countryside, and Emma had a bird's eye view of it plotting and bubbling. At night, columns of flame the height of the mountain shot into the sky alongside exploding clouds of peacock blue or buttercup yellow lightning, covering the windowsills with ashes.[87] She lay listening to the volcano's billowing sighs and the sound of rival gangs fighting in the caverns of rock under her window, trying to ignore the creaks as Sir William paced the floorboards in his upstairs room. Her new home was much more exciting than Edgware Row, in every way.

Next morning, there was a surprise: Sir William had a house guest, Mrs Anne Damer, a respectable sculptress whose ornamental heads still adorn Henley Bridge over the Thames. Even though his nephew's mistress was on his way to him as – according to Greville – a willing bedmate, William had spent March debating whether to propose to Anne. She was disconcerted by the appearance of a sexy woman of poor reputation who was nearly half her age. But Emma, since she had no idea that she had been sent as a paramour, was curious about Anne: it was her husband who had set tongues wagging at Kelly's and the other brothels after he had lavished money on food, drink and prostitutes before shooting himself dead.

Flirtation with Anne had inflamed Sir William, and he fell back into his old infatuation with Emma almost immediately. Mrs Damer found herself excluded from Sir William's attentions. 'The prospect of possessing so delightfull an object under my roof soon causes in me some pleasant sensations,' Sir William wrote to his nephew, on the day before Emma arrived. 'You may be assured that I will comfort her for the loss of you as well as I am able.'

'We have had company most every day since I came,' wrote Emma proudly to Greville, four days after her arrival. 'Sir Wm is never so happy as when he is pointing out my beauties to them.' Messengers on business, Ferdinand's courtiers, sellers bearing fragments of vases from Pompeii, and musicians poured through the doors, along with dozens of English visitors who treated their envoy's house as a tourist office, restaurant and private club. Warned by Greville that 'Emma's passion is admiration', Sir William invited his friends to praise his guest. He was, as Emma wrote, 'doing everything he can to make me happy, he as never dined out since I came hear, & endead to spake the truth, he is never out of my sight, he breakfastes, dines, supes, & is constantly by me'. Mrs Cadogan was left alone to sort out Emma's clothes and battle against the 'fleas and lice' of which Emma complained 'their is millions' infesting their ground-floor rooms. Only in her early forties, a little older than Mrs Damer, and fifteen years younger than Sir William, Mrs Cadogan was firmly demoted once again. Like Greville, Sir William needed to separate Emma from her background, and he did so by treating her mother as a domestic servant.

Emma was being treated like a princess, but she still yearned for Greville. 'I am sure to cry the moment I think of you.' No coach rides, plays or operas 'can make me happy, it is you that as it in your power.' Anxious that Sir William was becoming overly attentive, she begged her lover, 'For my sake, try all you can to come here as soon as possible.' His flirtations were much more intense than they had been in Edgware Row, for he was always 'looking into my face, I cant stir a hand, a legg, or foot, but what he is marking as graceful & fine'. She worried that he was angling for sexual favours and made it clear she would ignore him. 'I can be civil, obliding, & I do try to make my self as agreeable as I can to him, but I belong to you, Greville, & to you only.' Everything, she wrote, 'depends on seeing you' at the end of the summer, 'how happy shall I be when I can once more see you, my dear, dear Greville'.

Sir William had admitted to Greville 'some anxious thoughts on the prudent management of this business', but he was dismayed to find Emma ignorant of what he expected of her. When she begged him to send Greville money so he could travel over to collect her, he realised that it was time to tell her the truth. Overwrought at his revelation that Greville was not coming for her, Emma rushed to her writing desk. 'I have had a conversation with Sir Wm. that has made me mad. He speaks half I do not know what to make of it.' She could not believe what she had heard.

I hope happier times will soon restore you to me for enead I would rather be with you starving, than from you in the greatest splender in the world . . . I will not venture myself now to wright any more for my mind & heart is so torn by different passions that I shall go mad, onely Greville, remember your promise, October. Sir Wm. says you never mentioned to him abbout coming to Naples at all . . . I live but in the hope of seeing you & if you do not come to hear, lett what will be the consequence, I will come to England . . . Greville, my dear Greville, wright some comfort to me, pray do if you love me.

Believing she would be gone for just a few months, Emma had arrived in Naples with only a handful of holiday clothes and without having wished goodbye to her child. Now Sir William had informed her she had no lover and no home. She shut herself in her room, wept for days, and scrawled in desperation to Greville.

Sir William read her miserable letters.[88] Shocked by her reaction and angry that Greville had lied to him and her, he eased off on the sexual advances. He accepted that he was not going to succeed (or at least not immediately) at making her his temporary mistress, and focused on enjoying her company and showing her the city he loved. He dreaded her return to England. As he wrote to his niece, Mary Hamilton, congratulating her on her recent marriage to her old friend, John Dickenson, 'it is most terrible to live chiefly alone'. Although he teased that he had a '*female visiter* from England', he admitted 'it is probable the visit will not be of long duration'.[89] Soon Emma convinced herself that it had all been a mistake. She decided that Greville was coming after all, and, making an effort to be cheerful, concentrated on enjoying what she thought was a short vacation.

19

The Greatest Splendour
in the World

Naples was the third biggest city in Europe after London and Paris. About nine miles in circuit it contained just fewer than 400,000 inhabitants, as well as hundreds of foreigners and troops of soldiers. As a best-selling guidebook of the time put it, the 'gay and populous' city was 'one of the most agreeable places in the world to reside at'.[90] Naples was a town of glamour and spending, but it was a flimsy pack of cards, built on the slenderest of economic and political props.

Today, the Palazzo Sessa is in the wealthiest area of the city, just off the Piazza dei Martiri in Chiaia. Emma's old home is now an exclusive residential block, near via Filangeri and via dei Mille, which houses the boutiques of international designers. Exquisite women, fingers sparkling with jewels, wander the piazza with their dogs. The road to her home hosts Naples's best bookshop and a few chic wine bars and is flanked by a handsome cake shop. The window bursts with elaborate confections of cream and puff pastry and chocolate, topped with cherries or strawberries, all very like the sweet cakes full of ricotta, citrus peel and nuts that so thrilled eighteenth-century English travellers, long habituated to plum pudding. So many of the places that Emma lived are now changed entirely: Ness is a comfortable commuter village, Hawarden is a housing estate, Chatham Place, Arlington Street and Clarges Street are covered in office blocks, and Paradise Merton has now been demolished. Only in Chiaia are there remnants of the luxurious life Emma led there over two hundred years ago.

Neapolitan buildings were painted bright colours: garnet, sapphire blue, pink and mint green. Foreign visitors sighed after the clean lines of the buildings in Rome and declared themselves disgusted by the tacky, florid excess of the palaces, churches and the recently completed San Carlo Opera House. But the extravagant architecture suited Naples. People, noise, and colour spilled out of every doorway. Even travellers from London, a city more than twice as populous, gazed open-mouthed at the throngs. Unlike London, where the poor congregated in hidden slums, the Neapolitans seemed to live almost entirely out of doors. There were about 40,000 *lazzaroni*, the ragged unemployed who filled the streets, all fervent fans of the King and, to the horror of English visitors, rather fond of swimming and sunbathing naked.[91] At the other end of society were over a hundred princes and dozens more dukes, all obsessed by, according to one commentator, 'the brilliancy of their equipages; the number of their attendants, the richness of their dress, and the grandeur of their titles', despite the hot climate.[92]

The Kingdom of the Two Sicilies, which covered Naples and most of the area south of the city, including Sicily, had not been governed by a Neapolitan since the medieval period. Ruled instead by a seemingly endless succession of foreign dynasties, rich and poor Neapolitans alike had family histories of repression and resentment, and King Ferdinand was not the monarch to bring them together. He had ascended the throne in 1759, an eight-year-old boy king. At the age of nearly forty, he was still a big baby, spoilt and spiteful. As William Beckford observed, he needed only a 'boar to stab or a pigeon to shoot' to be entirely satisfied.[93] He laughed off protocol, teased his diplomats, devoted every day to hunting or fishing, and could not speak French or even correct Italian, sticking to a broad Neapolitan vernacular. Sir William sighed that his 'habits of dissipation have taken such a firm root that there is little probability of his ever changing'.[94] Largely ruled by his formidably intelligent wife, Queen Maria Carolina, sister of Queen Marie Antoinette of France, he occupied himself with setting up factories to make the splendid silk and china for the palace, specifying that they must be staffed by beautiful young girls who had to be very docile, sexily casting down their eyes when he happened to visit. He and his government neglected the city's infrastructure and hardly bothered to encourage trade. Tax revenues came only from the supply of ice and a toll on tourists. Most visitors believed the *lazzaroni* too idle to work, but the more astute realised that the city was utterly lacking in manufacturing industry.

The poor were ruined by terrible unemployment and the rich lost themselves in leisure.

Neapolitans devoted their energies to socialising. During the 'universal jubilee' of the *carnevale*, the Royal Family threw galas almost every night and the San Carlo theatre hosted a weekly masquerade teeming with shepherdesses, princesses, nuns and oriental queens. On one day, nobles drove along the main street pelting both each other and the spectators with balls of bread and plums frosted over with sugar. Always the most enthusiastic participant, Ferdinand led the bombarding, gleefully ambushing his long-suffering ministers and ambassadors with sticky fruit.[95] The most famous event in *carnevale* was the repellent Cocagna festival. Over a few days, workers made a giant mountain of bread, grain, cakes, pasta, fruit and vegetables, and used rope to tether freshly killed cattle and live birds and lambs to the mass, prettifying it with fountains of wine, grottoes made of fish and rolling pastures of vegetables. Guards held off the looters. Then, when the nobles were all assembled to watch, the guards left the mountain to the hungry crowds. In the ensuing bloody frenzy, birds were torn away from their posts so ferociously that only their wings were left behind and the people fought and crushed each other, with some even stabbed in the tumult. The rich spectators then returned to their palaces to enjoy a sumptuous dinner, their hunger piqued by the sight of poor women fighting over a loaf of bread. Some were sickened, but the majority enjoyed Cocagna, telling themselves that the Royal Family was generously allowing their subjects to satisfy their brutal desires.[96]

The author Laurence Sterne was entranced by Sir William's life of nothing but parties, operas and masquerades. Drink flowed, everybody gambled, parties broke up at around five in the morning, thousands danced in the streets on a Sunday night, and even respectable families caroused late into the night. 'If a young man is wild, and must run after women and bad company, this should be done abroad,' proclaimed Dr Johnson and Naples was seen as the perfect place for womanising. James Boswell admitted he chased girls unrestrainedly, his 'blood inflamed by the burning climate'.[97] Every gentleman who arrived in the city aimed to have an affair with one of its legendary *demi-mondaines* or even a singer or dancer from the Opera.

The English were the most eager participants in the Neapolitan parties. There were not quite the three thousand English that Stendhal later complained filled every available hotel (he had to search for five hours for a room), but there were hundreds, wandering with guides around Pompeii, bartering for vases, and fanning themselves in their carriages.[98] As Sir William grumbled, 'Go where you please on the continent, you are sure to find some straggling English tourists.'[99] Emma's countrymen packed hotels like the Ville de Londres, which comforted those daring souls returning from Vesuvius with a stodgy full English breakfast.[100] As one contented traveller reported, 'Everybody else here might be English, and Naples has more the air of London than any place I have seen on the Continent.'[101] Theatres even ran plays to please the English about the political scuffles between Whig and Tory.[102] But few amusements could drag the English from their main passion: shopping. Excited by shops piled high with everything from fine art to tacky reproductions, they stuffed their bags with jewellery and souvenirs from the new excavations at Herculaneum and Pompeii, snapping up statues of Hercules or busts of Augustus at rock-bottom prices. After his tour, Lord Burlington filled nearly 900 trunks with souvenirs. Only Johann Wolfgang von Goethe, the most famous author in Europe at only thirty-seven, after the publication of his *The Sorrows of Young Werther*, and the continent's most hard-working and cultured man, managed to resist the temptation of bargain-hunting on his visit to Naples. Already developing their reputation as the world's most determined shoppers, English travellers left the city weighed down with paintings, statues, carvings, jewellery, busts, manuscripts and even a painter or sculptor to decorate their newly inherited mansions.

By the time they arrived in Naples, most tourists were suffering from museum fatigue, their brows furrowed by days of trying to appreciate the treasures of Rome and Florence. After a gruelling six-day 'Course in Antiquities and the Arts' in Rome, Boswell happily became a 'slave to sensual pleasures' in Naples.[103] Fortunately, everybody agreed that, apart from Titian's *Danae* at the royal palace in Caserta, Naples had no worthwhile art and there was nothing to do but dance, drink, see shows and hunt for bargains. As one jolly traveller exulted, 'what is to be done at Naples, but to live and enjoy life?'[104]

20

Painful Truths

Sir William loved the Palazzo Sessa for the breathtaking view it commanded of the bay. A monastery until the monks were evicted by Ferdinand's chief minister, Tanucci, the house had been given to a fellow courtier who rented out all of the southern side and most of the west to Sir William for about £150 a year. There were fifteen main rooms in the house. The envoy's private apartments were on the first floor, as were those that used to be Catherine's, then occupied by Mrs Damer. Sir William's staff had been busy in the first months of the year, dusting, tidying and stuffing antiquities into boxes into the basement, clearing enough space to accommodate Anne, Emma, her mother and their maids.

Visitors to the Palazzo arrived in the antechamber and found it full of sellers and tourists. The chosen few were ushered in to wait in the gallery, where the envoy showed off his latest vases. When the paper-work became pressing, Sir William retired to the adjacent library, where his secretaries, Smith and Oliver, were busily planning parties and answering invitations. Perhaps the most exciting novelty for Emma and Mrs Cadogan was the proper WC (the waste simply flowed into the bay). When Emma arrived, her host was attempting to convert the upper floors into one large room. After months of arguing with workmen and searching for the right materials (he had a particularly tedious hunt for the perfect window), as well as spending nearly £3,000, he transformed his room into one of the must-sees of the city. At the corner was a circular tower, half of which was a large bow window which curved around, giving his guests a fabulous view over the bay almost as far as Sorrento. He added a backdrop of mirrors across the other wall, so Vesuvius was doubly reflected. The painter Wilhelm Tischbein felt as if he was sitting 'on the crest of a cliff above sea and earth'. When Goethe visited, he was quite delighted by Sir William's rooms, 'furnished in the English taste', praising the view of Capri, Posillipo, the Royal Palace and the wonderful view of the coast. He decided 'probably nothing comparable could be found in the whole of Europe'.[105]

In pride of place were the portraits of Emma: Romney's *Bacchante* of her in pink, the *Emma Hart in Morning Dress* and the Reynolds *Bacchante*. Sir William soon bought even more portraits – there were eventually fourteen adorning the walls of the Palazzo. A visitor in 1787 was impressed.

> It is furnished with many pictures by Sir Joshua Reynolds and Angelica Kauffman; a fine crucifix by Vandyke, and a most capital naked boy by Leonardo da Vinci in fine preservation. I could not but smile to hear what pains Sir William has been at to get commodious sash windows, in the English style.[106]

Emma marvelled at Sir William's 'pack of servants'. Benefiting from the low wages caused by massive unemployment, he employed around fifty men, as well as a large band of musicians to entertain him. Since men did the domestic work, the only females would probably have been Emma's and Mrs Damer's maids. Senior staff lived out or had their own rooms, and the rest slept in the corridor or on the floor in the kitchens. They were fully occupied in cleaning the house and ornaments, tending to the visitors, assisting at the regular parties and caring for the four or five carriages and fleets of fine horses. Like most eighteenth-century men, Sir William kept his servants busy buying new carriages, trading old ones, repainting and trying to improve speed and suspension.

Sir William shared his government's disparaging attitude towards the politics of the Kingdom of the Two Sicilies. Bickerings with Rome were, he complained, 'the only occurrences in this remote corner of the World'.[107] His letters to the Foreign Office in London described the life of a medieval courtier rather than a modern diplomat: he listed the sniffles of the princesses, glamorous parties, and the exact number of boars killed by the King and Court.[108] He hardly ever needed to write in code. Sir William was bored but he was grateful for the opportunity to develop his interests. Instead of competing with other envoys at dreary trade talks, he studied the volcano, hunted with Ferdinand,

flattered Maria Carolina and her ever-growing band of belligerent children, and became the world's best tourist guide. Hoping to make an
easy million, he collected cheap antique vases and cleaned them up in
the hope that there would soon be a demand (the market for statues
and paintings was so inflated that they could no longer be bought and
resold for a profit). After a few years in Naples, he was a man of culture,
the acknowledged English expert on both classical vases and Vesuvius.

From spring 1786, Sir William had a new hobby: Emma. Devoted
to his beautiful new distraction, he put off writing to the government
and his letters to the Foreign Office dwindled from around May. English
visitors chivvied to see the gorgeous lady herself. The Duke of Gloucester,
youngest brother of the King, arrived and straightaway desired to meet
the envoy's 'little friend'.

Feeling guilty that he had plotted with Greville, Sir William showered Emma with gifts. He gave her a beautiful horse, treated her to
fine dinners, took her to plays and operas, and to her amazement and
delight, ordered her a new painted carriage, and a staff of liveried
footmen and a coachman to match. He also bought her a whole new
wardrobe. Gleefully stuffing her sober Edgware Row outfits at the back
of the closet, she delighted in his present of a white satin gown (costing
25 guineas) and muslin dresses with 'the sleeves tyed in fowlds with
ribban & trimmed with lace'. On top of this, she received a luxurious
camel shawl, and some of Catherine's jewellery and ornaments. Sir
William had realised that if he wanted to please Emma and perhaps
win her heart, he would have to court her with kindness and presents.

In July, Emma wrote to Greville, eager to share the excitement of
her summer holiday. They had visited Pompeii and Posillipo and planned
to sail to the islands of Ischia and Capri. She had been bathing daily,
and her 'irruptions' were gone, leaving her, as she claimed, 'remarkably
fair'. Sir William had invited every artist and sculptor in Naples (apart
from Mrs Damer) to portray her. One, possibly Elisabeth Vigée le Brun,
was painting her in 'a Bacchante setting, in a turbin, a turkish dress'
and she was modelling for another in a blue silk gown and a black
feathered hat. The young Swiss-German Angelica Kauffman and two
others planned to paint her, and the cameo maker, Marchmont, would
soon carve her head into a stone that could be set into a ring. Sir
William had sent to Romney asking for more portraits to adorn his
rooms.

Every evening, Emma proudly paraded with Sir William along the
Chiaia and past the Royal Palace. As they did so, up to six hundred gilt

carriages jammed along the seafront while actors, singers, dancers and even preachers performed to the gathered crowd.[109] Each of the splendid carriages was led by a footman carrying a flambeaux and pulled by up to eight horses wearing ornate costumes of blue silk and silver, adorned with white ostrich feathers and strewn with flowers. The nobles waved graciously, dressed up in gold and silver lace and heavy jewellery. One traveller grumbled that the multitude of footmen, flambeaux and carriages looked like a grand funeral procession, but Emma was deeply impressed and spent hours preparing herself.[110] Excluded from the Court and aristocratic gatherings, she aimed to catch the eye of the Neapolitan elite on their public outings. She soon found a little circle of admirers. The debauched English aristocrat, Lord Hervey, became her devoted fan and the royal courtier, Prince Dietrichstein, begged for a portrait, promising he passed his time telling the Queen about Mrs Hart's remarkable beauty.

The King soon spotted Sir William's new friend and began sending her lecherous looks and bowing to her whenever he saw her out walking or sailing. On one occasion when she was accompanying her host in his boat, Ferdinand came beside her and 'took off his hat & sett with his hat on his knees all the wile & when we was going to land, he made his bow & said it was a sin he could not speak English'. Maria Carolina was recovering from childbirth at the Palace, and the full force of his schoolboy seduction efforts was directed at Emma. 'We are closely besieged by the K. in a round about manner,' she reported, sighing that he came to Posillipo every Sunday to ogle her. She declared she would 'never give him any encouragement', for she was hoping to 'keep the good will' of the Queen, who punished those of his lovers she could by banishing them. Deterring the King was not easy: he expected to get what he wanted. Emma decided to pretend she was too innocent to understand what the King desired, which was a delicate matter, considering she was neither married nor Sir William's mistress and could not claim that she had to be faithful. Still, her efforts were successful and when Maria Carolina heard about her pains to fend off her husband's advances, she declared Emma a pattern of virtue.

'The great heats are but just set in,' complained Sir William in July.[111] Emma had still not heard from Greville although she wrote to him that she had written fourteen times. The letters do not survive; perhaps she wrote and never sent them. She was desperate for a reply.

I have a language master, a singing master, musick etc etc, but what is it for, if it was to amuse you I should be happy, but Greville, what

Emma as *Circe* by George Romney.

WALTZING! or a peep into the Royal Brothel Spring Gardens dedicated with propriety to the Lord Chamberlain

Emma's days at Madam Kelly's would have looked very like this scene from a brothel a few years later: drink was flowing, the dancing was wild and the girls didn't wear very many clothes at all.

In *Lady H****'s Attitudes*, the cartoonist Thomas Rowlandson hints that Emma posed nude for London's Royal Academy of Art.

In *Cupid Unfastening the Girdle of Venus*, later snapped up by Prince Potemkin for Catherine the Great, Joshua Reynolds makes a sly joke on Emma's work at the Temple of Health.

Greville (*standing*) and William Hayley look on as Romney consults with Emma posing for *The Spinstress*. Romney later declared that his other models 'all fall short of *The Spinstress*, indeed, it is the sun of my hemisphere and they are but twinkling stars'.

Emma's mother, Mrs Cadogan, her faithful supporter and friend.

Engraving of Romney's own copy of Emma as a *Bacchante* – the painting comissioned by an admiring Sir William in 1784. Prints of the engraving of *Bacchante* were immediate bestsellers.

Charles Greville, aesthete and aristocrat, broke Emma's heart.

Emma as *The Spinstress* by George Romney –
a joke on her life as Greville's mistress in the country.

(*Facing page*) In George Romney's *Sensibility*,
later titled *Lady Hamilton as Nature*, Emma is the picture
of innocence – even though she had just given birth
to Sir Harry Fetherstonhaugh's illegitimate daughter.

Emma's view from her window swept the whole bay of Naples and gave her a bird's eye view of the bubbling volcano.
(*A View of the Bay of Naples, Looking Southwest from the Pizzofalcone towards Capo di Posilippo* by Giovanni Battista Lusieri (watercolour, gouache, graphite, and pen and ink on six sheets of paper) © The J Paul Getty Museum, Los Angeles.)

(*Facing page*) Study by George Romney of Emma as Miranda from Shakespeare's *The Tempest*.

(*Overleaf*) Sir William Hamilton, intellectual, connoisseur and ambassador to Naples, fell in love with Emma against all his instincts.

will it avail me. I am poor, helpless & forlorn. I have lived with you 5 years and you have sent me to a strange place & no one prospect, me thinking you was coming to me; instead of which, I was told I was to live, you know how, with Sir W. No. I respect him, but no, never, shall he peraps live with me for a little wile like you & send me to England, then what am I to do?

Finally, in August, Greville replied and her illusions were shattered.

'You have made me love you, made me good', wrote Emma in consternation, and now 'you have abbandoned me'. In his reply, Greville instructed her to be Sir William's mistress. 'If you knew what pain I feil in reading those lines whare you advise me to oblidge Sir Wm . . . nothing can express my rage, I am all madness, Greville, to advise me, you that used to envy my smiles, now with cooll indifferance to advise me to go to bed with him, Sir Wm.' Feeling as if she could 'murder you and myself boath', she could not believe that she had turned down offers from other men and struggled to obey Greville's rules, only for him to pimp her out. She threatened that she would return to the streets: 'I will go to London, their go in to every exess of vice, tell I dye a miserable broken hearted wretch & leave my fate as a warning to young whomin never to be two good.'

Emma could not believe his hypocrisy. Exploited from the age of fourteen, she had thought that Greville had saved her, and she had grown proud of her hard-won respectability. As she knew, mistresses tended to be passed on to progressively poorer protectors, and she expected that Sir William would keep her for no longer than a year and then pass her on.

Oh Greville, you cannot, you must not give me up, you have not the heart to do it, you love me I am sure & I am willing to do everything in my power that you shall require of me & what will you have more and I onely say this the last time, I will either beg or pray, do as you like.

How could he treat in such a way 'a girl that a King etc etc is sighing for'. She begged him to let her 'live with you on the hundred a year Sir Wm will give me'. 'I have ever had a foreboding, since I first begun to love you, that I was not destined to be happy with you,' she wrote. As she cried in her room, Sir William began to regret his part in the whole affair. He admitted to Joseph Banks that he thought it was a 'bad job to come from the Nephew to the Uncle'.[112]

By November, Greville realised he had underestimated his mistress. Emma had been at the Palazzo Sessa for over six months and she was still refusing to become Sir William's mistress. Unable to admit to himself that Emma was distressed by his cavalier behaviour, Greville decided she considered Sir William too old. He instructed his uncle to find her a middle-class protector, no 'boy of family', but a gentleman from '25 to 35, & one who is his own master', which implied married, rather than subject to parental control. He was willing for her to return home and live off a hundred pounds a year, but only if she lived nowhere near him.

Emma's choices looked bleak. She knew very well that pensions promised by men tended to dry up when the woman had no male relatives to pursue the debt. Greville's cruel treatment finally induced her to fall out of love with him. Deciding herself 'poor, helpless and forlorn', she came to understand that she could never win him back, however much she promised to be good.

In the months that followed Greville's brutal August letter, Emma saw Sir William anew. He comforted her and tried to distract her from her sadness and she became more dependent on him as a shoulder to cry on. She already had affectionate feelings towards him as a friend and she soon found herself increasingly attracted to him. He was interesting, kind, and still handsome and he treated her with tact and respect. In even her most vehement letters, she had never suggested she found him unattractive or unlovable, but stressed that she was not looking for another man since she was a faithful mistress to Greville. Now there was a vacancy in her heart. Emma was always looking for someone to love and she longed to be needed, and lonely Sir William seemed to need her so much. It would not be the first time a woman fell in love with a friend she knew desired her.

Sir William courted Emma intensely and just before Christmas, their friendship developed into a full-blown affair. Almost as soon as she became intimate with Sir William, Emma found herself becoming deeply dependent on him, surprising herself with the strength of her feelings. 'I love you & sincerely,' she confessed to him on Boxing Day. On Christmas night, Sir William had left her in Caserta and travelled to Naples to attend Court and she was missing him dreadfully. 'Yesterday, when you went a whey from me,' she flourished, 'I thought all my heart and soul was torn from me.' She was intent on becoming the type of woman he desired. 'If sometimes I am out of humer,' she entreated, 'forgive me, tell me, put me in a whey to be grateful to you for you[r] kindness to me.' She pledged that 'in a little time all faults will be corrected' and promised, 'you will have much pleasure to come home to me again, and I will setle you and comfort you'.[113]

In January, she returned to Naples and he followed the King and Queen to Caserta. She wrote regularly to him throughout the month and made strenuous efforts to prove that she spent her days in worthwhile occupation. From nine until ten she had a singing lesson, from ten until twelve, she was sitting for a portrait for Constanza Coltellini, and she took lessons in Italian from twelve to one, then lunch from two to three. After one similarly exhausting day, she collapsed into bed at eight. She was particularly pleased with Coltellini's portrait, noting that it will not 'be two naked' for then 'those beautys that only you can see shall not be exposed to the common eyes of all, and wile you can even more than see the originals, others may gess at them, for they are sacred to all but you'.[114] In her letters, as she confessed, 'everything flows from my heart, and I cannot stop it'.

Affection for Sir William spills from her letters. She teased him that she 'will bite your lips nor fingers no more', and promised, 'How I wish'd to give you some warm punch, and settle you in my arms all night, to make up for your bad day'. She even made a joke about playing on 'all fours'. When she received a kind letter from him, she was thrilled: 'Oh, what a happy creature is your Emma! – me that had no freind, no protector, no body that I could trust, and now to be the friend, the Emma, of Sir William Hamilton!' 'One hour's absence is a year, and I shall count the hours and moments till Saturday, when I shall find myself once more in your kind dear arms.' 'I owe everything to you,' she declared.

Gossip about the new relationship reached London. One of Sir William's dealers was telling anyone who would listen that the envoy had 'lately got a piece of modernity from England which I am afraid will fatigue and exhaust him more than all the volcanoes and antiquities in the Kingdom of Naples'. In Naples, Emma was being approached for favours. Even though the relationship had only just begun, she, as the Neapolitans and visiting English could see, had influence over Sir William.

Sir William had forgotten his plans to take Mrs Hart only as a temporary mistress. 'His *domestic hours have many charms to interest him,*' joked his niece. He had become so lackadaisical about writing to the Foreign

Office that he had to dash off an apology to the Foreign Secretary in November, lying that he had 'rather chosen to be silent than take up your time relating the trifling intrigue of this Court'.[115] He loved Emma's appetite for new experiences, and her fascination with Court gossip and the Neapolitan social whirl Catherine had reviled. Most pleasingly of all, she seemed to appreciate his love of hunting. Sir William considered almost daily bouts of slaughter as essential to maintaining relations with the Court and he reported the catches to the Foreign Office. Emma's time at Uppark had taught her that a man's love of hunting could never be overestimated and she was careful always to praise her new lover's haul.

Delighted by her efforts to please, he lavished praise on his mistress. All things considered, the 'experiment' had worked out rather well. Emma, he wrote to Greville in February, 'improves daily, & is universally beloved. She is wonderfull considering her youth and beauty.'

21

Sparing No Expense

*E*ven though Greville had discarded her, Emma continued to write to him, anxious to prove to him how successful she was in her new home. 'Sir Wm says he loves nothing but me, likes no person to sing but me and takes delight in all I do and all I say so we are happy,' she enthused. As well as devoting herself to being his perfect helpmate, she was practising her music. A scurrilous memoir later gossiped that Greville had sent her to Sir William to put her to the Opera. Emma was still hungry for stardom and she had dreams of becoming a singer.

Emma spent the first months of 1787 in Sir William's draughty, fifty-room hunting lodge at Caserta, twelve miles outside Naples. There, she dwelled on her good fortune. Only six months earlier, she had thought that her happiness had ended, but now she found herself more contented and more secure than she could have ever dared imagine for Sir William had promised not to cast her off. Even though she was so much younger, Emma had taken to mothering Sir William, worrying about whether he was eating enough and keeping warm while hunting. She wanted terribly to win his approval and good opinion, and she was determined to hide every trace of her origin, to appear exactly the type of woman who would be a fit companion to an ambassador: elegant, accomplished and well educated. While Sir William rode around Caserta, she tried to improve herself.

The Neapolitan court frittered away spring and autumn at the Royal Palace at Caserta, and spent the rest of the time at Portici, near Pompeii, or on Capri, returning only to Naples for galas or urgent political business. Built to rival Versailles, the palace at Caserta was set in nearly 300 acres of ornate parkland, with 1,200 rooms, its own full-scale theatre and 171 steps up its lavish staircase. Over 3,000 servants and courtiers awaited royal commands, and hundreds of dogs hurtled over the marble floors. The fountains crossing the lawns stemmed from a gigantic 'Grande Cascata' that poured down from a height of 78 feet. The nearby pond was so large that real ships were put on it to stage mock sea battles and the playhouse for the royal children was the size of a large family home. Goethe found the Palace ridiculously large and out of human scale while other visitors were shocked by its florid mass of building. One thought the cascade looked like 'linen hanging to dry'.[116]

At Versailles, Marie Antoinette had built the *Petit Trianon*, a little palace surrounded by a *Jardin Anglais*. Not to be outdone, her sister Maria Carolina planned an even larger English Garden on fifty acres near the royal playhouse and she asked Sir William to organise it for her.[117] Joseph Banks recommended a British garden designer, John Andrew Graefer, to oversee the project, and he arrived with his family just after Emma. Maria Carolina had never visited England, but she desired the ultra-fashionable landscaped garden of paths, flower beds, hedges and shrubs, and spent thousands of pounds on erecting an elaborate waterfall and a small valley, as well as importing nearly a million exotic plants that had to be watered in shifts by hundreds of servants. Now the most popular attraction in Caserta, the English Garden is a shady alternative to the exposed main grounds. At the time, its construction was a headache for Sir William, for the Queen could not understand why it all seemed to be taking so long.

Nowadays, Italian families enjoy ice cream near the fountain and travel around the gardens on a special bus. Then, ordinary Neapolitans could not enter and no foreigner could attend Court functions before he or she had been presented to his or her own sovereign. Emma waited at Sir William's lodge until he returned from his hunting parties, covered in blood. As Sir William reported to the Foreign Office, the King's 'Hunting and Shooting Parties are carried on with all the usual Ardour and Success'.[118] The royal army, gangs of peasants and around 400 dogs flushed out the animals, and Ferdinand and his chums killed on average 40 or 50 of the 'largest and fiercest boars' every day, as well as deer, hares, birds, foxes, wolves and bears. They also trampled a dozen hunting dogs to death.[119]

Caserta was then, as one person described it, 'poor and straggling', and Sir William's lodge was freezing in winter, sweltering in summer and plagued by malarial mosquitoes. Emma, knowing that Sir William had been disappointed in Catherine Hamilton's aversion to the house, was determined not to complain. Instead, she set about 'fitting it up eleganter' with a music room. Sir William paid for the costly alterations and encouraged her to invite her singing master to stay.

Sir William also summoned friends to keep her company while he was at Court in the evenings. John Graefer, struggling with his poor Italian and Maria Carolina's confusing demands, visited to play whist or cribbage, along with the German painter, Philip Hackert, then the court artist. Playing the role of respectable hostess, Emma sang to her new friends almost every night and probed them for gossip about the Queen. Catherine had described herself as a 'bad courtier' and her doctor decided her lack of interests made her 'a prey to ennui'.[120] Emma aimed to prove herself very different.

Anxious that the Palazzo Sessa should regain the reputation for musical excellence it had enjoyed when Catherine Hamilton was alive, Sir William encouraged Emma to sing and play on the harpsichord and guitar, as well as taking classes with the Queen's dancing master three times a week. The expensive Signor Gallucci coached her at eight, one and before supper with scales, exercises, and music he had written. Sir William soon engaged him as her exclusive tutor and Gallucci brought his musicians to play the guitar and harpsichord and singers to blend with her soprano. Her many songbooks, painstakingly coloured and designed by Gallucci's assistants, filled the shelves at the Palazzo. When she went to dinner with English visitors and Neapolitan grandees, she was nearly always asked to sing. By August, Emma received 'great offers to be first whoman in the Italian opera at Madrid where I was to have six thousand pounds for three years' and heard that she might be offered £2,000 to sing at the London opera house and at the Hanover Square concert rooms.

Sir William delighted in his makeover of his mistress. As he sighed, 'Who can scarcely believe she has only learnt 5 months.'

> I find my house comfortable in the evening with Emma's society. You can have no idea of the improvement she makes daily in every respect – manners, language, & musick particularly. She has now applied closely to singing 5 months, & I have her master (an excellent one) in the house, so that she takes 3 lessons a day; her voice is remarkably fine, & she begins now to have a command over it. She has much expression . . . there is no saying what she may be in a year or two; I believe [her] myself of the first rate, & so do the best judges here.

Their relationship had become even closer. Emma was now living in his apartments, leaving Mrs Cadogan downstairs in the ground floor rooms. She could not attend Court, but Sir William took her to every other party, assembly and outing. In an effort to improve her minimal education, she browsed Sir William's extensive library in English and, after making rapid progress with her tutor, soon began to read in Italian. She tried hard to retain a light, engaging manner with the daunting nobles who visited the Palazzo. 'Her behaviour', Sir William reported, 'is such as has acquired her many sensible admirers,' declaring that she had won over the city's male aristocrats and even 'the female nobility, with the Queen at their head, shew her every distant civility'. Neapolitans and English tourists alike were willing to socialise with her – a testament to Sir William's popularity and her efforts to make herself cultured and elegant. 'He goes no whare without me, he [h]as no diners, but what I can be of the party, no body comes with out they are civil to me; we have allways good company,' she informed Greville. Moreover, she pointedly added, Sir William 'is in raptures with me; he spares neither expence nor pain in any thing'.

Sir William and Emma spent every spare moment together. Emma had never been a tourist in her life and Sir William felt as if he was rediscovering his home city. Emma applied herself to learning from her cultured lover, he, in his turn, was melted by her maternal fussing over him, and her playful sense of fun lightened his previous seriousness. She had never been happier: she had a lover who adored her and a secure, stable home for her and her mother. Her only struggle was hiding her sadness when she thought of her daughter, little Emma, growing up without her in Manchester.

Emma kept the local painters in work. 'The house is full of painters painting me . . . All the artists is come from Rome to study from me that Sir Wm. as fitted up the room that is calld the painting room,' she boasted to Greville. By mid-1787, Sir William had nine new paintings of Emma by various painters and two more under way, as well as a wax model, a clay sculpture and various cameos. He invited dozens of guests to watch her model. Wilhelm Tischbein was so captivated by Emma's beauty that her likeness recurred in his paintings for the rest of his life. Other nobles commissioned portraits of her and soon a painting of Mrs Hart on the wall was a marker that its owner was absolutely up with the fashion. Emma claimed to Greville that one painting of her was even to be sent to the Empress of Russia. She was so sought after that when the great French portraitist, Elisabeth Vigée le Brun, quickly sketched Emma's head, Sir William immediately sold it. He also made a tidy sum from another head that Vigée le Brun sketched on a door, after he had his servants saw it off its hinges. Sir William had persuaded Vigée le Brun to meet Emma by extolling her ability to assume different poses. Queen Marie Antoinette's portraitist was now as eager as Romney had been for a model willing to portray moods. She wrote, 'I painted Mme Hart as a bacchante, reclining by the side of the sea holding a cup in her hand. She had a beautiful, very lively face and voluminous tresses of fine chestnut, which could cover her body completely, so she looked wonderful.'[121] The most exotic portrait of Emma ever produced, her *Bacchante* of Emma reclining on a leopard-skin rug was one of Sir William's favourites and he hung it in a central place in his magnificent reception rooms.

Vigée le Brun invited duchesses and princesses to watch Emma sit and painted her as the *Sibyl*, swathing her head in a turban. The *Sibyl* made painter and subject famous. Vigée le Brun sold Sir William one copy, auctioned others off to local grandees and then took the painting on show around Europe, displaying it in Italy, Vienna, Russia and Germany, keen to prove she could produce historical paintings as well as portraiture. Women demanded to be portrayed similarly to Emma in the *Sibyl*, and aristocrats in every city begged for copies. Emma, as the *Sibyl*, confirmed the turban as one of the most modish trends, soon satirised by Jane Austen as a fashion for self-obsessed young women.

Eager to see Emma dress in the opulent style befitting Neapolitan high society, Sir William bought her satin and silk, lace from Paris and feathers. He also gave her £200 a year for clothes, although she sent some of it secretly to her uncle, William Kidd, who was already demanding money. She found an excellent hairdresser, requested her hats and dresses from Greville and prepared her outfits days in advance. To attend a Royal gala at the opera house, she 'had the finest dress made upon purpose as I had a box near the K & Queen. My gown was purple sattin, wite sattin petticoat trimmd with crape & spangles, my cap lovely from Paris, all wite fethers.'

When Emma visited the ostentatious San Carlo opera adjacent to the Palace in Naples, she saw the stardom she desired. The house was a brilliant spectacle, dazzling with glasses, mirrors and thousands of candles. At the back of the theatre, the King and Queen were splendidly arrayed in their Royal Box (now reserved for the Italian Prime Minister). Every box contained a mirror, so the audience could follow the King's signs of appreciation. The opera was a social occasion for the benefit of a small group of nobles and they behaved in the same way as we do when watching TV with friends – they chattered, ate and drank constantly, stopping only at particularly dramatic moments.[122] The same opera would play for weeks in the expectation that the audience would talk through it, but attend most nights. Performances could last up for to five hours and although the audience gossiped, they were still acutely sensitive to the slightest change in repertoire or a mistake. Singers able to produce impeccable solos were highly fêted.

Emma thought Greville had forgotten her. He had not. As he confessed to Romney, the 'separation from the original of the Spinstress has not been indifferent to me, and I am but reconciled with it, from knowing that the beneficial consequences of acquirements will be obtained, and that the aberration from the plan I intended will be for her benefit'. Greville built a larger house near Emma's old home in Paddington Green and lived there for the rest of his life. He hung her portraits on his wall and kept every one of her letters.

In summer the Naples aristocracy and the most fortunate English travellers fled the desiccating heat to Posillipo, to the west of the city. Sir William kept a summer villa on a rock jutting on to the Mediterranean, near the modern-day Palazzo Donna Anna, now a grand apartment block. Emma's summer home was surrounded with poplars and vines, and trees bowed with figs, peaches and crimson cyclamen honeysuckle.[123] She spent hours gazing at the marvellous view of Vesuvius over the islands of the bay. 'You have no idea of the beautes of it,' she wrote to Greville. 'From this little Paridise, after breakfast we vewd the lava running down 3 miles of Vesuvua and every now and then black clouds of smoak rising in to the air, had the most magnificent appearance in the world.' She so loved the house that Sir William soon called it the Villa Emma for her.*

At Posillipo, Emma had a lesson in singing or Italian, then rode on horseback about the country, and dined at three. In the afternoon she sailed and swam, using the bathing machine Sir William brought from England to protect her complexion, and she usually sang in the evening. They travelled to visit a duchess friend of Sir William on the island of

---

* One visitor was so enraptured by the Villa Emma that when he returned to his castle in Germany, he built a miniature Vesuvius rising in his grounds, complete with a replica of the 'Villa Emma'. Once a year, he put fireworks on top and watched his volcano 'erupt'.

Ischia, packing the sailboats for the short trip with Sir William's entire band of musicians, her harpsichord, her music master, four servants and her lady's maid, as well as trunks of luggage. When Sir William paid calls, he always took his musicians with him, so intent was he that Emma's singing should be heard.

Emma's greatest adventure was a ride up Vesuvius one evening, reaching the top by dark. She was bubbling with excitement beforehand, writing, 'I fancy we shall have some very large eruption', noting how already 'the lava runs down allmost to Porticea; the mountain looks beautiful. One part their is nothing but cascades of liquid fire, lava I mean, red hot, runs in to a deep cavern that is beautiful.' The usual procedure was to ride as far as possible and then walk, with a sturdy Neapolitan pulling you along with a rope tied to a girdle around your belt (it took five men to haul the fattest travellers to the summit, two in front and three pushing from behind).

Unlike most other English travellers, Emma did not complain about the climb, which was, as one guidebook related, quite terrible, 'you sink up to the knees, and go two steps backward for every three' in the ground covered with loose ash and cinders.[124] Boswell was more succinct: 'on foot to Vesuvius. Monstrous mounting. Smoke; saw hardly anything.'[125] Only the bravest were able to admire the view from the top − one lady was too shocked by the billowing sulphurous smoke and the 'dreadful chasms, through which appear gulphs of liquid fire' throwing up stones as large as clothes presses.[126]

Sir William had compiled his studies of the volcano into a book that every English traveller consulted, so Emma was in excellent hands. After her climb, she reported, 'in my life I never saw so fine a sight. The lava runs a bout five mile down from the top . . . when we got up to the Hermitage there was the finest fountain of liquid fire falling down a liquid precipice & as it run down it sett fire to the trees and brush wood so that the mountain looked like one entire mountain of fire. We saw the lava surround the poor Hermits house & take possession of the chapel, not withstanding it was coverd with pictures of saints & other religios preservitaves against the fury of nature.' Although less hackneyed than many accounts, her description is exaggerated − the hut survived and the hermit continued to cook his famous omelettes for travellers, usually over the stream of lava.

Emma was enjoying herself but she was also making plans. Resentful that guests left her behind when they went to meet the King and Queen, she had ambitions to become a rival attraction to the Court.

22

Brandishing Daggers

On a warm night in spring 1787, Sir William Hamilton assembled his most distinguished guests in his fine rooms looking out to the bay. After a lengthy dinner, he plied them with the finest wines from his cellars and made them a surprising promise. If they joined him upstairs in the reception rooms, there would be unlimited port – and something he vowed they had never seen before. When they were all assembled, he called them to hush and servants snuffed a few of the candles. In the gloom, they could just catch sight of a female figure draped in white, her dark hair flowing around her shoulders. As she came closer, they recognised Mrs Hart, Sir William's pretty, witty mistress, who had been laughing at their jokes, flushed with gaiety, entertaining them with anecdotes about England. But now she was pale and almost ethereally composed. Taking up the shawls that lay at her feet, she began to swathe them around her, to kneel, sit, crouch and dance. They quickly realised that she was imitating the postures of figures from classical myth. First, she pulled the shawls over her like a veil and became Niobe, weeping for the loss of her children, then, using them to make a cape, she was Medea, poised with a dagger, about to stab. Then she pulled the shawls around her into seductive drapes, becoming Cleopatra, reclining for her Mark Antony.

Almost as soon as they had begun to predict her next pose, she disappeared. They sat open mouthed, as the servants relit the candles and offered more wine. Some of them shook themselves out of their dazzled state to nudge Sir William. Where had she learnt it? they pressed him. Could she do it again? Behind the scenes, readying herself to come out and bask in their praise, Emma smiled as she heard her lover say that if they wanted to see her again, they would have to come on another evening. That was, if he could find the space. There was already something of a waiting list to see Mrs Hart's Attitudes.

Emma began developing her Attitudes soon after she settled at the Palazzo Sessa. Early on, she asked Greville to send out more shawls for 'I stand in attitudes with them on me'. Romney's sketches had given her an awareness of Greek and Roman dress, and she had struck classical poses for Greville when she was not playing the repentant Magdalen. He boasted to his uncle that 'Lacertian or Sapphic, or Escarole or Regulus; anything grand, masculine or feminine, she could take up'. Sir William's collection of statues, the paintings of nymphs on the wall of the Villa dei Papyri at Pompeii, and the antiquities for sale in Naples gave her the opportunity to study classical forms at first hand. She would also have noticed the modern Italian tradition of pantomime, often performed on street corners, in which the performer acted out moods with the use of masks. At the same time she took regular lessons in dance, learning ballet steps including sweeping turns and bends. She naturally progressed to borrowing postures from the pictures and statues of nymphs and goddesses she had seen. She combined her dance training and her modelling at the Temple of Health and for Romney, with influences she collected in Naples to create her Attitudes, an extraordinary fusion of eighteenth-century dance with classical costumes and references, and a truly innovative art form.

Ballet dancers often practised in plain shifts and shawls, and Emma would have worn a similarly loose dress that tied around the waist with shawls draped around her shoulders. When designing her outfit for the performances, she remembered the pattern of her tunic at the Temple of Health and the draped costumes she wore while modelling for Romney, as well as the local peasant costume, a Grecian style dress, worn particularly on the islands in the Bay of Naples. Emma employed her dressmaker to produce dance dresses that were fuller at the waist and arms, giving a more gathered effect.

For her first performances to friends, Emma held poses in a black box rimmed with gold. She soon made use of the whole room. By the spring of 1787, she felt ready to show Goethe, travelling Europe to enjoy some of the celebrity of his smash-hit *Sorrows of Young Werther* and relax after a punishing schedule of work. The great man watched the Attitudes two nights in a row and he was quite delighted, praising the Greek costume, her 'beautiful face and perfect figure' and dubbing her performance 'nothing you ever saw before in your life'.

> She lets down her hair, and, with a few shawls, gives so much variety to her poses, gestures, expressions, etc, that the spectator can hardly believe his eyes. He [the viewer] sees what thousands of artists would have liked to express realized before him . . . standing, kneeling, sitting, reclining, serious, sad, playful, ecstatic, contrite, alluring, threatening, anxious, one pose follows another without a break. She knows how to arrange the folds of her veil to match each mood, and has a hundred ways of turning it into a head-dress.[127]

Once the gossips found out that Goethe loved the Attitudes, hundreds, perhaps thousands of tourists followed in his wake. Nearly twenty-five years later he included a scene in his novel, *Elective Affinities*, in which beautiful young Luciane thrills her audience with Attitudes. Emma's performance for Goethe when she was twenty-two ensured that she would be asked to present Attitudes for the next thirty years – a move she only occasionally regretted.

Another early spectator was Elisabeth Vigée le Brun who marvelled at Emma's ability to 'suddenly change her expression from grief to joy . . . With shining eyes and flowing hair she appeared perfect as a bacchante; she could then change her expression immediately and appear as sorrowful as the repentant Magdalene . . . I could have copied her different poses and expressions and filled a gallery with paintings.'

Soon, every guest at the Palazzo demanded to see the Attitudes. One raffish French visitor, the Baron de Salis, related how Emma covered herself with flowers and 'gives a living spectacle of masterpieces of the most celebrated artists of antiquity. She is very obliging and gave a performance to a little group of us. You have to have seen her to conceive to what degree this lovely figure enabled us to enjoy the charms of illusion.' Adelaide d'Osmond, later the Comtesse de Boigne, a young refugee from Paris, described how Emma clad herself in a white tunic, her hair over her shoulders, and took up two or three cashmere shawls, an urn, a lyre and a tambourine.

> With this scanty equipment and in her classic costume, she would take up her position in the middle of the drawing room. She would throw over her head a shawl which trailed to the ground and which covered her entirely, and thus hidden she draped herself with others.

Then she would lift the shawl suddenly or sometimes throw it aside altogether; at other times she would half slip it off, and it then served as a drapery for the model she personified.

To the little girl's excitement, Emma sometimes used her in her perform-ances.

One day she made me kneel before an urn with my hands joined in an attitude of prayer. Leaning over me, she seemed to be absorbed in grief and we were both dishevelled. Suddenly she stood upright and, withdrawing a little, she seized me by the hair with such a sudden movement that I turned round in surprise and even a little fear, for she was brandishing a dagger! Enthusiastic applause from the artist spectators was heard, accompanied by the exclamations of 'Bravo le Medea!' Then, drawing me towards her bosom with the semblance of protecting me from the wrath of heaven, she wrung from the same voices the cries of 'Viva la Niobe!'[128]

The Comtesse's report shows how the Attitudes worked as an elite type of parlour game or charades, in which the audience competed to guess the posture Emma assumed. As Emma knew, there were hundreds of visitors in Naples eager to show off their classical knowledge.

Mrs Hart soon became one of the biggest tourist attractions in Naples, and the political and cultural elite of Europe flocked to see her. Modern researchers claim that Sir William created the Attitudes but there is no evidence for this. No spectators, even those who found her dismay-ingly vulgar, credit the idea to her lover, for they knew he was igno-rant about fashion and dance. As they recognised, Emma borrowed poses she had struck in Romney's studio, recalling the artist's quest to unite classical models with modern sex appeal. Some implied that she learnt to pose in the brothel and indeed the word 'attitude' was often used to refer to postures by courtesans. As one put it, she 'improved her skill in Attitudes by the study of antique figures, from which she learned a variety of the most voluptuous and indecent poses'.[129] Like the gossip columns in the newspapers already dropping teasing hints about Emma's performances, the guests describe Sir William as an enthusiastic admirer, awed by his lovely mistress's skill. If he took a role, it was to encourage her to dance around his finest vases in the hope that one of his visi-tors might want to buy them.

The Attitudes reflected Emma's endeavours to educate herself about classical culture by reading in her lover's library and accompanying him on his trips to Pompeii, Herculaneum and Portici, as well as to excavations of tombs in search of new vases. In an illustration at the front of one of his catalogues, Emma is pictured in her signature white muslin, peering into a tomb. After listening to Sir William and his friends, she soon had the same smattering of knowledge about classical myths and history as any travelling squire, and her performances were created to please just such an average chap. The Attitudes were neither esoteric nor even accurate, but a hit parade of popular classical stories: Clytemnestra and Niobe, the more attractive goddesses, Iphigenia preparing to sacrifice herself, Helen of Troy, women seduced by Zeus, and Cleopatra waiting for Antony, as well as a Magdalen. Since all travellers hoped to see Titian's *Danae* at Caserta, the corresponding attitude was always a reliable crowd pleaser as Emma posed as the title figure, a princess visited by Zeus disguised as a shower of gold.

Travellers wandered around Pompeii and Herculaneum hoping to be, as William Beckford put it, 'transported bodily into the realms of antiquity', but feeling guiltily bored by the mass of soil and dirt. Much remained overgrown because the King refused permits to excavate, dreading anyone finding anything better than his own collection of antiquities. Although guides hunted out the sites of brothels and cafés to please the tourists, few were able to imagine Pompeii as a Roman city.[130] Without films or plays to depict classical times (the Neapolitans hardly ever performed classical plays, for they preferred comic farce), they craved a performance that might give them an idea of classical Italy – and also encapsulate the essence of the modern country and its people. Emma fulfilled their desire. As the Comtesse de Boigne suggested, she showed them 'the poetic imagination of the Italians by a kind of living improvisation' in easily digestible form. The Attitudes soon became crucial to any self-respecting visitor's Grand Tour and essential to his descriptions of his encounters with classical culture.

Actors in England and Europe were pigeonholed into either comic (usually sexy) roles or parts as a tragic hero or heroine and were seldom allowed to perform both. Emma's audiences were stunned by her ability to move swiftly from tragic to comic postures. One onlooker rhapsodised that he had

> never seen anything more fluid and graceful . . . at one moment I was admiring her in the constancy of Sophonisba in taking the cup of poison . . . afterwards, changing at a stroke, she fled, like the Virgilian

Galates . . . or else she cast herself down like a drunken bacchante, extending an arm to a lewd satyr.[131]

Male spectators wished that Emma would strike erotic poses. A Parisian aristocrat, Comte d'Espinchal, declared she should forget dreary Minerva and dance about as lovely Hebe, Venus, and the Graces, then recline in a sumptuous boudoir and pretend to be 'Cleopatra ardently welcoming Mark Antony'.[132]

Since Emma performed from her early twenties until her late forties, the Attitudes were constantly changing. Her performances never fell out of favour because she kept up with the latest fashions, styles and issues, incorporated new references and altered her props and costumes. As she became more experienced, she gave roles to guests and servants, retained hairdressers to vary her look and added songs. She tried hard to use her face to show the change of mood. Her audience were habituated to seeing acting at a distance on stage in which loud noise and exaggerated movement often took the place of communication, and they found her ability to show different emotions through facial expression truly startling.

Emma tailored her Attitudes to her audiences. To spectators in Naples, fresh from art history courses and tours of Pompeii, Emma showed classical postures. In England, she aimed for a populist audience by pretending to be a Neapolitan peasant woman, posing as a captive in a Turkish harem, or, capitalising on her fame as a model, imitating famous statues and paintings. She also chose her attitudes to promote her ambitions. As a mistress and then newly married, she performed Magdalen, the woman penitent for her early life. After 1791, when she was advocating Maria Carolina's desire to defend Naples against the French, she imitated figures from classical history who resisted tyranny and invasion. When she returned to England, she emphasised her pregnancy by performing postures of a mother and showed herself as Cleopatra, matching the media's representation of her as the sexy, powerful, exotic Queen.

In 1794, Friedrich Rehberg, a German artist living in Rome, sketched twelve of her poses, including a Sibyl, Mary Magdalen and Cleopatra. There was such demand for prints that engravings of his drawings were published as a book and distributed across Europe. Ladies in their salons, courtesans and dancers had poses to copy and guidance on dress and they all tried to imitate Emma's performances. Soon guests were balancing on chairs to see the great beauty of Napoleonic France and intimate of the Empress Josephine, Juliette Recamier, performing similar poses in her Paris salon. Her elderly banker husband trotted around placing napkins under their feet to protect the upholstery. Increasingly, women began to adopt Grecian dress in imitation of Emma's fashions in Rehberg's pictures and abandon their hobbling high-heeled, point-toed shoes for her signature flat pumps. The Attitudes were equally influential on styles of dance. As ballet in the eighteenth century was formal and stilted and the dancers paused frequently between positions, Emma's plasticity and rapid movement were revolutionary. When Isadora Duncan reworked her techniques, performing sensual, fluid dances in classical garb, she set Victorian London on fire.

Incorporated into books, pictures, cartoons and caricatures, the performances inspired artists and writers. *Corinne* by Madame de Staël, Europe's most influential writer during the Napoleonic Wars, features a tall, slightly plump Englishwoman living in Italy who has become the most famous woman in England through reciting poetry and performing her Attitudes. Wearing a white dress and a turban, like Emma, she performs the sufferings of a Sibyl. Her performances entrance the English sailor and great leader Lord Nelvil (a name too reminiscent of Nelson to be coincidental). Corinne's performances underline her belief that Italy should resist Napoleon's armies. By the 1790s, Emma too performed Attitudes that extolled the virtues of martyrs and those who resisted tyranny. Unlike Staël's heroine, however, Emma never subsumed herself in the figures she represented. She was constantly giving her audience a wink, always saying, 'Look at me.' Her aim was to showcase her talents.

Emma knew that the guests at the Palazzo wanted to see her, the famous mistress and muse. She guessed that her notorious past meant that guests would be staring at her body and making suggestive comments about her. By developing the Attitudes, she exploited their attention and ensured that their reports about her focused on her performances rather than her previous behaviour. Many arrived determined to judge her as immoral but left seduced by her skill and eager to pass on the word. The Attitudes turned Emma into a European star.

Sir William's admiration for Emma deepened every day. He was allowing her to act as his hostess and he gave her grand dresses and jewels in order to do so. On top of his basic allowance to Emma and her mother for clothes and washing of £200 a year, (over £12,000 by today's standards), he bought her day dresses and formal gowns and 'every now and then a present of a gown, a ring, a feather, etc'. Once, he wrote, 'she so long'd for diamonds, that, having an opportunity of a good bargain of single stones of a good water [carat] & a tolerable size, I gave her at once £500 worth', and then paid again to set them in necklaces and bracelets.

When he planned a trip to Puglia in 1789, she begged to join him, even though they would be walking and riding on 'execrable roads' and sleeping in tents. Emma claimed that she could never be upset by poor accommodation, since she had lived in very rough lodgings in her youth. While her lover investigated the area's infrastructure and found the roads in ruins and the port of Brindisi abandoned, Emma watched the women in the town perform the tarantella, a dance inspired by the energetic movements of a tarantula.[133] The performer shook a tambourine as she twirled and danced in a circle. She became more and more frenzied and sometimes collapsed at the end. When Emma returned to the Palazzo in May, she incorporated the tarantella into her Attitudes, much to the delight of her audience. The Comte d'Espinchal decided that the beauty and voluptuousness of her performance could inflame the 'most insensible man'. Sir William envisioned happy years ahead spent indulging his graceful mistress.

But Europe was changing.

On 14 July, crowds stormed the Bastille in Paris and thrust its governor's head on to a pike. In October, the King and Queen of France were dragged from Versailles and imprisoned. Parisian nobles fled for their lives and Sir William reported, 'French refugees drop here apace.'[134] Neapolitan aristocrats were terrified for the French Royal Family and worried that their own masses cherished similar revolutionary fervour. As Sir William worried, the Revolution 'cast a visible Gloom upon the face of this Court'.[135] Ferdinand, however, quickly bored of the despondent mood of his acolytes, banned all mention of France at Court. His ludicrous attempt to live in a happy bubble was a failure. France remained agonising, 'the only Topic in every Conversation'.[136]

Within three years, Emma had emerged as a talented performer and a confident hostess. Glittering with diamonds, she was the image of an ambassadress and she combined natural style with ladylike accomplishments of music and languages. Now all she needed was the title. 'I will make him marry me,' she had warned Greville in 1786. As revolution engulfed France and began to tear across Europe, Emma began to realise her desire.

23

Manipulating Sir William

'All my ambition is to make Sir Wm happy & you will see he is so,' Emma wrote to Greville. She lied: she wanted to be more than his mistress. Emma sought to share his work as the ambassadress, to visit the English Court and to settle down with him for good. Eighteenth-century women were trained to wait modestly for a proposal, but Mrs Cadogan was hardly able to play the role of the pushy mother, intent on wringing the question out of the envoy. In late 1788, however, after only two years of living with him, Emma was convinced that she could persuade him to make her Lady Hamilton.

Emma never lost an opportunity to stress to Sir William how she loved him and longed for him to marry her. She emphasised that her sense of gratitude would make her an excellent wife and, as she put it, she would be the 'horridest wretch in the world not to be exemplary towards him'. In the hope of sprinkling rumour in the newspapers, she began to encourage gossip that they were secretly married (reports that reached the horrified ears of Sir William's family and friends). The English tourists who arrived in the winter of 1789 believed they were already married, and Sir William made no effort to stamp out the rumours, knowing that such illustrious guests would flinch from being entertained by a mere mistress. As he boasted, 'many seek Emma's acquaintance, & we have the best company in Naples at our house. The Duchess of Argyle & that family doat upon Emma, & really she gains the heart of all who approach her.' Sir William was so intent on promoting an intimacy with the new Spanish ambassador and his wife, that he had implied to them he was married, enabling Emma to charm the stolid Señora, gloating 'we are allways together'. Feeling newly respectable because everyone believed her married, Emma revelled in her role of hostess. 'Every night our house is open to small partys of fifty and sixty men & women. We have musick, tea etc, etc.' She welcomed guests to 'the first great assembly we had given publickly', a ball for nearly four hundred, 'all the foreign ministers & their wives, all the first ladies of fashion, foreyners & neapolitans, our house was full in every room. I had the Banti, the tenor Casacelli & 2 others to sing.' The other ladies dripped with diamonds and brocade, but she was proudly resplendent in white satin, with her hair loose and unpowdered, in the fashionable Grecian look she herself had popularised.

When his friends wrote demanding the truth, Sir William declared they were not married and never would be. His mistress, he told Greville, was 'welcome to share with me, on *our present footing*, all I have during my life, but I fear her views are beyond what I can bring myself to execute; & that when her hopes on the point are over, that she will make herself & me unhappy, but all this entre nous, if ever a separation should be necessary for our mutual happiness, I would settle £150 a year on her, & £50 on her mother'. He explained to his friend Joseph Banks that 'I have no thoughts of relinquishing my Employment and whilst I am in a public character, I do not look upon myself at liberty to act as I please.'[137] Marrying her might affect his position at Court. Moreover, as he wrote to Mary Dickenson, 'of all Women in the World, the English are the most difficult to deal with abroad. I fear eternal tracasseries, was she to be placed above them here, & which must be the case, as a Minister's Wife, in every Country, takes place of every rank of Nobility.'[138] The problem was Emma's famous reputation: every visitor knew about Amy Lyon of the gossip columns, and Mrs Hart, star of Romney's studio, and the Queen of Attitudes.

Women, Sir William claimed to Banks, were 'subject to great change according to circumstances and I do not like to try experiments at my time of life. In the way we live we give no Scandal, she with her Mother and I in my apartment, and we have a good Society. What is to be gained on my side?'[139] Sir William told his friends what they wanted to hear — lying to Banks that Emma lived with her mother, when she was actually installed in his apartment. His letters veer between declaring he would never marry and praising her excessively, emphasising how she 'really deserves everything and has gained the love of everybody', as well as 'universal esteem'. When he admitted that Emma 'makes my house more comfortable', he inadvertently revealed the truth of the whole matter: he could not bear to lose her and pension her off in the country. As the year wore on, Sir William realised she was not going to settle for being his mistress much longer. He had a choice: a comfortable house or the approval of his society friends in England. He began to plan a journey to England to check on his Welsh estates. Senior diplomats could not marry without the permission of their sovereign and he aimed to test the waters with King George about the possibility of taking Emma as his bride.

By late 1790, all London was gossiping about the imminent arrival of the ambassador and his mistress. The *Town and Country Magazine* gave Emma and William starring roles in its scandal column, 'Tête a Tête', as 'The Consular Artist and the Venus de Medicis'. According to the article, Emma was a shrewd and beautiful artist's model with expensive tastes and Sir William a buffoon, prone to making risqué jokes that offended his guests. 'Industry, without much taste or genius, has gradually conducted him to the top of the ladder' and he was conspicuous proof that 'success is not always the result of great talents'.

Although Sir William, the journalist declared, 'may not be able to execute, he is said to be a competent judge of the performances of others'. In other words, he was neither an artist nor a sexual partner, able only to watch the acts of others (a joke about his interest in penile cults). He had refused to marry because, the article continued, 'the term *wife* was offensive to his ear, as it implied the natural consequences which would probably ensue – the immoderate increase of his expenses'. So obsessed by statues, his idea of a compliment is 'Madam if you were mine, I would put you into one of my best frames'. He then sees Emma, at a lubricious 'exhibition, at which he is more than an indifferent spectator' – a quip about the Temple of Health. She 'was in the last year of her teens and seemed to have been cast in perfection's mould'. 'Seized with a kind of infatuation, he presented her with one of his best catalogues and begged he might be permitted to attend her and explain to her the embellishments of his gallery. The fair one granted his petition, and May and January formed a temporary alliance.' Emma was 'not insensible of the honour conferred on her by a man of consular dignity' and, the journalist declared, their mutual happiness was enhanced when she performed her Attitudes:

A tender intimacy commenced; and when our hero chooses a relaxation from severer duties, he pays his devoirs to our beautiful young heroine. But in these agreeable *rencontres*, nothing impure or impassioned is admitted: as an *artist*, he admires the figure of the lady, not as a *lover*, as an *artist* his adoration is enthusiastic, as a *lover* his sentiments are too refined to relish sensualities. His fair advocate is however, infinitely serviceable to him in his professional line. She is the standard of female perfection, a comparison is therefore made between her limbs and those of the ideal females which his ministers delineate for him on canvas.[140]

Sir William ignored the barbs of the gossip magazines. Since he had given up expecting a promotion to Paris or Madrid, he was more tempted to marriage. He would have had an uphill struggle introducing Emma to French or Spanish society, but the Neapolitans loved her and would accept her as his wife.

Emma shared Sir William's interests in music, sailing and travel and his fascination with the Neapolitan Court, and they had realistic expectations of each other. She knew she had to keep cheerful and could not make emotional demands on him. Tolerant of her noisy restlessness, he ignored her tendencies to take on too much, to interfere and to hog the limelight. Fully aware of her history, he knew that if she had been a respectable young lady, he never would have met her, and she would not have the same energy and willingness to please. He was also grateful to her: she had been faithful to him in Naples despite offers from elevated men and she had been good-natured and uncomplaining about his frequent absences to visit the Court or hunt. 'No Princess cou'd do the honours of her Palace with more care and dignity than she does those of my house,' he declared.

A visit from Greville's friend Heneage Legge cemented his resolve. Emma had become fond of Legge when he visited Edgware Row – she had written in an early letter to Greville from Naples that Legge and his friends had better 'take care of their hearts when I come back'. But when he arrived, Legge bluntly informed Sir William that Emma would be 'inadmissable' to his wife's company for they 'had no reason to think her present different from her former line of life'. He was utterly scandalised to find his old pet as Sir William's hostess, 'much visited by ladies of the highest rank, & many of the *Corps diplomatique*', and he dashed to inform Greville. 'Her influence over him exceeds all belief; his attachment exceeds admiration, it is perfect dotage,' he spluttered. Although he admitted she 'does the honour of his house with great attention & desire to please' and described the Attitudes as 'beyond description beautifull and striking', he still considered her as a mistress, hinting salaciously 'you will find her figure much improved since you last saw her'.

Legge reported:

She gives everybody to understand that he is now going to England to sollicit the K.'s consent to marry her, & that on her return she shall appear as Ly H. She says it is impossible to continue in her present dubious state, which exposes her to frequent slights & mortifications; & his whole thought, happiness & comfort seems so center'd in her presence, that if she should refuse to return on other terms, I am confident she will gain her point, against which it is the duty of every friend to strengthen his mind as much as possible.

He told Emma that 'she could never change her situation for the better, & that she was a happier woman as Mrs H. than she would be as Ly H., when, more reserved behaviour being necessary, she would be depriv'd of half her amusements, & must no longer sing those comic parts which tend so much to the entertainment of herself & her friends'. Little was more likely to convince Emma in her resolve to cajole William into marriage than Legge declaring she would be happier (and more amusing to men like him) as a mistress. He admitted, 'She does not accede to that doctrine.' Legge instructed Greville that 'unless great care is taken to prevent it she will in some unguarded hour work upon his empassion'd mind, & effect her design of becoming your aunt'. Greville did not protest. He guessed it would be futile and he hoped that Emma, unlike a society lady, would agree to Sir William settling his estate solely on him.

At the same time, William's friends in Naples, including the Queen herself, encouraged him to marry Emma. Maria Carolina had not forgotten Emma's tactful rebuff to her husband and also guessed that she would be a more malleable conduit to British influence than Catherine Hamilton had been. By February, the journey to England had been planned. Sir William had become increasingly infuriated by the gall of pompous English visitors telling him what to do. Their efforts to dissuade him had only pushed him further towards marriage. 'She will be my wife, no matter what they say,' William confided in secret to Elisabeth Vigée le Brun. But he had one condition: King George had to agree.

By April, Emma, Sir William and Mrs Cadogan were visiting Venice, where the lovers toyed with more art and socialised with embittered

French émigrés, including the Comte d'Artois, Louis XVI's brother, the future Charles X. They continued through Brussels and, on 16 May 1791, arrived in London's Nerot's Hotel – the same hotel where William had stayed when he first met his 'Fair Tea Maker'. In geographical terms, Emma was just around the corner from Madam Kelly's and not far from the house that had been the Temple of Health. But she was a different person from Amy Lyon. 'Mrs Hart' was about to become Lady Hamilton.

24

Engaged for Life

*W*hen Emma arrived in London, everyone wanted to meet her and find out whether she had hooked the 'consular artist' as a husband. Greville's sister, Lady Frances Harpur, comforted her relations that his 'making a Shew of her *Graces & Person* to all his *acquaintance* in *Town*' was hardly '*a preliminary for Marriage*'.[141] She was wrong.

A few days after her return, Emma burst into Romney's studio dressed in a fantastic Turkish dress and turban. He immediately cancelled his other engagements. 'At present, and the greatest part of the summer, I shall be engaged in painting pictures from the divine lady. I cannot give her any other epithet, for I think her superior to all womankind,' he enthused. Romney painted her throughout sweltering June and July, thirty-eight times in all. Emma's arrival was serendipitous: John Boydell wanted paintings for his paying gallery of Shakespearean scenes in Pall Mall. Romney had already worked from memory and sketches to paint Emma as Miranda in a scene from *The Tempest*, unveiled to great excitement in the previous year. Now, he took sittings for her to be *Cassandra* in drapery wielding an axe (which William Hayley later praised as showing her 'beauty blazing in prophetic ire') and *Joan of Arc*, in which she poses similarly to *Circe*. He also painted her as *Ophelia* and *Titania* from *A Midsummer Night's Dream*, as well as *Terpischore*, the Muse of Dance, and, half-topless, as *Euphrosyne* or *Mirth*. He had to hurry for, as Emma had told him, 'everything is going on for their speedy marriage'.

By July, Romney could hardly believe how 'all the world [is] following her and talking of her'. People crowded into his studio to see paintings of Mrs Hart. He promoted her effusively, inviting guests to watch her model and hosting parties to showcase her singing and Attitudes. After one performance, he declared the 'whole company were in an agony of sorrow'. Ever keen to be fashionable, the Prince of Wales commissioned him to paint her as *Calypso*, reclining in a cave and wrapped in pale purple drapes, and also as *St Cecilia*, a limpid-eyed nun, gazing to the heavens, a wry joke about her life as one of Madam Kelly's nuns. The Prince liked to spend time with her in Romney's studio but that was as far as the relationship went: he did not invite Emma or Sir William to his brilliant thirtieth birthday gala on 29 July.[142]

Soon Romney began to detect signs of 'neglect'. Emma had other claimants on her time. Many painters wanted to enhance their portfolios by taking sittings from her. Thomas Lawrence had heard that she was 'the most gratifying thing to a painter's eye that can be'. Jibing that Romney's paintings were more revelatory of the 'artist's feebleness than her grandeur' and 'frightened . . . she will soon be Lady Hamilton and that I may not have such another opportunity', he pressed Richard Payne Knight to introduce him. After a few short sittings at Knight's Downton Castle he produced a full portrait,[143] *La Penserosa*, which caused a sensation when it was exhibited at the Royal Academy in 1792.

Emma was the talk of the town. Sir William Lock reported that 'All the Statues & Pictures he had seen were in grace so inferior to Her, as scarce to deserve a look.'[144] A Mrs Preston was so eager to 'hear her softly sing & see her sweetly smile, & exhibit a variety of attitudes & passions' that she put herself 'as much as possible in the way to see Mrs Hart but always faild'. Many were disappointed in the crush to see the new superstar.

Sir William was excited by the adulation Emma received and deeply relieved that she did not demand to meet his family. When Emma showed no sign of distress after meeting Greville, the last twinge of jealousy disappeared. He visited his friends, and the Society of Dilettanti presented him with twenty-five copies of his work on penile cults, *The Worship of Priapus*, a sly reference to his life with Emma. Otherwise he parried his family's questions about his marital intentions. Although unhappy about Emma's background, they would have detested the thought of any wife, for they wanted his fortune intact. He promised his sister that he 'did not think it Right to marry Mrs Hart; from respect to his King', even though she was the 'Happiness of his Life'.[145] He was playing for time. In May, he had written to the Archbishop of Canterbury to request a special licence to be married in a place other than a church for 'I wish my marriage to be secret untill I have left England'.[146] The Archbishop refused his request, but did allow him to escape the exposure of having the banns published. Sir William made a new will, settling a yearly income on his wife-to-be and bequeathing his estate to Charles Greville. Without a new will, Emma could try to claim more of his fortune after his death.

In August, Sir William, Emma and Mrs Cadogan visited Mary Dickenson, Sir William's favourite niece, and her husband, in Derbyshire, then travelled to stay with his friend and relation, William Beckford, England's richest man and biggest hedonist, at his eccentric mansion, Fonthill, near Bath. Fonthill cost the extortionate sum of £250,000 (somewhere around £15 million today). Covered with oriental trappings, it was staffed by a pet dwarf, and – gossips claimed – slaves. Very few were allowed to enter its opulent doors. The visit was a great success. Beckford wrote to Sir William, 'The only glorious object I have set my eyes upon since my arrival in this foggy island is the Breathing Statue you have brought over.'[147]

The party travelled on to Bath. Emma met Georgiana, Duchess of Devonshire, who was holidaying in the town with her sister, Lady Harriet Duncannon, and Lady Elizabeth (Bess) Foster, sometime mistress to the Duke of Devonshire, along with their children and Bess's daughter by the Duke. The usually sparkling Devonshire set was in anxious disarray. Lady Harriet was suffering, reviled by society after an affair with Emma's old manager, Richard Brinsley Sheridan. The Duke of Devonshire was so furious with his wife about her debts that he had stayed away, and Georgiana was reeling from her discovery that she was four months' pregnant by the young Whig politician Charles Grey.

The Duchess aimed to cultivate the future wife of the envoy to Naples, for she thought she might have to flee to Italy with her illegitimate child. She believed Emma's claim that she had been married to Sir William for two years, and sympathised with her that she had not been invited to meet the Queen of England. Bess jealously decided that the 'celebrated Mrs Hart' was 'a very handsome Woman', but 'vulgar'. The word vulgar had a particular meaning: a social *arriviste* who behaved above her station and was insufficiently humble. Like most of those who met Emma, Bess praised her Attitudes wildly but slyly referred to her past: 'as an excuse for that vulgarity and as a further proof of the superiority of her talents that have burst forth in spite of these disadvantages, that Mrs Hart was born and lived in the lowest situation till

the age of 19, and since that in no higher one than the mistress of Sir
W. Hamilton'.[148]

Emma did not dare visit her daughter. She could not risk the press
discovering the existence of the little girl and she knew that Sir William
wanted her by his side. So Mrs Cadogan, possibly accompanied some
of the way by Greville, travelled to Manchester. Nine-year-old little
Emma had heard that Mrs Hart and her husband-to-be were in England
and hoped they might visit her, even take her away with them. Eager
to show she was an accomplished young lady, she had spent days ornamenting a box with filigree. A complex and time-consuming task, especially for a child, filigree involved rolling up strips of coloured paper
into tight curls and sticking them over the box to create an overall
picture of flowers. Her effortful display of her industry, patience and
feminine skills went to waste. Mrs Cadogan arrived alone and little
Emma was deeply disappointed and blamed herself. After a difficult
visit, Mrs Cadogan battled the heat and travelled on to Hawarden.
Emma's grandmother was seventy-six and wanted to see her daughter
before she died.

Emma returned to London from Bath on 22 August, after what one
friend described as a 'frenzy' for her, with people going 'mad about her
wonderful expression'.[149] 'She is the talk of the whole town', Romney
declared:

> she really surpasses everything both in singing and acting, that ever
> appeared. Gallini [master of the London Opera] offered her two
> thousand pounds a year if she would engage with him, on which
> Sir William said pleasantly, that he had engaged her for life.

Sir William confessed to his friends that he had decided to 'make an
honest Woman of her'. He promised that he would never set her above
visiting female aristocrats by allowing her to present them to Maria
Carolina. Declaring himself entirely confident about the future, he cheerfully knocked two years off Emma's age. He wrote to his friend,
Georgiana, Countess Spencer, mother of the Duchess of Devonshire:

> A Man of 60 intending to marry a beautifull young Woman of 24
> and whose character on her first outset in life will not bear a severe
> scrutiny, seems to be a very imprudent step, and so it certainly would
> be 99 times in a 100, but I flatter myself I am not deceived in Emma's
> present character – We have lived together five years and a half, and

not a day has passed without her having testified her true repentance for the past.[150]

On 28 August, Sir William attended Court at Windsor and gained the King's consent to the marriage. It was always a good sign when George made jokes and he was quietly jubilant when the 'King joked him about Em. at a distance' and teased him 'that he was not quite so religious as when he married the late Lady H'. Queen Charlotte was less easily mollified. She made it clear that she would not receive the new Lady Hamilton. Emma had damaged her cause by insisting on sharing hotels with Sir William rather than maintaining propriety by living separately in the weeks before the wedding. She could only console herself with the hope that when her admirer, the Prince of Wales, ascended the throne, she would be received at Court with all the trappings.

Emma listened patiently to lectures about getting above her station. Mr Dickenson, husband of Mary, advised her to remain intent on pleasing in order to maintain in Sir William 'that warmth of attachment which he entertained for her'. He hoped, sternly, he would 'find Emma & Lady H. *the same*'. Even Sir William, Dickenson implied, who had risked his position to marry her, would never love her unconditionally.[151] He was right: she knew she had to flatter and cosset, not make emotional demands. She agreed to a small, secretive wedding. Sir William dreaded publicity and feared a mob at the church. He did not want people to hear the proof, when the names of the couple were read out, that Mrs Hart had indeed been the notorious Amy Lyon.

Early in the morning of Tuesday 6 September, Mrs Cadogan and Emma's maid dressed the bride in white muslin with a turquoise sash and arranged her hair loosely under a handsome blue plumed hat. They hired a carriage and Emma travelled to St Marylebone Church on the Marylebone Road, Greville's local church and conveniently distant from town. Once featuring in William Hogarth's series of paintings, *A Rake's Progress,* as a ramshackle, unkempt church famous for clandestine marriages, St Marylebone had smartened up its image but still fell short of Emma's dreams of grandeur. She said 'I do' in a plain small building, only slightly more impressive than humble St Mary's in front of her old house in Paddington Green (then under renovation), bearing no resemblance to the graceful high late Regency church that now stands proudly across from Madame Tussaud's near Baker Street. The witnesses were the Marquis of Abercorn, Sir William's relation and friend, and Louis Dutens, Rector of Elsdon in North-umberland and formerly secretary to the English Minister at Turin. Two friends of Sir William were witnesses. Mrs Cadogan was probably present and possibly Mary Dickenson's husband (who was in London on business) and Greville also attended. At about half past nine, the 'Right Hnble Sir Willm Hamilton of this Parish, Widower and Amy Lyon of the same Parish, Spinster' were married.

While Sir William celebrated with his witnesses, Emma drove to Romney's studio and sat for the last portrait he would create of her from life. Frantic to capture her on canvas before she left, he had painted her on the two days before her wedding. On 6 September, for the first and last time, he wrote 'Lady Hamilton' rather than 'Mrs Hart' in the sitter's book. *The Ambassadress* is one of his most elegant portraits of her. He marks her marriage by allowing her, like a genteel lady, simply to represent herself, rather than Sensibility or a goddess such as Circe. Still wearing her wedding dress, Emma looks over her shoulder, her hands folded in front of her, Vesuvius behind her. Despite her elegant appearance, her position is still winsome for she looks up at the viewer over her shoulder. Romney captures her at a moment of transition: from alluring young muse to grande dame and ambassadress.

Emma's departure plunged Romney into depression. Although September was a busy time for portrait painting, he did not take another sitter for nearly six weeks. Locked up in his Cavendish Square studio, he tried to exorcise his feelings of loss by drawing Emma in frenzied sketches, which grew increasingly nightmarish and sexual. In some, she swirls her drapery like a goddess, in others, she is a nude or weeping woman. In one, he let his tormented imagination flow and drew a nymph being stripped by a grimacing satyr who has Romney's face. Trying and failing to forget her with a French mistress, Thelassie, Romney began to work up the studies he had made during the summer of 1791 into full portraits. Emma was becoming respectable as Lady Hamilton and moving toward her thirties, but in Romney's portraits, she remained laughing and malleable, for ever young.

Sir William's effort to avoid publicity by marrying in the early morning failed. The news was flashed around London. Sir James Burges, the foreign under secretary of State, was shocked that Emma, whom he had visited with William at Romney's studio, had married the King's envoy.[152] Beckford marvelled that his friend had 'actually married his Gallery of Statues'. An old school friend wrote to congratulate Sir William on the 'manly part you have taken in braving the world and

securing your happiness and elegant enjoyment in defiance of them'.
Sir William had no regrets. As he declared robustly to Horace Walpole,
'It has often been remarked that a reformed rake makes a good husband.
Why not vice versa?'

Most couples spent the weeks after marriage paying wedding visits
to relatives. Sir William ensured they left London for Italy after two
nights. Their speedy departure only fanned the flames of press speculation. The three most popular magazines recorded the wedding: the
European Magazine, the *Lady's Magazine* and the *Gentleman's Magazine*.
All called Emma 'Miss Hart' rather than Amy Lyon and the *Gentleman's
Magazine* declared her 'much celebrated for her elegant accomplishments and great musical abilities'.[153] The gossipy *New Lady's Magazine*
noted the marriage alongside 'An Essay on Second Marriages', a virulent attack that suggested that the widower who remarried 'must stand
convicted in a deficiency of affection and gratitude'. The journalist illustrated the stern advice with a prediction, disguised as a tale, of Emma's
fate. Although the heroine's 'only qualifications' were beauty and grace,
she captured a top aristocrat at a ball but soon regretted marrying a
man so much her social superior because she could never be his equal.[154]
The *Morning Herald* jibed how Mrs Hart, of 'whose feminine graces
and musical accomplishments all Europe resounds, was but a few years
back the inferior housemaid of Mrs Linley'. Richard Newton produced
The Wife Wears the Breeches, a caricature of a newly married couple who
look like Sir William and Emma: he waits in bed while she dons a pair
of trousers, a reference to her theatrical past and a clear suggestion that
she controlled him. One poetically inclined wit suggested that Emma
would be unfaithful and might even return to work as a Covent Garden
streetwalker:

> O Knight of Naples, is it come to pass
> That thou hast left the gods of *stone* and *brass*,
> To wed a Deity of *flesh* and *blood*?
> O lock the temple with thy strongest key,
> For fear thy Deity, a *comely* She,
> Should one day ramble in a frolic mood –
>
> For since the Idols of a *youthful* King,
> So very volatile indeed, take wing;
> If his to wicked wanderings can incline,
> Lord! who would answer, poor old Knight, for *thine*?

> Yet should thy Grecian Goddess fly thy fame,
> I think we should catch her in Hedge-Lane.

One of Sir William's friends had complained that Emma used to be a common streetwalker in Hedge Lane (an alley off Drury Lane notorious for prostitutes); this wag implied she would take up the job again if she grew weary of her husband.

The Times weighed in more supportively, if still salaciously, reporting that Lady Hamilton had departed, leaving 'six portraits behind her which are done by Romney. Two of these are for the Prince of Wales, in which she is drawn in her most elegant attitudes.'[155] In October, the paper published 'To Lady Hamilton' by H.F. (perhaps a sly joke about her affair with Sir Harry Fetherstonhaugh). The poet produced a eulogistic version of what was by now a hackneyed description of the relationship: Emma was a beauteous statue, desired by the impotent Sir William as an aesthetic object. The word 'Aether' is a coy reference to the Temple of Health.

> What time the fairest Dame of Athens came,
> To give the Artist's eye of the mould of grace,
> The matchless texture of the harmonious frame
> The perfect features and the luxuriant face
>
> One brilliant eye-ball shot a beam of fire
> Another languished blue as Aether's light,
> Here Dignity and Heaven his touch inspire,
> There dimpling laughing beauty charms his sight.

In the poem, the Artist or Sir William sees Emma and is thrilled by 'A form by early majesty inform'd / O'er which the hand of Grace had passed from you!'

> His eye had caught thy fascinating smile,
> Thy seraph eye and features touch'd by Heaven,
> Th'enamour'd Gods had left their thrones awhile,
> And deathless honours to thy name been given.

The poem concluded generously with 'sweet Stranger, Praise shall mark thy way'. In England, she was not so much the object of praise as of gossipy insinuation and sartorial imitation. Alerted by *The Times* and by gossip columns, people flocked to see her portraits. Prints sold wildly and more and more women adopted her signature look of a loose, draped white muslin dress and 'Grecian style' pumps. Emma's marriage and her busy schedule of shows of Attitudes in London and Bath had ensured she was headline news.

William's first wife had brought him a huge dowry and a life of ease. Emma, as the *Town and Country Magazine* had suggested, only increased his expenses. But she made him happy, which Catherine had been unable to do. Sir William would have found a genteel virgin tediously dependent. He soon recommended to Emma that she 'harden' her 'good and tender heart', admitting that, as for his own, 'I will allow it to be rather tough'. Emma knew she had a tricky job ahead of her, both in public and in private. As John Dickenson reported to his wife, Emma told him she knew that the 'eyes of many people were upon her' and she promised that 'gratitude, inclination, & every consideration wd compel her to do everything in her power to please him & She was certain she'd do it'.[156]

25

A Difficult Part to Act

'Am I Emma Hamilton? It seems impossible,' Emma marvelled as she journeyed to Naples. 'Surely no person was ever so happy as I am.' The new Lady Hamilton arrived in Paris in September 1791. Like all visitors to the city, she and Sir William hoped to see the revolution at first hand. Emma also had a plan: she wanted to meet Queen Marie Antoinette.

Only a year before, Romney and his friends had revelled in Paris, deciding it the most splendid place in Europe, but since then much blood had been shed.[151] Sir William and Emma took rooms in the expensive and very central Hôtel de l'Université, where Lord Palmerston, William's old friend, was also staying. He secured them seats at the Assembly on 14 September when the King was forced to accept the constitution, which classed him as a constitutional monarch and his family as commoners. The King was humiliated because he had to sit on an ordinary chair and everyone retained their hats. Few sympathised: public support for the Royal Family was at an all-time low after they had attempted to escape in June.

After the constitution was passed, the city was thrilled. Elite Parisians planned to seize positions in the new republic, and everybody else hoped that the settlement would bring the bloodshed to an end. A large hot-air balloon was raised above the city centre in celebration, buildings blazed with illuminations, and relieved citizens flung themselves into music, feasting, dancing and cooing at a grand display of fireworks. Palmerston, the Hamiltons, and an ex-courtier, the Marquis de Noailles, wandered around until ten o'clock, surprised by the widespread 'Enthusiastical attachment to the new Constitution', as

Sir William put it.[158] Over the next few days, Emma visited the many English nobles in town and sang or performed her Attitudes. Palmerston was appreciative. 'I have seen her perform the various characters and attitudes which she assumes in imitation of statues and pictures, and was pleased beyond my expectation, though I had heard so much. She really presents the very thing which the artists had aimed at representing.' He commissioned Thomas Lawrence to alter a painting by Reynolds in order to put Emma in the centre, and he kept the painting until he died. He decided Emma 'very handsome', 'very good humoured, very happy, and very attentive' to her new husband.[159]

All the while, Emma was pressing for an introduction to Marie Antoinette. If Emma could meet the Queen, she would score an amazing coup and increase her chances of being received at the Neapolitan Court. Like every woman in Europe, she was fascinated by the glamorous French Queen, who was doubly appealing now she was imprisoned at the rambling palace of the Tuileries. The novelist and antiquarian, Horace Walpole, had described both Emma and Marie Antoinette as a statue of beauty, but Emma was very different from the Queen: she knew how to satisfy her husband but had no idea how to please the Court. Meeting Marie Antoinette would prove a crucial stage in her training.

Under her mien of graceful resignation, the Queen was begging her brother, Leopold, the Emperor of Austria, to threaten the French into reinstating Louis XVI as monarch. Throughout September, she wrote letters in code and sometimes in invisible ink to Leopold and various European Royals, collaring passing aristocrats to pass them on. She was intent on winning the support of her favourite sister, Maria Carolina of Naples, only three years her junior. Emma's visit came at an opportune moment. Marie Antoinette neither knew nor cared that Queen Charlotte had not received Emma: she wanted a favour from the woman she believed to be an ambassadress.

Few women (and no man other than her husband) could resist Marie Antoinette. Trauma had wrecked her beauty: she had grown gaunt and her luxuriant hair had thinned and turned white at only thirty-six. But her limpid blue-grey eyes were enticing, her sweet, hesitant voice still tempting, and her soft smile – once able to charm the most embittered courtier – had won the hearts of her guards. Deeply emotional, she kissed and embraced frequently. Ardent revolutionaries faltered when they thought of Marie Antoinette, and Emma fell in love with her on sight. Ambitious to be at the centre of politics, she dreamed of a Queen restored to the throne, thanks partly to her efforts. Despite her impoverished childhood, Emma believed in opulent courts, and she thought, like many others, that the King was vital to maintain the correct order of society. She saw the French political conflict in personal terms as the bloodthirsty Jacobins against her beautiful, victimised new friend. When she heard that peasants had thrown stones at the Royal Family when they were caught trying to escape from Paris, she was utterly incensed. She left her meeting bursting with indignation, desperate to be of service to the Queen.[160]

Marie Antoinette's letter safely stowed, the Hamiltons departed for Geneva, Rome, then Venice. In every city, Emma performed her Attitudes and in Rome, she made her final sitting for Angelica Kauffman's *Lady Hamilton as the Comic Muse*, which became her wedding portrait. Then they rolled on to Naples. The English were still eager to hear about the fascinating Lady Hamilton and on 8 October, *The Times* reported that the bridal couple had arrived in Naples, although Sir William claimed to his managers in the Foreign Office that he did not arrive until the beginning of November.[161] The newspapers argued over whether Emma had been received by Maria Carolina and whether she was introducing ladies at Court, the role of an ambassador's wife. One traveller, Lord James Wright, tried to inform the Foreign Office that the gossip in the newspapers was 'wanton and false': Lady Hamilton had not forced herself on the Queen or the English travellers and Sir William continued to present women as well as men.[162]

Emma confided in Mary Dickenson who, in a traditional courtesy to a bride from a member of the groom's family, had solicited her as a correspondent, telling her that, 'before the 6th September I was always unhappy and discontented with myself'. Now, however, she wrote, 'I feel every moment my obligations to him and am always afraid I can never do enough for him since that moment. I say to myself Am I his Wife, and I can never separate more?'

The codes of high society that Emma had to negotiate as Lady Hamilton were labyrinthine. The slightest mistake in dress or manner could mean disfavour and she needed to train herself in the correct behaviour and self-presentation for the Neapolitan Court. Fresh-faced innocence was not enough. Ladies at court had precise standards of elegant movement and performance that required time and practice to perfect. A woman was expected to carry her head artfully, her arms curving gently away from her torso, and walk gracefully with small steps, without jostling her skirts or appearing stiff or inelegant. Even simple activities like entering a room, or exiting it, sitting, drinking tea, or waiting in line at a reception were highly embellished and ritualised.

Sir William was blind to the minutiae of female fashion and behaviour and Emma had to discover the secrets of courtly speech and manners for herself. She learnt how to greet acquaintances with the right degree of formality and familiarity, speak subtly and softly, and found out when to listen attentively and when interruptions were permitted. More important still were the non-verbal skills, the touch of the hand, the curtsy and the subtle deployment of the fan. Ushering together all her energies, Emma worked hard to transform herself into a lady of distinction.

A month after Sir William's arrival, the Queen communicated to him that, as she had heard much of Lady Hamilton's 'exemplary good Conduct and Humility', she would receive her privately. At the meeting, when the Queen invited her to sit beside her to discuss Marie Antoinette, Emma was so overcome that she burst into tears and the Queen was deeply touched.[163] 'I have been presented to the Queen of Naples by her own desire she as shewn me all sorts of kind & affectionate attentions,' Emma wrote. She advanced her position in the Queen's favour by declining Maria Carolina's first invitation: a dinner in honour of Prince Augustus, the youngest son of King George, to which only the most eminent English travellers were invited. Sir William went alone and introduced the aristocrats to Maria Carolina.

When the Hamiltons were invited to spend the hunting season and Christmas at the Palace at Caserta, Emma had her chance to become accepted as Lady Hamilton, rather than as the private wife of Sir William. Most courtiers had been steeped in courtly behaviour since childhood, but Emma had been picking up every piece of gossip about the Court over the last five years. She knew the power structures she faced and was ready to be thrown into a treacherous environment where every conversation contained hidden dangers and a kind suggestion was often a stab in the back. By January, Sir William declared, the Queen had 'become quite fond of her & has taken her under her protection'.

By March, Sir William was gratified by her success at negotiating the complex social codes. Aristocrats queued to visit her and Emma was careful always to dress well, seem humble and obliging, and flatter her guests with attention. She described Lord and Lady Malmesbury, Lord and Lady Plymouth, Lord Dalkeith and Lord Bruce as 'very kind and attentive' and 'remarkably civil to me'. Sir William enthused to Joseph Banks that the King and Queen

> are so good as to receive & treat her as any other travelling Lady of distinction – She has gained the hearts of all even of the Ladies by her humility & proper behaviour, & we shall I dare say go on well – I will allow with that 99 times in a hundred such a step as I took would be very imprudent but I know my way here . . . I am sure you will hear from every quarter of the comforts of my house.[164]

Sir William had made a similar comment about imprudent steps and 99 times out a hundred to his friend, Georgiana Countess Spencer – he took a defensive stand so often that he even repeated the same lines. As Sir William suggested, Emma had 'a difficult part to act'. She had to preside over the dinners for her illustrious guests and ensure everyone was looked after. Emma sat at one end of the table, Sir William at the other, with the principal guests seated along the sides. Dinners usually began at three o'clock in the afternoon and could last for over four hours. Food did not come in successive courses but in two servings of around twenty or more dishes, both sweet and savoury. The savoury plates included fish, carved meat, a ham, a turtle and plentiful game. Sweet dishes were cakes, and on a gala occasion, sorbets or fruit in ice sculptures. Meals were at best lukewarm for the kitchens were situated some way from the dining room, but no guest expected the food to be sizzling. Very hot food was thought to damage the constitution and it also signified poverty. Only the lowest classes ate food straight from the fire. Throughout the dinner, Emma had to keep an eye on the servants to ensure they served everyone correctly, monitor the guests for boredom or difficulty with the food, and keep up a sparkling and informed but tactful conversation. The guests expected the dishes to be artfully arranged in patterns and decorated with flowers. Hostesses were expected to lead the entertainment after dinner, so Emma sang and performed her Attitudes or the tarantella. Emma excelled in her role, and reports soon reached England that she was 'much respected & beloved on account of the proofs she gave of a benevolent heart'.[165]

'I am the happiest woman in the world,' Emma told Romney in a long letter, soon after she had arrived back at the Palazzo. She wondered if the Prince of Wales had said anything about her, promised she was 'interested in all that concerns you' and asked him to send the portrait of her in a black hat to Louis Dutens, the witness at her wedding, for 'he took a great deal of pains and trouble for me'. She then implored his help.

I hope I will have no corse to repent of what he [Sir William] as done, for I feel so grateful to him that I think I shall never be able to make him amends for his goodness to me. But why do I tell you this? you know me enough; you was the first dear friend I open'd my heart to, you ought to know me, for you have seen and discoursed with me in my poorer days, you have known me in my poverty and prosperity, and I had no occasion to have lived for years in poverty and distress if I had not felt something of virtue in my mind. Oh, my dear friend, for a time I own through distress my virtue was vanquished, but my sense of virtue was not overcome. How gratefull now, then, do I feel to my dear, dear husband that has restored peace to my mind, that has given me honors, rank, and, what is more, innocence and happiness. Rejoice with me, my dear sir, my friend, my more than father, believe me I am still that same Emma you knew me. If I could forget for a moment what I was, I ought to suffer.

She begged him to ask for 'anything I can do for you'. 'Come to Naples, and I will be your model, anything to induce you to come, that I may have an opportunity to show my gratitude to you.' Emma offered her services and solicited his pity because she wanted him to keep her secrets, now that she had new 'innocence and happiness'.[166] Although there had been hints about her life as a courtesan and a prostitute in Covent Garden, Romney was the only person who could confirm the rumours without impugning himself, and he could also spill the beans about her daughter. Emma wanted to sustain good relations with the English aristocracy, but she also had a bigger prize in view. She wanted to win Queen Maria Carolina.

26

Loving Maria Carolina

aria Carolina was the most powerful Queen in Europe. Although her room was adorned with a tapestry depicting 'Innocence' and Ferdinand's room was bedecked with one portraying 'Conjugal Fidelity', her husband was a lascivious layabout and she was a sharp political operator. In aiming to supplant the Marchesa di San Marco, the Queen's long-time friend who had controlled the Court indirectly for years, Emma was aiming high.

Charismatic and ruthless Maria Carolina was ten years Emma's senior. She had arrived in Naples at 1768, at the age of fifteen, eighteen months younger than her royal bridegroom. Stately and mature beyond her years, she had been raised in the backbiting Austrian Court while her mother, Queen Maria Theresa, ruled the country. She grew up accustomed to seeing women obeyed. Maria Theresa demanded that her daughter be allowed a place on the Neapolitan state council after she gave birth to a son and when she took her position in 1777, Maria Carolina quickly assumed power over her childish husband and the hidebound Court. Napoleon mocked the monarchs of Europe as useless puppets, but made an exception for her, praising her intelligence and vigorous appetite for work. She knew, as Sir William put it, that 'unless she applied to the business which the King avoids, the whole state would fall into confusion' and she gave 'the greatest part of her time in looking minutely into every paper'.[167] She had little help other than John Acton, the stolid English general and de facto Prime Minister. Her aim was to ensure she controlled the distribution of patronage, favours and positions in the Neapolitan Court and that Europe continued as it always had: reigned over by her relations and offspring. It was the type of absolute monarchy Britain had endured in the Tudor period, in which ritual took the place of decision and the only way to achieve any influence in government was to flatter the King or Queen.

The Queen was no great beauty but she embodied majesty in every sense of the word, awing courtiers with her grandeur. Her exquisitely jewelled silk dresses made the most of her abundant pale chestnut hair, brilliant blue eyes, and famously white and delicate hands. Underneath her glamour, she was often suffering. She endured eighteen pregnancies and was often sick with migraines and in pain from what the surgeons declared a benign tumour in her breast. Her children were weak and many died in early childhood. Ferdinand hunted every day, leaving her alone, and she relied on her female confidantes for support. The wives of ambassadors and daughters of powerful families fought bitterly for the position of Maria Carolina's favoured female friend. Sir William was close to the King and John Acton but his relationship with the Queen was uneasy and tainted with distrust and she hated the intimacy he gained with her husband through hunting with him.[168] He encouraged his new wife to win the Queen's favour. Catherine Hamilton had been reluctant to fawn over Maria Carolina but Emma, adaptable as ever, jumped to refashion herself as a courtier.

Emma had a significant advantage over her rivals, for she was feminine and warmly emotional, as the Queen liked her friends to be. She also had an innate sense of style, and Maria Carolina relied on her confidantes for assistance with her wardrobe and advice on dress. And, unlike many of the women at Court, Emma had not slept with the King. The Queen's motives were, most of all, strategic. The Neapolitan Court, Sir William nervously reported, was 'actively employed in preparing against any sudden attack' and Maria Carolina was flurried by 'alarm and uncertainty' that the French would invade Naples.[169] Intent on finding out the plans of the British government and suspicious of Sir William, she paid particular attention to the new Lady Hamilton, who seemed to have unlimited influence over her wily husband.

At the same time, she worried constantly about Marie-Antoinette and implored Emma for details about her sister's health. As Emma later wrote, 'At Paris, I waited on the Queen there at the Tuilleries, who entrusted me with the last letter she wrote to her Sister the Queen of Naples; this led to an ascendency in Her Majesty's Esteem.'[170] Maria Carolina wept that she could not respond to her sister's plea for help. Emperor Leopold of Austria, their brother, refused to intervene, and if he would not act, she had no chance of encouraging Ferdinand to do so. Emma was her ally in her grief and in the process, managed to gain the Queen's sympathy. According to Sir William, she 'very naturally told her whole story & that all her desire was by her future conduct to shew her gratitude to me, and to prove to the world that a young, beautiful Woman, tho' of obscure birth, could have noble sentiments and act properly in the great World'.

Maria Carolina was attracted to Emma as a political ally and also as a personal friend. Surrounded by jaded aristocrats, cynical courtiers almost from the moment they were born, the Queen took pleasure in Emma's genuine excitement about her new surroundings. By late 1792, to the shock of the jealous Court, Lady Hamilton had become the Queen's special favourite, a spy at the heart of plush Caserta.[171] The Queen began to sign her letters to Emma 'Charlotte' as she did only to her siblings and closest friends. Sir William was thrilled. 'Altho we have had many Ladies of the first rank from England here lately & indeed such as give the Ton in London, the Queen of Naples remarked that Emma's deportment was infinitely superior. She is often with the Queen, who really loves her.'

Emma boasted that the Queen esteemed her for being 'simple and natural', but the friendship was political. They shed tears together over Marie Antoinette, swapped fears about anti-monarchist riots and the advance of the French, and quickly began to plot to advance a relationship between Britain and Naples. To be the Queen's friend, Emma needed an elaborate wardrobe of dresses, shoes and necklaces, tiaras and bracelets of gold and diamonds worth thousands of pounds, a look very far from 'simple and natural'.[172] The journalist from the *Town and Country Magazine* had been spot on: the consequence of the marriage was a striking increase in Sir William's expenses.

The new Lady Hamilton became the ideal courtier: willing to be at the Queen's beck and call, always ready to flatter and entertain, and attentive to her smallest concern. As an actress's maid, Emma had learnt how to serve demanding women with sensitivity and her skills came in doubly useful with the Queen. Just as the King issued his commands on the hunting field, so the Queen's affairs of state were intermingled with dressmaking, childcare and social gossip. Emma and the Queen read together, talked in French and exchanged mementoes and tokens of friendship. The Hamiltons were soon invited to every Royal occasion and were in daily attendance. In private, she and the Queen were very intimate but in large assemblies, as she described to Greville, she pretended to be just one of the crowd, keeping a prudent distance. Discretion was crucial: the Court was humming with spies reporting back to the French on whether the Neapolitans would capitulate, and the French ambassador was vigilantly alert to the burgeoning intimacy between the British envoy and the Royal Family.

Maria Carolina became more intent on developing relations with the British in 1792, after the sudden death in March of her brother, Emperor Leopold of Austria. Only twenty years before, it had all been wonderfully cosy – the monarchs of Europe intermarried into one big chummy family, devoted to hunting, squandering their fortunes on ludicrously enormous buildings, and parading their kingly roles in pompous processions. Now they were falling. The Queen believed Leopold had been poisoned by French agents. With his death, another monarch with the power to resist her great enemy was gone.

The position of the French Royal Family deteriorated fast after Emma's visit to Paris with her new husband. In August 1792, Marie Antoinette and Louis XVI were taken from the Tuileries and imprisoned. The mob began to attack their friends, beginning with the Princesse de Lamballe, Marie Antoinette's close friend. In September, inflamed by scurrilous cartoons depicting her in lurid sexual positions with the Queen, the crowd brought the Princesse before their tribunal and sentenced her to death. There was no dignified death by guillotine for the gentle, dippy Princesse. She was immediately knocked down by a hammer. The crowd then fell on her and hacked off her breasts and raped her to death, so frenzied that they continued to violate her corpse. Her head was torn from her body, and plunged on to a pike, and her body ripped open and the intestines hung on another pole. The people hoisted up the pike and paraded her head through Paris to show Marie Antoinette in the tower. News of the Princesse's horrific fate swept across Europe in sensational reports and sickening cartoons depicting the mob eating her heart.

When the French republic was declared on 22 September 1792, Ferdinand and Maria Carolina refused to recognise it and snubbed their new French ambassador. The Queen was desperate to declare war against the French but Ferdinand was doubtful. A proposed alliance against France of the Italian states, Spain and Austria collapsed. The Neapolitan navy was weak and the army had spent the last decade assisting with Ferdinand's hunting expeditions. It seemed to the Queen that only Britain, with its huge navy and intimidating empire, had the power to protect them.

The Hamiltons spent much of 1792 at Caserta, often up and dressed for attendance as early as seven o'clock in the morning. Emma rambled around the English Garden with her husband, waiting for Maria Carolina to issue a summons. Despite her admission to the heart of Neapolitan affairs, she was intent on never losing her Englishness. As she reassured Greville, 'we allways drink tea'.

27

A Very Extraordinary Woman

ℬack in England, Emma was a style leader. At Queen Charlotte's birthday gala a few months after Emma departed, almost every woman was dressed 'à la Lady Hamilton' in flowing, simple white crêpe and satin, embroidered in silver, gathered with a silver or diamond belt, with their hair arranged in a loose Grecian style, circled with a jewelled headband and a few feathers. The Queen's birthday fashions had the influence of the Hollywood awards ceremony and the style reports set women rushing to their dressmakers for copies. The Duchess of York's dress 'à la Lady Hamilton' was, according to one reporter, 'the most magnificent and tasteful which her Royal Highness has worn in Britain': a petticoat of white crêpe 'embroidered with lilac stones and silver spangles', drapery embroidered with flowers, edged with a deep fringe of lilac beads and silver, and ornamented with chains of diamonds falling across the body. She wore flat slippers and her hair was simply gathered and adorned with a feather and a few diamonds.[173]

The *Lady's Magazine* was the lead fashion magazine, consulted by fine ladies, dressmakers and genteel women alike, and it began to promote the 'à la Emma' look in earnest. In October, it declared the essential autumn outfit for the 'most elegant women' was 'white linen or muslin petticoats, scalloped at the bottom without any flounces' with flat slippers, like those for dancing. The ensemble was topped with a cap similar to that worn by Emma in the *Town and Country Magazine* caricature of 1790: small, set low on the forehead, and short at the ears, with narrow borders of fine edging. The journalist sternly instructed readers that the Emma-dress 'has already been adopted by the Duchess of

Rutland, Lady Anne Fitzroy, Lady Smith, Mrs Robinson, Lady Charlotte Lennox, and many other elegant women, and it is to be hoped, will abolish the *enormous* head-dresses of the *last three winters*'.[174] A style Emma had developed to flatter her taller figure and wide hips became modish for women of all sizes. The fashion frenzy struck even Charles Greville. In June 1793, he reported to Sir William that all the dresses at the King's birthday gala in the same month 'had been evidently an imitation of her'. He declared his ex-mistress's style as the first and the most superior: 'far more adorning than all the trappings of French milliners on awkward inanimate damsels'. Emma's portraits, her performances, and her appearances in London had turned her into a fashion leader, even though she was many miles away. Some reports were more salacious: *The Times* declared Emma had begun a fashion for padding the bosom that had 'lowered the characters of many young ladies', for it was thought that they stuffed their cleavages to confuse suitors during heavy petting. Soon, the journalist joked, the Lady Hamilton vogue for 'pads will not leave an unsullied female, married or unmarried, reputation in the circle of fashion'.[175]

The English gossip columnists used Emma to sell papers, snickering about her friendship with Maria Carolina and her influence over her husband. Only one aspect of Emma's life remained a secret. Little Emma, now known as Miss Carew, a young lady of twelve, was still living in Manchester. Greville transferred the cost of her upkeep for six months, just over £32, to his uncle. The money was a trifle to a man of Sir William's expenditure, and Greville gently suggested he might move the girl to an establishment befitting the stepdaughter of an envoy. She was already learning French, music and dancing and had a maid, and he knew that the more education she received, the more likely William would be to bring her to Naples and the better were her chances of a good marriage. But Sir William preferred to forget about her and she remained at the Blackburns'.

Visitors flocked to see the new ambassadress. As Emma sighed, 'Our house at Caserta as been like an inn this winter, as we have partys, that have come either to see the environs, or have been invited to court.' In the winter of 1792, Sir William collapsed with exhaustion and stomach fever, the first of his severe bouts of dysentery, although he did not know the cause of his illness. As one traveller reported, he had 'been in some danger'.[176] Emma nursed him with the help of her mother. She declared 'I have been almost as ill as him with anxiety, apprehension, & fatigue,' and was 'eight days without undressing, eating or sleeping'. She was 'in hopes he will be better than ever he was in his life, for his disorder has been long gathering'.

In the hours of sitting by his bedside, Emma had dwelt on her good fortune. 'What cou'd console me for the loss of such a husband, friend, & protecter,' she wrote to Greville. 'We live but for one another, but I was to happy, I had imagined I was never more to be unhappy, all is right, I now know myself again & I shall not easily fall in to the same error again, for every moment I feel what I felt when I thought I was losing him for ever.' She gloated that Lady Plymouth, Lady Dunmore, Lady Webster and others had offered to assist her, and even the 'King & Queen sent constantly, morning and evening, the most flattering messages'. The Hamiltons ended their first year of marriage with their bond sealed by a shared aim to gain influence at the Neapolitan Court. Anxious to claim that Emma was worthy of her position and to ensure his friends knew she was more than his 'private wife', Sir William wrote in the spring of the following year:

> Emma goes on perfectly to my mind, but she has made our house so agreeable that it is more frequented than ever, &, of course, I am at a greater expence. However, I may safely say that no minister was ever more respected than I am here, & the English travellers . . . feel the benefit of our being so well at this Court, for Emma is now as well with the K. & Q. as I am, & of many parties with them. You will be glad to hear as I am sure you must from every quarter of the prudent conduct of Emma − She knows the value of a good reputation which she is determined to maintain having been completely recovered. She knows that beauty fades & therefore applies daily to the improvement of her mind.

Emma endeavoured to be his perfect hostess and courtier, always telling him how grateful she was for his kindness to her. She never stopped working to make herself the perfect lady, practising music and French and studying the exquisitely fashionable topic of botany, as well as developing her charitable interests.

The English observed Emma's effusively affectionate behaviour towards her husband and watched for signs of a pregnancy. A baby would ensure her position with her 'husband, friend & protecter' and be her financial security after his death. Sir William's family dreaded a pregnancy: he would not cut Greville's inheritance for Emma but he would for their son. Motherhood would enhance Emma's endeavour to appear respectable and would strengthen her position with Maria Carolina, mother of many. The Neapolitan Court was child-friendly and Emma had a willing nanny on hand in Mrs Cadogan. Yet there was no suggestion of a pregnancy and there is no evidence of any illness that might have been a miscarriage. It seems most likely that Sir William was infertile. Catherine Hamilton never conceived, and there is no trace that any of the courtesans he used did so either. Perhaps that was why he felt grateful to Emma for marrying him. Unlike many men his age, he had courted widows rather than young girls, knowing that his wife must sacrifice any wish to have a family.

There was no way of diagnosing infertility, and Emma might have thought that she, as a healthy young woman, could conceive by Sir William. If she was hoping to fall pregnant, she kept her efforts private. Otherwise, her time was consumed by the work of an envoy's wife. 'I literally have been so busy with the English, the Court, & my home duties, as to prevent me doing things I had much at heart to do,' she flustered to Greville. When the Duchess of Devonshire blazed into town, with her mother, Lady Spencer, and assorted children and hangers on, there were 'fifty in familly for four days at Caserta'. She and Sir William had lived for eight months at Caserta to be near the Royal Family and commuted twice weekly to town, 'to give dinners, balls, etc, returning here at 2 or 3 o clock in the morning after the fatige of a dinner of fifty, & ball & supper of 3 hundred, then to dress early in the morning, to go to court, to dinner at twelve a clock, as the Royal familly dine early, and they have done Sir William and me the honner to invite us very, very often'.

Maria Carolina wanted to meet most of the English visitors, for many of them, such as the Devonshires, wielded considerable influence over key English ministers in Parliament. Aristocrats had heard of Emma's influence with the Queen and demanded an audience. 'Tis true, we dined every day at court, or at some casino of the King; for you cannot immagine how good our King and Queen as been to the principal English who have been here.' She gave her visitors something more exclusive than an introduction at Court: a private audience. 'I have carried the Ladies to the Queen very often, as she permitted me to go to her very often in private, which I do. And the reason why we stay now here is, I have promised the Queen to remain as long as she does, which will be the tenth of July. In the evenings I go to her, and we are tete a tete 2 or 3 hours. Sometimes we sing. Yesterday the King and me sang duettes 3 hours.'

Emma and Sir William conducted their visitors around the city, to Court, to dinners and assemblies, and to their box at the opera. Scattered in archives and collections across the country are dozens of affectionate invitations from Emma to her guests. In one warm letter, she promised Lady Throckmorton that, had the Countess of Plymouth come to visit, 'I wou'd have ciceronised her all day & at night music and attitudes wou'd have diverted her'.[177] All self-respecting tourists called on *ciceroni*, famously learned and devoted guides, to show them the city and take care of their every need. Most of her visitors required 'ciceroning' to shops and dealers, help with buying and bargaining and many sent requests to the Palazzo Sessa for the envoy and his wife to pick up souvenirs they had forgotten and send them on. Some important visitors behaved like film stars, accustomed to constant attention. Many travelled to improve their health and Emma was called upon to tend the ill and comfort the bereaved. Lady Spencer had fond memories of Emma's assiduous nursing of her daughter, Harriet, Lady Duncannon, who was suffering from pneumonia.[178] When they recovered, they wanted to see the attractions Emma had visited tens of times – the ceremony when the holy blood held at San Gennaro Church liquefied, the coast and islands, the King's china factory at St Leucio, the Court and one of the King's country seats, Carditello, where Ferdinand pressed his guests to spend hours examining his cows and pigs.

Emma was excited to entertain the Devonshire set and she sympathised with Georgiana, for her husband had exiled her for giving birth to Charles Grey's child, but she was less entranced by the many other dreary and boorish guests, sometimes up to eighty at a time. They all required chaperoning and expected to attend an opulent party at the Palazzo. Many times a week, Emma, radiating smiles and sparkling with diamonds, presided over a bout of gambling or whist, sang Handel and presented her Attitudes. One astute squire spotted that Emma was weary of performing her famous poses, but most had no recognition of how much their visits drained Emma's patience and her husband's purse. Sir William continued to spend, believing that the English government would compensate him in due course and also hoping the same aristocrats would repay him with hospitality when he returned to England.

Everyone was eager to judge Emma, particularly the younger women. Lady Palmerston thought her not as beautiful as she had expected, but exquisitely dressed and 'very good humoured' and decided that 'her desire to please and her extreme civility is very uncommon'. She thought – like everyone else – that the couple was 'rather too fond'.

Emma hosted a dinner for the Palmerstons and more than fifty others, and Lady Palmerston decided she looked 'extremely handsome, and really does the honours exceedingly well . . . Sir William perfectly idolises her and I do not wonder he is proud of so magnificent a marble, belonging so entirely to himself.'

Lady Palmerston gives us a rare insight into how the guests perceived Emma's mother. Mrs Cadogan, she wrote to her brother, 'looks like a lady you have more often found useful than I could ever have done'. Her brother was a terrible reprobate and the women he found useful were prostitutes, madams and the odd cookshop owner as he was stumbling home. Perhaps Mrs Cadogan put Lady Palmerston in mind of all three occupations at once. She and her fellow travellers were perhaps a little insulted for many had heard that Sir William permitted Mrs Cadogan to attend the English parties but not those of his Neapolitan friends. Lady Palmerston slipped in a note of Emma's background. 'Lady H. is to me very surprising, for considering the situation she was in, she behaves wonderfully well. Now and then to be sure a little vulgarness pops out, but I think it's more Sir William's fault, who loves a good joke and leads her to enter into his stories, which are not of the best kind.'[179]

Most people describe Emma similarly: she was a friendly hostess and eager to please, well-mannered and attractive and Sir William was too fond of her. One minor squire reported, 'as we knew her story you may conceive we did not expect so much'. Entranced by Emma's spontaneous sense of fun and her actressy ability to mimic voices and personalities, he enthused that as well as her wonderful talent for attitudes, she 'has that of countenance to a great degree. I have scarcely know her look the same for three minutes together, and, with the study she has made of characters, she mimics in a moment everything that strikes her, with a versatility you have not a notion of.'[180] Everybody knew about Emma's previous life as wild Amy Lyon of the Temple of Health and Romney's model, but they tended to treat her origins as proof that she was, in Lady Palmerston's words, 'a very extraordinary woman' to have escaped.

The Kidds were living reminders of Emma's squalid background and Sir William rather wished they might disappear. Emma felt guilty about her grandmother, sickly and struggling for money, and she was trying to help her without Sir William discovering. She fretted to Greville that she wore a Court dress in November that cost £25 (nearly £1,500), and felt 'unhappy all the while I had it on', since she had '2 hundred a year for nonsense, & it wou'd be hard I cou'd not give her twenty pounds when she as so often given me her last shilling'. She begged him to send her grandmother £20 at Christmas, and asked him to 'write to her a line from me or send to her & tell her by my order' for 'if the time passes without hearing from me she may imagine I have forgot her & I wou'd not keep her poor old heart in suspense for the world'.

Emma vowed to send her grandmother money every Christmas. But throughout the first half of 1793, Sarah Kidd grew frailer and finally died in July, at the age of seventy-eight. Her grave is nowhere to be found in the large graveyard of Hawarden church. She was probably buried very simply with only a wooden cross marking where she lay. Mrs Kidd's life could hardly have been more different from that of her granddaughter. She could never read or write, married young and brought up a large family in a mining village, moving from village to village as her husband tried to find work as a collier. After his death, she supported her entire family. Throughout her life, her mind was focused on finding the next meagre meal, and her days were almost entirely limited to the four walls of her hovel and the mile or so around. She had never seen London, or any more of England than Chester for the last sixty years and Emma's adventures in London and beyond were something like a fairy tale: far away and utterly bewildering. She could not comprehend the lives of her daughter or granddaughter, but she understood all too well the sad situation of poor lonely little Emma, deemed too genteel to live with her, but not genteel enough to stay in the Palazzo with her mother. Humbly marked down in the parish register as 'widow of Thomas, Collier', the grandmother of England's most famous woman was given a simple funeral and burial at Hawarden, where she had lived for all of Emma's life.

Emma had not seen her grandmother for ten years. But there was no way she and her mother could journey across revolutionary Europe for a funeral – at least not on their own. Mrs Cadogan and Emma had to comfort each other in private.

In January 1793, Louis XVI of France was executed and Ferdinand commanded the Court to go into mourning. The Queen was doubly determined to encourage her husband to fight the French and declared that she hoped Louis's death 'will implore a striking and visible vengeance . . . and that on this account the Powers of Europe will have no more than a single united will'. She wrote to Emma that she looked to Emma's generous nation to provide this vengeance.[181]

In February, the new government of France, determined to be

respected as the European superpower, declared war on England and Holland. The English government began sending envoys to Naples to encourage the King and Queen to ally with England. At the end of the previous year, the French had sent out warships to threaten the King and Queen with invasion, forcing them to recognise the new regime, and they were nervous about inflaming their enemies any further. Emma struggled to persuade the Queen that the British could assist and, after a series of debates, an Anglo-Neapolitan treaty was signed on 12 July. Britain would maintain a fleet in the Mediterranean and Naples was required to provide ships and men and no longer trade with France. Sir William's comfortable backwater was about to become crucial to the battle for dominance over Europe.

Emma's support for Maria Carolina's aversion to the French would change her life. In August, Admiral Lord Hood, Commander-in-Chief of the British fleet in the Mediterranean, decided to call in troops from Naples, to assist his men in defending the French town of Toulon. As his messenger, he sent HMS *Agamemnon* and its young, ambitious captain, Horatio Nelson.

III. Neapolitan Nights

28

The Hero Visits

Since 1787 Horatio Nelson had been retired and miserable, on half pay in muddy Norfolk, making model ships, reading the newspapers, and feigning patience with his sickly, unfulfilled wife, Fanny. When he arrived in Naples on the evening of 10 September 1793, at the age of thirty-five, he knew it was his chance to grab back the glory that had seemed so secure before his marriage. 'I have only to hope I shall succeed with the King,' he worried.

Ferdinand came to meet Nelson's ship, resplendent in full court dress, accompanied by the Princes and Princesses, numerous courtiers, and Emma and Sir William. Since leaving Britain four months before, Nelson had been on shore only twice, and he had hardly seen a woman. He described himself as 'sick with fatigue', but he soon perked up when he spotted Lady Hamilton, the glamorous star of the gossip columns, sparkling in her court finery. Emma ushered him back to the Palazzo Sessa and into the apartments prepared for him and his thirteen-year-old stepson Josiah. They probably occupied the handsome suite with the sea view and the ceiling painted with stars that she first used when she arrived in 1786. Nelson slept in a room adorned with portraits of Emma as a Bacchante and a goddess, as was every room in the Palazzo, and Vigée le Brun's celebrated portrait of Emma as a *Sibyl* glowed softly over his bed.

Still stung by Queen Charlotte's refusal to receive her, Emma strained to prove herself to the visiting captain by planning entertainments and trying to anticipate his every need. Nelson had not eaten fresh meat or vegetables for weeks and he gleefully tucked into the silver plates of the finest fish, turtle and exotic sweetmeats arriving regularly from the Palazzo's kitchens. Emma accompanied him to Court and listened rapt to his stories of bravery, overwhelming the shy sailor with tricks of flirtation and allure she had perfected with hardened Neapolitan courtiers. Obsessed by social rank and terrible at languages, he was immediately impressed by her intimacy with the Queen and by her fluent translation from Italian and French.

In just four days, the King pledged Nelson his troops and wrote an obliging letter to Lord Hood. Nelson exulted that the King called him and his company 'the saviours of Italy'. Exhilarated by his social success and Ferdinand's cooperation, Nelson planned an elaborate Sunday breakfast on his ship. The King was to attend, along with the Court, but the pregnant Queen probably stayed behind. Also in attendance were Sir William and Emma and the most distinguished English visitors: the Bishop of Winchester and family, Lord and Lady Plymouth and various other aristocrats. The meat was roasting in the ovens, the table laid with china borrowed from the Palazzo Sessa, and Sir William and Emma were already on board, when John Acton sent the urgent message that a French man-of-war had arrived at Sardinia.[182] Detecting a chance for glory, Nelson hustled his guests off the ship, rushed to up the anchor and set off in pursuit. He wrote to his hosts twelve days later, thanking Sir William for organising some prints for him and apologising for dashing off with the embassy's butter pan.

Fanny, alone in her empty Suffolk home, Roundwood, needed to be reassured about her husband's meeting with the woman the newspapers declared no man could resist or forget. 'Lady Hamilton has been wonderfully kind and good to Josiah,' he wrote, carefully concealing his attraction to her. 'She is a young woman of amiable manners and who does honour to the station to which she is raised.' Sexual guilt always prompted Nelson to buy Fanny a gift, and he found time in his hectic few days to purchase some rich sashes of Naples silk. One of Emma's trademark fashions was a thick coloured silk sash tied tight around a muslin dress, an almost childish style. Romney painted her in the same outfit for *The Ambassadress*, and she wore a similar style for her wedding and then repeatedly in Naples. Nelson was even thinking of Lady Hamilton as he bought his wife a gift.

The English gossip columnists rushed to exploit the meeting between the ambassadress sex bomb and the virile captain. The scandalous *Bon Ton Magazine* made fun of Sir William, Nelson and Emma in a tale about 'the lovely Syren'. A young, newly-married woman who is sexually unsatisfied by her elderly husband, Lord E—, who, like Sir William, has a 'violent rage for private theatricals and dramatic representations', falls in love with a captain when he visits. A cartoon depicts a small man who looks like Nelson helping a lady descend down a wall to him, accompanied by the scurrilous tale of how the visiting captain becomes a

> professed adorer of the lovely Syren, whose beauty, about three years ago fascinated Lord E— in such a bewitching manner, that his lordship, actually forgetting what he owed to himself, his family and rank, after a courtship of a few months, led her . . . a willing victim to the Temple of Hymen [i.e. he married her, a joke on Emma's work in the Temple of Health]. But though Lord E— may be as great an admirer of female charms as most of his compeers, he is certainly but ill qualified to do homage to the power of beauty, in that way that the ladies generally expect.

The 'reports in general circulation' imply that Lord E— 'sleeps at night with a pound of raw beef stakes clapt on each cheek, to give them a fresh and ruddy appearance', and wears silver thimbles to 'render his fingers conical and tapering'. Although, however, he 'might secure the *appearance* of youth and vigour . . . we greatly doubt whether the whole *Materia Medica* can recall the actual enjoyment of those enviable blessings', for he is impotent. After a few weeks, the new wife was deeply disappointed by the failure of her husband's 'bag-pipes' (the Hamiltons were initially Scottish) and, because women are 'ill qualified to put up with crosses and disappointments', frolics with the handsome captain.[183]

Infatuations with married women were Nelson's speciality. 'This Horatio is for ever in love,' he had once imagined himself described, although his amorous obsessions were not generally matched by success. Small at just under five foot six, thin and pale, he had a shock of unwieldy ginger hair and his Norfolk drawl was very pronounced. Nelson's sharp, chiselled face and small, sunken eyes disappointed when the ideal of male beauty was Lord Byron with his limpid eyes and sensual plump mouth. At least two young ladies had snubbed his offers of marriage and his friends derided the courtesans and mistresses he chose after his marriage. When he took up with a young opera singer, Adelaide Correglia, when stationed in Leghorn, now Livorno, a strategic port on Italy's Tuscan coast, his colleague Captain Fremantle complained he made himself 'ridiculous' with his excessive devotion to her, ruining the whole dinner by gazing devotedly into her eyes.

Horatio Nelson was born in 1758, the third son (he was technically the fifth, but two elder brothers had already died) of a country rector in Burnham Thorpe, a small village in Norfolk, ten miles from the coast. When he was nine, his mother died, aged only forty-two, after producing eleven children in seventeen years. Little Horatio claimed to remember no more about her than that she 'hated the French'. Most widowed fathers remarried as quickly as possible, but Edmund Nelson remained single and brought up his family with stringent discipline. Horatio grew up competing for attention and he escaped home at the age of twelve to become a midshipman, thanks to his uncle who paid for his commission. He travelled to the West Indies, the Arctic, India and the Mediterranean and did not see his father or his siblings for six years.[184] Starved of affection since childhood, he fell desperately in love with nearly every woman he met. Neither good-looking, well-connected nor rich, he was ignored by the girls he tried, and he had no chance with his grand passion, the belle of Quebec town, Mary Simpson. As he grew up, he was increasingly attracted to young married women with a maternal gleam in their eye. While stationed in the Caribbean, he became infatuated with the beautiful young wife of the elderly Commissioner of Antigua, declaring, 'was it not for Mrs Moutray, who is *very very* good to me, I should almost hang myself at this infernal hole', and extolling that 'her equal I never saw in any country'. His desires piqued by days of flirtation with her, Nelson sailed for the Caribbean island of Nevis. There he met John Herbert, a rich planter and President of the Island Council, and developed a crush on his niece and housekeeper, Fanny Nisbet, a widow with a young son.

A fractious only child, Frances Herbert Woolward had enjoyed a leisured childhood in Nevis, but in 1779 her father died, leaving her nothing, and she was forced to accept the marriage proposal of the doctor who had attended him, Josiah Nisbet, ten years her senior. The newly-weds travelled to England. Most Nevisians who moved to England did so in the hope that the cold climate would cure their sufferings from lead poisoning, caused by drinking rum that had been distilled in lead pipes, and Josiah Nisbet was probably similarly afflicted. She quickly fell pregnant, but Dr Nisbet sickened, probably with syphilis, and died in 1781, hallucinating wildly in his final months.[185] Left a widow at twenty-one, with a son, Fanny had no choice but to return and become her uncle's housekeeper. Two years later, Nelson arrived and, touched by her bruised sadness and impressed by her fortitude after losing both father and husband in quick succession, he began to enjoy Fanny's company. She had the mature, maternal air he loved, and he admired her petting her young son, imagining him doing the same to him and their brood of children. He was enjoying just another pleasant crush – but he had no idea that the Herberts saw him as the answer to their prayers. Herbert wanted his disillusioned niece and her son off his hands and she was desperate to flee the stultifying routine of her life as his housekeeper. Any man with reasonable prospects would have done. Fanny knew her youth was fading. In the excitable young captain, she saw her last chance of escape from growing old as her uncle's servant.

To Nelson, Nevis was a romantic paradise. Over 3,000 feet high, Mount Nevis towered over 36 square miles of lush vegetation, fruit trees and hot springs. According to *A Description of the Island of Nevis*, dedicated to John Herbert and compiled in consultation with Dr Nisbet, the island was 'altogether pleasing and agreeable'.[186] Sugar cane grew thick on the rich volcanic soil, and the Herberts, owners of the Montpelier Plantation, were the island's first family. The beauty hid misery and pain and ten thousand beaten, abused slaves. Nevis's population was small, with only 1,000 whites, and out of every five people who came to Nevis, free or as a slave, three were dead before the end of five years, and few white inhabitants lived past fifty. Fanny had no chance of meeting new men. Since most women married before twenty, Fanny was old. The white population was in decline, and, because English servants were unwilling to travel out, most women had more domestic work than their English counterparts. Fanny knew she had to turn Nelson's crush into a desire to marry her. Her uncle was more than willing to encourage the match by throwing them together and declaring her four years younger than she actually was. Nelson turned out to be less easily swayed than he had hoped, but Herbert was not to be daunted. He played his trump card: the offer of a massive dowry.

Nelson, like all the English, believed the white inhabitants of the Caribbean to be wildly rich, as well as more sexual, thanks to their acquaintance with the black arts of witchcraft and their torrid climate. Prime Minister Pitt declared that four-fifths of Great Britain's overseas wealth came from the West Indies, but the income of the Nevisian planters was actually in decline because the soil was losing its fertility through overcultivation. Herbert hid his worsening fortunes and let Nelson believe that he would 'provide handsomely' for Fanny: a large gift on marriage, £300 a year, and £20,000 on his death (over £1.2 million today).[187] Nelson also anticipated that she would inherit the bulk of Herbert's estate.

Tempted by the prospect of catching an heiress to millions, Nelson began to imagine himself a husband. After all, he was an age to be married and he longed to start a family. Most importantly, while every other woman had turned him down, Fanny was a sure thing. Although she was no beauty and could never be called vivacious, she was wealthy, fertile, and seemingly possessed of the self-control, poise and maturity vital for a navy wife. Nelson was very much in the dark. He had no idea that Fanny and her uncle were engaged in an effort to show her off as independent – in reality, she was tremulous and nervous. Neither did he realise that she was no longer fertile, her womb wrecked, probably by an infection contracted from syphilitic Josiah Nisbet. He was also utterly ignorant that Herbert's famed riches were a lie.

Once they were engaged, Herbert offered nowhere near the money he had promised. Breaking an engagement was always reviled as a dishonourable act, so Nelson could only complain – and anyway, he had high hopes that Fanny's uncle would shower money on her in the future. Their marriage took place on 11 March 1787, in Montpelier House, across the road from the sugar plantation where the slaves still toiled. The hell-raising twenty-two-year-old Prince William Henry, the future King William IV, was visiting and agreed to give away the bride. The wedding was celebrated in his honour and a hundred dined on the island's best produce and watched cock-fighting and horse-racing, toasting the Prince with imported wines and gallons of rum.

The bridal couple returned to London to begin their life together. Disaster struck almost immediately. Nelson was retired and put on half pay of eight shillings a week. In Nevis, he had leap-frogged over his superior's head to request that the Admiralty uphold the law and prevent the islands from trading with America. His fault as a subordinate was what later made him great: convinced he was right, he refused to conciliate. Nelson's tactless accusations of fraud (to the extent of writing to the Prime Minister) had annoyed the Admiralty. Even worse, King George blamed him for failing to stop Prince William's irresponsible behaviour and ludicrous spending in the West Indies. Nelson was firmly out of favour. As it was a period of peace, there were not many ships available and he had no chance of the few that came up.

Fanny had believed that her acquaintance with the Prince would give her an inroad into a position in the Queen's household. It was an outlandish idea: Queen Charlotte despaired of her wild son and wanted nothing to do with those he had befriended on his travels. Fanny was marooned in Norfolk, far from London and the fashionable life she had dreamt about. To her distress, Josiah was sent away to school, and the couple moved in with Nelson's father, Edmund, still the rector at Burnham Thorpe. As the weather turned cold, she was entirely debilitated by the Norfolk damp and mud. Wracked by chills, rheumatism and nervous fevers, she wept her weeks away in her room. 'Mrs Nelson takes large doses of the bed,' sighed Edmund in exasperation. Fanny made no friends in the tiny village and she was not helped by the English prejudice that West Indian ladies were leisured and self-indulgent. Back in Nevis, Herbert was nursing a grudge that he had been pushed aside at the wedding by limelight hog Prince William, and he refused requests for money.

Horatio occupied himself with examining nautical charts, reading Dampier's *Voyages* and the newspapers, modelling ships, and writing to the Admiralty. Fanny tried and failed to embroider and paint, disappointing Edmund's wish for entertainment by declaring she was too miserable to sing or play. She had bravely borne her father's death and husband's insanity and illness, but as she reached thirty, she seemed to lose her spirit. Her hopes of genteel comfort as mistress of her own home had crumbled. Nelson, in turn, was dismayed by her sickliness and lost all hope of her becoming the wife he had hoped for: an efficient, wealthy mother of sons.

Girlish Frances Nisbet would have been the ideal wife for a quiet country vicar, but she was wrong for ambitious Nelson. She always counselled moderation and he began to perceive such advice as disloyalty. Before they were married, she urged him not to pursue the issue of American trade with the Caribbean islands, but he wrote to her firmly that if he had done as she advised, 'I should have neglected my duty'. As their marriage wore on, he was irritated by Fanny's failure to praise him as he desired and he was increasingly baffled by her lethargy and depression.

Five years dragged by and there was no sign of a baby. Fanny had conceived two months after her first marriage. Fertility problems were not uncommon, but what was rare was the Nelsons' refusal to investigate a cure. In the eighteenth century, since infertility was always deemed to be the fault of the woman, scores of desperate childless wives of the middle and upper classes clustered in Bath taking the waters, consulted doctors, submitted to peculiar regimes of diet and exercise, and even paid James Graham £50 for a night on the Celestial Bed. A woman who was not a mother was considered a failure, and so a baby was thought to be ample recompense for the indignity of being probed by doctors and quacks. But Fanny and Nelson appear not to have tried any remedy. Their marriage was simply too fraught to embark on the stresses of treating infertility. Within a year of arriving in England, they were trapped in a bitter round of mutual blame.

When the revolution began in France in 1789, war with France seemed inevitable, but Nelson felt as if every man but him was called to sea. With inactivity and illness all around him, he sank into depression and no longer wrote to ask for places. Salvation came for him in 1793. Understaffed and in crisis, the navy could ignore him no longer (by 1795 naval demand was so great that the authorities had to open their gaols and send in criminals as seamen). He received his orders and left Norfolk for Chatham, Kent, to join the *Agamemnon*, jubilant to escape the slow drag of his marriage. While he was preparing the ship for sea, Fanny had devastating news: her uncle Herbert had died and had left her only a token amount of money and £500 for Josiah. Nelson plunged himself into provisioning and staffing, trying hard to quash his anger over the thousands he had expected. He had to accept that his wife would always be poor and would never bear another child.

Nelson returned to sea in May determined to pursue glory. He was delighted to meet a woman who was Fanny's complete opposite: uncomplaining, vivacious, flattering and obsessed with fame. As Nelson's success with King Ferdinand confirmed him back in favour with the Admiralty, he would have adored Lady Hamilton for her assistance in procuring him the promise of troops even if she had been a dumpy matron with ten grandchildren. When he set sail for Sardinia on 15 September after only five days in Naples, Nelson was already a little in love.

29

War Approaches

*E*mma's time with Nelson was soon little more than a pleasant memory to recall occasionally. Only a few days after he departed, her life became more frenetic than it had ever been. Marie Antoinette was in terrible danger in France and it seemed as if Napoleon was finalising plans to invade Naples. Emma's every hour was devoted to Maria Carolina. 'Owing to my situation here,' she scrawled to Greville, 'I am got into politicks and I wish to have news for our dear much loved Queen.'

Maria Carolina was obsessed with the plight of Marie Antoinette. 'Every time they enter her room,' she agonised, 'my unfortunate sister kneels, prays and prepares for death. The inhuman brutes that surround her amuse themselves in this manner . . . I should like this infamous nation to be cut to pieces, annihilated, dishonoured, reduced to nothing for at least fifty years. I hope that divine chastisement will fall visibly on France.' On 14 October 1793, Marie Antoinette was hauled up before a public court, accused of treachery and of sexually abusing her eight-year-old son Louis Charles. The audience, expecting her to be plump and pampered, were shocked by the pale and emaciated woman in front of them, dressed in a threadbare black dress. Fifty witnesses were called to the two-day trial, and although Marie Antoinette's spirited defence, particularly against the accusations about her son, won the crowd's sympathy, she was summoned back into the court at four in the morning to hear that she was condemned to death. At eleven o'clock on the following day, her hair cut short and her hands bound, the Queen was driven along the long route to the guillotine in an open cart to the derisory shouts of the crowd. Through it all, she kept her composure, stepping gracefully from the cart and walking lightly to the block. At twelve fifteen, her head was cut off and displayed to a jubilant crowd. Many had expected her to escape execution, and aristocrats and ordinary people alike across Europe were stunned by her fate. They rushed to buy the newspapers, pouring over the detailed transcripts of the trial and the Queen's death.

Maria Carolina was prostrate with grief. Eight months' pregnant, furious with the failure of her husband and late brother to mount a rescue, and paralysed at the death of a sister she had not seen for so long, she could hardly be compelled to leave her apartments. 'My poor sister,' she mourned uncomprehendingly. 'Her only fault was that she loved entertainments and parties.' Under a picture of Marie Antoinette in her study, she inscribed, 'I shall pursue revenge until the grave'. The Court was devastated, Sir William reported, thrown 'into the utmost grief and indignation'. Ferdinand ordered four months of mourning and closed the theatres.[188]

When she was not weeping for her sister, the Queen dwelt on her terror that she might share her fate. Students, respectable burghers, and members of the armed forces, as well as intellectuals, were forming clubs dedicated to bringing in a republic. Maria Carolina knew that she was a particular focus for resentment. According to Giuseppe Gorani's *Secret Memoirs of the Courts of Italy*, rushed off the Paris press in 1793 to a public avid to give their political grievances sensual colour, the lazy King lived in a moral vacuum, caring only for hunting. Shrewd John Acton was the Queen's lover, governing Naples despotically for his own gain. The Queen, 'like her sisters', was concerned only to 'increase the power of the Austrian Royal Family', disdaining her husband and his kingdom alike. 'Hard, capricious', she was a second Catherine de' Medici without Catherine's administrative skills. Emma had a starring role in Gorani's best-seller: she was 'a charming orphan from the most notorious nunnery in London'. He ridiculed her low background and dubious education, but noted her extreme beauty and her rare mix of affability and dignity.[189] Everything about her was, he decided, as extraordinary as her almost unbelievable history. Gorani trotted out the usual salacious biography of Emma to lend ammunition to the representation of the Court as obsessed by pleasure. It was fortunate that he had had little access to the Palace, for the comparison between Marie Antoinette's *Petit Trianon* and Maria Carolina's English Garden was impossible to miss: both Queens spent absurd sums of money on exotic plants while their subjects lived in squalor.

The price of foodstuffs was spiralling, and the people begged the

King to use some of his wealth to subsidise the cost of oil and maca-
roni, the staples of the Neapolitan diet. When Ferdinand refused, the
lazzaroni, traditionally royalists, began to pay attention to the angry
students preaching liberty on their street corners.[190]

Determined to defend her dear friend, Emma wrote to Greville:

> no person can be so charming as the Queen, she is everything one
> can wish, the best mother, wife & friend in the world. I live constantly
> with her & have done intimately so for 2 years & I have never in
> all that time seen any thing but goodness and sincerity in her & if
> ever you hear any lyes about her contradick them & if you shou'd
> see a cursed book written by a vile french dog with her character
> in it don't believe one word.

Instead of making concessions to those who felt, in the words of an
English journalist, 'the allurements of liberty', or supplying the poor
with food to compensate for the inflation, Ferdinand and Maria Carolina
employed a repressive chief of police and sent spies into every part of
the city.[191] They intensified their security by changing their bedrooms
frequently, employing many more bodyguards and only leaving the
palace under massive guard. Believing themselves fighting a hidden,
deadly enemy who wished for nothing more than total destruction of
the Court, they ordered terrible reprisals against the demonstrators.
They commanded troops to imprison or kill every inhabitant of rebellious towns and villages in the country.[192] Those simply suspected of
anti-monarchist ideas were thrown into gaol, languishing indefinitely
without trial, and no doubt dozens were tortured. The King and Queen
demanded their secret services find hard evidence of Jacobin plots and
Naples seethed with false accusations and denunciations.

Emma had her hands full. The Queen needed her more than ever,
and Sir William's attacks of gout and stomach upsets were becoming
very frequent. He was often too ill to attend Court, let alone gain privileged access to Ferdinand by hunting and partying with him. He needed
his wife to care for him, act as his secretary (he was often too ill to
write), and attend Court with redoubled vigour to make up for his
absence. If all this was not enough, more English visitors arrived than
ever before. Since Paris was in bloody chaos, there was nowhere else
for the tourist bent on self-indulgence. Emma sighed that her 'breakfast, dinner & supper is like a fair'.

She was becoming weary of performing her Attitudes for clamouring guests. Although they wanted to see her famous poses of Niobe and Cleopatra, they were rather discomfited by her performances, now that she was married. When she had been a mistress, they praised her unreservedly (they were used to enjoying performances by actresses with dubious pasts). But once she was their equal (often superior), as Lady Hamilton, women, particularly of the minor aristocracy, became uneasy about expressing approbation. Just so no one might think them taken in, they now made a point of declaring that she betrayed her humble past, wrecking the wonderful feelings she had inspired in her audience by exclaiming, 'Ah, Sir Willum, I've dropped me Joug.'[193] Men tended to be more forgiving, one young dazzled squire proclaiming that her performance 'joins every grace that ever was united to the greatest beauty of face and person'.[194]

The Palazzo hit a new level of social glitter when Mrs Elizabeth Billington arrived, trailing glamour and luscious blonde hair. The highest paid opera singer in England, she was famous for her extraordinary three-octave range and expressive acting and she aimed to take advantage of the city's new status as Europe's favourite aristocratic playground. The Hamiltons eagerly introduced her at Court. She was soon appointed prima donna at the city's San Carlo Opera and the Neapolitans fell in love with her – so much so that when their priests later declared that Vesuvius erupted to express God's displeasure at seeing a Protestant on the stage of a Catholic city, they ignored them. She and Emma had much in common for both knew the power of an image (indeed, she had copied her hostess's St Cecilia pose when she had sat for Romney). After performances, Mrs Billington always directed her carriage to whisk her to Emma's home. In Sir William's handsome rooms, she struck up an intimacy with the plump asthmatic young Prince Augustus, George III's sixth son, who was in disgrace after recently marrying Lady Augusta Murray without his father's permission. When the sumptuous carriages of Mrs Billington and the Prince were outside the Palazzo, Emma's salon was more of a fair than ever. An invitation to hear the opera singer and the runaway Royal singing duets was the hottest ticket in town.

As in England, Emma's most frequent visitors and closest friends were Whig supporters: Sir Charles Blagden, Lord Cholmondeley, Lord Palmerston, Lord and Lady Plymouth, the Duchess of Devonshire, Lady Foster, Lady Webster, and Lord Bristol, Emma's particular friend. After King George had refused to receive Emma at Court, Sir William had become somewhat less staunchly loyal to the Tory party, and he raised no protest as his wife turned his home into a salon for Whigs abroad, all of them intent on their principle that wealth and property, not simply aristocratic title, should confer power. Any gathering attended by the Whigs soon became a gambling party, and thousands were squandered at faro, quinze and hazard, games of pure chance played in groups. The frisson of play lay in trying to second-guess your neighbour's hand, and in acting, pretence and double bluff – all skills at which Emma excelled. She loved gaming. In 1793, Sir William gave her a birthday present of a necklace of fabulous diamonds as a bribe to stop her from throwing down so many notes on to the gambling table.

There were other matters to worry about. In France, a diminutive Corsican, Napoleon Bonaparte, had risen to be Commander-in-Chief of the army. His troops were rampaging through Europe and they were heading for Naples.

30

In Fear of Napoleon

*M*aria Carolina was frantic. She vacillated between fear of being overthrown by a Jacobin mob and terror of a French invasion. The King retreated to the hunting field and, as Sir William wrote in exasperation, 'accustomed to a life of continued dissipation, gives but little attention to the Affairs of State, which are transacted chiefly by the Queen of Naples and General Acton'.[195] Casting about for a way to save herself, the Queen turned to Emma.

Most English notables who visited Naples were related to Members of Parliament and the Queen wanted Emma to introduce them to her and help persuade them that Britain should assist in the defence of Naples. Emma dropped heavy hints to Greville, hoping her ex-lover might pass the information to his friends in government. The Queen, she wrote, 'loves england and is attached to our ministry and wishes the continuation of the war as the onely means to ruin that abominable french council'. Maria Carolina ran a clever publicity campaign, presenting herself to smitten English visitors as a vulnerable Queen and a great admirer of Britain.[196] In England, Whig leader Charles Fox, convinced that the French wished for peace, was the voice of the anti-war movement. Tories and supporters of the war-mongering Prime Minister Pitt did not generally need to be persuaded that the French desired to subjugate all Europe. By introducing the Duchess of Devonshire, the Hollands, Blagden and the rest to Maria Carolina, Emma hoped to inspire Fox's friends to support the cause of war.

In 1794, the Queen wrote to Emma asking her to tell the company at their commemoration of King George's birthday that 'I wish and desire all happiness to the King, to whom I have vowed a friendship without limits'. She was delighted that the Neapolitan alliance between Naples and Britain 'permits me to express the sentiments which I have always cherished in my heart towards England'. She requested to see English visitors, such as Mrs North, presumably a relation to Lord North, former Prime Minister. Sir William sent a copy of the letter to England, as Maria Carolina had hoped he would. The Queen also deputised Emma to find out more from her visitors about the plans of the English government.

Many of Emma's new friends became her admirers. She escorted the Earl of Bristol, who was 'very fond of me', to Maria Carolina with whom 'we spent four hours in an enchantment'. Lady Holland observed Bristol was 'a great admirer of Lady Hamilton, and conjured Sir William to allow him to call her Emma'. She was surprised by Bristol's interest in such a commoner, although she thought that his attraction to her 'beauty and her wonderful attitudes is not singular'. Bristol sneered at Sir William as a shrivelled 'piece of walking *verd-antique*', a cruel joke that he could not keep up with his handsome wife, but Sir William trusted Emma and encouraged her close friendships with powerful men.[197] For him, they were perfectly innocent, a natural extension of her warm, outgoing personality.

Emma always set out to make people fall in love with her. She was tactile and loved to flatter. In private, she could not stop gushing about Maria Carolina as 'the Queen whom I adore' and claimed 'nor can I live without her', and to the Queen's face she was even more excitably emotional. She declared her a 'mother, friend & everything', her 'talents are superior to every woman in the world', 'she is the first woman in the world'. The Queen addressed her intimately. As she wrote to her when Sir William fell ill, 'I would fain keep you company, my friendship might comfort you.'

The Hamiltons spent their third wedding anniversary with Maria Carolina in Quisiana, a smaller seaside palace that Ferdinand used as a base for fishing trips, and Sir William told her, as she wrote to Greville, he 'loved me better than ever & had never for one moment repented'. She continued with her music and rode out regularly with the Queen, who supplied her with horses, an equerry and her own servant. If not entertaining at home, her evenings were occupied by crowded balls and concerts at Court. Although she was busy, she was also trying to fill her time, trying to stave off unhappiness. After four years of marriage, Emma was realising that the Palazzo would never be full of children. 'He is the best husband and friend,' she later wrote. 'I wish I could say father also; but I should have been too happy if I had the blessing of having children, so must be content.' As Emma could persuade Sir William to nearly anything, we have to presume that the hints in the English gossip columns were correct: he was sterile (male infertility was discussed as impotence) and could not impregnate even a healthy young partner.

Her childlessness was doubly painful for Emma because she had a better chance of bringing her daughter to Naples if she could have babies with her husband. She turned to Greville for help, begging him, 'Do send me a plan how I could situate little Emma, poor thing.' Little Emma knew that her stepfather was a great aristocrat and ambassador, and she was desperate to live with her mother. Although Greville had instructed her guardians to tell her that she should expect nothing 'beyond the quiet & retired life', he was hopeful that his uncle might change his mind. He told Sir William that, since her health was too delicate to put her into service, he should bring her to live in the Palazzo Sessa, as Mrs Cadogan's niece, or give her a dowry and marry her to a 'good sort of man', like a clergyman. Sir William refused to bring her to the Palazzo and was adamant he would not expose himself by making enquiries in England about suitors. Little Emma had no choice but to accept that her future would entail what she most dreaded: work as a governess.

Emma's daughter had to find out about her mother through the fashion magazines. The dresses at the English royal birthday galas throughout 1794 and 1795 were 'à la Emma': white satin crêpe and petticoats, simple drapery, gold headbands, while the fashionable hairstyle was a simple arrangement of curls around the head. Rehberg's book of Emma's Attitudes had become a fashion magazine. As one journalist reported in 1796, by 'following the style of dress, and the arrangement of drapery, in the fine remains of antiquity, the present taste has happily emancipated the ladies from the ridiculous lumber of the late fashions, from powder, whalebone and cork, flounces and furbelows'.[198] Even actual items were named after Emma's favourite poses: a special 'Iphigenia Veil' was very popular, as were 'Minerva Lapels'.[199] In 1795, the *Lady's Magazine* fashion reporter described how Emma's outfit, as in the Romney portrait *Emma Hart in Morning Dress*, had become the latest look: a bonnet of black velvet over hair combed into light curls, a full cravat around the neck and a black satin cloak.[200] The *Bacchante* of Emma running with a dog, celebrated because everybody knew Greville commissioned it in an attempt to foist Emma on to Sir William, was finally engraved from Romney's private copy in which Emma's left breast was almost entirely exposed. Prints were soon selling wildly.

Hack writers and popular novelists continued to work Emma into their fanciful narratives. A magazine serial, 'The Adventures of Emma', published in 1796, tells the story of a wholesome country girl who 'blended the artless simplicity of rural life with the more refined sentiments of cultivated education', and succeeds in marrying her much more aristocratic lover after she proves herself by escaping seduction.[201] The real Emma, however, had come a long way from such a sentimental representation. She was an active participant in the turbulent politics of the Neapolitan Court. As she boasted to Greville, her situation there was 'very extraordinary & what no person as yet arrived at'.

In 1795 Emma turned thirty and the Palazzo Sessa became a hothouse for spies. Charles of Spain, King Ferdinand's brother, was considering an alliance with France, and he was secretly trying to encourage Ferdinand to join him. But the Queen had not softened towards the French as the 'murderers of my sister and the royal family' who have 'put poniard and poison into the hands of all classes and peoples against legitimate authority'. The British navy, however, was overstretched and the government was increasingly preoccupied with defending its own territories in the Mediterranean. They suggested Naples make peace with France.

Emma made almost daily trips to the Palace, carrying letters and news or introducing diplomats and dignitaries. Her task was complex: along with John Acton and the small pro-English faction at Court, she promised the apprehensive Queen that the British were trustworthy and could protect them. At the same time, she was trying to persuade the British government, by means of letters and strong hints to visiting diplomats, that if they did not make a commitment, then Naples might well unite with Spain. She vouched that if Naples partnered with the English, Ferdinand and Maria Carolina would fulfil the terms of the treaty.[202] She was also gathering information for her home government. Maria Carolina gave Emma information about King Charles's plans from her spies in Spain and Emma was able to send to England copies of signed letters from the King of Spain to Ferdinand in which he confirmed he would ally with the French.[203] She wrote to Greville, 'we have been 3 days 7 nights writing to send by this courier letters of *consequence* for our government. They ought to be gratefull to Sir William & myself *in particular.*'

The British government recognised that Maria Carolina was a vital source of information and employed Emma to mediate between her and their visiting spies and representatives. For Sir William to pay a call on the Queen with an English visitor would arouse everybody's suspicions, but Emma could pretend the diplomats were only her admirers, wishing to flirt with the Queen. When in early 1796 an important English diplomat, Earl Macartney, came to investigate the latest intelligence that Spain was allying with France, Emma wrote that she 'will be alone, and you will see her in the family way. You will be in love with her as I am.' She meant that they would discuss politics in private, but to the Court – and to anyone reading the letters – it would seem like an evening between two silly women and one gallant man.

In October 1796, Ferdinand's nerve gave way and he signed a treaty with the French, bribing them from attacking with sixty million francs, vases and statues and the rights to excavate at Pompeii, Herculaneum and Portici. But people soon began to whisper that Napoleon would break the treaty. Northern Italy was falling fast to the French throughout 1797. Napoleon seized Italian art for the Louvre, and his men, marching with no supplies, robbed from petrified villagers and city dwellers alike, attacking and raping as they went. Ferdinand declared himself and the Queen 'ready to spill our blood and perish for our subjects, we expect them to reciprocate'. He offered new army recruits the bounteous salary of a shilling a day, and the Neapolitans hurried to join up (in England and France men were better fed and had to be press-ganged and conscripted into fighting). Ferdinand's fine words came too late: after years of underinvestment in the army and general poverty across the kingdom, the troops were malnourished and much less effective than Napoleon's determined, disciplined men.

Rome fell in February 1798, and the Pope was bundled out of his apartments and taken to France to die in ignominy. Napoleon's armies began trekking south. All the English travellers in Italy fled to Naples. Maria Carolina insisted that her subjects would see the French as their liberators, declaring there was 'general unrest, all classes, especially the best educated, entirely corrupted' and that the city buzzed with 'hothouses for running down the government'. Afraid that the French would attack his home, Sir William took an inventory of his belongings. Emma conjured terrible scenarios of the Queen seeing 'her friends sacrificed, her husband, children and herself led to the Block'. Pamphlets published around the city accused Emma of having been a spy from at least 1792, initially as a payback to the English government for leaning on John Acton to introduce her at Court. Accused of lesbianism and manipulating Maria Carolina and portrayed as a prostitute, Emma believed she risked sharing the fate of the Princesse de Lamballe.

Then, in the spring of 1798, Emma heard that Horatio Nelson was returning to the Mediterranean. Nelson's mission had nothing to do with Naples: he was charged with investigating reports of French ships being assembled in Toulon to attack. Sir William and Emma had corresponded with him over the last few years in a businesslike fashion. Now she saw her chance. Emma resolved to do everything in her power to persuade Nelson and his superiors to defend her dear Queen.

31

The Battered Hero

'I feel myself highly honoured and flattered by your lady-ship's charming letter,' enthused Earl St Vincent, Nelson's commander, to Emma in May 1798. 'The picture you have drawn of the lovely Queen of Naples and the royal family, would rouse the indignation of the most unfeeling of the creation, at the infernal designs of those devils, who, for the scourge of the human race, are permitted to govern France. I am bound by my oath of chivalry to protect all those who are persecuted and distressed.' Luckily, he had a 'knight of superior prowess in my train, who is charged with this enter-prize, and will soon make his appearance'.[204]

St Vincent was not by any stretch of the imagination a gallant man. In the same year he was waging bitter war against women on British ships for wasting clean water on laundry (Nelson tactfully diverted his attention to more important matters). Emma's carefully constructed letter persuaded him that the ships at Toulon were intended to attack Naples. They were wrong: the armament was intended for Egypt. But the die was cast: Nelson, the 'knight of superior prowess', was sent to Emma in Naples.

'I cannot describe to you my feelings on your being so near us,' exulted Emma to the knight on his way. She enclosed a letter of the Queen's in which 'with her whole heart and soul she wishes you victory', and flirtatiously instructed him to '*Kiss it*, and send it back'.[205] Coyly, Nelson replied that he hoped to be 'kissing her hand' soon.[206] Her request for British help coincided with Nelson's decision to fight Napoleon in the Mediterranean, and he was eager to reach Naples. On the way, however, he heard that Bonaparte was heading for

Egypt and he changed his plans to set off in hot pursuit. He sailed so fast that he arrived before his prey and, rather than wait, a sitting target, he turned the ships around and headed back to Syracuse in Sicily to restock with food and water. When he attempted to enter, however, the governor refused him entry, believing that Ferdinand's kingdom was still keeping to the treaty with the French. Nelson wrote to Sir William for help, and Emma sent him a deeply sympathetic letter while encouraging the Queen to press her husband to order the governor to allow Nelson to take the supplies he needed. The Queen and Emma together were successful. Bulging with food and drink, Nelson's *Vanguard* and his ten accompanying ships left Syracuse and sailed once more for Egypt.

On the night of 1 August, Nelson and his company shattered the French fleet off the coast of Alexandria at Aboukir Bay. In what came to be known as the Battle of the Nile, nine ships were taken, two were sunk and only two escaped. 'Victory', Nelson declared, 'is not a strong enough name for such a scene as I have passed.' He instructed Sir William to 'communicate this happy event to all the courts in Italy'. Emma immediately wrote to Maria Carolina, who declared herself 'wild with joy'. 'Gratitude is engraven on my heart,' she wrote, begging Emma to find her a portrait of Nelson. Emma scrawled on the back of the letter that she received it on 'the happy day we received the joyful news of the gret Victory over the infernal french by the brave gallant Nelson'. The city was illuminated for three days in honour of the amazing victory.

Nelson set sail for Naples, ready to be fêted. Emma made plans to celebrate him, struggling a little to imagine how he would look on his arrival. She knew he had been badly wounded in the battles against the French, but she had no idea of how ravaged his body had been. Since she had last seen him in 1793, he had lost what little good looks he had. At the Battle of Calvi in Corsica, in 1794, stone splinters from an enemy shot hit Nelson's right eye and he was immediately blinded although he could soon distinguish objects as well as light and dark. His eye was heavily scarred, the iris and pupil were so static as to seem dead, and it gave him terrible pain in times of stress. In July 1797, when leading a rash assault on the town of Santa Cruz on Tenerife by night, his right arm was destroyed by grapeshot. Josiah bound it with handkerchiefs and the surgeon amputated the arm in a dark, freezing and flooded ship's cabin, where nothing would hold still under a weak, flickering light. Nelson returned home in agony from his infected wound, tormented by hallucinations caused by the laudanum he took for the pain. Fanny was a devoted nurse and the period of Nelson's convalescence was the happiest in their marriage. To her misery, he recovered only to seize fame with doubled fervour.

Nelson trumpeted his triumph against the Spanish fleet at the Battle of Cape St Vincent, a Portuguese peninsula near Gibraltar, on 14 February 1797 by presenting himself as the champion of the hour, dramatically boarding the enemy ship and shooting his way to the quarterdeck until the crew surrendered. His version appeared in *The Times* and the *Sun*. Most English soon believed that he lost his arm at Cape St Vincent. The newspapers gushed praise for Nelson's bravery, engravings of him were sold across the country, and London, Bath, Bristol and Norwich voted him the freedom of the city. He was promoted to the position of rear admiral and was given a knighthood. Fanny, newly Lady Nelson, hoped that Nelson's promotion would encourage him to desist from 'boarding', leading parties of armed men on to enemy ships, a dangerous job that most admirals delegated to their captains. Nelson ignored her: he loved the excitement of the risk and was determined to pursue glory at all costs.

When the news of the Battle of the Nile was confirmed on 2 October, England went wild. Their Nelson had won the most cataclysmic victory of the Napoleonic Wars so far. He became Baron Nelson of the Nile and of Burnham Thorpe in Norfolk, his home town. Every newspaper praised him and even scabrous James Gillray produced congratulatory caricatures. The fashion for Nelson merchandise that began after his victory at Cape St Vincent became a craze, an unprecedented hysteria for one man that has never been equalled. Shop windows exploded with Nelson memorabilia. Manufacturers put his face and figure on any possible item and worked overtime to satisfy demand. Within a month or so of the Nile victory, virtually every house owned an image of Nelson, whether on paper, porcelain, cloth, silk, wood or stone. As well as busts, bronzes and portraits, there were Nelson tea sets, dinner sets and home accessories such as doorknob handles, flower pots and vases, along with less delicate ware, cheap jugs, mugs in Pratt ware and pewter plates. Ladies embroidered tapestries of England's hero and others bought Nelson jigsaws. When they were not buying Nelsonia, they treated themselves to Egyptian-themed homeware and fashions. Wedgwood even produced a blancmange mould that made a pudding topped with an Egyptian symbol. In England's most exquisite drawing rooms, ladies wore crocodile ornaments and seated themselves on a sofa shaped like a sphinx while mummies decorated the walls. One satirist ridiculed the 'Dresses a la Nile', showing a gentleman resplendent in a crocodile coat and boots like webbed feet conversing with a woman festooned in feathers, both blazoning 'Nelson and Victory' on their ludicrous head-dress.

Nelson was suddenly a heartthrob. Fashionable ladies hurried to dress themselves 'alla Nelson' in Nelson-themed shawls, hair ribbons, rings, brooches, earrings, charms, scarves, bags, necklaces, pendants, hats, and petticoats. They wore gold anchors that celebrated their hero, who 'relieves the World at the Mouth of the Nile'. Particularly sought after was the Nelson riding habit, a blue jacket with gold buttons, a near exact copy of his uniform.[207] He featured on thousands of enamel boxes, used to store beauty patches, as well as on other intimate objects such as jewellery and pomade boxes. Patriotic ladies turned up at social functions festooned with Nelson jewellery and knick-knacks. They snapped up fans commemorating him that also bore lists of the English and French fleets and details of new dances, including 'Sprigs of Laurel for Lord Nelson'.

England wanted Fanny to be the high priestess of the new Nelson cult, but she declined. The new Lady Nelson refused to wear fashions after her husband, crocodile earrings or *Vanguard* buttons and she had no intention of ornamenting her home with life-size mummies. Accosted by fans when she was shopping and besieged by dignitaries wishing to praise her husband, Fanny struggled with the social demands made upon her. She dreaded being caricatured and she was horrified to find that her name was being used to dub a quickstep 'Lady Nelson's Fancy'. Nelson was deeply disappointed by her efforts to ignore the avalanche of tacky goods in his honour and fan worship. He wanted her to cultivate his fame while he was away, cover her house and herself in tributes to him, and report back on the eulogies in the papers.

Emma knew that Nelson's arrival in Naples was her opportunity to catapult herself on to a world stage. She desperately wanted to grab his attention and share some of his incredible fame. At the same time, she was determined to confirm him as the defender of her dear Queen, proving herself the key political machinator of the court. Intent on captivating him, she wrote an extravagantly passionate letter:

How shall I begin, what shall I say to you 'tis impossible I can write . . . I am delerious with joy, and assure you I have a fervour caused by agitation and pleasure. God, what a victory! Never, never has there been anything half so glorious, so compleat. I fainted when I heard the joyfull news, and fell on my side and am hurt, but well of that. I shou'd feil it a glory to die in such a cause. No I wou'd not like to die till I see and embrace the Victor of the Nile. How shall I describe to you the transports of Maria Carolina, 'tis not possible. She fainted and kissed her husband, her children, walked about the room, cried, kissed and embraced every person near her, exclaiming, Oh brave Nelson, oh, God bless and protect our brave deliverer, oh Nelson, Nelson what do we not owe to you, o Victor, Saviour of Itali, that my swolen heart cou'd now tell him personally what we owe to him!

The Neapolitans are made with joy, and if you wos here now, you wou'd be killed with kindness. Sonets on sonets, illuminations, rejoicings; not a French dog dare shew his face. How I glory in the honner of my Country and my Countryman! I walk and tread in the air with pride, feiling I was born in the same land with the victor Nelson and his gallant band . . .

We are preparing your appartment against you come. I hope it will not be long, for Sir William and I are so impatient to embrace you. I wish you cou'd have seen our house the 3 nights of illumination. 'Tis, 'twas covered with your glorious name. Their were 3 thousand Lamps, and their shou'd have been 3 millions if we had time . . . For God's sake come to Naples soon. We receive so many sonets and letters of congratulation . . . I woul'd rather be an English powder monkey or a swab in that great victory than an Emperor out of it.

My dress from head to foot is alla Nelson. Ask Hoste. Even my shawl is in Blue with gold anchors all over. My earrings are Nelson's anchors; in short, we are be-Nelsoned all over. I send you some Sonets . . . I am afraid you will not be able to read this scrawl.[208]

After the Battle of the Nile, every woman – in England and Naples – wanted Nelson but Emma made sure to get there first. Nelson was deeply gratified by her letter. Puffed with pride, he wrote to Fanny that on hearing the victory, Lady Hamilton 'fell apparently dead and is not yet recovered from severe bruises'.

32

Falling into His Arms

Nelson arrived at Naples in the *Vanguard* on 22 September 1798. Five hundred boats spilling musicians and cheering courtiers flocked to meet him. Crowds lined the shore, and bands played 'Rule Britannia' and 'See the Conquering Hero'. Emma staged her own dramatic welcome. To the delight of the watching audience, she arrived on deck and flung herself against him, exclaiming in happiness and shedding sympathetic tears over his wounds. 'Up flew her ladyship,' Nelson spluttered in excitement, 'and exclaiming "Oh God is it possible" fell into my arms more dead than alive.' Entranced by the display, he temporarily forgot he had only one arm.

Emma swept Nelson and also Josiah, now eighteen, back to the Palazzo Sessa. Nelson had bought Emma the present of a black maid, perhaps a Sudanese girl from a dealer who had set up shop on his ship after the Battle of the Nile. A black maid was a mark of extreme sophistication in England, kept by fine ladies to make their complexions look paler. Ecstatic about her new gift, Emma called her Fatima. Almost as soon as he arrived on shore, the battle-scarred hero collapsed with exhaustion. Emma devoted every hour to caring for him: serving him nourishing meals and warming drinks and helping him to sleep by soothing his brow. Hamilton had written to him before he arrived, promising that 'Emma is looking out for the softest pillows, to repose the few wearied limbs you have left.' She plumped up the pillows and patted his hair.

While she had him prostrate before her, Emma exerted all her seductive powers to encourage Nelson to protect Maria Carolina and the kingdom of Naples. Nelson had other missions in the

Mediterranean, namely to warn France away from Egypt and protect Malta, but Emma aimed to ensure he focused on her.[209] She pulled out her most alluring muslin dresses from the closet, wearing every item that could be even vaguely 'alla Nelson'. When two of his captains had arrived in Naples with the news of the victory of the Nile, she accompanied them to the opera wearing a headband embroidered with 'Nelson and Victory' in gold. Since then, she had turned herself into a living tribute.

Nelson had been excited to receive such an inviting letter from the famous sex bomb. Indeed, he had written to Sir William rather weakly offering to lodge in a hotel.[210] Now he could hardly believe that she was tending to him so closely in her home. He was soon wrapped around her little finger, dazzled by her warm attentions. Beautiful, flirtatious, sexy, witty and young, as well as frank and not easily offended, she was a great contrast to the dreary, stiff wives of ambassadors and other superiors who usually dismissed him as a vulgar little man. 'She is an honour to her sex,' he wrote to Fanny, 'one of the best women in this world'. To Earl St Vincent, his commander, he was more honest. 'I am writing opposite Lady Hamilton, therefore you will not be surprised at the glorious jumble of this letter,' he admitted, describing his heart as fluttering with confusion. 'Naples is a dangerous place, and we must keep clear of it.' Nelson was ready for a little infatuation, for he had seen his wife for seven months in the last seven years. He no longer loved her and he was lonely.

Unlike sybaritic, rank-obsessed playboys at the Neapolitan court, Nelson's charisma inhered in his passion for his work and his serious ambition. He radiated blunt honesty and he was probably the least cynical guest the Palazzo had ever entertained. Unlike every other person in Emma's social circle, he was from a humble background, and his education was patchy. He was a man of action: he could not play music, sing or dance and he was a terrible dresser. Neapolitans and English aristocrats cut a dash in pastels, exotic pink suits and gold shoes but out of his impressive dress uniform, gaudy with medals, Nelson wore dull black, grey and brown wool and his hair was unstyled and unpowdered. He was smaller than most men, so thin as to seem emaciated, and he had a large bald patch where he cut his head at Aboukir, which he tried to hide by combing over some of his unruly shock of white hair. Covered with scars and wrinkles from sun exposure, he was neither attractive nor suave. Emma didn't care.

Emma worked hard to bring Josiah out of his shell. Rebellious and unhappy, convinced that others mocked him for not being up to his job, Josiah drank heavily and refused to obey his stepfather's commands. He was sullen and defensive and Nelson, who had no patience with depression or anxiety, was simply infuriated. But Emma was soon working wonders with her spotty teenaged guest. 'He likes Lady Hamilton more than any female,' boasted Nelson to his wife. His bluster that Emma would 'make more of Josiah than any woman', and that she would 'fashion him in 6 months in spite of himself' was hardly calculated to win over his wife. Fanny was deeply worried about the tense relationship between father and stepson and Emma's breezy promise that although she and Josiah might 'quarrel sometimes, he loves me and does as I would have him' twisted the knife.

Fanny had to read lashings of praise about Emma. 'How few could have made the turn she has,' Nelson marvelled to his wife, 'proof that even reputation may be regained, but I own it requires a great soul.' Nelson knew Emma's history – everyone did – and he hardly cared. Thanks to his humble upbringing, he was sympathetic toward women who had to make their own way, and aware that there were few choices for a poor girl but prostitution. He had worried that his sister, Anne, had been exposed to insult when she worked as a lacemaker's apprentice in London. Nelson's attitude towards prostitution was pragmatic. Whenever a ship came ashore, traders arrived to set up stalls on the deck, and hundreds of prostitutes flocked on board, rowed out in 'bum boats' and then taken down by the men to their hammocks in the huge orlop deck where they all slept. The officers went onshore to meet expensive courtesans or local actresses. As Nelson knew, in the ranks of the men there was no dividing line between 'virtuous woman' or wife and prostitute: many men married women who came on ship or entered into alliances with the hundreds of prostitutes in Greenwich, who looked after their money, checked their lottery numbers, and cared for them when they returned.

Real life in the navy was nothing like the dignified oil paintings. Many of his men were very young, some no more than thirteen, high on their rations of a gallon of beer a day, pimply adolescents starved of female company, unable to write home, their only possessions the clothes they were wearing when they had been seized by the press-gang. They were often drunk, the ship resounded to the sound of the cows, sheep and hens packed into cages, women dressed as men worked as sailors (without anyone guessing), men with a little money and seniority took prostitutes as 'wives' for the journey, and sex was not always consensual:

in the Caribbean, plantation owners sent out their slaves to work as prostitutes. Having ruled over a ship that was at times a floating brothel, menagerie, pub and shopping centre, Nelson was less hypocritical than the average eighteenth-century man. When he had an affair with the singer Adelaide Correglia in the Italian port of Leghorn between 1794 and 1796, he demanded his superiors acknowledge the importance of the intelligence about ships' movements that she gave him. Rather than goggle at Emma as an ex-courtesan or joke about her background, he accepted her as he saw her: a woman who had made a great turn in life.

'Ten thousand most grateful thanks are due to your ladyship for restoring the health of our invaluable friend,' St Vincent wrote skittishly to Emma. 'Pray do not let your fascinating Neapolitan dames approach too near him, for he is made of flesh & blood & cannot resist their temptation.' Emma did not need any warnings. She was determined to monopolise Nelson's attentions.

While Nelson recovered his health, Emma planned her most spectacular party ever to celebrate his fortieth birthday. She spent thousands of pounds on food, decoration and entertainment so opulent that even Nelson worried it might make him vain. On 29 September, the Palazzo Sessa played host to eight hundred Neapolitan dignitaries and select English guests, and nearly a thousand more joined them for dancing. 'Such a style of elegance as I never saw, or shall again probably,' wrote an overwhelmed Nelson to his wife. Emma adorned the courtyard with elaborate arrangements of flowers, lights and candles and a column inscribed with 'Veni, vidi, vici'. Every ribbon and button bore a picture of Nelson, and one of the English travellers composed a new verse to be added to 'God Save the King', which began 'Join we great Nelson's name / First on the roll of fame'.

Under the twinkling lights in the courtyard, Nelson and Emma were obviously absorbed in each other. Josiah began to suspect that Lady Hamilton had been kind to him only to win his stepfather. He was equally horrified that nobody seemed offended by his stepfather's obvious infatuation. Used to the culture of the *cicisbeo*, in which young married women had platonic male friends to squire them around, the Neapolitans thought Nelson just another of Emma's *cicisbeos* and quite naturally so, since he was a British naval captain and she was the wife of the British envoy. Sir William was equally sanguine, believing it was yet another of his wife's passing flirtations with a powerful man. He trusted Emma for she had always been faithful to him. If she had resisted some of England's wealthiest aristocrats, why would she want a grubby, half-blind, one-armed little sailor? Eighteen months short of his seventieth birthday and doggedly hanging on to influence, he knew that if he was seen as influencing the great naval hero, his position at the Neapolitan Court would be unassailable. He showered his new friend with compliments, hailing him as the 'Guardian Angel from the Ruin with which it has been long menaced'.[211] Nelson, Emma and Sir William described themselves as *Tria Juncta in Uno* (three joined together as one). Sir William plotted for Naples, while Emma and Nelson wallowed in flirtation – and stardom. Every time Nelson went outside, he attracted a mob of tearful, grateful Neapolitans, wearing their Nelson shawls and crying 'Viva Nelson!'[212] Nelson was soon intoxicated by Naples and completely obsessed by Emma.

After the party, Emma became Nelson's secretary and political facilitator. She translated from French and Italian for him, guided him around the Court, and escorted him to the Queen. 'Lady Hamilton is an angel,' he wrote to St Vincent, describing her as 'my Ambassadress to the Queen'. She had been his nurse, companion and social hostess, and now she was his assistant. When they were not working, they were confessing all to each other. Emma confided her fears about invasion and her sadness at not having children with her husband. She and Nelson had shared aims, they were no longer deeply in love with their partners, and they were both susceptible to romantic attachment. They were soon hopelessly in love with each other.

Hints about the relationship between the glamorous mistress-ambassadress and the hero of the Nile began to appear in the English newspapers. By November 1798, less than two months after his arrival in Naples, everybody was gossiping that the two biggest sex symbols of their day were having an affair. Female figures who closely resembled Emma soon began to feature on the commemorative Nelsonia – boxes, pendants, pictures, and ribbons. The phrase *Tria Juncta in Uno* began to appear in caricatures and pictures, with sly puns turning 'joined' into a sexual innuendo. In lonely Roundwood, Lady Nelson stared at the gossip in the newspapers and read her husband's letters overflowing with extravagant praise for the Hamiltons and reports of glamorous balls and the adulation he had received. 'Lord Hood expressed his fear that Sir W and Lady Hamilton would use their influence to keep Lord Nelson with them, they have succeeded,' she lamented.[213] She laid much of the blame on Josiah, believing his truculence had finally infuriated his stepfather enough to push him into the arms of Emma and Sir William.

Fanny decided to act. First she instructed Josiah to remember he was lucky to have 'such a father to bring you forward'.[214] Then she went to Alexander Davison. As Nelson's prize agent, financial wheeler dealer Davison administered the money his client was awarded when he captured ships as well as attending to his wider financial and administrative affairs and he wrote frequently to the Palazzo. Fanny begged him to communicate her threat to her husband that, if he did not return, she would come out to Naples.[215] Davison did not offer, as she had expected, to accompany her. Europe was dangerous and it might take her four months to reach Naples. Nelson's Admiralty superiors also refused to assist. Fanny gave in and consoled herself that going out would confirm all the rumours and only annoy her husband. She hoped that if she stayed put and kept sending regular, chatty letters, Lady Hamilton would turn out to be just another irrelevant dolly.

Nelson had little experience of royalty, and he was excited by his intimacy with Maria Carolina and his privileged entry into the gilded heart of the Neapolitan Court. Here he felt appreciated, whereas the Admiralty had retired him for years and the government had made him only a Baron after his victory at the Battle of the Nile. Emma wrote to Fanny that Sir William 'was in a rage with the Ministry for not having made Lord Nelson a viscount' and she added, 'Hang them I say!' To Nelson, she rhapsodised, 'If I was King of England, I would make you the most noble puissant Duke Nelson, Marquis Nile, Earl Alexandria, Viscount Pyramid, Baron Crocodile, and Prince Victory.'[216]

'Baron Crocodile' was yearning for another fix of glory. He could see a chance to lead the war against Napoleon by taking a key role in an offensive against the French planned by John Acton and the Neapolitan Court and endorsed by Sir William, with Emma as a passionate devotee. It was necessary: Nelson's arrival in Naples trailing the battered French ships captured at Aboukir contravened Ferdinand's treaty with France and made a French invasion almost inevitable. Ferdinand would send thirty thousand Neapolitan soldiers to capture Rome and Nelson was to support them by delivering four thousand soldiers (the Neapolitan navy carried another six thousand) to take Leghorn back from France. Emma, convinced that Nelson was invincible, enthused about the plan. Nelson's commander did not intervene, even though the mission in Naples should have been purely defensive. Almost as infatuated with the Queen as he was with Emma, Nelson went to rouse the land troops before they set off, with Emma as his interpreter, and Maria Carolina at his side.

On 29 November, Ferdinand entered Rome, accompanied by his soldiers. Within a week, the French had beaten him and taken ten thousand prisoners. The King's failure forced Nelson to abandon the attack on Leghorn. 'Viscount Pyramid' was furious, declaring that the Neapolitan officers ran the first thirty miles out of Rome. The King fled back to his palace and by 15 December, the French troops were closing in on Naples from the north. Emboldened by the approach of the French, pro-republican Jacobins began to demonstrate more virulently against the King. The Royalist mob was equally violent, incensed by rumours that the King and Queen intended to flee. When a Royal messenger was murdered right under Ferdinand's windows, the Queen began telling anybody who would listen that the Neapolitan Jacobins would soon storm the palace.[217] Emma declared she would go to the block with the Queen, but Maria Carolina was not planning to be seized from her home like her sister. She and the King decided to flee to their palace in Sicily, although the stormy December weather made it the worst time to travel. Many of the courtiers were elderly and the Hereditary Princess had recently given birth, but the departure of the entire Court with their belongings and retinues had to be organised in under a week. Emma took charge. It was her most daunting challenge to date.

Royalist mobs roamed the streets in search of Jacobins to attack and there were pitched battles between the two sides. Passions were running so high that no one, not even a stranger, was safe in the streets. Afraid of capture, Sir William and Nelson refused to visit the King and Queen. They sent Emma in their place, consoling themselves that the mob was used to seeing her go to the Palace every day and would think that, as a woman, she was irrelevant to politics. Emma prided herself on never being afraid, especially now she was trying to impress Nelson, and was eager to take on the role of messenger.

Sir William's task was to evacuate the British citizens in Naples, and he arranged three transports from Nelson for those who wished to leave. He was even more preoccupied in ensuring that his pictures and vases were packed and sent to England. Nelson was concerned with military matters and readying the ships to take their Royal cargo. With the male duo of the *Tria Juncta in Uno* preoccupied, Emma had to take care of the logistical nightmare of preparing the Royal Family to leave.

Maria Carolina dwelt obsessively on her sister's botched flight from Paris and Emma tried to allay her fears. The entire Royal Family and Court had never moved en masse and there was brutal competition over who was allowed on the same boat as the King, how much luggage they would take, and even the order in which they would embark.

Ferdinand and Maria Carolina declared that they needed all their treasure, china and glass, pictures, clothes, jewels, and hunting paraphernalia, and much of their furniture. When they declared they did not trust their own navy to take them, they offended their remaining loyalists and upset the British who had expected to travel on Nelson's ship. Terrified of a last-minute crush, Maria Carolina made an invitation card for those she wished to accompany her, which she designated a ticket of admission to Nelson's boat.[218] She wrote to Emma on the 17th that she was sending her 'all our Spanish money, both the King's and my own'. Sixty thousand gold ducats and the diamonds were to follow. Emma inscribed on the back, 'My adorable unfortunate Queen!' Maria Carolina declared she was drowning in tears and worried that it was all right to send so much. Emma spent six nights waiting for contraband deliveries of the 'jewells, money & effects of the Royall familly' and giving them to British sailors to transport to the ships. Carriages bumped up into her courtyard, packed with jumbles of clothes, jewels, linen, sculpture and toys. Emma packed them up in boxes, disguising most of them as 'Stores for Nelson'. She told Greville of her 'many such strategems' for hiding her work from foreign spies and the angry mob, hoping he would mention her to those influential in government. She explained how 'I got those treasures embark'd and this point gain'd, the king's resolution of coming off was strengthened; the queen I was sure of'. Sir William judged their stash worth the incredible sum of £2.5 million. Emma had helped to smuggle out the contemporary equivalent of over 15 billion pounds of gold and millions of pounds worth of jewels.

The Neapolitans spotted the ships waiting in the bay and convoys of goods heading to the Palazzo Sessa. Many cheered while others became riotous, crowding around the palace and begging the King not to leave, 'I am overwhelmed with misery and confusion,' the Queen wrote desperately to Emma. 'I've lost my head tonight, I'm sending some more trunks . . . believe me the saddest of mothers and queens but your sincere friend, Charlotte.' Emma scrawled on the back of the letter, 'God protect us this night'.[219] The Queen sent her a final passenger list, adamant that Emma keep a hawk's eye out for anyone of a lower station trying to sneak on.

Emma and Sir William, Mrs Cadogan, and their servants slipped away from the Palazzo Sessa on 21 December and walked to the shore, where they boarded a boat to travel to the *Vanguard*. The ship was anchored safely out of range of the forts, and, thanks to the rough weather, the journey there took over two hours. Meanwhile, the King and Queen, convulsed by panic about leaving, threatened to stay put. Nelson took matters into his own hands, and, as Emma described to Greville, travelled to the Palace by armed boat, 'got up the dark staircase that goes in to the Queen's room & with a dark lantern, cutlasses, pistol, etc, etc, brought off every soul, ten in number to the *Vanguard*'. The lesser servants, including priests and the King's surgeon, arrived a few hours later and the minor courtiers were taken to a ship captained by the Neapolitan Francisco Caracciolo. Everybody else bundled on to twenty transport ships. It was a ridiculously cumbersome operation, hundreds of travellers from England and elsewhere, perhaps a thousand aristocrats, the extensive entourages of two French Princesses, and the massive Neapolitan Royal Family plus all their loot and servants were piled on to warships. All Naples knew they were leaving, but the loyalists who wished them to stay were far outnumbered by those who welcomed their flight.

At the last minute, Ferdinand demanded that his servants bring over yet more gold and treasures from the Palace. The boat was groaning with the Court treasures, and there was no room for the belongings of his humble ambassador. Emma and Sir William left behind three elegantly furnished houses and all their many carriages and horses.

Nelson had prepared the ward room for the King, the Crown Prince, John Acton, a few key male courtiers and Sir William and the admiral's quarters for the women, girls and younger boys, but there were few home comforts and not enough linen to go round. Emma had presciently brought practical items, and she had sheets, blankets, pillows, crockery and food to spare. She did her best to make the Royal Family comfortable.

Rain fell hard, the sea churned, and the captains battled to keep their vessels upright. The passengers became hysterical with seasickness not long after they embarked. Terrified that the mob might come out in boats and attack and rob them, everybody was desperate to leave Naples but the weather was too stormy to sail. After being buffeted about for a day and a night, they eventually set out on the 23rd in tossing seas that ripped at the masts. Sailors were expected to work – and fight – under worse conditions but the *Vanguard* carried plumped-up Royals unused to discomfort. Convinced they were about to capsize, Maria Carolina cried, Ferdinand raged, and the courtiers spent the journey 'frightened & on their knees praying'. Sir William huddled alone with a loaded pistol in each hand, declaring that he would not 'die with the guggle guggle guggle of salt water' in his throat. The King's confessor fell out of his bunk and broke his arm and the Duchess of Castelcicala cut her head on Nelson's sideboard. As Emma despaired to Greville, the 'few women Her Majesty brought on board were incapable of helping her' and there was only 'poor I to attend & keep up the spirits of the Queen, the princess Royall, 3 young princesses, a baby six weeks old & 2 young princes Leopold & Albert, the last 6 years old, my favourite'. Emma gave them beds, helped to arrange for food, and became their full-time servant, tending to the useless courtiers and soothing the fractious Maria Carolina. Nelson claimed later that she did not enter a bed the whole time she was aboard and 'became their slave'. Mrs Cadogan assisted her with the nursing and was so gentle and efficient that according to Emma, the King hailed her as an angel.

Emma only slept for a couple of hours at a time, after nights of waiting up to receive the treasures at the Palazzo. Refusing to let the experience of being sick defeat them or to droop under the atmosphere of panic, mother and daughter tried to comfort peevish courtiers who had never known hardship, and struggled to keep some kind of order in the rolling ship. Emma tried to snatch every moment she could for her 'favourite', little Prince Albert. Maria Carolina had been eight months' pregnant with him when Marie Antoinette had been executed. When he was born, she had been lost in a cloud of grief and despair and so Emma, newly the Queen's confidante, spent hours petting him, playing with him and trying to make up for his mother's inability to pay him much attention. Her heart was deeply touched by his weak health. As a young child, he had been frequently confined to bed. Emma had visited him regularly and the two became firm friends. She had high hopes that the move to Sicily might improve his health, but almost as soon as he boarded ship, he fell sick. As they set sail, he retreated into sickness and misery, vomiting hopelessly even though he could hardly eat. Soon unable to drink, he was so dehydrated that he fell into convulsions. All she and the Queen could do was hope that they would reach land soon. Amongst all the grown men and women claiming that they were terribly ill and could not go on, Prince Albert was actually in danger of death.

When Christmas Day dawned, Sicily was nearly in sight. Affected by the new spirit of optimism in the boat, the little Prince managed to eat some breakfast. But he quickly fell ill again as the boat smashed over the waves. Emma nursed him all day, but in the evening he fell into hopeless convulsions and died in her arms. Maria Carolina had lost another child less than a year before and she was shattered. Emma and Mrs Cadogan had to take the little body away so that it could be cleaned and prepared for burial. Emma tried to comfort the Queen, but she was struggling with grief, guilt and an acute sense of failure that she had not managed to keep Albert alive.

Emma had spent five days exhausted and covered in dirt. She had hardly had a moment to think about Nelson. He, however, had been watching her and was deeply impressed by her efficiency and fortitude. When the *Vanguard* anchored at Palermo, on Sicily's northern coast, at 2 a.m. on Boxing Day, Nelson was in love with her and anxious to turn their heady flirtation into a full romance.

33
Passions in Palermo

'*G*od onely knows what yet is to become of us, we are worn out,' lamented Emma to Greville after two days in damp and freezing Palermo. Overwhelmed by 'anxiety & fatigue', she was worried about Sir William who 'had 3 days a bilious attack' and moreover, 'my dear adorable Queen whom I love better *than any person in the world*, is allso unwell'. When the ship arrived, Maria Carolina could not bear to stay aboard one moment longer and she, Emma, the other women and the sad bundle of Prince Albert's corpse were rowed ashore in secret before dawn. At nine that morning, the King was ceremonially disembarked to a warm welcome from the Sicilian people, who had long resented his reluctance to visit the island. They expected him to live in the royal apartments in the city, but they were disappointed. Ferdinand was not about to sit about in dreary Palermo when there were crowds of wild boar to be killed. The Royal Carriage sped to his hunting grounds just outside the city, now in the Parco della Favorita, less than two miles north of the city centre. His family and their entourages, the Hamiltons and Nelson huddled together in the dilapidated buildings of his hunting lodge, battling to keep warm in a house without fireplaces.

Within a few days, Emma and Sir William moved to the Villa Bastioni, another summer house nearby, the last place the Hamiltons would live without Nelson. Plump cupids bounced in ornate frescoes over the ceilings and walls but the furniture was dirty and cracked, and there were once more no fireplaces. Shivering amongst the peeling gilt and dusty stucco, Sir William took to his bed, fretting about the fate of his belongings and distressed by stomach pain. Emma had to care for him and take over his duties with the Royals and the hundreds of English who had fled, as well as thousands of Neapolitan nobles and loyalists.

Albert weighed heavily on Emma's mind. She was always on the brink of tears – much to the irritation of her husband – and when the Queen gave her a mourning pendant with hair and the inscription, 'Prince Albert died in my arms, 25th Dec, 1798', she refused to take it off. She spent every moment she could with the Queen, who was wounded by Ferdinand's seeming indifference to Albert's death. 'We weep together & now that is our onely comfort,' Emma mourned to Greville. But she could not lose herself in grief for she had work to do. Maria Carolina quickly become utterly reliant on her as organiser, assistant, cheerleader and friend. In the confusion of arrival, the Queen had lost much of her luggage and she sent Emma to find her Court dresses before an official reception on Sunday afternoon. Then she needed her dear friend to find a way of hiding the treasure of £2.5 million. The English visitors in Naples were no less demanding. Many were piqued that they had not been invited to travel with the Royals and Emma was expected to make up for the slight by procuring them good but cheap lodgings, a difficult job when every property owner in Palermo was profiting from the influx of wealthy refugees by raising rents.

Only Ferdinand was happy. The hunting was quite excellent, and he had decided that his first task on the island should be to transform his lodge into a palace fit for a king. He was intent on showing himself off as at the forefront of fashion and design. The Versailles look was passé, and Europe's most fashionable grandees were beginning to build homes in the oriental style. Ferdinand was not to be outdone. He employed Palermo's foremost architect, Giuseppe Venanzio Marvuglia, to rebuild his home as a fantastic bright orange and gold Chinese Palace, peaked with fake pagodas, complete with technicolour murals of oriental scenes and twinkling lights. He planned to spend thousands of pounds turning the overgrown land into graceful grounds of walks and fountains, a version of Caserta's garden with added oriental trappings.

The new arrivals in Sicily were as eager to forget as Ferdinand. They dissipated their fears in balls, gambling and infidelities. Looking more radiant than ever, Emma dazzled at the card table and on the dance floor, intoxicated by her feelings for Nelson. He sat at her side, wrapped up in her games of faro and hazard, putting up hundreds of pounds for her bets. They gambled long after Sir William had gone to bed. Nelson was wholly absorbed in Emma. Too honourable to seduce a woman under her husband's roof, he began to hint that they might live together as they had in the Palazzo Sessa and share the bills.

Sir William was worried about his finances. He had lost his home and his belongings and his money was being squandered on Emma's entertainments and on the English hangers-on who streamed through his doors expecting food and amusement. Nelson, he thought, should fund more of Emma's extravagant lifestyle than her losses at faro. The gossips were whispering about the late-night visits of their 'dear friend' and about Emma's carriage rides to his residence. Sir William thought that if the three of them lived together, they could split expenses and quell the talk. He accepted that the relationship between his wife and his friend had become deeper in Palermo, and he knew that he was powerless to end it, for the Royal Family was dependent on Nelson and would ostracise anyone who upset the great hero. If Nelson lived with them, he hoped Emma might rest at home some evenings to keep him company. It seemed a perfect arrangement: no scandal, profit and happiness all round. Emma was soon eagerly searching for new lodgings.

Within a few months, the pair moved with Nelson to the Palazzo Palagonia, a vast palace of nearly fifty rooms in deep countryside to the east of the city, now in the bustling town of Bagheria. Despite years of neglect, the Palazzo is still breathtakingly bizarre – a huge stone double fronted mansion adorned with a sweeping staircase to the front door, covered in gargoyles and strange statues. The walls are a riot of statues of hybrid monsters, half gods, half goats, half sea monster and mermaids, while the interior is no less ornate, entirely covered in coloured marble and jewels. The bedroom apartments were particularly spectacular, covered in erotic murals of Venus and Leda loving Zeus when he was disguised as a swan. The owner, the Prince of Palagonia, had packed it with garish bulky furniture in clashing colours, a chandelier made from cups and saucers, and secret spikes under the cushions of the chairs. The villa was one of the 'must-sees' of Palermo, and when Goethe had visited, he had felt quite faint at its rambling excess.

Nelson, Emma and Sir William were showing they had arrived in style by choosing the most extravagant and costly house on the whole island, after the Royal Palace, awing their friends with grand rooms and eye-popping decor. They moved into the Palazzo Palagonia along with Mrs Cadogan and Josiah, Maria Carolina's gardener, John Graefer, and his family and various other English dependents, two English bankers (handy to have on call during gambling parties) and secretaries, musicians and staff. The rental was wildly expensive, as was supporting this newly expanded household, but the *Tria* were living for the moment, convinced that their government would heap rewards on them. At the Palazzo Palagonia, Emma threw even more lavish entertainments, and gambled recklessly, captivating her new Sicilian friends and Neapolitan visitors. Nelson's men declared themselves equally bewitched. One of Nelson's captains dubbed her 'Patroness of the Navy', trilling, 'you fascinate all the Navy as much at Palermo as you did at Naples'. Only Josiah was miserable, confused by his admiration for Emma and his loyalty to his mother.

Sir William tried to ignore Emma's growing intimacy with Nelson. His relations with her had been fraternal for some time and they had long slept in separate apartments, so he could shield himself from the evidence that – as everybody knew – his wife was on the brink of having an affair. He focused his resentment on Maria Carolina for encouraging her friend to charm the hero, and, most of all, on his ill-health. As he grumbled to Joseph Banks, everybody suffered from the 'thick air' of Palermo and had frequent bilious attacks, but 'owing to my age, I do not recover as soon as they do'. Suffering from a 'shattered constitution', he informed the Foreign Office that the 'whole confidence' of the King and Queen 'entirely reposes on . . . Lord Nelson'.[220] When he heard in early March that the ship carrying his collection to England had been wrecked off the Scilly Isles in December, he was devastated. Although some good pieces and his best paintings were on another ship, the collection he valued as worth over £6,000, and into which he had poured so much devotion and money, had sunk to the bottom of the sea. As his ill-health worsened under the weight of depression, he lost his influence over Ferdinand. Leaving the entertaining and political caballing to his wife, he tried to retain some semblance of authority at Court by implying that he influenced Nelson, which living with him suggested. He boasted that he had the 'temper to stem the torrent of his impetuosity, even against his best Friends, and in that respect he is just enough to own that I have been of infinite use to him'.[221] He lied. As one shrewd visitor reported, 'the little consequence he retained as ambassador was derived from his wife's intrigues; but as long as he could keep his situation, draw his salary, and collect vases, he cared little about politics; he left the management of them to her Ladyship'.

Emma had remained faithful to Sir William to this point but she could no longer resist her feelings. Nelson had been true to Fanny in the way that his contemporaries defined male fidelity: he had used only courtesans and prostitutes. Although we have definite proof that the relationship between Nelson and Emma had become physical by early 1800, the affair must have begun in the Palazzo Palagonia. Sir William would never have allowed Nelson to pay Emma's expenses unless they were having an affair. At some point early in 1799, Emma and Nelson began a full-blown sexual affair. They were so close that he began to address Mrs Cadogan as *Signora Madre* (pleasing Emma greatly, for Sir William had never been able to treat her as a mother-in-law). The exhilaration of having survived the journey to Palermo, the anxiety induced by the fraught political situation, the long nights of gambling and drinking, and the close living arrangements transformed a mutual sexual obsession into love. They were caught up in each other, swept away by a passion neither of them had ever felt before. They were like two lovers who had lost their virginity to each other, constantly touching and staring at each other, swapping pet names and secret anecdotes, talking endlessly, desperately seizing every chance to be together.

In the warm Sicilian spring, the Royal gardens sprang into bloom and men, women and children came to Palermo from all over Sicily to sell handicrafts, perfumes and fine foods to the flocks of rich leisured refugees from Naples. Emma was the centre of attention, pursuing what a travelling Scotsman dubbed her 'attitudinal celebrity'. She welcomed him by a display after dinner in which, as he wrote, she 'dropped from her chair on the carpet' after having removed the 'comb which fastened her superabundant locks'. He decided 'nothing could have been more classical or imposing than this prostrate position'. Another guest was so convinced by Emma's faint that he dashed to douse her with water. The Scotsman judged their 'introduction to the fascinating Lady Hamilton' was 'got up with considerable stage effect'. When he saw Sir William again later in the evening, 'on his shoulder was leaning the interesting Melopomene, her raven tresses floating round her expansive form and full bosom'. Emma declared to her startled guests that she was 'dying' of sorrow for her 'beloved Naples'. On another occasion, the Turkish envoy of Emperor Paul of Russia, who was seated by Emma at a dinner held in his honour, held up his sword and claimed he had used it to execute twenty French prisoners in one day. Emma took the sword, kissed it and handed it to Nelson.[222] Her guests cringed at her dramatic displays of devotion to him, but Nelson adored her for them. He soon added a codicil to his will leaving Emma a rare gold box covered with diamonds as a 'token of respect for her every eminent virtue'.

Emma as a dancing *Bacchante*
by Elisabeth Vigée le Brun.

Pietro Novelli's drawing of Emma performing her Attitudes shows how Emma used her shawl to transform herself from a tragic queen to a demure young lady in prayer, finally turning from Agrippina holding the ashes of Germanicus into a drunken Bacchante.

Emma as the Muse of Dance, in a page from the bestselling 1794 book of her Attitudes.

A dancer in a Neapolitan brothel in 1945
performing her version of Attitudes.
(Inset) Emma dancing her famous Tarantella.

Elisabeth Vigée le Brun's portrait of Emma as a
reclining Bacchante was Sir William's prize possession.
(*Inset*) Emma begs Nelson to come to Naples and
rescue her friends from Napoleon – making it clear
she will welcome him with passion.

Tête à Tête: The Consular Artist and the Venus de Medicis, from the *Town and Country Magazine*, May 1790. As the gossip columnist suggested, the Consular Artist had been reluctant to marry his lovely model, afraid of 'the natural consequences which would probably ensue – the immoderate increase of his expenses'.

Maria Carolina, Queen of Naples, pictured here with one of her many children, was magisterial, ruthless and hungry for affection.

(*Facing page*) Nelson arrived in Naples, resplendent in his medals, fresh from success at the Battle of the Nile, and Emma was determined to capture his heart.

Nelson enjoying a drink with his sailors. Life on ship was fuelled with gallons of beer and wine. (*Below left*) Fanny, Nelson's quiet and reserved wife had none of Emma's glamour. Nelson had fallen out of love with her and he was craving affection.

In James Gillray's *A Cognocenti Contemplating ye Beauties of ye Antique*, Sir William examines a broken statue of Emma. Gillray had a simple point to make: Sir William was the biggest cuckold in England.

It seemed to everyone that Emma had the power. 'Sir William, Lady Hamilton, and myself, are the mainsprings of the machine which manages what is going on in this country,' boasted Nelson. Since the Queen took care of the details of government while the King hunted, the only way to gain some influence was to address her, and Emma was besieged by people begging favours. Her old admirer, Lord Hervey, described to her the French manoeuvres around Venice, in the hope that his information would be passed on to the Neapolitan Royal Family, and he begged her to inveigle an introduction to Prince Charles, commander of Austrian forces in the area.[223] Everybody was equally intimidated by her influence over Nelson, believing, in the words of one visitor, 'never was a man so mystified and deluded'.[224] In Sicily and England, the trend for 'à la Emma' fashions hit a new high.

Fanny, alone in her chill Suffolk home, pined for a letter from her husband. The Admiralty bigwigs despaired of their errant genius, groaning how 'the world says he is making himself ridiculous with Lady Hamilton and idling his time in Palermo when he should have been elsewhere'.[225] In April, Nelson received the letter from Alexander Davison in which his agent passed on Fanny's wish to come to Naples. Her attempt to win back her husband finally prompted him to write – but not in the way she hoped. Nelson furiously scribbled to her that he would find her visit 'unpleasant' and that the minute she arrived, he would have immediately sent her home 'for it would have been impossible to have set up an establishment at either Naples or Palermo'. By then it was too late. Nelson was Emma's lover. As he wrote later, 'I want not to conquer any heart, if that which I have conquered is happy in its lot: I am confident for the Conqueror is become the Conquered.'

34
Neapolitan Rebellion

*W*ithin two weeks of the Royal Family abandoning the Palace, French troops invaded Naples and Ferdinand's viceroy surrendered. Those remaining mostly welcomed the invaders. When the theatres staged a play that mocked the flight of the Court and the English to Sicily, they prolonged the curtain calls with, as Sir William noted unhappily, 'the greatest applause'.[226] Matters were not much better in Palermo. Ferdinand had found his Palazzo Cinese far too near to the city for his liking, and he took the Court on an indefinite vacation to another hunting lodge at the tiny town of Ficuzza, in the deep Corleone forest, thirty miles south of Palermo. Angered by the King's selfish behaviour and aggression against anyone he considered disloyal, many Sicilians were already whispering about revolution – and were ready to welcome the French when they came. Ferdinand battered the island's wildlife while his wife lay panicking in darkened rooms. 'The dangers we run here are immense and real,' she agonised. 'Before forty days revolution will have broken here. It will be appalling and terribly violent.' 'The priests are completely corrupted,' Emma wailed, 'the people savage, the nobility more than uncertain and of questionable loyalty.' She felt 'quite desperate'.

Only after much pressing from his wife, Nelson, the Hamiltons and John Acton, as well as many of his courtiers, did Ferdinand stop hunting long enough to send Cardinal Ruffo, minister of war, to lead an army of Calabrians and Turks, accompanied by royalist Neapolitans, to attempt to recapture the city. By June, Ruffo had trapped most of the Neapolitan rebels and the French fighters in the city's castle. They offered their surrender, on condition that they received a pardon. Ruffo and Nelson's

Captain Foote signed the agreement and congratulated themselves on restoring order with minimum bloodshed. On 24 June, Nelson arrived on his ship, the sparkling new *Foudroyant*, recently arrived to replace the battered *Vanguard*, itching to shatter the city's uneasy calm. Fired up by the commands of the Queen and the King's obsession with his divine right to rule, he decided the agreement was invalid. 'Rebels and traitors', he thundered, 'must instantly throw themselves on the clemency of their sovereign, for no other terms would be allowed them.'

Emma had accompanied Nelson and Sir William on the boat to Naples at the request of Maria Carolina. The Queen had demanded Emma write daily informing her of what was going on, and also, according to Sir William, charged her with 'many important Commissions'.[227] The King, Queen and John Acton demonised the rebels as evil traitors who deserved no mercy. Hamilton agreed and called the truce a 'shameful capitulation'. Chivvying for a 'second Aboukir', Maria Carolina declared that no one could 'deal tenderly with this murderous rabble'. The British government had recently come down hard on insurrections in Ireland, nervous that the Irish might ally with the French, and the Queen exhorted Nelson to handle Naples 'as if it was a rebel city in Ireland behaving in like manner'. She instructed him to 'make an example of the leading representatives' with an 'exact, prompt, just severity'. Any female rebels should also be treated without pity.[228] Captain Foote pleaded with Acton to show mercy, but to no avail.

Convinced he was defending Europe by following the orders of the Neapolitan King and Queen and believing himself the man able to stop Jacobin fury, Nelson assumed the mantle of divine vengeance and described himself as 'the happy instrument of His punishment against unbelievers'. All the rebels in the castle were arrested and threatened with execution. The city exploded into violence once more. Royalist mobs, operating with unofficial sanction, roamed the streets, beating and burning suspected republicans. Officers arrested anyone who held a position in the Republic. Middle class and poor, men and women alike were sentenced to death, and about a hundred were executed. Among the rebels apprehended was Caracciolo, admiral to the Royal Family and old friend of the Hamiltons. Intent on showing that not even the most elevated Neapolitans could escape punishment, the court assembled on Nelson's ship sentenced him to death by hanging. Nelson refused Caracciolo's plea for execution by gunfire – the customary mode of death for a commander – and also his request for time to prepare.

He commanded that the Admiral be hanged the same day from the fore yardarm of his own ship, *La Minerva*. His body would remain there until sunset and then be thrown into the sea.

The crowds were already waiting on the shore by the ship, to hear Caracciolo's sentence. When it was announced, there were hysterical cheers while those sympathetic to him slunk away, too fearful of arrest to express their horror. Waiting in the *Foudroyant*, Caracciolo knew he would be hung in front of a jeering crowd and then left to be circled by the seagulls. Like most Catholics, he believed that without a proper confession, ceremony and grave, he would not reach heaven. He begged for a moment apart from a guard to pray, but he was roughly refused. It was midday. All he could do was wait for the frame to be readied on the *Minerva*.

The Neapolitan sun was still hot at five o'clock. As the Admiral waited to mount the block, he saw the crowds jeering on the shore. Dozens of little boats had drawn up beside the ship, spilling with spectators. Sailors hung off the rigging of the *Minerva* and the *Foudroyant*, intent on seeing his death. When the officer put the hood over his head, it was a relief to be no longer able to see.

Sir William reported that the Neapolitans greeted Caracciolo's death with 'loud applause', praising 'so speedy an act of justice'.[229] Others were less persuaded. To the eighteenth-century mind, the commander's code of honour had the same standing as the Geneva Convention: it guaranteed decency in war. The code was simple: treaties should be honoured and officers treated with respect. After breaking the treaty with the rebels and hanging Caracciolo, Nelson had flouted it twice and English observers were scandalised. Sexual confidence tended to make Nelson more rash (he had been imprudent in the West Indies after Fanny had agreed to marry him), and he was reckless in Naples. He applied the tactics he used in his sea battles: hunt down and destroy every enemy. To him, the treaty had always been invalid, since the King and Queen had instructed Cardinal Ruffo not to settle with the rebels. Nelson was a poor politician for the same reason that he was a great fighter: he saw matters in black-and-white terms as loyalty and disloyalty, good versus evil.

Emma was seen as the Queen's representative, and she was visited on the *Foudroyant* by streams of Neapolitan women proclaiming their loyalty to the throne and imploring forgiveness for supporting the rebellion.[230] Desperate people addressed her as *Signora excellentissima, Bella Milady*, and *Excellenza*, pressing her to use her influence over Nelson to commute sentences.[231] Nelson angrily complained to Mrs Cadogan that Emma 'has her time so much taken up with excuses from Rebels, Jacobins, & Fools, that she is every day most heartily tired'.[232] Emma, however, could do nothing for these women unless the Queen felt generous and Maria Carolina would not be swayed. She asked Emma for a detailed list of Jacobins, and pages survive where Emma added names in her own hand, including Domenico Cirillo, her old friend and physician, who was also a friend of the Queen.[233]

Like Nelson, Emma had come to believe that they would save the city by purging it. Cirillo and the others were, to her, potential murderers of the Royal Family, who had helped cause the death of Prince Albert, and whose equivalents had killed Marie Antoinette. Even if she had hated the idea of a purge and had begged Nelson to desist, he would not have listened to her. He always ignored questions and doubts, even from his superiors at the Admiralty, and perceived pleas for moderation – as when Fanny begged him to soften his campaign against corruption in the West Indies – as a weakness, a failure of a woman's essential duty of support and loyalty.

As the reprisals subsided, the citizens of Naples began to feel guilty. Many declared it unlikely that the rebels would have attacked again, and others were tormented by guilt, claiming they saw Caracciolo's corpse bobbing in the harbour. Nelson, however, congratulated himself for 'driving the French to the devil, and in restoring peace and happiness to mankind'. Maria Carolina wrote to Emma that she had 'done wonders' and assured her she was 'gratefully sensible of your exertions'. Her excitable correspondent inscribed on the back of her note, 'my blood if necessary shall flow for her! Emma will prove to Maria Carolina that a humble born English woman can serve her Queen with zeal and a true soul, even at the risk of her life.'[234]

When Nelson and the Hamiltons returned to Palermo, the Royal Family and the Court showered them with gratitude for Nelson's success. They were all rather pleased with themselves. Sir William boasted to his superiors that he and Nelson had restored 'tranquillity to the distracted city' and placed the King and Queen back on their throne.[235] 'We return with a Kingdom to present my much loved Queen,' Emma vaunted to Greville. The King called Emma his *Grande Maitresse* and the Queen told her she was her deputy. They both gave her a miniature of themselves set in diamonds, the Queen's inscribed *Eterna Gratitudine*, as well as a lock of Maria Carolina's hair set in diamonds, diamond and pearl earrings, a brooch of diamonds in the shape of the

Queen's initials, a complete dress of finest lace, baskets of gloves, and a selection of ornate Court gowns.[236] Having lost many of her own clothes in the flight from Naples, Emma welcomed her new presents, dreaming of captivating the Neapolitan Court in her swathes of exotic silk, resplendent with the Nile hero by her side. She was taller and more busty than the Queen, so the ever-reliable Mrs Cadogan was set to work letting down the hems and taking out the seams.

'Emma is really the Queen's bosom friend,' boasted Sir William.[237] Emboldened by Maria Carolina's promises of never-ending affection, Emma asked for the ultimate favour: she wanted her daughter, Emma Carew, now eighteen, appointed to the Queen's house as a lady of the bedchamber. Emma assured Greville that 'the Q. has promised me'. She was deluded: Maria Carolina, however much she doted on Emma, would never take an illegitimate daughter of a minor English aristocrat as her lady-in-waiting.

Nelson wrote jubilantly that the King had 'created me Duke of Bronte and has annexed an Estate of 3000 pounds Sterling a year, both Title and Estate at my disposal together with a magnificent diamond hilted sword'.[238] He was thrilled with Bronte, a large estate on the western slopes of Mount Etna on Sicily's eastern coast. Bronte now produces Italy's best pistachio nuts, but it was then a chilly, poverty-stricken estate, days by cart from any large town and cut off by terrible roads. Thanks to years of chronic underinvestment by Ferdinand, the tenants lived miserably, and the buildings were collapsing. The yield was nearer £30 than £3,000. Bronte needed a tough estate manager, experienced in agriculture, fluent in Sicilian, ready to rebuild every building and replant every field. Nelson, however, with no time to undertake the lengthy journey to Bronte, believed Ferdinand's claims that the estate was in perfect condition. He sent hypersensitive landscape gardener John Graefer to turn the grounds into a beautiful landscaped garden fit for a great gentleman. If Ferdinand's gift was a joke, since the original Bronte was, in Greek myth, a one-eyed Cyclops, Nelson, like every member of the Court, was accustomed to Ferdinand's puerile sense of humour. Deeply satisfied with the gift, he saw it as compensation for the refusal of the English government to make him a viscount and for the rest of his life signed himself 'Nelson & Bronte'.

The Court celebrated the end of the rebellion at a giant party at the Palazzo Cinese. Maria Carolina commissioned three life-size waxworks of Emma, Sir William and Nelson as the centrepieces. The Emma statue wore a purple gown embroidered with the names of the captains of the Nile. Bewitching lamps were strung all across the Palace gardens, exotic ices were arranged in fabulous sculptures and guests feasted on exquisite sweetmeats and downed decanters of fine alcohol. The grateful, happy Court danced in their most sumptuous outfits and marvelled at a lavish firework display imitating the Battle of the Nile, which ended with the blasting of a tricolore into red, white and blue sparks. When Ferdinand's youngest son, nine-year-old Prince Leopold, crowned Nelson's statue with a laurel wreath covered in diamonds, Nelson burst into tears, believing that he had finally found a Court to truly appreciate him. His body had paid the price for his victories: he was now minus his top teeth and his remaining eye was filming over, but at moments like this the sacrifice seemed worth it. He made sure to send glowing accounts of the party to *The Times* in England.

After living with his wife and Nelson closely on the *Foudroyant* in Naples from 21 June to 13 August, Sir William was used to taking a back seat to their intense relationship. He was secretly grateful that the little sailor had taken flamboyant Emma off his hands and relieved him of her bouts of hysteria. When Nelson sailed briefly to Minorca in October, Sir William sent him a letter begging, 'Emma is tired of the Colli for God's sake come back as soon as possible.' He felt he was fading, and he recognised that Nelson loved Emma in a way that she needed and he was unable to give her. Naturally sanguine, he had always been out of step with her expressive and demonstrative nature and he had resented the emotional demands she made. 'My shattered constitution now calls for some little repose and relaxation,' he groaned.²³⁹ He was simply too tired to protest.

Sir William had been asking the government since March to allow him leave for a holiday in England. Once at home, he would 'consult with my Friends what is best for me'. For, as he confessed to Charles Greville, 'to keep on as I have done for 35 years – it is impossible . . . even with Emma's assistance, which is infinite'.²⁴⁰ He suffered from frequent diarrhoea and bouts of sickness that he blamed on the 'intense heats and damp' but were actually caused by dysentery. When he was not fretting about his health, he was worried about money. He owed well over £19,000 (£1.15 million) to bankers in Palermo, Naples and London and the rents from his estates hardly covered his interest payments. He longed to return home, but declared he could not for it was 'impossible to quit Lord Nelson who does not understand any languages but his own and fairly said that if we went he could not stay here'. The King and Queen wanted Nelson to remain, so Sir William had to wait, but he lamented to Greville that it was 'at an Expense I can no means afford'. Not only did 'all Foreigners and the Nobility of this Country flock to this house' but also Nelson's 'numerous train of officers that come to him on business'.²⁴¹ Tired of the round of celebrations and Emma's relentless sociability, he complained that 'a Comely Landlady calls more company than I could wish to my House'.²⁴²

'I shall finish my Diplomatical Career gloriously,' he declared, believing his acts to quell the rebellion confirmed him worthy of the highest honour from the British government.²⁴³ He wanted to return to England, relax for a year, and ensure his comfortable retirement by extracting compensation and a bigger salary from the government. If it failed to comply, he would appeal directly to King George. The Foreign Office manoeuvred to head off Sir William's attempt to hold the government to ransom by removing him from his post. Lord Grenville wrote in December to grant the leave and added he had arranged a permanent replacement.

Nelson was entirely happy, puffed up by the attention from the Neapolitan ladies and flirtations with Maria Carolina's daughters, who were frequent visitors to the Palazzo Palagonia. A twenty-five-year-old travelling English artist. Henry Barker, compared him and Emma to Hercules and Omphale, the Lydian Queen who held the Greek hero captive. When Barker paid an afternoon visit, he found Emma and one of the Princesses spinning together. At dinner, 'Lord N. sat on L.H's right & she cut his meat. He was very lively.' Nelson thought it a huge joke to tell the Princesses that 'Damn your eyes' was a good way to greet an Englishman.²⁴⁴ Barker was dazzled by the array of nobility but shocked by the gambling, in which 'Lady H. & Lord N. were principal actors'.

Emma adored gaming and Nelson loved to sit by her, offering whispered advice, brushing his hand against her, touching her hair, intoxicated by her glamour and falling ever more desperately in love. Excited by the illicit thrill and the midnight secrets of the long hot Sicilian nights, they seized every chance to be together.

35

Days of Ease and Nights of Pleasure

'*H*eroes and conquerors are subdued in their turn,' joked *The Times* in November 1799. 'Mark Antony followed Cleopatra *into the Nile* when he should have fought with Octavius and laid down his laurels and power, to sail down the *Cydnus* with her in the dress, the character, and the *attitudes* of Venus.'[245] It later reported that 'the admirable Attitudes of Lady HAM-T-N are called *Admiral-attitudes*'.[246] English readers were hungry for every salacious detail about Nelson's affair with glamorous Lady Hamilton.

Caricatures began to appear in the print shops. In the eyes of eighteenth-century satirists, mistresses and courtesans could do as they pleased, but a wife who was unfaithful was beyond the pale. Emma received some harsh treatment. One of the most scabrous depictions of Emma and Nelson ever produced appeared at some point in late 1798 or early 1799. *The Night Mare on the Source of the Nile* is a parody of *The Nightmare*, the famous gothic work by Swiss painter Henry Fuseli, in which a woman lies on a bed, a small demon balanced over her. Emma is shown in the same position on a large round bed (perhaps an allusion to James Graham's Celestial Bed) and Nelson, as a crook-nosed little demon, perches on her midriff and pulls up her skirt. The affair between Nelson and Emma sold newspapers and prints, and few missed the chance to exploit it.*

---

* As pornographic cartoons tend not to survive, since they are hardly items people treasure for their relations, it is very likely that dozens of similar cartoons appeared.

The ordinary seamen adored Emma, and begged her to intercede in disputes. Nelson's officers, however, began to fret. Admiral Goodall branded Emma an 'enchantress'. Captain Troubridge warned Emma that her 'enemies' in London were whispering about her unseemly influence over Nelson and he implored Nelson to stop gambling at 'nocturnal parties' for 'Lady Hamilton's character will suffer; nothing can prevent people from talking'. Lord Elgin was travelling through Palermo on his way to take up a position as ambassador to Constantinople, and the new Lady Elgin, just twenty-one, judged Emma according to the gossip columns: she decided Emma managed Nelson entirely while he behaved 'as if he had no other thought than her'. She derided 'the fuss the Queen made with Lady H.'. She thought Emma buxom, described her dress as showy and revealing, and decided she would be just her father's type: a 'fine Woman' of 'good flesh and blood'; a phrase used at the time to imply sexual susceptibility.[247]

By January, Lord Keith, the commander of the British fleet in the Mediterranean, was sick of the antics of the 'silly pair of sentimental fools' and ordered Nelson to meet him in Leghorn. Emma clung to him before they parted, no doubt aware that he had conducted an affair there with the singer Adelaide Correglia, and begged him not to sleep off ship or to socialise for 'there is no comfort their for you'. She had no need to worry. He wrote the earliest of his love letters to her that survives:

last night I did nothing but dream of you altho' I woke twenty times in the night, in one of my dreams I thought I was at a large table you was not present, sitting between a Princess who I detest and another, they both tried to seduce me and the first wanted to take those liberties with me which no Woman in this World but yourself ever did, the consequence was I knocked her down and in the moment of bustle you came in and taking me to your embrace wispered I love nothing but you my Nelson, I kissed you fervently and we enjoy'd the height of love. Ah Emma I pour out my soul to you. If you love any thing but me you love those who feel not like your N . . . no separation no time my only beloved Emma can alter my love and affection for you, it is founded on the truest principles of honor, and it only remains for us to regret which I do with the bitterest anguish that there are any obstacles to our being united in the closest ties of this Worlds rigid rules, as we are in those of real love. Continue only to love your faithful Nelson, as he loves his Emma, you are my guide I submit to you.

The 'Princesses' are probably Maria Carolina's daughters, Amelia and

Antoinette, young, single and teasing (future Queens of France and Spain respectively). Later in the letter he uses his small appetite to beg her attention. 'I never touch even pudding you know the reason, no I would starve sooner, my only hope is to find you have equally kept your promises to me.' He is 'confident of the reallity of your love and that you would die sooner than be false in the smallest thing to your own faithful Nelson who lives only for his Emma'. She missed him terribly, and her letters to him were probably even more passionate and explicit. He burned them to protect her honour as soon as he could bear to do so.

In January, to his utter shock, Sir William read in the *Morning Chronicle* that he had been relieved of his post. He tried to hope that the newspaper had been mistaken, but he became increasingly worried. When Lord Grenville's letter reached him some time afterwards, probably in late January, he realised despondently that his bid for security and a large payout had failed. Disoriented and feeling wounded and underappreciated by the government, Sir William planned with Emma to travel to England and then return quickly to live on the Bronte estate, with Nelson either fighting in the Mediterranean or retired. Emma worried about returning to England where every woman wanted the hero of the Nile. As Nelson's nephew later remarked, 'His warm heart eagerly strove to attach itself to some object of primary affection; if Lady Hamilton had not artfully endeavoured to inveigle it, some other female would.'[248] Anxious that she might lose him, she aimed to have his child.

Nelson had probably been asking for the intimacy of unprotected relations for some time. In mid-February, he had his wish. As he reminisced to her later, 'I did remember well the 12th February and also the months afterwards. I shall never be sorry for the consequences' (then going on to discuss their child). She no doubt promised him a son to inherit his dukedom and his aptitude for leadership. But she needed to become pregnant quickly. She was nearly thirty-five and Nelson was forty-two, and couples of a similar age usually have regular intercourse for over six months or a year before they conceive.

Emma made her decision just in time. Nelson was also about to be recalled. His commanders were angered by gossip in the newspapers that they could not control him. In May, Lord Spencer commanded Nelson silkily, 'You will be more likely to recover your health and strength in England than in an inactive situation at a foreign court, however pleasing the respect and gratitude shown to you for your services may be.'

'We are coming home; and I am miserable to leave my dearest friend, the Queen,' Emma wrote to Greville on 25 February. Their last months in Sicily were a turmoil of arrangements. Emma was concerned by the plight of the people of the island of Malta, south of Sicily. After Napoleon's troops had invaded and looted the island in 1798, the furious Maltese had decided to attempt to force the French troops to surrender by blockading them in the garrison. British ships arrived to surround the island and prevent the French bringing in men or supplies. Then King Ferdinand, concerned about rising food prices in Sicily, refused to let the British take grain to the Maltese. The islanders were soon starving. When Nelson begged Ferdinand to reconsider, he promised the moon but gave nothing. Emma stepped in, sending supplies of food and inveigling £10,000 from Maria Carolina to give to the Governor.[249] In gratitude for her efforts, Emperor Paul I of Russia awarded her the Cross of the Knights of St John, or the Maltese Cross. When she received the solid gold cross, the Queen took it to set it with diamonds. Emma gloated, 'I am the first Englishwoman that ever had it. Sir W. is pleased, so I *am happy*.' She was a Dame of the Order of Malta, or *dame petite croix*. It was a title that was entirely her own (she was Emma, Lady Hamilton, rather than Lady Emma Hamilton because her title was her husband's). She used Dame when she was behaving at her very grandest.

Sir William tried to pretend he was merely returning to England for a well-deserved break. After thirty-seven years in his post, he believed that he had turned a minor ambassadorial post into a major one. He thought himself essential and could not believe that the government would not accede to his request to take a sabbatical of a year or two and then resume the position when he pleased. Maria Carolina, whom Sir William had welcomed from Austria thirty-two years before, begged her husband to protest to the Foreign Office. Lazy Ferdinand did not write, but his intervention would not have carried much weight in any case. The British government wanted to distance itself from the controversial reprisals after the rebellions. The new envoy, Arthur Paget, only twenty-nine years old, had promised to represent the interests of his country, rather than those of Maria Carolina. Lord Dalkeith teased him that he should not only take Hamilton's place but 'occupy Lady Hamilton too, a place you are much better fitted to fill than the old knight'.[250] After fending off similar schoolboy jokes, Paget arrived in April to find that Sir William not only refused to present him at Court but also appeared to have destroyed his files. All the records and correspondence had vanished. Paget would resign within a year.

Desperate to grasp a few last moments together, Nelson and Emma planned a voyage to Syracuse and Malta on Nelson's ship, setting out on 23 April with Sir William and an assortment of English tourists. The ostensible purpose was to join the ships blockading Malta. In reality the ship on which Caracciolo had been sentenced now hosted a honeymoon cruise of, as Nelson put it, 'days of ease and nights of pleasure'. On the journey out, Emma claimed to be suffering from palpitations. Nelson consoled her ardently. Soon her declarations of illness were excuses for them to escape the other guests and languish in the cabin. Emma celebrated her thirty-fifth birthday on the way and recovered sufficiently to throw a party, with toasts and songs.

In Syracuse, Nelson and Emma wandered around like teenage lovers, leaving Hamilton alone with the other guests. Sir William struggled with his thoughts: he hoped that the affair might wane, but he also knew that, now he was retired, keeping friendly with Nelson was his only chance of retaining some influence back in England.

Emma fell pregnant after only a few weeks of unprotected sex. The baby was conceived between late April and early May, either on the cruise or just before departure. Emma wanted to give Nelson a child, and she threw away every worldly advantage she had gained in order to do so: her respectable status as Sir William's wife, her chances of social advancement and her 'virtue'. If she had not become pregnant, no one could have proved her affair was anything other than the friendship that she and Nelson declared it to be. Emma's first baby caused her nothing but stress and heartache. Her second would change her life.

After a few days in Syracuse, the party travelled to St Paul's Bay on Malta's north coast. Now built up with high-rise hotels and cafés, the bay was then a quiet fishing port. As the *Foudroyant* entered, the blockading ships fired off spectacular welcoming salutes, and villages across Malta were illuminated. After a week, Nelson and Emma sailed to the capital, Valletta, hurrying off when they were fired at to join the southern blockade at the scenic Marsa Sirocco Bay. They returned on 1 June to hear that Ferdinand had pardoned all those who participated in the Neapolitan rebellions. Sir William added to his debts by hosting a sumptuous banquet at the Palazzo Palagonia in honour of the birthday of George III. Unwilling to part with her friend, Maria Carolina decided to visit her daughter and son-in-law, the Empress and Emperor of Vienna, accompanying the Hamiltons as far as Leghorn.

When Emma had first arrived abruptly in Naples, she thought it was merely a holiday destination. Now she was about to leave her dear Queen, many close friends, and her home for thirteen years to return to London.

36

Baron Crocodile's Roadshow

When he heard that Nelson planned to transport Maria Carolina on his ship to Trieste and accompany the Hamiltons home, his commander, Lord Keith, exploded that Lady Hamilton had ruled the fleet long enough. Despite his opposition, fanfares sounded across the harbour as the *Foudroyant* set off on 10 June 1800, weighed down with the Queen, her four youngest children and three marriageable daughters, together with eighty ministers, nobles, attendants and servants, doctors, ministers, cooks and nannies. The Hamiltons had about twelve secretaries and servants, as well as Mrs Cadogan and various English friends who expected the *Tria* to pay for their trip home. It was Emma's homeward journey, and she looked forward to showing off, but she was seven weeks' pregnant and feeling weak and very nauseous.

At Leghorn, on the Tuscan coast, Maria Carolina said goodbye to Emma, showering her with heaps of jewels, including a diamond necklace containing locks of her children's hair, giving splendid presents to Sir William and Nelson. Then the British navy refused permission for Nelson to sail the *Foudroyant* back to England. As Nelson fumed and tried to work out how to reach home (there were no ships he could charter to take them, even if he could have afforded to), the Queen grew increasingly afraid of the nearby French forces and begged Nelson to take her entire party back to Sicily in the *Foudroyant*. While the Queen cajoled and Emma tried to encourage Nelson to negotiate with his superiors, the French continued to advance. On 8 July, the terrified inhabitants of Leghorn seized the city's stock of arms and surrounded their Royal visitors in the Governor's Palace, declaring that they would keep them prisoner until Nelson led them into battle against the enemy. The hero locked himself into a back room and Maria Carolina, the Princesses, and the ladies of the court fell into hysterics.

Emma had to come to the fore – and her skills as an actress would never be more necessary. Dressed in white, she appeared on the palace balcony and extolled her friend's innocence and delicacy, pleading with them against 'violently surrounding an amiable and illustrious queen'. Her heartfelt appeal won over the crowd. But they still wanted Nelson, and Emma had to tell them he would not speak to them until they returned their weapons to the city's stores. They straggled home, most welcoming the excuse to turn back with honour. Maria Carolina, relieved but still piqued that Emma had failed to win her the *Foudroyant*, dashed inland to Florence, with Nelson and the Hamiltons hot on her heels. They decided to travel over 150 miles east to Ancona, on the Adriatic coast, from where they could catch a ship to Trieste.

The Hamiltons and friends rambled within two miles of French military posts, through swarms of people fleeing the enemy advance. At Ancona, they discovered that the Queen had dismissed the Austrian frigate that had been fitted out to receive her. The giant party drummed their heels for three weeks until Nelson managed to commandeer enough Russian boats to transport them. Once they had piled on to the ships, their unhappiness only increased. The weather was terrible, and the first lieutenant, a close friend of Caracciolo, reviled the Royal Family for fleeing Palermo and executing his friend and he and his Neapolitan crew had no interest in making the journey more comfortable. There was so little space that some of the passengers had to sleep on the orlop deck among the ordinary sailors. Sir William lay in bed groaning, declaring he was dying. Nelson, who knew that Emma stood to be impoverished by the terms of his current will, encouraged him to amend it to make more generous provision for her. Sir William refused, determined that his estate would be Greville's.

At Trieste, the Nelson party collapsed into bed in their luxury hotel as cries of 'Viva Nelson' echoed around the bay. When they departed on 10 August, the city blazed with more than four thousand wax lights and oil lamps, in Nelson's honour. They had a long route ahead of them through the Austro-Hungarian Empire: Trieste to Laibach (now Ljubljana, capital of Slovenia), Klagenfurt to Graz (now Austria), through Baden to Vienna, then to Prague, capital of Bohemia, then up the great Elbe river from Dresden, capital of Saxony, through Magdeburg in

Prussia, to Hamburg, where they would catch a ship to England's south coast – a journey of well over seven hundred miles.

It was stardom and chaos all the way as the fourteen carriages and three baggage wagons rumbled through the pretty valleys and mountains of Slovenia and Hungary. At every place they stopped, everybody came out to goggle at the hero of the Nile and his glamorous mistress, as well as the Queen and her ninety-two horses. Usually quiet roads were jammed with traffic as carts and horses tailed along the roads behind them. Almost every evening, Emma had to assemble her finery from a trunk and sparkle at a dinner and play or concert put on by local dignitaries in Nelson's honour. She always wore a 'Nelson outfit' or converted one of the fine Court dresses Maria Carolina had given her by accessorising with anchor earrings or necklaces, and she never tired of praising him and singing about him. Everyone watched her lead her lover, take hold of his hand or whisper into his ear. In public she cut his food, opened doors and held items he wished to see and in private, she arranged his hair and trimmed the nails on his fingers and toes. She now understood the price of falling in love with a public hero. No longer able to control her own exposure through stage-managing her parties and appearances, she had to smile through dinners and walkabouts during which people grabbed at her clothes. She had to be ready at any time to play the role of Lady Hamilton, Nelson's heroine. Left behind at the hotels as her daughter dazzled, Mrs Cadogan continued to let out the waists of the Queen's old dresses.

After a musical celebration commemorating the Battle of the Nile and a sumptuous commemorative dinner at Laibach, the Hamiltons and Nelson set off north after a few hours' sleep for the Karawanken mountain range, a rocky route notorious for its bloodthirsty bandits. They walked to the top, to save the horses. After another four days of travel, they arrived in Graz. Crowds of people had been waiting for hours to welcome Nelson, many on the brink of tears. 'The manifestation of esteem and affection so moved the hero', gushed Graz's local newspaper, 'that he not only invited many people into his own room but even went into the street amongst the crowd – with the beautiful Lady Hamilton on his arm,' pressing hands, kissing babies and accepting little presents.[251] After they had recovered from the shock of realising that the great man was tiny, pale and scrawny, Graz's journalists decided they had never seen such a hero. To their delight, Emma staged her own personal walkabouts, playing to the image of her as Cleopatra, flanked by her glamorous Nubian maid. 'The respect which the hero universally inspired was equalled by the admiration for Lady Hamilton's beauty.'

Before dawn, the Nelson and Emma show departed for Gloggnitz, intending to meet up with the Queen in order to enter Vienna in a triumphal progress. They burned into the quiet town only to be bitterly disappointed: she had already left. Her son-in-law, Emperor Leopold of Austria, was afraid of offending Napoleon and he had instructed her to come alone. Nelson was infuriated by the Queen's decision to hurry on without them, and when they arrived at the luxury spa resort of Baden Baden, he decided they had no time to bathe, even though his hernias were giving him pain and Emma's limbs were swollen.

Despite the Emperor's attempt to play down the hero's arrival, the Viennese treated Nelson and Emma as the biggest stars they had ever seen, decking themselves in Nelson memorabilia. Fashionable shops were decked with muslins embroidered in gold and silver to commemorate his victories. Portraits of the hero seemed to hang over half of the city. The Viennese ladies were resplendent in the latest look, a 'bonnet a la Nelson', which resembled a crocodile.[252] 'À la Lady Hamilton' led fashion: short haircut, no bonnet, light muslin dress, earrings in the shape of anchors and a replica Maltese Cross. The newspapers threw up their hands, declaring that 'many women now refuse to wear any dress other than their "Nelson"'.[253]

Even though they had travelled more than three hundred miles in a week, Nelson and Emma gamely welcomed the cheering crowds. Snowed under by invitations to soirées, concerts and dinners, they found that everybody tried to pay for their food and wine, and presents arrived at their hotel. Lord and Lady Minto, the British envoy and his wife, entertained their new guests, stunned at the frenzy for the hero. 'The door of his house is always crowded with people, and even the street whenever his carriage is at the door,' Lady Minto reeled, equally stunned that Emma led 'Nelson about like a keeper with a bear'.[254] People thronged the route when Nelson and Emma travelled out in their carriage and the audience stood and cheered when they arrived in their box at the theatre. Every artist offered to paint the hero and his mistress, musicians and composers waited for Emma's and Sir William's attention, and Mrs Cadogan and Emma's maids were besieged by jewellers, dressmakers and milliners hoping for favour. Tradesmen offered Nelson goods in order to claim him as a customer and named their shops, cafés and hotels after him. They had no time for most of the offers, but Nelson did pay attention to the painters. He tried to distract Emma from her resentment at Maria Carolina's neglect by arranging for her to sit for the state painter, Heinrich Füger. In London, the *Morning Post* joked that Füger was 'drawing Lady Hamilton and Lord Nelson at full length together. An Irish correspondent hopes the artist will have the delicacy to put Sir William between them.'[255]

On the Thursday after Nelson and Emma arrived, the Empress invited them to tea with her children and Maria Carolina at the recently built Schönbrunn Palace. Soon after, they received good news. Stunned by the outpouring of support for the Nile hero, the Emperor had decided he could no longer ignore his visitors, and he had invited Nelson and the Hamiltons to a grand Court reception.

Emma's pregnancy was beginning to show. Although she was not sharing a room with her husband, he would have realised the reason for Emma's nausea and Nelson's protectiveness by the time the party reached Vienna. Under eighteenth-century law, custody of a child, even an infant, was always the mother's husband's and she had no rights of access if the pair separated. The baby inside Emma was legally Sir William's possession. But he and everybody else knew it was not his child. Sly comments appeared in the newspapers about Emma's size: reporters praised the wonderful face of 'the most beautiful woman in Europe' but tittered that her figure had swelled.

At the end of August, the Royal Family moved to their summer residence at Baden. Nelson and the Hamiltons visited for Court dinners and smaller lunches, but Nelson was growing increasingly frustrated by Emma's efforts to catch the Queen's attention. It was quite obvious to him that Maria Carolina, preoccupied by the advance of Napoleon and marrying off her children, had no more use for Emma, the wife of an ex-envoy. He steered his darling toward accepting an invitation from the young Prince Esterházy, a friend from Naples, to his splendid palace in Eisenstadt, a day or two's drive away. At Esterházy's glittering receptions, upward of sixty dined every evening, and a hundred Hungarian bodyguards waited behind the banqueting table. After dinner, Emma performed her Attitudes, whipping guests into states of high emotion, according to the effusive reports in the newspapers. The Prince put on fanfares and salutes and balls for his guests. Sir William hunted (to the amazement of the other guests, he shot 122 birds in a single session) and Emma won a great prize: the admiration of Josef Haydn, Esterházy's Court musician and one of the most illustrious composers alive.

Sixty-eight-year-old Haydn was captivated by Emma's voice and her powers of expression, and practised songs with her every day. She sang

'Ariadne auf Naxos', one of his favourite pieces, and they tried out some of his new songs. Emma even managed his mournful 'The Spirit's Song', a difficult piece in a high register. She asked him to set to music a poem by one of her English hangers-on, the impecunious would-be writer, Cornelia Knight, and he did so in two days and named it 'The Nelson Aria'. He also revised part of a piece he had already written to create 'The Nelson Mass'. A beaming Nelson gave Haydn his watch in exchange for the pen used to create the composition. Pretty girls with good singing voices often accosted Haydn, and he was frequently called upon to entertain the Prince's female visitors. His interest in Emma was different: he found something original in her approach to perform-ance. Just as Romney had been delighted by her plasticity, her imagin-ation, and her willingness to try new creative experiments, so Haydn relished her open expressiveness. Fine ladies were almost always stolid singers: they refused to alter the usual rendition of a performance and were particularly nervous about expressing fervent emotion, running the risk of being accused of exciting the passions of the men in the audience. Emma threw her emotions into her performances and sang madness, anger, fear and love as if she was really feeling them.

One Hungarian visitor was bowled over by 'her clear, strong voice with which, accompanied by the famous Haydn, she filled the audi-ence with such enthusiasm that they almost became ecstatic. Many were reminded of pictures of the 'Goddesses Dido and Calypso'.[56] Haydn came to her inn to wish her a fond farewell as they prepared to leave Vienna at the end of September. He gave Emma her own copy of 'The Spirit's Song' and presented Nelson with a copy of 'The Nelson Aria'. The Princess Esterházy wrote to Emma 'you will always exist in my heart and in my memory, and that I shall never forget your kind friend-ship to me'. She cherished 'the flattering hope of seeing you here again in the spring'. They all thought they would be on their way back to Italy in the New Year.

Now that Emma was leaving, Maria Carolina was terribly sorry to see her go. 'At all times and places and under all circumstances, Emma, dear, dear Emma shall be my friend and sister,' she effused. She paid her the compliment of begging her to return to Naples with her, and wrote a letter to give to Queen Charlotte, which Emma presumed was a letter of recommendation guaranteeing her entry to the English Court.

In Prague, crowds draped in Nelson regalia mobbed them as soon as they arrived. Weary after their two-hundred-mile journey from Vienna, Nelson and Emma were thrilled to find that their hotel was covered in illuminations to celebrate their arrival. They were later startled to see the cost of the lights charged to their bill. Without Maria Carolina to cover the travel expenses, both Nelson and Sir William were living well beyond their means. Charles Greville's blood pressure shot up as he read about their extravagance in the English newspapers. 'I had prepared a plan for cheap residence but this establishment confounds all,' he fumed, almost weeping to see his long-desired inheritance squandered on turning the *Tria* into megastars.[257] The party's expenses were mounting well past £4,000. Still, in Prague, it was Nelson's birthday and it was no time to economise – after a large dinner at the palace of the Archduke Charles, where Emma sang a version of 'God Save the King', adding a final stanza commemorating Nelson, they invited their fellow guests back to their hotel for a second dinner and more singing.

At Dresden, people spotters, autograph hunters and ordinary people craving a glimpse of Nelson surrounded the hotel. According to the newspapers, the Electress of Saxony refused to receive them on account of Emma's rakish past, although the truth was that the Elector worried about antagonising Napoleon. Nelson did not care, cheerfully blustering that if there was 'any difficulty of that sort, Lady Hamilton will knock the Elector down', socialising instead with the recently appointed British envoy, Hugh Elliot, and his wife, and their guest, Melesina St George Trench. Elliot became rather a fan, admiring Emma's lack of airs and graces and comparing her to Nell Gwynn, recalling the story in which the King's mistress allayed the anger of the masses by identifying herself as the Protestant Whore. Like many, he decided her a second Cleopatra, manipulating her Antony, and he believed she had bigger fish to fry than Nelson. 'She will captivate the Prince of Wales, whose mind is as vulgar as her own, and play a great part in England.'

Melesina was in love with Elliot and painfully jealous of Emma's electrifying effect on him, resenting her flamboyant behaviour and her efforts to steal the limelight by flattering her lover. 'It is plain that Lord Nelson thinks of nothing but Lady Hamilton, who is totally occupied with the same object,' declaring him 'a willing captive, the most submissive and devoted I have seen'. Emma, she mocked, 'puffs the incense full in his face; but he receives it with pleasure, and snuffs it up very cordially'. Sir William was dismissed as 'old, infirm, all admiration of his wife' and Mrs Cadogan was a trial. 'Lady Hamilton's mother, is what one might expect from the purlieu's of Dr Giles's whence she really comes,' an accusation so shocking that it was cut from the version of her journal later published by her son, but remains in the original manuscript in Hampshire Record Office.

Melesina wished she had Hugh Elliot and his malleable wife to herself, but she could not deny Emma's beauty. 'She resembles the bust of Ariadne, the shape of all her features is as fine as her head, and particularly her ears' and even the brown spot in one light blue eye 'takes nothing away from her beauty of expression'. The pregnancy was now obvious: her feet were heavy and swollen and she was 'exceedingly embonpoint' or bosomy, a phrase used to signal pregnancy. Although Melesina admitted that Emma was entertaining and that she 'did not seek to win hearts, for everyone's lay at her feet', she complained she was more 'stamped with the manners of her first situation than one would suppose, after having represented Majesty and lived in good company, for fifteen years'.

Melesina was, however, won over by her Attitudes, for which Emma cunningly made them wait five days.

Several Indian shawls, a chair, some antique vases, a wreath of roses, a tambourine, and a few children are her whole apparatus. She stands at one end of the room with a strong light to her left, and every other window closed . . . her gown a simple calico chemise, very easy with loose sleeves to the wrist. She disposes the shawls as to form Grecian, Turkish and other drapery, as well as a variety of turbans. Her arrangement of the turbans is absolute sleight-of-hand, she does it so quickly, so easily, and so well . . . Each representation lasts about ten minute. It is remarkable that, though coarse and ungraceful in common life, she becomes highly graceful, and even beautiful during this performance.[258]

In the cold light of morning, she judged her dress 'vulgar, loaded, and unbecoming'. Emma preferred an obvious look – bright colours, cleavage, heavy jewellery, and tight drapes – but there were few men who were not attracted by it. Melesina's scornful remarks are often quoted but she was acerbic about everybody else she met, other than Hugh Elliot, and much nastier about many of them. And Melesina's pen did not reflect her behaviour to her visitor's face: she was a frequent visitor to Emma's homes after both had returned to England. While Emma flattered the Elliots, Nelson ordered Dresden porcelain in his honour and arranged for Saxony's foremost artist, Johann Schmidt, to paint him and his Emma. He was determined to have his own set of portraits of her in which she was herself, not a model playing glamorous roles, tainted by the paw marks of William or Greville.

On 10 October, Nelson and the Hamiltons caught a barge along the Elbe. Spectators crowded along the bridge and the shore and the crushes when the party disembarked were so intense that those at the front almost fell into the river. When they disembarked at Magdeburg, further up the Elbe, Emma was the star of their lunch engagement, interpreting for her lover, showing where he had been wounded, and boasting about his 120 sea battles. Onlookers jostled to peer in while Nelson dined and boats full of cheering spectators escorted his boat as it set off once more.

On 21 October, they finally reached Hamburg. The frigate that Nelson had requested the Admiralty send to transport them home was nowhere to be seen, and they had to buy places on a ship transporting mail. Amongst the dignitaries they met in the ten days they waited to depart was the poet Friedrich Gottlieb Klopstock. Utterly charmed by Lady Hamilton, the elderly intellectual would not let her out of his sight. He enjoyed a private performance of the Attitudes and wrote to a friend that she had given him a kiss.

The English in Hamburg put on a play depicting the Battle of Aboukir and then threw a party in Nelson's honour for over a thousand guests, including a twelve-year-old Arthur Schopenhauer, already showing hints of the genius that would make him the age's most respected philosopher. Nelson was so carried away by the riotous celebrations that he lost a giant yellow diamond from the sword that Ferdinand had only recently given him. Just before they embarked on the *King George* on 31 October, the hungover hero sheepishly bought his wife a black lace cloak and a package of fine lace to decorate a Court dress. None of the fashion reports ever noted that Fanny wore it.

They arrived home on 6 November. The triumphal journey was only a trial run. Emma was about to become the most famous woman in England.

IV. Scandal and Stardom

37
Cleopatra Arrives

The whole of East Anglia seemed to have arrived at Yarmouth to welcome the Hero of the Nile and his friends. It was Emma's first glimpse of England in nearly ten years. Boats flying every colour came out to meet them and excited crowds teemed on the shore. When they landed, burly men removed the horses from Nelson's carriage and dragged it to the inn. There, to the delight of the crowd, Nelson and Emma waved from the balcony as the local infantry struck up a congratulatory march. No representative from the Admiralty was present to greet the hero, but the Mayor of Yarmouth staged a lavish banquet in their honour and offered Nelson the freedom of the city.

Undeterred by the November chill, crowds in Nelson hats and badges thronged their route through Norfolk, waving flags, singing and weeping with joy. Emma delighted in the adulation. She dreaded meeting Fanny. Nelson vowed that he adored her because she was so different from his wife, but she was anxious that he might feel a twinge of guilt when he saw her again. She was nervous that Nelson at heart was too conventional to abandon his marriage.

Nelson had written to Fanny telling her to anticipate them for dinner on Saturday. He expected her to put the servants to work and welcome him and his friends with a sumptuous meal. But Fanny had not received the letter. Unsure of what to do, she had hurried to London with Nelson's father to wait for him. The homecoming hero's party reached Roundwood to find only a few servants in the kitchen, little food, no fires, and hardly any candles. Nelson flew off the handle, suspecting his wife had left his home cold and empty to humiliate him.

After a dismal and anticlimactic evening, the party set off for London the next morning, narrowly avoiding the worst storm since 1703. Trees were torn out of the ground, signs flew off shops, and houses collapsed, but nothing could halt the progress of Nelson and his fan club. They arrived in London by early afternoon, and Nelson, Emma and Sir William took suites at Nerot's Hotel in St James. Mrs Cadogan and the others went to a cheaper lodging house nearby. Admirers surrounded the hotel and cheered through the rain to see the Hero of the Nile and the Cleopatra who had won his heart and, some said, directed the English fleet. Gossip columnists and reporters skulked at the back doors, recording their every move. After a lightning visit from Sir William's relation, the hugely rich debauchee the Duke of Queensberry, Fanny arrived, accompanied by Nelson's father, seventy-eight-year-old Edmund Nelson. She now knew that Nelson had been to Roundwood and she was almost paralysed by nerves. Every print shop she passed was selling images of Emma and the newspapers were churning out jokes about her Attitudes and the same old story about her meteoric rise to fame. Fanny shrank from meeting the famous Emma. Forty-two and conscious that she was ageing, she had lain awake through long, lonely nights seething with hatred for her younger rival. She was painfully aware that she had put herself at a terrible disadvantage by missing the chance to receive Emma on home ground.

The meeting was even worse than she had feared. Emma swept in, overexcited and effusive, her dress outlining the now resplendent swell. Fanny finally saw what everybody had kept from her: Lady Hamilton had succeeded where she had failed. She could hardly retain her composure. Nelson received her politely but, although they had been apart for three years, he refused to retire and see her alone. He could not bear to leave Emma, the woman pregnant with the child he had longed for almost as much as he desired glory. Fanny withdrew into herself and seemed cold and Emma claimed her eyes were icy with an 'antipathy not to be described'. In Sir William's favourite hotel, surrounded by cheering crowds wielding flags, Fanny was faced with the bitter truth: she had lost her husband.

Emma was comforted to see that Nelson's ardour for her never faltered, but she knew she had to press her advantage. Lady Nelson joined the Hamiltons and Nelson for dinner at Nerot's at five o'clock. Emma talked nineteen to the dozen, making sure to attract all the attention, even though she had to let Fanny sit by Nelson's side. He left in the early evening to report to Lord Spencer, the First Lord of the Admiralty, and Fanny followed him in her carriage, tormented by the situation and deeply unhappy that Nelson's commanders had underplayed the affair as a mere crush.

Nelson had hoped that his wife would behave like Sir William, recognise that their marriage had ended, stepping back to allow the lovers to pursue their mutual adoration. But Fanny, disgusted by Sir William's placid acceptance of the affair, decided to fight. She was Lady Nelson, Baroness Nelson, and Duchess of Bronte, and she was not about to let her husband go. To the delight of the newspapers, the women began fighting for his heart under an increasingly flimsy mien of polite friendship.

William Beckford offered the Hamiltons use of his mansion, 22 Grosvenor Square, and Nelson and Fanny took an expensive furnished house a comfortable walking distance away at 17 Dover Street. Relations between him and his wife rapidly deteriorated. As Fanny knew, if she had been the mother of his children, he would have treated her with greater respect, and more journalists would have taken her side. She was in a weak position because she was childless. Nelson visited Emma daily and praised her endlessly to his wife and to anyone else who called at Dover Street. Fanny was too unhappy to pretend to be sweet and forgiving, and in retaliation Nelson refused to behave as her husband in public. He came to hate the sight of her. He tried to dispel his anger and frustration by walking for hours around London late at night before arriving at Emma's house in Grosvenor Square. The autumn of 1800 was such a strain that he declared in the following spring that 'sooner than live the unhappy life I did when last I came to England, I would stay abroad forever'.

Meanwhile, Emma was winning the media war. There were around fifty daily newspapers in circulation and Emma, looking ever more resplendent, was the toast of every one. Many newspapers had a print run of over 4,000 and, as editions were usually shared (Robert Southey estimated that every paper had five readers), we might make a conservative estimate that over a quarter of a million people read about her antics over their meals. Journalists followed her everywhere. The *Morning Herald* extolled Emma's expressive face, beautiful teeth, deep eyes, and her 'immensely thick' hair of the 'darkest brown' that 'trails to the ground', and decided her 'the chief curiosity with which that celebrated antiquarian, Sir William Hamilton, has returned to his native country'.[259] The *Morning Post* gallantly defended her against the *Herald*'s slur that she was forty-nine, declaring that she looked no more than twenty-five. She was only made more beautiful by her mysterious 'tawny tinge', a quip alluding to Cleopatra.²⁶⁰ Comparisons of her with the Egyptian Queen appeared almost every day. The joke was on the difference between the two women as shown in Shakespeare's play: Cleopatra, exotic, powerful, seductive and fertile versus Octavia, Antony's dreary, childless wife (who, like Fanny, also came to him as a widow), able to offer only 'a holy, cold, and still conversation'. Emma even took to wearing Turkish dress to capitalise on the associations with the exotic East.

The English public was enthralled by Emma's growing figure. The loose, low muslin fashions of the time made it impossible to hide the truth: the hero of the Nile was about to become a father, at the age of forty-two. Emma was hardly ever mentioned without a pointed comment on her 'rosy health' and 'plump figure', and typically a version of the phrase '*embonpoint*'. In the words of the *Morning Herald*, 'Lady Hamilton has been a very fine woman; but she has acquired so much *en bon point* and her figure is so swoln that her features and form have lost almost all their original beauty.' As another journalist put it, 'Lady Hamilton's countenance is of so rosy and blooming a description that, as Dr Graham would say, she appears so far a perfect *Goddess of Health*.'* It was traditional to lay straw outside the homes of women in labour. The *Morning Chronicle* published a story about Lady Hamilton next to a joke about ladies who were often 'in the straw' and 'laid in sheets'. Another noted how an 'unfortunate personal extension' was making her less quick and graceful than she had been.²⁶¹

Now that Emma was in England, every fine lady was experimenting with her look: either dresses in the Turkish style or white draped gowns, headbands rather than hats, and shawls and anchors 'alla Nelson'. Those still wearing hoops and corsets gave them up. Emma's pregnancy had led her to adopt the French fashion of the empire-line dress and she pulled the waistline outrageously high. As Melesina Trench sniped, 'her waist is absolutely between her shoulders'. Women across the country were besieging their dressmakers, demanding copies of what was, tech-

---

* The reporter could not resist adding, 'It was her figure for which she was particularly celebrated and in consequence of which her reputation commenced. She served for a model in the Academy of Painting and Sculpture. She was then Miss Hart. It was then doubtless that she acquired this taste and talent for fine attitudes and antique positions in which she has displayed so much skill.' 'Antique positions' implied that the Attitudes were partly erotic (*Morning Herald*, 5 December 1800).

nically, a maternity dress. Ladies in quiet Suffolk villages and large towns alike tied their dresses under their bosoms.

Hundreds dashed to buy Rehberg's book of her Attitudes to borrow ideas for the classical style of dress. The *Lady's Magazine* noted English women's 'enthusiastic partiality for the forms and fashions which were preferred among the ancient Greeks and Romans'. They even modelled their footwear on Emma's buying 'slippers in imitation of Etruscan ornaments'.[262] The Maltese Cross, pinned to Emma's now expansive bust, inspired particularly wild imitation. Cheap gilt versions of the cross were sold throughout England and the very wealthiest ladies had their own made out of diamonds. Even Caroline, Princess of Wales followed Emma's fashion and wore a white dress with a Maltese Cross brooch to attract the attention of the newspapers. Her estranged husband, the Prince, hated everything about her, except for the fashions she copied from Lady Hamilton. He gave a diamond Maltese Cross to his youngest sister Amelia in 1806. Poor Fanny was surrounded by women imitating her showy rival in transparent dresses and heavy jewellery. She was utterly isolated.

Printing presses worked overtime to produce cartoons, ballads and bawdy pictures about the affair. The newspapers had suggested before Sir William's marriage to Emma that he was infertile, even impotent, and it seems as if everybody agreed, for nobody assumed that the child she carried was his. On 18 November, the windows of the print shops exploded with a new caricature by Isaac Cruikshank, *Smoking Attitudes*, in which Emma, Sir William, Prime Minister Pitt, Nelson and the Lord Mayor are smoking pipes, following Nelson's recent attendance at the Lord Mayor's Reception. Smoking was a particularly exotic habit of the upper classes, associated with the East, and the pipes suggest that they are louche and extravagant. Hamilton's pipe is conspicuously unlit, and Emma, dressed in muslin and assuming an Attitude, effuses to Nelson that her husband's 'pipe is always out but yours burns with full vigour'. Her lover's reply is characteristically blunt. 'I'll give you such a smoke I'll pour a whole broad side into you.'*

Every time they opened a newspaper, Sir William's family, friends and ex-colleagues were shocked to see him represented as a cuckolded,

---

* Broadside was a term for a cheap printed song or pamphlet, as well as a naval term describing the moment when a battleship fired all its guns (from one side) into the enemy. Partly a comment on the outpouring of satiric material the publicity-seeking pair inspired, it was a very rude joke about Nelson's virility.

bamboozled, out-of-touch old antiquarian. They were even more scandalised by his sanguine acceptance of the situation. Sir William ignored
their complaints, perhaps because he thought them too concerned about
whether he would leave his money to Emma. Lady Frances Harpur,
Charles Greville's sister, visited Grosvenor Square with every resolution
to disapprove, but admitted 'She appears much attached to Sir Wm &
He is in much admiration & I believe She *constitutes* his *Happiness*.' Lady
Frances acknowledged that Emma was treating Sir William kindly, but
had to '*lament* this *Idolatory*'.[263] William's motives in forgiving the affair
were complex. He owed Nelson more than £2,000 (well over £120,000
in today's money), for expenses accrued in Naples, Palermo and the
journey home. Unable ever to pay it back, he hinted that Emma was
responsible for the expenses by complaining in front of her lover that
she gambled too much and would make herself a pauper. He was also
genuinely fond of Nelson and, furthermore, he knew their friendship
gave him social consequence.

Society commentators found Emma's behaviour bewildering, although
they hardly blinked when a man kept both mistress and wife, like the
Duke of Devonshire who lived at Devonshire House with both his
wife and Bess Foster, her friend and his mistress. Sir William excused
his wife because he loved her, valued her companionship, and welcomed
not having to be her sole support. And, as he knew, his only alternative was being alone. 'A man of my age ought not to be attach'd to
any worldly thing too much,' he wrote, 'but certain it is the greatest
attachment I have is the friendship and society of Lrd N. and my dear
Emma.' He also felt a little guilty for asking her to sacrifice her desire
for children. Because Emma was happy with Nelson, she was kinder
and more solicitous to him than she had been for some time. He always
defended his wife and told everyone how much he loved her. He could
have sought to harm the relationship by telling Nelson about Emma
Carew, but he never disclosed the secret.

The Nelsons and the Hamiltons spent most evenings together at
parties, dinners or theatre trips. Fanny sat bolt upright with misery as
she watched her husband in ecstasies over Emma's singing and dancing.
At his box in Covent Garden, after a musical performance of *The Mouth
of the Nile* Nelson forced his wife to sit on his left, with Emma on his
right, so that, as everybody saw, his mistress could help him eat when
he wanted to enjoy a snack in the interval. As one newspaper put it,
'Lady Hamilton sat on that side of Lord Nelson on which he is disarmed.'
The *Morning Herald* reported that Emma was '*embonpoint*' but 'extremely

pretty' in a blue satin gown and plumed headdress, while Fanny wore a white dress and small white feather.[264]

Emma also planted stories in the newspapers and encouraged her friends to do the same. The *Morning Post* reported, 'Lady Hamilton is fitting up a room for the purpose of displaying her *attitudes* and in a short time she will give large *attitude parties*. Attitudes, it is thought, will be much more in vogue this winter than *shape*' (a reference to Emma's lost figure).[265] On 18 November, *The Times* predicted she would soon be received at Court, and reminded its readers that the Queen of Naples had written to Queen Charlotte praising Emma, adding it was thanks to Emma's 'exertions' that Nelson's fleet was victualled and then able to win at the Battle of the Nile.[266]

Nelson bought a black terrier dog from a shop in Holborn, adorned him with a silver collar, called him 'Nileus' and gave him to Emma. Emma patched up her old disagreement with Anne Damer, and commissioned her to sculpt a huge marble bust of Nelson. The *Morning Post* joked about his flirtatious sittings for the 'fair artist' and compared the nose of the statue to Nelson's manhood.

When he was without Emma, Nelson behaved cruelly to his wife. At a dinner with Lady Spencer, wife of the Lord of the Admiralty, whom he thought took Fanny's side, Nelson was sullen. When Fanny offered him a walnut she had shelled for him, he refused it so roughly that it flew across the room and smashed a glass. Fanny fled and wept outside the door. Only Emma was allowed to prepare his food for him, to love him. He no longer cared who knew it.

38

Show Time

O n 24 November, the Hamiltons and the Nelsons arranged to
see Richard Sheridan's version of *Pizarro*, a play by the popular
German playwright August von Kotzebue. A tragic drama of
love and revenge, *Pizarro* had become inordinately popular during the
conflict between England and France. The audience cheered any possible
allusion to fighting the good fight, the players delivered their speeches
as pro-war tirades, and the actor playing Pizarro hammed up comparisons of the heroic main character to Nelson by wearing Nile dress and
swashbuckling around the stage. Announcements that the hero had
ordered a box caused a huge crush for tickets, even on a Monday night.
The house was crowded in every part by a 'splendid assemblage of beauty
and fashion', trilled the *Morning Herald*. The excitable crowds burst into
applause when Nelson arrived and did so repeatedly throughout the
play.[267] Fanny attempted to concentrate on the stage as Nelson and
Emma whispered together and petted. She was miserable and longed to
be back at 17 Dover Street – but there was much worse to come.

Jane Powell, Emma's old friend, starred as Elvira and Pizarro was
John Kemble, whom Emma had already met and charmed.* Like Emma,
Jane had come far since days of scrubbing at Dr Budd's and she was
now an accomplished tragedienne, second only to the great Sarah
Siddons. It was a set-up. Either Emma had met Jane a few days before
and plotted with her, or Jane had guessed at the way to please Nelson's
mistress and gain herself some notoriety into the bargain.

---

* Emma knew well in advance that Jane had taken the lead role, for it would have
been advertised.

The high point in the play came when the actress playing Elvira threatened vengeful Pizarro that she would defeat him if he attacked her. The audience was expectant. Jane waited for a degree of quiet, and then delivered the killer line. She taunted Pizarro to 'wave thy glittering sword'; then to the amazement of the crowd, she paused, and turned to look straight at Lady Nelson before crying 'and meet and survive – an injured woman's fury'.

Fanny let out a scream of shock. She had been demeaned repeatedly and now an actress was dubbing her an 'injured woman' in front of everybody. The theatre dissolved in uproar. Fanny fainted. Nelson refused to leave the box and Fanny suffered the indignity of being carried out by their servants. Nelson was infuriated with his wife for making a scene but everybody else could hardly believe it and journalists went wild for the news. One newspaper reported that Emma helped Fanny and Nelson's father away from the theatre and into the carriage. Poor Fanny was so bereft of her husband's support that she had to depend on the woman she hated more than anyone in the world. The *Morning Herald* remarked Fanny was 'for some days in a very indifferent state of health'.[268]

Emma was beginning to feel the strain of keeping up appearances. At a dinner she was seized with nausea and vomited repeatedly in a basin in front of Fanny. It was looking increasingly unlikely that she would be received at Court as Queen Charlotte showed no signs of caving in to media pressure. Nelson had not improved his popularity with the Royals by his predilection for converting 'God Save the King' into a hymn to his own victories. They could not refuse to see him, but they could snub Emma. In an effort to cheer her up, Nelson accepted an invitation to spend Christmas with Sir William's friend and relation, William Beckford, at his crazy Gothic-style mansion, Fonthill Abbey. Rumours abounded about Fonthill, and only Britain's chosen few stepped inside its luxurious doors. Leaving Fanny alone in London, with only her pompous brother-in-law, William, and his wife for company, Emma, Nelson and Sir William set off for an eccentric winter break. Beckford promised that Nelson and Emma could stay free from 'the sight and prattle of drawing room Parasites', but it was impossible to escape the reporters.[269] The public was always hungry to read every slavering detail about Nelson and Emma; where they stayed, who they met, and what they wore, ate and drank.

Local volunteers in army dress playing 'Rule Britannia' welcomed the visitors from London. Friends from Naples also attended: soprano

Brigida Banti, Emma's old duet partner, French émigrés along with various nobles and dignitaries. The *Gentleman's Magazine* reported the entertainment in luxurious detail to readers across England. After a tour of the flamboyant rooms led by hooded servants carrying torches, the guests were ushered to Beckford's sumptuous purple-draped reception rooms. Sitting nervously on priceless ivory chairs around ebony tables, they enjoyed an exquisite dinner served from huge silver dishes, expensive wines and 'confectionery served in gold baskets', under glittering gold lights. At eleven at night, when everybody's attention was heightened:

> Lady Hamilton appeared in the character of Agrippina, bearing the ashes of Germanicus in a golden urn, as she presented them before the Roman people [...] Lady Hamilton displayed with truth and energy every gesture, attitude, and expression of countenance which could be conceived in Agrippina herself, best calculated to have moved the passions of the Romans on behalf of their favourite General. The action of her head, of her hands, and arms in the various positions of the urn; in her manner of presenting it before the Romans, or of holding it up to the Gods in the act of supplication, was most classically graceful. Every change of dress, principally of the head, to suit the different situations in which she successively presented herself, was performed instantaneously with the most perfect ease, and, without returning or scarcely turning aside a moment from the spectators.[270]

Half drunk, satiated with sweetmeats and dazzled by Beckford's elaborate decor, Nelson fell in love with Emma all over again. The delighted company wept at her 'pathetically addressed' speech as Agrippina. Heavily pregnant, Emma emphasised her condition by playing maternal roles instead of more provocative nymphs. The journalist compared the experience of watching her to 'magic' and decided, 'I can scarcely help doubting whether the whole of the last evening's entertainment were a reality or only the visionary coinage of fancy.' Behind her back, Beckford joked she was 'Lord Nelson's Lady Hamilton or anybody else's Lady Hamilton', but to her face, he eulogised 'that light alone which beams from your Image ever before my fancy like a Vision of the Madonna della Gloria'.[271]

On 26 December, they returned to a bleak London. Nelson went back to Dover Street where Fanny awaited him. Emma could not give birth in 22 Grosvenor Square, for it was not their own house but Beckford's, so Sir William quickly rented a large and handsome town house in the prime location of 23 Piccadilly, facing Green Park. Emma was still just about able to get around and they began to pack up their belongings. Their old friend, Louis Dutens, acting as their assistant, took charge of furnishings. He worried that there were not enough beds for the eight servants, arranged to dye the dining-room curtains and wrote that he would move her bed from the room facing north to 'be placed in that fronting the South, looking onto the Park'. The bed had presumably been in the room adjoining Sir William's chamber and she wished to give birth in a room farther from him.[272]

On 1 January, Nelson's promotion to Vice Admiral was confirmed and he prepared to receive new orders to go to sea. Emma tried to be pleased for him, but she was miserable that he would not be with her for the birth, and perhaps would not return for a year. The promotion prompted Fanny to make an ultimatum. She could no longer bear the humiliation of her position, and she dreaded Nelson returning to sea with the situation unresolved. She begged him to tell her if he had ever mistrusted her or doubted her fidelity, covertly implying to Nelson that he might doubt Emma's ability to be loyal to him while he was away. She declared she was weary of 'dear Lady Hamilton, and am resolved that you shall give up either her or me'. Nelson was livid that Fanny had dared tell him what to do. He chose Emma and decided to take steps to formalise his separation from his wife. That same night, he left for Plymouth to embark on his ship, the *San Josef*. Fanny had lost Nelson for good. He never saw her again.

39

A Pledge of Love

As the *Morning Post* joked, Lady Hamilton had arrived in London in the 'nick of time'.[273] With only a month of her pregnancy to go, Emma was big and uncomfortable in her new home. Carrying a baby was much more difficult than when she was seventeen and, like any woman at the time, she was afraid of dying in childbirth. Only a few years before, Mary Wollstonecraft died after a doctor tore out her placenta with his bare hands. Mrs Cadogan cared for Emma and told inquisitive visitors and journalists that she was in bed with a cold. The doctor came secretly to escape the attention of the press. Amid the confusion, Nileus hurtled off into the Park. Emma frantically advertised for her dog in the newspapers, offering a guinea reward, but he was never found.[274]

Nelson arranged to sell Roundwood, his home with Fanny. Unlike many men, who left their wives no property or money on separation, he gave Fanny half his income, the equivalent now of about £120,000 a year. Although taking half his income signified their separation, Fanny refused to be beaten. On receiving her first payment on 13 January 1801, she wrote warmly to thank the 'man whose affection constitutes my happiness'. When she heard that Nelson was ill with eye pain, and knowing that Emma was in no fit state to travel, she offered to come and comfort him. Enraged, Nelson replied, 'Whether I am blind or not, it is nothing to any person, I want neither nursing, or attention. And had you come here, I should not have gone on shore nor would you have come afloat. I fixed as I thought a proper allowance to enable you to remain quiet.'[275] He told Emma that he had sent Fanny such a stinging rebuff that he worried 'you will think I have gone too far', begging her not to be 'angry at the strength of my letter'.[276] Fanny continued to promote herself as the perfect wife to Nelson's friends. She had already implied to him that Emma would be unable to endure the prolonged separation and would find fresh company elsewhere, and she hoped fervently this would come true.

Nelson wrote regularly to Emma, sometimes twice a day, brimming with 'all the affection which is possible for man to feel towards Woman and such a Woman'. He was lonely and overworked, complaining that his 'business' was 'endless'.[277] His captains were trying to discipline the youths caught by press-gangs into reasonably efficient seamen. Furious wives and incensed mothers battled the press-gang with sticks and other makeshift weapons and sometimes stormed docked ships to reclaim their men, rather than see them condemned to five years at sea, usually unable even to disembark. Nelson's eye became inflamed, as it did in periods of stress, and he begged Emma to sew him some green shades to shield it from the light.[278] Lord St Vincent, less than thrilled to be in charge of England's most famous lover, grumbled he was so obsessed with Emma that he wrote four letters a day. Far from her, he was becoming fretful about the child due to be born.

In their letters, Nelson and Emma established an elaborate secret code to discuss Emma's condition. They pretended he wrote to Emma on behalf of a sailor on his ship called Thomson or Thompson, whose pregnant wife was under Emma's protection. William Hamilton became Mrs Thomson's uncle. Since the publication of Jean-Jacques Rousseau's *La Nouvelle Héloïse*, English aristocrats had rushed to adopt pen names to conduct their amorous correspondence, enjoying the frisson of speaking in code and pretending to be a member of the lower classes. The code of the 'Thompsons' was more of a mutual thrill than a useful strategy. Firing off letters late at night, Nelson was often so carried away by feeling that he wrote 'I' instead of 'Thompson'.

Nelson instructed his friend and prize agent, Alexander Davison, to hustle Fanny out of town. 'I *will* stay on purpose,' she protested. But Davison increased the pressure, and none of Nelson's family or friends would support her, so she was forced to leave. Nelson wrote to a triumphant Emma, 'Let her go to Brighton or wherever she pleases, I care not; she is a great fool and thank god you are not in the least like her.' The stage was clear for Emma to give birth.

Emma locked herself in her room and crossed her fingers, praying for a boy. Only the wealthiest women, whose heirs were of paramount importance, paid for a doctor to attend a routine childbirth, but Emma paid £100 for medical services, so she must have hired a doctor, midwife and nurse. The child was born around 28 January 1801. It was a girl. Emma was not too disappointed for she planned to get pregnant again very quickly and give Nelson a son. Now that the baby was born, she was relieved that he was away. She did not want to risk him developing any sort of familiarity with the doctor and midwife, to whom it was evident that she was not giving birth for the first time. Nelson wanted to call the baby Emma, but she overruled him and named her Horatia. A very rare name for a girl, it was the most ridiculously obvious declaration possible that the baby was Nelson's child.

'I believe poor dear Mrs Thomson's friend will go mad with joy,' bubbled the new father when he heard. He 'does nothing but rave about you and her'. Most men in the period were fathers by thirty. Nelson, exulting 'I never had a dear pledge of love til you gave me one,' was embarking on fatherhood at forty-three.[279] Surrounded by men with families of five or more, Nelson had been burningly conscious of his childlessness. Now he had proof: Fanny was infertile, not him. Bursting with glee, he suggested that his daughter should be registered as born of Johem and Morata Etnorbe, the surname being Bronte backwards and the former anagrams of 'Emma' and 'Hora', with an extra few letters added to make it sound more like a name. It was accepted practice for astute mistresses – particularly those who had essentially obtained the status of common-law wife – to press for the establishment of a settlement for their child as soon as possible after the birth. Emma did not do so because she was sure that there was no need: Nelson, she thought, would never fail to provide for Horatia and herself.

Doctors and midwives told women to shut themselves up in their rooms for weeks after birth, keeping the fires burning high and never opening the windows. Nelson instructed her to stay in bed for a week and at home for a fortnight, but Emma wanted to reveal her victory to the nation. Defiant and triumphant, she retrieved a glamorous evening dress and made a spectacular appearance at a concert at the house of the Duke of Norfolk in St James's Square on 1 February, only a few days after the birth. Sir Harry Fetherstonhaugh and Charles Greville were among the guests.[280] Gossip columnists scrambled to file suggestive reports about Lady Hamilton's lovely new figure. Emma was flaunting the return of her beauty and also demonstrating that, because she was not hiding at home, she was well and the baby was alive.*

Emma had played a difficult game, ensuring everyone knew she was the mother of Nelson's child, but without suggesting she had intended to court newspaper attention. Aware that women could be elevated one day and eviscerated the next, Emma worked hard to keep the newspapers on her side by pretending to be a woman who did not actively court their attention but 'allowed' it if it came her way. A flurry of gossip and jokes in the newspapers followed the birth. Caricaturists were just as quick. James Gillray worked overtime drawing Emma as *Dido in Despair* and it was immediately displayed in pride of place in the print shops. A heavily pregnant Emma in her nightdress (a joke on her revealing muslin dresses) throws an attitude of misery. Out of the window, we see Nelson's ships sailing away.[281] Gillray portrays Emma's bedroom as littered with Sir William's broken statues, erotic art and a book of her Attitudes. Sir William slumbers on in bed, oblivious. Emma's poor ankles are heavily swollen from pregnancy. It was impossible for anyone to misunderstand Gillray's point: Emma was massively pregnant and about to give birth. Like Dido (and not Cleopatra), Emma weeps alone, keeping her grief to her bedroom, just as society believed a woman should.

Five days later, Gillray produced another caricature exploiting the birth of Nelson's child. In *A Cognocenti Contemplating ye Beauties of ye Antique*, a wizened Sir William hunches in his collection rooms surrounded by broken stone phalluses and cracked pots, examining a bust of Emma missing a nose. A pot was a figure for the (unsatisfied) woman in caricatures, and Gillray means his reader to infer that Emma's husband was impotent. On the walls in front of him are three portraits: a topless Emma in a version of Romney's *Mirth*, Nelson looking manly, and Vesuvius exploding with the fire Sir William lacked. He had, as everyone now knew, been well and truly cuckolded.

Emma quickly recovered her health. Convalescing in close, hot rooms put women at severe risk of catching puerperal fever and Emma's decision to venture out undoubtedly improved her health. A romantic man like Nelson might hope that his children would be breast-fed, believing

---

* Women who wanted to give birth covertly hurried abroad or to a country retreat. Because she needed to prove she had been pregnant by showing herself off as swollen and then recovered, Emma had chosen to have her baby in one of the most conspicuous houses in London.

that breast milk carried spirit and character, but Emma could not keep the child at 23 Piccadilly. Everybody loved to joke about her baby but no one would visit her home if they thought the baby was present and she would be publicly reviled if she was ever seen with her child.

A few days later, Mrs Cadogan wrapped her granddaughter in a muff and furs and, perhaps accompanied by Emma, hurried in a hired cab from 23 Piccadilly, to the home of a Mrs Gibson at 9 Little Titchfield Street, Marylebone. Mrs Gibson seemed to be discreet. Her lack of a husband was a bonus, for men tended to be more alert to the opportunities for selling stories to the newspapers. Emma paid Mrs Gibson handsomely to care for Horatia and hire a wet-nurse. The gentry routinely sent children out of the home for the first eighteen months or so. Only the upper aristocracy had nannies and wet-nurses living with them, and Emma's behaviour would have been little different if her child had been legitimate. She had to express her milk at home to ease her discomfort, once again separated from a baby daughter only a few days after her birth.

Soon, Emma had a second problem to deal with. The Prince of Wales had decided she had 'hit his fancy'. He had admired Emma for years and, to Nelson's intense jealousy, owned portraits of her. 'I know his aim is to have you for a mistress,' moaned Nelson to Emma on 4 February. The Prince was separated from the Princess of Wales and his only other regular lover since 1800 was modest Mrs Fitzherbert, who lacked the sexy, blowsy allure he adored. There was a definite vacancy for a new and glamorous woman in his life. Emma was just his type: strong-minded, stylish and adored by the public. Nelson was terrified. It seemed to him that Fanny's insinuation that Emma was incapable of the fidelity needed to be his partner might well prove true after all.

40

The Prince and the Showgirl

'Oh God, why do I live?' Nelson wailed about a week after the birth of Horatia. 'I am mad, almost dead . . . God strike him blind if he looks at you.' Even the newspapers were beginning to hint at the Prince of Wales's passion for Nelson's Cleopatra. 'I am in tears, I cannot bear it.'

The Prince could give Emma anything she desired: a Mayfair mansion, her own carriage with six white horses, showers of diamonds, Court dresses, and introductions to anyone she desired. An affair with the Prince would make her very famous, courted by aristocrats, mobbed in her carriage, the toast of dressmakers, the star of every fashion plate. Nelson mournfully decided himself a poor prize in comparison. 'I am only fit to be second or third, or four' in Emma's heart. It was obvious to him – and to the newspapers – that becoming the Prince's mistress would be Emma's revenge on the Royal Family for not inviting her to Court, and it would also solve her financial problems. Even worse, she might have her eye on marriage. Nelson rued, 'you would grace a Court better as a Queen than a visitor'. The Prince was a fabulous prize. As Nelson whimpered, 'no one, not even Emma, could resist the serpent's tongue'.

Emma was still uncomfortable after the birth, longing to be with her child, and trying to play hostess while pandering to a fretful Sir William. Even worse, a nurse, probably one of the wet-nurses, was threatening to talk and had to be bribed. And now Nelson, only a few days after he claimed to be dancing with joy, was bombarding her with frantic letters full of explicit references to her as the Prince's courtesan. Most women did not resume sexual relations until at least four weeks after giving birth, and Emma was in no state to be making love with anybody, let alone the party-loving Prince of Wales. Nelson could not think rationally. Suffering from stress and searing eye pain, which he could only dull with opium, he implored, 'I cannot, will not believe you can be false. No, I judge you by myself; I hope to be dead before that should happen, but it will not. Forgive me, Emma, oh, forgive your own dear, disinterested Nelson.' In a muddle of feelings he scribbled she was 'kind and good to an old friend with one arm, a broken head, and no teeth'.[282] 'Hush, hush my poor heart keep in my breast, be calm. Emma is true!' He declared that his coded alter ego, Mr Thompson, 'is almost distracted; he wishes there was peace', so that he could 'instantly quit all the world and its greatness to live with you a domestic, quiet life', because he 'doats on you and the child'. Nelson even promised to sacrifice the chance to beat Bonaparte just to be with Emma.

The prospect of the Prince coming to dinner tipped him into hysteria. 'I would bawl with my whole strength and my last breath should say do not suffer him into your home.'[283] He had visions of Emma performing the suggestive songs to her Royal guest that she had once sung to him. Late at night he scrawled, 'Will you sing for the fellow, The Prince, unable to Conceal His Pain? No you will not . . . He will propose if you – no, you will not try; he is Sir Wm's guest.' Before he could send the letter, he received one from Emma. He replied:

> I have just got your letter, and I live again. DO NOT let the lyar come . . . May God Blast him! Be firm . . . Do not, I beseech you, risk being at home. Does Sir William want you to be a whore to the rascal? Forgive all my letter; you will see what I feel, and have felt. I have eat not a morsel, except a little rice, since yesterday morning, and till I know how this matter is gone off. But I feel confident of your resolution and thank you 1,000,000 of times . . . Did you sit alone with the villain for a moment? No, I will not believe it! Oh, God! oh, God! keep my sences. Do not let the rascal in.

The Prince could not attend and instead Greville invited Emma to attend a soirée with the Prince at the house of another aristocrat, probably the Duke of Devonshire. 'Tell the Duke that you will never go to the house,' Nelson thundered. 'Mr G must be a scoundrel; he treated you once ill enough, & cannot love you, or he would sooner die.'

Nelson hardly ate, abandoning himself to lurid fantasies. 'I might be trusted with 50 virgins naked in a dark room,' he raved. He suspected that Sir William was using Emma as bait to encourage the Prince's assistance in his efforts to gain a pension and some compensation for his losses. After all, if Sir William had turned a blind eye to Nelson's frantic courting of Emma in Palermo, he was hardly about to start playing the jealous husband over visits from the Prince of Wales.

Emma was deeply hurt by Nelson's accusations. She had been unfaithful to Sir William only once – with him. It was rumoured that King George's madness was returning and everybody believed the Prince might soon be Regent. All London wanted to invite him for dinner. Nelson was being naive: if Emma did manage to become friendly with the Prince, it would also assist his position. Infuriated that he had called her a whore, Emma accused him of cruelty, and suggested that he was the one with the wandering eye. Nelson wrote, 'I am alone with your letters, except the cruel one, that is burnt, and I have scratched out all the scolding words, and have read them 40 times over . . . again I intreat you never to scold me, for I have never deserved it from you, you know.' But he had – Emma was his faithful lover, struggling to keep life together without him, and she did not deserve to be called 'a whore to the rascal'.

Emma was flattered by the Prince's attentions. He courted women intensively. One reported he writhed on the floor in front of her, sobbing and vowing eternal love, promising to break with all his other ladies and swearing that she 'should be his sole confidante, sole advisor – private or public'.[284] Most women responded to his pleas, flattered by such emotional attentions from the heir to the throne. Emma might sing for him, show him her Attitudes, flirt, and allow him to tease her that he had been her client at the Temple, but it went no further.

As 23 Piccadilly was bombarded with Nelson's letters, Sir William grew concerned about Emma. Then Nelson hit a new level of frenzy when he ranted, 'rather let the lowest wretch that walks the streets dine at his table than that unprincipled lyar . . . Sir William never can admit him into his house, nor can any friend advise him to it unless they are determined on your hitherto unimpeached character being ruined. No modest woman would suffer it. He is permitted to visit only houses of notorious ill fame.' Emma was devastated by his comparison of her house to one of 'ill fame'. Even the man who claimed to love her more than life seemed obsessed with her background. She wept so violently that she gave herself a migraine. It was the last straw for Sir William.

Whether Emma will be able to write to you today is a question, as she has got one of her terrible sick headaches. Among other things that vex her is that we have been drawn in to be under the absolute necessity of giving a dinner to the Prince of Wales on Sunday next. He asked it himself having expressed his strong desire of hearing Banti's and Emma's voices together . . . Emma would really have gone to any lengths to have avoided Sunday's dinner, but I thought it would not be prudent to break with the prince who really has shown the greatest civility to us . . . and she has at last acquiesced to my opinion. I have been thus explicit as I know your lordship's way of thinking and your very kind attachment to us.

Sir William added he was 'well aware of the danger that would attend the prince's frequenting our house', not because he thought Emma might 'ever be induced to act contrary to the prudent conduct she has hitherto pursued' but for fear that the newspapers might misinterpret her hospitality. His is a remarkable letter: a husband writes to his wife's lover, assuring him that she is being faithful. It shows how much the *Tria Juncta in Uno* depended on each other. When he remarked that 'the world is so ill-natured that the worst construction is put upon the most innocent actions', he implied Nelson was being similarly unfair.

Around 23 February, a very remorseful Nelson wrote to Emma that he had 'forgot all his ill health, and all his mortifications and sorrows, in the thought that he will soon bury them all in your dear, dear bosom'. He declared, 'I daresay twins will again be the fruit of your & his meeting. The thought is too much to bear. Have the thatched cottage ready to receive him, & I will answer that he would not give it up for a queen and a palace.' The 'thatched cottage' was his pet name for her genitalia, while 'twins' was a sexual joke. At the time, intercourse was sometimes described as being 'twinned'. Nelson was fond of Shakespeare and often recited entire passages and he was perhaps thinking of the line in Othello where sexual intercourse is described as the 'beast with two backs'. Sorry at having hurt her, Nelson anticipated a night in bed together.

On the same day as he wrote to Emma to prepare the 'thatched cottage', Nelson was given leave to return home. Travelling through the night by carriage to reach 23 Piccadilly by 7 a.m., he hurried to Emma's arms. King George was ill and the attention of the press was – briefly – diverted. Dreading a recommencement of Fanny's campaign for his attention, he wrote to command her to remain in Brighton. She dared not disobey him. He stayed at Lothian's Hotel in Albemarle Street and Emma introduced him to Horatia at Mrs Gibson's in Marylebone. Nelson fell in love with his infant daughter on the spot, rhapsodising 'a finer Child never was produced by any two persons, it was in truth a love begotten Child'. He decided 'She is in the upper part of her face so like her dear good mother' and burbled, 'If it is like its mother it will be very handsome . . . I think her one, aye, the most beautiful woman of the age.'

41

Precious Jewels

*T*he excited new father returned to his ship at Yarmouth bubbling with happiness. 'My own Dear Wife for such you are in my Eyes and in the face of heaven,' he wrote

there is nothing in this World that I would not do for us to live together and to have our dear little Child with us. I firmly believe that this Campaign will give us peace and then we will sett off for Bronte, in 12 hours we shall be across the Water, and freed from all the nonsense of his friends or rather pretended ones . . . it would bring 100 of tongues and slanderous reports, if I seperated from her which I would do with pleasure the moment we can be united. I want to see her no more. Therefore we must manage till we can quit this Country, or your Uncle dies.

They were still dreaming that they would soon be able to return to Sicily and live in bliss on his estate at Bronte. 'I never did love anyone else,' he promised. He was already quivering with anticipation for his next home leave, 'My longing for you, both person and conversation, you may readily imagine what must be my sensations at the idea of sleeping with you. It setts me on fire even the thought, much more would the reality. I am sure my love and desires are all to you, and if any woman naked was to come to me even as I am this moment thinking of you, I hope it might rot off if I were to touch her even with my hand.'[285] Mr Thompson, he wrote, was 'more in love with her than ever' and 'sorry that she was a little unwell when he was in London as it deprived him of much pleasure, but he is determined to have full scope when he next sees her'.[286]

Nelson's sexual obsession with Emma was tinged with concern about Sir William's power. The law allowed Sir William to banish Emma and keep her daughter. Had he chosen to do so, neither Emma nor Nelson would ever have been able to see their daughter again and after Sir William's death she would go to his heir – namely, Greville. Sir William might have owed his 'dear friend' money, but he technically owned his child and Nelson detested the uneasy balance of power. Hopefully, Emma's husband never found those letters in which his cross friend wished his rival would hurry up and die. Nelson busied himself with pursuing the dream of living with Emma by making provision in his will for her and Horatia. As he wrote, Sir William owed him £927 for expenses in Palermo, £255 lent him in 1800 and £1,094, his half share of expenses of the journey home in 1800. He left this debt in trust (i.e. William would pay it back to Emma, not to Nelson), as well as £1,000 a year for Emma in her lifetime. Nelson guessed that Emma would live for only another twenty years: she would, as it happened, live another fourteen, so he was prescient – strangely so, considering she was only thirty-six.

Nelson's provision for Emma was shoddy. Sir William could not re-imburse the debt and Nelson should have guessed that Greville, as Sir William's heir and executor of his will, would never pay it. In the eighteenth century, property and money, like votes and power, were the business of men, and they guarded them jealously. A man left his estate to his male heirs or relations and they were supposed to care for his wife and female offspring. Nelson may have been sufficiently unconventional to desert his wife and have a child with Emma but he was not independent-minded enough to leave her adequate money to live after his death. Glowing with visions of them living together in his brand new home on the Bronte estate, enjoying his fame after he had beaten Napoleon, he thought he was never going to die.

Nelson was breaking his ties with Fanny. The Admiralty was exas-perated with Josiah's brawling, insubordination and laziness, and not even Nelson's intervention could secure him another ship. Nelson raged to Fanny that he had done all he could for Josiah and commanded her to stop writing to him: 'I neither want nor wish for any body to care what become of me, whether I return or am left dead in the Baltic, seeing I have done all in my power for you . . . my only wish is to be left to myself.' She called it 'Lord Nelson's letter of dismissal' but refused to take 'the least note of it'. She begged sympathy from Nelson's prize agent, Alexander Davison, as well as from Nelson's family, and the

Admiralty Board, declaring she found Nelson's behaviour utterly incomprehensible.

Fanny did just as any other canny eighteenth-century woman would: she ensured that Nelson and all his friends knew he had no grounds to divorce her. She pursued a careful strategy by emphasising to everyone how she was the perfect wife: 'faithful, affectionate, and desirous to do everything I could to please him'.[287] Divorce was difficult and costly. A husband could divorce his wife for adultery, a wife could cite only non-consummation and cruelty. Fanny's letters made it clear: the marriage was 'affectionate' and consummated, she had been entirely faithful, and always his deeply loving wife. She also stressed that she wished the marriage to continue: even if Nelson chose to present himself as cruel, she would refuse to divorce him on such a basis. Her status, her social preeminence and the respect she gained from her peers were contingent on being Nelson's wife, and if she lost him, she lost everything. Fanny stepped up the public relations war against Emma by stressing her excellence to anyone she could find. But she dared not go too far: she wanted to keep her £1,800 a year. Incensed, Nelson instructed Davison, 'Before I arrive in England, signify to Ly N that I expect, and for which I have made such a very liberal allowance to her, to be left to myself, and without any enquiries from her.'

Although Horatia had secured her position in Nelson's heart, Emma felt vulnerable. Her lover hated to hear even the mention of his wife's name so she kept her jealousy secret and plunged her energies into trying to fulfil his dream of a home filled with his family and friends. She infuriated Fanny by attempting to employ Nelson's French butler from Roundwood and trying to win over his siblings. Nelson's clergyman brother, William, wrote unctuously to Emma, 'Your image and voice are constantly before my imagination, and I can think of nothing else . . . It is no wonder that my good, my great, my virtuous, my beloved brother should be so attached to your ladyship.' Nelson's family knew about Emma's pregnancy (William had seen it for himself), guessed it meant he had transferred his loyalties for good, and they were fully prepared to follow.

Emma's lifestyle was ruinously expensive. She and Sir William had chosen one of London's premium rental properties. The lease for a year cost £1,000, and Emma had spent over £2,000 furnishing the house, including £300 on repairing the coach, £300 on wine and coal and £28 on employing an exquisitely fashionable French cook. The named staff included Oliver, Emma's maids, Fatima, Julia and Marianne, a valet and

In Isaac Cruikshank's risqué 1800 caricature, the Lord Mayor of London, Sir William Hamilton and Prime Minister William Pitt enjoy Egyptian tobacco together – but Nelson and Emma only have eyes for each other.

In *Dido in Despair*, published a few days after the birth of Horatia, James Gillray showed Nelson sailing away while Emma weeps, heavily pregnant with his child.

Fanmakers, haberdashers, fashion designers and dress makers were just a few of the manufacturers cashing in on the wild craze for Nelson goods.

Before long, Emma was featuring on commemorative Nelson goods, clutching a picture of the hero or waving him off from the quayside.

Paradise Merton: Emma's beloved home with Nelson.

Horatia Nelson, Emma's daughter
with her lover, aged about four.

Thomas Rowlandson's *Modern
Antiques* ridiculed the set-up at
Merton, showing a crabbed old
Sir William protesting as the
lovers frolic in a mummy's case.

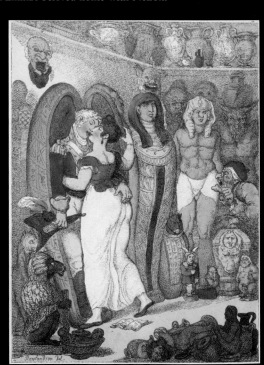

Emma covered Merton
with representations of
her lover and herself –
such as her embroidery
of Nelson and herself
as the famous
sentimental lovers,
Yorick and Maria,
from Laurence Sterne's
novel, *A Sentimental
Journey*.

James Gillray's *Assemblée Nationale; or, Grand Co-operative Meeting at St Ann's Hill*. Emma,
wearing a Nelson miniature around her neck and a feathered headdress gossips with the
Duchess of Devonshire as plump little Charles James Fox and his wife receive the luminaries.

The Death of Admiral Lord Nelson – in the Moment of Victory by James Gillray.
The nation's artists drew Emma into the scene of Nelson's death.

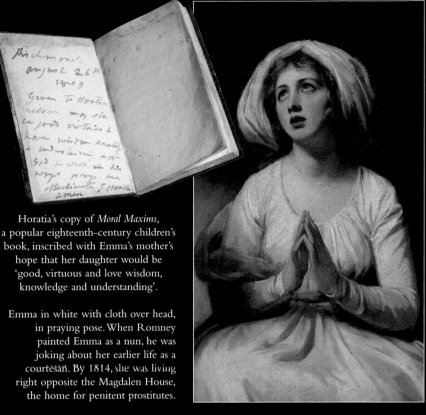

Horatia's copy of *Moral Maxims*,
a popular eighteenth-century children's
book, inscribed with Emma's mother's
hope that her daughter would be
'good, virtuous and love wisdom,
knowledge and understanding'.

Emma in white with cloth over head,
in praying pose. When Romney
painted Emma as a nun, he was
joking about her earlier life as a
courtesan. By 1814, she was living
right opposite the Magdalen House,
the home for penitent prostitutes.

King's Bench Prison, painted by Thomas Rowlandson in 1808,
not long before Emma arrived there.

Emma Hart as *Circe* by George Romney.

butler, coachmen, footmen and housemaids, scullery maids, and kitchen maids. Hiring singers and musicians for evening parties sent costs soaring. Emma opened a bank account with Thomas Coutts, a social climber, known for his generous terms to the Prince of Wales and the aristocracy, although he would not give her a loan. Believing he would soon return to Naples, Sir William was still renting the Palazzo Sessa and the Villa Emma and paying his staff, and he owed more than £6,000 to his bankers. He also had belongings and a coach waiting for him in Palermo. At the end of 1800, no longer able to hide from his debts, he instructed his agent in Naples to give notice on the lease for the Posillipo house and to sell the furniture and other effects from the Palazzo Sessa.

Sir William still hoped for compensation from the British government for his losses at Naples, estimated at around £13,000. Beckford instructed Emma to 'pursue your object with those omnipotent looks, words and gestures with which Heaven has gifted you. By such persevering Efforts, and by such alone, we shall obtain justice.'[288] Emma's flirtatious smiles were hardly going to sway the Foreign Office, who resolutely refused to pay out. The bills for setting up 23 Piccadilly had to be paid, and so Emma agreed to sell most of her diamonds, beginning with those Maria Carolina had given her in Naples. She rewarded her husband for his supportive behaviour over the birth of Horatia with jewels they believed worth £30,000 (£1.8 million) and in return Sir William allowed her to bring Horatia to Piccadilly for a visit. The press were always watching the house and Emma warned Mrs Gibson to ensure Horatia was 'well covered getting in and out of the coach'.[289] In the event, the diamonds were sold for only £2,500 (presumably they were not quite as precious as Maria Carolina had implied) and the Hamiltons soon fell into debt again. Sir William heard that the coach he had bought just before they fled Naples was 'so heavy no tolerable offer was ever made for it', and the furniture from the Palazzo Sessa was equally unsaleable.[290] They hoped Nelson would capture enemy ships in the North Sea and return with prize money, but in the meantime Sir William was forced to take drastic measures. He advertised an auction of his belongings at Christie's. Aiming to generate huge publicity, he made it known that he would be selling most of his portraits of Emma.

'I see clearly, my dearest friend, you are on SALE,' Nelson agonised to Emma. 'I am almost mad to think of the iniquity of wanting you to associate with a set of whores, bawds, & unprincipled lyars.' He was wretched at the thought of his darling exposed to the crowds at Christie's.

'I am really miserable, I look at all your pictures, at your dear hair, I am ready to cry.' He begged Davison to remove one portrait from the auction, the notorious *Bacchante* by Vigée le Brun in which Emma reclines on a leopard-skin rug. Vigée le Brun's works sold for spectacular prices, particularly because she had painted few English subjects. Christie's demanded £300, but Nelson would have paid any sum. Exhilarated by his catch, Nelson wrote to Emma that if it 'had cost me 300 drops of blood I would have given it with pleasure'. He was blunt as ever. 'If you was single and I found you under a hedge, I would instantly marry you. Sir Wm has a treasure, and does he want to throw it away? That other chap [Greville] did throw away the most precious jewel that God Almighty ever set on this earth.' The sudden disappearance of one of the most celebrated paintings set tongues wagging – and made Emma even more notorious. While Nelson was away, she cut her hair to match the latest Paris fashion for short hair. When she revealed her new look, a boyish cut curling around the ears that left the neck enticingly bare, women dashed to hairdressers to follow her lead.

A visit to 23 Piccadilly was the hottest ticket in town, particularly thanks to the patronage of the Royal brothers and the Whig circle of the Duchess of Devonshire. Nelson was gratified she was courting London's fashionable set and welcoming his family and friends but he had no clue about the costs of being a grand hostess. Emma was borrowing heavily, but this time she was doing so against the prospect of Nelson's next win, receiving credit by presenting herself as his mistress.

On 12 March, Nelson departed for the Baltic. As the *Morning Herald* joked, 'A celebrated *female attitudinarian* ever since our Northern Squadron has put to sea has thrown aside all the lighter airs, and positions of gaiety, confining her imitative talents to those of a graver cast. Cleopatra arrayed in *mournful graces* is now the model that she daily copies.'[291]

'I burn all your dear letters because it is right for your sake,' Nelson hinted to Emma. 'I wish you would burn all mine. They can do no good and will do us both harm if any seizure of them, or the dropping even one of them would fill the mouths of the world.'[292] But Emma kept every letter, lovingly dwelling on his every word, although perhaps not when he wrote to her that he saw her crying, dressed in black, and then 'I dreamt last night that I beat you with a stick on account of that fellow [the Prince of Wales] and then attempted to throw over your head a tub of Boiling hot water, you may believe I awoke in an agony.'[293]

The jealous hero soon had fighting to distract him. The government suspected the Danes might ally with the Tsar of Russia and the French and sent Nelson to Copenhagen to look threatening and do some sabre rattling. He ended up engaged in a full-scale attack on a country with which England was not officially at war. The Battle of Copenhagen was an equivocal victory and a public relations disaster. Nelson's enemies claimed he had proposed a truce because he could no longer fight and that he had in fact capitulated. Three hundred and fifty of his men were killed and a thousand injured. The English government advised citizens to spend their money not on celebratory flags but on donations to the many widows and orphans of the dead seamen.

When she heard the news on 15 April, Emma threw a dinner party for a Neapolitan duke, the actor John Kemble and various socialites. She entertained the guests by performing a tarantella with her glamorous Sudanese maid, Fatima. Writer, Nathaniel Wraxall, felt rather faint watching her perform a scene about a nymph and satyr or bacchante and faun (a pose in which Emma had posed for Romney). He decided it 'certainly not of a nature to be performed except before a select company, from the screams, attitudes, starts, and embraces with which it was intermingled'.[294] Now Emma was no longer pregnant, the Attitudes became risqué once more.

Nelson wrote to Emma after his victory at Copenhagen, 'very tired after a hard won battle', and sent her a few sweet lines, addressing her as 'Lord Nelson's Guardian Angel'. 'I leave my anchor in my Angel's heart,' he continued and reminisced how 'this day twelve months we sailed from Palermo on our tour to Malta. Ah! those were happy times, days of ease and nights of pleasure.' On 26 April, he gave a party on his ship to celebrate Emma's birthday and had his mates and superior officer, Sir Hyde Parker, raise champagne toasts to 'the Birthday of Santa Emma'. Convinced she brought him good luck, he heaped her with compliments, declaring 'there is certainly more of the angel than the human being about you'.[295]

42

Paradise Merton

No detail was too insignificant for Nelson's passionate letters to Emma. He described how he had not cut his nails since February for 'I should have thought it a treason to have them cut, as long as there was a possibility of my returning for my old dear friend to do the job for me.' He was nervous, suffering from palpitations and was 'more emaciated than you can conceive'.[296] Intent on spending every possible minute on his return with Emma, he was tired of snatching time with her in Sir William's house and hotels. He wanted Emma to find him a home.

Even though she had Horatia, Emma's position was not secure. Crowds of starstruck girls, powerful aristocrats, respectable wives and fine ladies were desperate for a piece of England's hero. Nelson, always a social climber, was most attracted by the aristocrats. Emma knew his fondness for kissing hands, bowing, flattering and making suggestive comments, and she had to ensure that no rival stole his heart, as she had done. She felt stronger on her own territory, and she knew that sharing a house with Nelson would confirm her as his mistress, controller of his patronage and head of his domestic life.

Sir William continued to take on the cost of caring for Emma Carew while Nelson remained unaware of her existence. In April, taking advantage of Nelson's absence, Emma paid for her ever-reliable mother to visit the Kidds in Hawarden and then Manchester, to see Emma, now nearly twenty. It would seem that she had been unhappy as a governess or had retired because of ill-health for she was living back with Mrs Blackburn and no longer working. There were still no precise plans for her future.

When the hero of Copenhagen arrived in England on 30 June, he immediately hired a decorated post-chaise drawn by six fine stallions, rattling to 23 Piccadilly where the lovers were reunited. Emma planned a break at Box Hill in Surrey, along with her husband where, Nelson wrote 'we are all very happy'. The party then set off for a fishing holiday on the Thames along with William Nelson and his wife and daughter, two of Nelson's officers and Captain Edward Parker, Nelson's latest protégé. They spent a fortnight soaking up the sun, staying at the Bush Inn in Staines. Sir William fished contentedly while the lovers boated and walked, joining up with the rest of the party for raucous dinners at the inn. The holiday came to an abrupt end with the news that Napoleon was preparing to invade England. Nelson was called to Whitehall and sent to protect the south coast between Orfordness and Beachy Head. There he waited dolefully, obsessed with his desire for a home.

Nelson wanted a palatial mansion and grounds in which he could play at being a country squire. It also had to be comfortably furnished, situated on a good road to London and not too expensive. 'I am very anxious for a house and I have nobody to do any business for me but you, my dear friend,' he chivvied. Emma was enthused by the responsibility of choosing a house and by 1 August, he authorised her to buy one she had seen at Turnham Green. The newspapers followed her efforts – *The Times* reported that on an outing to Harrow with Sir William's relation, the Marquis of Abercorn, the horses tipped Emma and the Marchioness into a hedge.[297] On the 15th, she was considering another property in Chiswick. At the same time, Nelson led an attack on Boulogne that ended in disaster: no French boats were taken, and 44 English sailors were left dead with 128 wounded. Although Nelson had brushed off criticism of the Battle of Copenhagen, he knew that his attack on Boulogne had been a terrible failure. He sailed back to Deal on the Kent coast, deeply depressed, begging his friends to come and comfort him.

Emma had good news for him. She had spotted what she thought could be their dream home in the village of Merton in Surrey. Nelson eagerly put in an offer. No one else wanted to buy it. The upkeep of the house had proved too much for its widowed seller, Mrs Greaves. The rooms needed modernising, the land was uncultivated, and there was no stabling or coach house. The surveyor was horrified by the situation of the house, judging it 'the worst place under all its circumstances that I ever saw pretending to suit a Gentleman's family'. When his solicitor advised him to demand a discount on the price, Nelson exploded with frustration against equivocating lawyers and their 'hard bargains'.[298] Claiming to admire the man who could make a decision on the spot, he commanded, 'I cannot afford a fine house and grounds therefore I wish for Merton as it is.'[299] Desperate to live with Emma, he refused to be delayed by petty disagreements.

So that Emma could visit Nelson without any impropriety in the eyes of society, Sir William rushed down from a business trip in Wales to be her chaperone. They took suites in a luxury hotel along with Nelson's brother's wife, Sarah. Emma had been busily winning the affections of Sarah and her two children, Horace and Charlotte. Bowled over by Emma's connections and riches, Sarah leapt to take advantage of an all-expenses paid trip to the sea. Nelson was gloomy, despite their efforts to make him smile. Young Captain Parker was dying from a wound he had received at Boulogne, and his state was a daily reminder to Nelson of the failure at Boulogne. After her morning dip, Emma rushed to tend Parker's brow with soothing milks and warm poultices, but there was little she and Sarah could do for the little 'Nelsonite' as she called him.

When she set off back north in her carriage after over a fortnight with Nelson, Emma was determined to win him his house. On 18 September, Nelson bought Merton Place for £9,000, borrowing money from his friend Davison, with the expectation of moving in on 10 October. 'I hope you will always love Merton,' he wrote excitedly to Emma.[300] Her first task was to find his belongings at Dod's warehouse and separate them from Fanny's. Nelson had been infuriated by Fanny's habit of asking for his help and advice about the tiniest decision: Emma resolved to manage alone. He ordered her to spend freely on furniture and supplies without bothering him with the details, instructing, 'I entreat I may never hear about the expenses again . . . at Merton I must keep a table.'

Mrs Greaves, the owner of Merton Place, had heard that Lord Nelson was the buyer, and she desired to remain in her home. Emma, however, was impatient to occupy the house and was eager that Nelson should see it furnished to his taste. She wished Mrs Greaves to move out immediately and instructed her lawyers to force her to leave. Furniture was arriving from Portsmouth, trees and shrubs were about to be delivered, and the painters were ready to start work. After some tense arguments, Mrs Greaves finally agreed to move. Emma and Sir William rattled down in their carriages a few days later. He was looking forward to relaxing in the country, she was ready to start work.

'I am in silent distraction,' wrote Nelson to Emma at the end of September, looking despondently around his cabin. 'The four pictures of Lady Hn are hung up, but alas! I have lost the original . . . How can I bear our separation?'[301] His mood was so fragile after the debacle at Boulogne that Emma worried that he might be disappointed. Sir William aimed to buoy her confidence and wrote to Nelson to extol Merton as a superb bargain: 'perfect retirement' only an hour from Hyde Park, requiring only cosmetic improvements and full of excellent furniture. 'I never saw so many conveniences united in so small a compass.' He promised Nelson he would 'enjoy immediately'. If all this was not enough, since the purchase, it had become public knowledge that Napoleon was unlikely to invade, so the house had increased in value by at least £1,000 (more than £60,000 in today's money). With Sir William's help, Emma promoted herself to Nelson as the antithesis of Fanny: efficient, shrewd and indomitable. 'Well done farmer's wife!' the hero bubbled. 'You will make us rich with your economy.' Nelson the publicity lover paid her his ultimate compliment: he imagined her turned into a caricature to be sold in the print shops. He decided 'the Beautiful Emma rowing the one-armed Admiral in a boat' around the grounds 'should certainly be caricatured'. But Emma would need all her energy to turn ramshackle Merton into a home for a hero.

A heavy, symmetrical Queen Anne style square, Merton Place was rather like a smaller, much cheaper version of Sir Harry Fetherstonhaugh's Uppark. Similar homes dotted all of Britain – but Nelson's was bigger and far more chaotic. Off the large entrance hall, there was a dining room to the left and a drawing room to the right. Behind the drawing room were a breakfast room and a room that Emma would transform into a library, then pantries and servants' quarters.[302] Upstairs was the main drawing room, five large bedrooms and a sizeable attic space. Divided by a road that is now Merton High Street was an expanse of good, but rather unkempt land. The small canal running through the grounds was, according to the anguished surveyor, a 'broad ditch, which keeps the whole place damp'.

Nelson described the house as the 'farm', and he wanted the fashionable country life. Emma planned to turn the land around the house into expensive landscaped gardens, and use the rest as pasture for animals. She set about discussing plans with gardeners, buying shrubs and trees, filling the stream and ponds with fish and filling the grounds with chubby pigs, poultry and sheep. Sir William conjured a bucolic image of 'Emma and her mother fitting up pig-sties and hen-coops, & already the Canal is enlivened with ducks & the cock is strutting with his hens about the walk'. Emma renamed the 'ditch' the Nile and built an Italian bridge over it. She arranged to rent the nearby fields and granary for £55 per annum so that Nelson could control the land he saw from his window.[303] Emma was soon growing vegetables and brewing beer, although their milk, cheese and meat, as well as fruit, came from neighbourhood farmers. Merton was not far from Marie Antoinette's fantasy of playing shepherdesses: it looked like a pretty farm, but it was neither self-sufficient nor economical. The rustic vision depended on Emma buying animals ready grown and putting fish into ponds in which they would not breed.

Emma planned to transform the house into a spectacular celebration of Nelson's genius, lavishly stuffed with mirrors, thick carpets, gold trimmings, and memorabilia. She obeyed Nelson's command to spare no expense and decided it should be an imposing double-fronted mansion atop a long sweep of drive and graceful gardens. They would build an enormous modern kitchen, suitable for extravagant entertaining, and develop a cubby into a proper cellar for their vintage wines. The bedrooms would be completely remodelled – fit to house the most eminent guests – and she planned to add a dressing room and modern water closet to the master bedroom, as well as putting eight servants' rooms in the attic to house her visitors' staff. Ambitious to make the house as light as possible, she resolved to add glass doors at the front, a long passage with glass doors opening into the lawn behind, and mirrored doors on the principal rooms. Large mirrors were a great luxury, and this was a crazily expensive innovation. Although the house was Nelson's, Emma used her husband's credit, as well as borrowing money herself, to pay for the extravagant alterations. She had one ambition: to turn Merton Place into a representation of her overwhelming love affair with Nelson, and cancel every trace of Fanny from his life.

The interior was soon transformed into a temple to kitsch. Along with mirrors and gold, Emma adorned it with Nelson memorabilia. Her lover instructed her to take from Piccadilly only the portrait of her and a painting of the Battle of the Nile, and to buy the rest. Remembering the chill dreariness of his home with Fanny, Emma adorned Merton Place with Nelson-themed curtains, tea sets, draperies and hangings, as well as paintings of him, swords and relics such as pieces of his ships. Bursting with brand-new goods, souvenirs of Nelson and tributes to his great career, her home was a snub to those who decreed that interior decor should be restrained. Giant 'N's festooned the walls, windows, crockery and ornaments, as well as Emma's dresses. After spending her youth in Sir Harry's Uppark, which was covered wall to ceiling with pictures of the Fetherstonhaughs and their horses, she wanted to show that she owned Merton. Sixteen trunks of Emma's belongings and dresses were still floating around Europe (they ended up back in Naples), but she no longer needed her old things. One early visitor, Lord Minto, the ex-envoy to Vienna who had entertained them on their visit to the city, was struck dumb by the decoration. Minto, who came from a class who inherited houses ready furnished, goggled. 'Not only the rooms, but the whole house, staircase and all, are covered with nothing but pictures of her and him, of all sizes and sorts, and representations of his naval actions, coats of arms, pieces of plate in his honour, the flagstaff of L'Orient etc.' He dubbed the house a 'mere looking-glass to view himself all day'.[304]

Lady Hamilton's taste in decoration set the tone for a nation deep in the throes of a Nelson cult. Thousands of women expressed their fervent admiration for the hero by stocking their homes in Nelson dinner plates, drawer handles, plant pots, chests and pictures. Fashion plates showed whole rooms decorated in the style of Nelson and offered suggestions on how to decorate windows to pay tribute to him – blue curtains with anchors, gold ties with anchors and a red swagging. In decorating their homes 'alla Nelson', Emma and the thousands of other Britons who followed her were displaying their political loyalties for all to see. Since there were no restaurants in which to entertain clients, friends, and family, nearly all social occasions from board meetings to job interviews, secret business coups and meetings with lawyers to firing employees, christenings to marriage proposals was carried out in the home. The ways in which a couple decorated their house directed the ways in which they were perceived by friends, relations, colleagues and clients. Led by Emma, British homes in the period of the Napoleonic Wars were a riot of brand-new glitz and colour. Very far from our modern vision of the eighteenth century as the age of elegance and taste, homes were gaudy and cluttered, covered in bright clashing colours, the ornaments a mishmash of souvenirs and tacky impulse buys.

Emma's taste chimed perfectly with the desire of those of the middle classes, many newly rich, to display their wealth and show themselves as Nelson's fervid supporters. She was the high priestess of the Nelson cult, and he loved her for it. A man who preferred watching theatrical versions of his own triumph at the Nile to any other play, he was enchanted by a house in which everything he saw bore a picture of him.

On 23 October, Nelson arrived at dawn in a post-chaise and four horses, through a triumphal arch erected by the villagers at the front of the house. Emma had encouraged them to welcome her lover in style by covering their homes in lights, lining the road to cheer and setting off fireworks when they saw him approaching.

In awe of their illustrious neighbour they – with Emma's encouragement – had organised a grand fête. They set off fireworks and illuminated their houses. Delighted by his new home, he was quick to take on the role of village squire by instructing Emma to use only local tradesmen and planning to patronise the parish church. 'We are all so joyous today, we do not know what to do,' Emma gloried. She arranged for him to meet Horatia at 23 Piccadilly. It was 10 o'clock on a Monday and Sir William tactfully arranged to pay a visit to his dealers. Now a sturdy ten months old, Horatia was not shy. Father and daughter were immediate friends.

The bustle of Merton made Sir William feel old. He knew he was too infirm to return to his beloved Naples so he instructed his agent in the city to discharge the servants still waiting for him at the Palazzo Sessa. Vincenzo, his valet, was devastated that Hamilton had not offered him a pension for years of faithful service. He was soon, as the agent pleaded, struggling 'in very narrow Circumstances, with a large family', but Sir William ignored his plight. Neapolitan tradesmen tried to call in their debts from him.[305] The government had awarded him a pension of just over £1,000 a year, but he still owed over £12,000. Fortunately for him, Nelson was adamant that Emma's husband would not own a single item in the house, although they split the day-to-day expenses of the house. Despite his debts, Sir William was a spendthrift and too old to change. Freed from the bother of having to buy new furniture, still convinced that the government would compensate him for the loss of his possessions in Naples, and confident that Nelson would secure a big prize at sea, he spent wildly on food, clothes and antiques.

At Merton, Emma addressed herself to winning over Nelson's elderly father, inviting him to stay for ten days in November. The visit went off perfectly. Ill and weak, eighty-year-old Edmund welcomed Emma's tender nursing, falling head over heels in love with her. He was tempted to move in full time, but he could not bear to leave his beloved Norfolk. Emma was also trying to mould Nelson's greedy relations into the loving, unselfish, worshipping family he desired. His sisters, Kitty and Susanna, had married George Matcham and Thomas Bolton respectively, men of energy but not much money, and they were always looking for help for their packs of children. Susanna had twin girls in their early twenties, a young son, and two pre-teenage daughters, and Kitty had five children under the age of twelve, and gave birth to another girl in 1801, naming her Horatia as a tribute to Emma's daughter. Kitty was almost constantly breast-feeding or pregnant throughout the early 1800s and she relied on her brother and his mistress to help her make ends meet.

Emma entertained the Matchams and Boltons to lavish dinners at Merton and 23 Piccadilly and tried to mediate the demands of his brother, William, and his wife Sarah. 'If we could but get some little addition to our Income, we should be more independent & be in Town whenever you liked,' pressed Sarah Nelson.[306] She extracted favours from Emma by promising to win Nelson's sister, Susanna Bolton, over to her side by telling her 'how *pleasant* & good you are & that I loved you dearly, & tell them every thing you gave me. I did bring down one of Charlotte's Frocks, which you gave her, which they shall see I Love.'[307] Nelson paid the fees at Eton for their son, Horace, and she wanted Emma to transform her lumpy daughter into a society debutante. Emma, presumably using Sir William's money, paid for thirteen-year-old Charlotte's education at an expensive girls' school in Chelsea, as well as dancing lessons, a singing teacher, outings and plays for her and her school friends and cousin at weekends.[308] Sarah wrote to Charlotte, without the 'accomplishments' gained with Lady Hamilton, 'you would be nothing'.[309]

Nelson anointed Emma 'Lady Paramount of all the territories and waters of Merton, and we are all to be your guests, and to obey all lawful commands'. Her frantic efforts won her his total loyalty. It appears that she finally felt sufficiently secure to tell him about Emma Carew. She found she had been worrying for nothing: Nelson was unruffled by the secret and was happy to meet her. Emma invited little Emma for a visit, but her husband worried about gossip if she stayed at 23 Piccadilly. As Nelson wrote to Emma, 'if your relative cannot stay in your house in town, surely Sir William can have no objection to your taking [her] to the farm'. Emma's female relations, such as Mrs Cadogan's sister Connor and her children, tended to visit in groups: this sole relation, unwanted by Sir William, was most likely Miss Carew. Nelson soon became fond of her. As he later wrote when away at sea, 'I would not have my Emma's relative go without seeing her.'

Fanny heard the news that her husband had set up home in Merton. She made a last-ditch attempt to regain her position. 'Do my dear husband, let us live together,' she wrote. 'I can never be happy till such an event takes place.' Alexander Davison returned it to her and curtly inscribed on the back, 'Opened by mistake by Lord Nelson, but not read', without adding another word of comfort.[310] Nelson never wrote to Fanny again.

Emma planned an elaborate first family Christmas. On 14 December, Emma sent an urgent message to Mrs Gibson, demanding that she bring Horatia to Merton in a post-chaise on the following day. 'Do not fail,' she begged.[311] A document found buried in an archive shows the similarly painstaking preparation that went into her dramatic extravaganzas. To perform her piece 'The Favourite Sultana', Emma planned every detail of the opulent dress for herself and the company, writing down extensive wardrobe notes on her own outfit and those of her attendants. She kept her hair loose (although she had a turban behind the scenes, ready to whip it on at any moment), and braided with strings of pearls, with two long locks of hair curling on the breast. A circlet of diamonds sparkled on her forehead, and draped over her head was a fine crêpe or muslin shawl so long that it reached the floor. Her pantaloons were twilled silk in bright colours – blue or green suited her – and she wore embroidered square-toed Turkish slippers and gold ankle bracelets. Over her pantaloons, she wore a coloured shift and tied the ends of the wide gauze sleeves behind her back. The outer gown was half one colour and half another, perhaps pink and red, and her jacket was a rich satin. Her arms glittered with dozens of bracelets, thick gold rings adorned her fingers, and her necklace was a long gold chain bearing a small perfume flask. The effect was truly spectacular.

Emma gave intricate commands to her assistants. Nelson's two little nieces, Kitty and Lizzy Matcham, as Moorish ladies, wore long pantaloons, gowns striped in two colours, embroidered slippers and veils over their heads. Even dowdy Mrs Cadogan became a Grecian lady, attired in a long white gown with wide embroidered sleeves, and a short bolero-type jacket, and she wore her hair in small curls, pinned under a cap. A 'Miss K', perhaps Emma Carew or the daughter of a neighbour, played a Negro Sultana, dressed in a 'negro mask', a black dress, gold sandals, a coloured turban with a long veil, gold girdle and jewellery, and a rainbow train. The men had roles too: a Major Magra and Nelson's secretary, Mr Tyson, were 'as magnificent as they can dress themselves; whiskers and no beards', neighbours Blow, Cumyng and

Jefferson were 'Moors of Quality' and the artist Thomas Baxter and any other spare gentlemen played slaves, wearing Negro masks, long, wide sleeves, shawls, and 'long pipes and bags'.[312] After a sumptuous dinner, the lights were turned down, the candles were lit against the glittering glass windows and Emma was the star of the show. She made sure that everybody knew that Nelson was her faithful devotee, wholly absorbed in her, his own 'favourite Sultana' and lady of Paradise Merton.

Soon the 'favourite Sultana' had the answer to her prayers. On 25 March 1802, France and Britain agreed the Treaty of Amiens. The war was over.

43
Keeping Nelson

*T*he new peace released Nelson from service and he contentedly settled at Paradise Merton. Although he was on half pay for he was no longer on active service, he wanted to keep his new-found position in society by maintaining an aura of incredible wealth. 'Nelson cannot be like others,' the hero insisted. 'Everybody knows that Lord Nelson is *amazingly rich*.' Emma had to be the proof: fashionable, glamorous, and dripping with expensive jewels, a generous hostess to his relations, his friends, his captains and the aristocrats he needed to cultivate, as well as being a doyenne of the arts, a charitable patroness, his tireless domestic manager and a doting mother. In the four years after he bought Merton, Emma worked hard to live up to his dream.

'I am as much amused by pigs and hens as I was at the Court of Naples,' Emma wrote to a friend.[313] Nelson, she declared, 'seldom goes to town and for that reason is much desired and sought for. "Keeping men off as you keep them on" will do for men as well as women.'* Emma splurged attention on her lover. As Lord Minto sneered, she was always 'cramming Nelson with trowelfuls of flattery, which he goes on taking as quietly as a child does pap'. She invited writers and social commentators to report on their home, adorned with images of their love. Denied a lush wedding or an appearance at Court on his arm, she staged extravagant entertainments. The newspapers reported her every move. She, rather than Lady Nelson, received all the requests for

---

* Emma quotes a famous description of coquettish techniques recommended by Mrs Peachum in John Gay's *The Beggar's Opera*.

patronage, favour and money that streamed toward the great Nile hero. Minto, now a frequent visitor, thought she wanted a reward for her exertions. 'She looks ultimately towards marriage,' he decided.

At the end of April 1802, Nelson heard that his father was seriously ill. Edmund wrote to his son he hoped to recover and 'with the assistance of the May sunshine get able to travel and smell a Merton rose in June'. But he grew sicker and by 24 April, it was clear he was dying. Nelson did not visit him. Although Fanny was not nursing Edmund for relations between them had cooled, Nelson dreaded encountering her if she returned to the deathbed. He was suffering from stomach pain and worried that the coach journey might make it worse. He stayed at Merton to celebrate Emma's thirty-seventh birthday. To distract him from his worry, Emma threw a big party and they gave themselves even more of an excuse for a celebration by christening Emma's Sudanese maid. Fatima Emma Charlotte Nelson Hamilton was recorded in the parish register as 'a negress, about 20 years of age'.[314] On the same day, Edmund Nelson's fragile grip on life loosened and he died at Bath. Many men tried to avoid deathbed scenes (it was seen as women's work), but Nelson declined even to attend the funeral. Distressed that Nelson's behaviour might be considered callous, Emma publicly excused him by declaring that his stomach was causing him such pain that he might need a surgical operation.

Meanwhile, Sir William was making plans to visit his Welsh estates. Emma decided to turn his summer business trip into a triumphal tour for Nelson. Tours were the business of royals, and the idea that a mere admiral might saunter around the country charming the ordinary people was unprecedented. Emma's plan was shrewd: the King hated travelling and visited only Weymouth and the surrounding area for holidays, and his provincial subjects were starved of glamour and celebrity. In planning their tour to cities that never saw anyone from London but merchants, she was determined to capitalise on public affection for Nelson and make herself as famous as the Queen.

Emma invited the William Nelsons to accompany them, and left her mother in charge of Merton. On 21 July, four carriages loaded with servants, maids, secretaries and endless changes of outfit rolled out of London and westwards to Wales. Oxford awarded Nelson the freedom of the city, and he and Sir William received the honorary degrees of Doctor of Civil Law. Shops along the way did a roaring trade in Nelsonia and the whole population of Gloucester came out to wave Nelson portraits, hats and ribbons at them. At Ross on Wye, the party took a boat garlanded with laurel for the seventy-mile journey to Monmouth, escorted by hundreds of little boats, while thousands of fans cheered from the banks of the river. The Mayor of Monmouth received them on the banks while cannons sounded a salute from a nearby hill. After travelling up through mid-Wales, they reached Milford Haven by night-fall, where a cattle show, a rowing match and a fair had all been laid on in their honour. Nelson and Emma basked in the adoring atten-tion.

Sir William checked on his estates, and the party set off home through South Wales. Pembroke, Swansea, Cardiff and Newport welcomed them with feasts, receptions, fireworks and colossal banquets – where Emma always performed songs in Nelson's honour, often the version of 'God Save the King' converted to praise him. Hysterical crowds unhitched the party's horses and dragged the carriage through the streets. As they progressed through Hereford, Leominster, Ludlow, Worcester and Birmingham, press packs from the London papers followed behind, eager to keep their readers up to date with the extravagant tour. The *Morning Post* reported that Nelson received a branch of an apple tree from the city of Hereford and 'his Lordship, with all the gallantry of Paris, presented the apple to Lady Hamilton, thereby acknowledging her Ladyship a perfect VENUS'.[315] Emma was showing the country that she was the wife of Nelson's heart and the woman who shared his fame.

In Worcester, Nelson treated himself to a dessert service decorated with his coat of arms, and in Birmingham's jewellery workshops, they gathered dozens of rings, necklaces, and bracelets and bought trunks of toys for Horatia at Theophilus Richards's toy warehouse. At Coventry, gushed the *Coventry Mercury*, 'every heart overflowed with gratitude'.[316] After visiting Towcester, Dunstable, St Albans, Watford and Brentford, they arrived at Merton Place on 5 September. Their Tour had cost nearly £500, around a year's pay for Nelson at his current rate, and they had spent even more on souvenirs. It had been worth every bruise and every penny. 'Oh, how our Hero has been received!' Emma exulted to Kitty Matcham.[317] As the *Morning Post* reported, 'It is a singular fact that more eclat attends Lord Nelson in his provincial rambles than attends the King.'[318]

The Tour ensured that Emma's fashions were copied across England and Wales. The *Lady's Magazine* declared early in the following year, 'Such has been the progress of good taste among our leading belles of fashion, that all the heavy appendages of dress, which used to encumber rather than adorn, have been judiciously relinquished for decorations more delicate and appropriate.'[319] The most fashionable dress was 'à la Lady Hamilton', an empire-line style made from 'white satin, gauze and muslin'. Voguish women now wore their hair cut close around the ears, with no hat.

In cartoons depicting Nelson rescuing Britannia, the beleaguered country now looked very like Emma: a statuesque woman with long dark hair in a white dress, often throwing a dramatic pose. Novels, now quite forgotten, featured heroines that exploited Emma's fame. Mary Charlton's *The Wife and the Mistress* (1802) excused the love triangle. Horatio Nelson became Horace Nevare, a romantic hero superior to trivial amusements, who follows the truth of his heart, and courts virtuous Laura without caring that her parentage is obscure. Charlton also added a character named Mrs Hamilton, who is the absolute epitome of virtuous behaviour, and she also included a Fanny and a Sir William. Emma clearly enjoyed the portrayal: she bought *The Wife and the Mistress* and kept it until nearly the very end of her life.

In the following year, an even more uncompromising defence of the affair appeared in the *Lady's Magazine*. Emma, Nelson, Horatia, Sir William and Fanny all had starring roles, and Emma was triumphant. The hero, Horatio, a figure of Nelson, is a perfect man, 'not more respected for his immense wealth than his amiable and gentle manners'. He has a toddler daughter, who was 'the most perfect of nature's children', but his shrewish, 'cruel, treacherous, and resentful' wife 'embittered' his life with 'peevish jealousies'. The 'manly Horatio scorned to use a husband's power towards her' but his 'soft rebukes' make 'not the least impression on her adamantine heart'. He gains his only happiness from a virtuous friendship with a beautiful, innocent girl, Miss Emily Lewis, the daughter of his sister, Emma Lewis. The journalist perhaps had an inkling about Emma's daughter, Emma Carew, who had been to stay with Emma at least once, and the suggestion that Horatio derived his only pleasure from talking to young Miss Lewis verges on implying an incestuous attraction.

If this was not enough, Emma Lewis's early life reflects that of Emma Lyon's experience as a courtesan, mistress to Greville, and wife. As a young girl, Emma travels to London, and 'pursued with eager avidity its luxuriant pleasures'. After her lover abandons her, she meets gentle Mr Lewis, who, like Emma's real-life Sir William, had a 'prepossessing and mild exterior, joined to the most profound knowledge, which he had improved by travelling, and the sensible converse of the most enlightened men'. Emma confesses that 'for him I felt not that ardent passion I had done for the regretted Alfred, no the passion which the worthy Lewis inspired was respect, which soon ripened into a pure attachment, never to be severed till death should part us'.

There could hardly be a more blatant version of the story of Emma Lyon-Greville-Sir William-Nelson, in which everything happens just short of Emma Lewis herself actually enjoying Horatio's admiration, which instead went to her daughter, Emily. In case any particularly slow reader had still failed to spot the resemblances to England's favourite love triangle, the author has the entire party go to watch Horatio's wife act Elvira in *Pizarro* (a play indelibly associated with Nelson and Emma since the shocking spectacle at Drury Lane of Fanny's humiliation, eighteen months before). The point is simple: Emily (Emma) gives Horatio (Nelson) optimism and relief from his sufferings from his cruel and spiteful wife. Poor Fanny could not pick up even a magazine without reading about Emma's triumphs. The years 1801–3 were truly her years of despair. The mistress had won a resounding victory.

44

Changes

'**I**was sensible, & said so when I married, that I should be superannuated when my wife would be in her full beauty and vigour of youth,' lamented Sir William in September 1802. 'That time is arrived, and we must make the best of it.' Exhausted by the recent tour, he was tired of watching her indulge Nelson's grasping family and preside over the social whirl of Merton, 'seldom less than 12 or 14 at table, & those varying continually'. Her energy, her appetite for society and her excellence as a hostess had once excited him. Now he wanted only to live quietly.

Emma tried to please her husband by holidaying with him in the fashionable beach resort of Ramsgate. But everywhere she went, she was pursued by the press and besieged by crowds, people hunting for a favour, and crazed obsessives, greedy to touch the star's mantle. As the *Morning Herald* reported, 'A Lady *swimmer* at Ramsgate, who is said to be a perfect *attitudinarian* in the water, is now the morning gaze of the place.' The reporter claimed she was such an excellent swimmer that she was 'secure against any *marine enemy*, but as she is young and beautiful, she is perhaps more in danger from the *land sharks*'.[320] Journalists followed her friends and bombarded them with questions. Emma had instructed Mrs Gibson to bring Horatia to nearby Margate incognito. On her first attempt to visit her daughter she forgot the address as soon as she arrived, but later managed to travel to play with her daughter when she could escape the gossip columnists.[321] Anxious to protect Horatia from the news hounds, she implored Mrs Gibson 'on no consideration to answer any questions about Miss Thompson', the name they used to discuss Horatia, and certainly not 'who placed her' with her faithful nurse.

Miserable in the bustle of bathers and fashion, Sir William wished he were alone with her. 'I care not a pin for the great world, and am attached to no one so much as you.'[322] Emma was exasperated with him, complaining she had her hands full with trying to dodge the journalists and see Horatia. Sir William decided he had no choice but to threaten her with separation. 'I am fully determined not to have any more of the very silly altercations that happen but too often between us and embitter the present moments exceedingly,' he insisted. 'If realy one cannot live comfortably together, a wise and well concerted separation is preferable; but I think, considering the probability of my not troubling any party long in this world, the best for us all wou'd be to bear the ills we have.' He wanted to fish, visit his friends and tour picture auctions, making the most of every moment because he felt he was fading fast. 'I have but a very short time to live, and every moment is precious to me.' Only two years earlier, he had been hunting with the Esterházys and dancing with the Elliots, but now he declared he was dying. Emma was shocked for she had hardly realised that she had been neglecting her husband. She tried to make more time for him and no longer pressured him to attend her parties. He went fishing on the Thames and treated himself, as the *Herald* noted, to an 'elegant new chariot'.[323]

Although Nelson enthused in his romantic moods that they could 'live on bread and cheese', he was adamant that Merton should always have 'good wine, good fires, and a hearty welcome for our friends'. Emma was overspending as usual. As most of her guests stayed overnight and travelled to London next morning, the parties continued late into the night, and she had to accommodate and feed her visitors' servants and horses. She hosted their neighbours at Merton, mostly wealthy bankers, as well as London aristocrats and foreign Royals, including Prince Leopold of Naples. The press were particularly interested in the regular visits of the Prince of Wales's brothers, the portly womanising twenty-nine-year-old William, Duke of Clarence, who had been star of the show at Nelson's wedding to Fanny, and his wheezy younger brother, the Duke of Sussex, who as Prince Augustus had been a regular guest at the Palazzo Sessa. Nelson's family came frequently, and Charlotte Nelson was living with Emma almost full time. Politicians also attended, keen to tempt Nelson to their interests. One night the talk would be of Pitt, the next Drury Lane. Jane Powell often swept through the porch, along with other great actors and actresses. Opera stars such as the great Brigida Banti came to sing with Emma and Mrs Billington often graced

Emma's soirées, for she had fled Naples just after Emma. London had missed her and she was soon singing at both Covent Garden and Drury Lane, for stratospheric fees of £10,000 a season. She was very friendly with the Duke of Sussex, and there were whispers she was also indulging his brother, the Prince of Wales. Emma pressed invitations on her glamorous female friends – tableaux like 'The Favourite Sultana' needed plenty of extras.

After his isolated childhood, Nelson wanted the house filled with family and friends, and Emma ensured carriages were always rattling into the drive. She invited all those she thought might give Nelson patronage including the Devonshire set and, to Nelson's fury, the Prince of Wales. Even when she was up to her ears in boxes moving to Merton, Nelson fulminated about 'that fellow's wanting you for his mistress, but I know your virtue too well to be the whore of any rank stinking king's evil; the meanness of the titled pimps does not suprize me in these degenerate days. I suppose he will try to get at Merton, as it lays in the road, I believe, to Brighton; but I am sure you will never let them in.' Her ebullient guests were high-stake gamblers at faro and hazard. By the end of the year, her banker Thomas Coutts informed her that the balance in her account was an unacceptably low twelve shillings and elevenpence.

The *Morning Chronicle* reported Nelson's birthday party in breathless detail, rhapsodising about Lady Hamilton's singing. Emma spent over £60 (nearly £3,600) a week on food alone, and coals, wines, candles and decorations cost her hundreds.[324] She was expected to set trends not only in fashion, acting and dance but also in entertaining, balls, table decoration and dining. As the *Oracle* reported in March, the exotic delicacy of sows' udders from Sicily had arrived at the Customs House in London and 'The Lady of a *celebrated Antiquarian* has lately imported a large quantity, flattering herself that their salubrious effects will ever continue her the blooming *goddess of health*.'[325]

By the autumn of 1803, the Peace of Amiens was disintegrating. Nelson expected to be back at sea in the New Year. Emma knew she was about to lose him – and she could not bear it. 'I love him, adore him, his virtue, heart, mind, soul courage', she scrawled, busily trying to organise an extravagant Christmas for him.[326] She pressed Kitty Matcham that they had '3 Boltons, 2 Nelsons, and only need two or three little Matchams to be quite *en famille*'.[327] Determined to have Horatia at Merton, she invited all the nephews and nieces to cover their daughter's presence. Nelson's family and friends expressed their pleasure in Nelson's 'god-child', although the William Nelsons saw her as a potential rival as Nelson's heir and prayed there would be no son. The Children's Ball after New Year, which continued until 3 a.m., was thrown in Horatia's honour. Now that she was nearly one, her resemblance to Nelson was striking. She behaved beautifully for her first Christmas and entranced both her father and Sir William who, as Nelson later wrote, thought her 'the finest child he had seen'.

Sir William seemed to be recovering from his recent bout of ill-health. In the first month of 1803, the *Post* spotted him and Emma enjoying a winter walk near the Serpentine, in London's Hyde Park. 'Among the fashionable, Lady Hamilton was much noticed for the elegance of her dress and appearance. Her Ladyship was in plain white, with a rich white satin cloack, trimmed with ermine and lined with amber.'[328] In February the Hamiltons staged a grand concert at home for a hundred guests, and the newspapers reported that her performance at the pianoforte 'electrified her auditors'. But within a week, Sir William collapsed at 23 Piccadilly. By late March he was dying. Emma spent every night nursing him with Mrs Cadogan, and Nelson also assisted. There was little she could do except keep her husband comfortable, but she refused to go to bed, determined to be with him through the final days. Still lucid in spite of the painkilling drugs, he instructed Greville he did not want to see a clergyman. A few days later, on 6 April, he died in Emma's arms with Nelson holding his hand. 'Unhappy day for the forlorn Emma,' she mourned. 'At ten minutes past ten, dear, blessed Sir William left me.'

Her grief was real. Sir William had been her loyal partner since she was twenty-one, and her husband for twelve years. He had been the first man to treat her with respect, ignoring the judgment of his family and friends and risking his social status to marry her for love. Although sometimes remote, he had always indulged her. 'I feel truly bereaved of all comfort', she wrote, 'my wounds bleed afresh in writing & thinking on what I have lost in such a man, such a husband.'[329] The intense devotion she had initially felt for him had mellowed, but although her passions were engaged elsewhere, she loved him, depended on him and had never imagined being without him.

Emma threw herself into arranging the funeral and hung a hatchment depicting Sir William's armorial bearings outside 23 Piccadilly to inform everyone of his death. Elisabeth Vigée le Brun visited and could hardly see the widow under her vast black veil. Nelson had moved from Emma's home to lodge nearby at 19 Piccadilly – with Greville, to the awkward dismay of both men – and Sarah Nelson came to assist Emma. Sir William was buried next to his first wife in the chapel of Slebech Castle in Pembrokeshire, their graves looking out to sea. Almost immediately after Sir William's death, Emma's creditors closed in. She begged Greville to tell her if he would pay her debts and how much he would give her of Sir William's estate, so that she could, in her words, 'reduce her expences and establishment immediately'. Greville instructed her to vacate 23 Piccadilly directly but gave no answer about the debts. For the sake of respectability, Emma needed her own residence separate from Merton, which was officially Nelson's home, so she took another house in an only slightly less expensive location, 11 Clarges Street, just off Piccadilly, still near Green Park and the Duchess of Devonshire's London home. The street was heavily bombed during the Second World War and number 11 was finally demolished in the early 1960s, but there are still some surviving examples of the graceful four-storey house in which Emma once lived.

'I hope she will be left properly, but I doubt,' Nelson wrote gloomily. Emma had previously complained to Sir William that the will left her to 'poverty and distress' and she had no pleasant surprises when it was read. She received £300 – hardly enough for three weeks of entertaining at Merton – and an £800 annuity, out of which £100 had to be given to Mrs Cadogan. In a codicil, Sir William asked that when the Treasury paid out compensation for his losses, Emma should receive £450 to pay her debts. As the *Morning Herald* put it, Lady Hamilton 'had not been left in independent circumstances'.[330] Emma's debts far exceeded £450 and the Treasury were unlikely to pay, even if Greville had been willing to press the claim. Sir William had kept to the usual eighteenth-century principle of wills: keeping estates intact. Charles Greville finally had what he had desired, and for which he had, in effect, exchanged Emma and broken her heart so long ago. He also inherited the paintings of Emma that Sir William had not sold: Romney's *Emma Hart in Morning Dress* and the *Bacchante* that he had made Romney paint over and over until he thought it perfect enough to sway his uncle to adopt his lover as mistress.

Sir William's kindest act was to bequeath to Nelson an enamel version by Henry Bone of the portrait by Vigée le Brun of Emma as a *Bacchante*. Pained to see erotic images of Emma on sale, Nelson had sent Alexander Davison to buy the original from Christie's in 1801. Sir William was well aware that Nelson was wildly jealous of Greville and would detest the thought of Emma's ex-lover possessing such a portrait of her, or even worse, selling it. Nelson treasured the enamel, and it now hangs on the walls of the sumptuous Wallace Collection in London's Manchester Square.

Charles was infuriated to find that his uncle had squandered his inheritance and amassed debts of over £5,000. As both executor and sole beneficiary, he was not about to give his old mistress any more money than she had already received. Quickly realising that Greville was too angry about the debts to do much for her, and newly poor, since Sir William's pension from the government ceased at his death, Emma redoubled her efforts to extract money from the government for services rendered at Naples. It was usual to give a pension to the wife of an ambassador but the government were proving reluctant to accept Emma's claim, still infuriated that the envoy and Nelson had been dragged into putting down an internal rebellion.

Emma had no idea of the truth: her husband had put up the greatest obstacle to her ever receiving any financial recompense for her work. In his letters to the Foreign Office, Sir William never mentioned any of the acts for which she claimed a pension, including her contribution to victualling the fleet before the Nile and her efforts in assisting the Royal Family to flee. Despite the fact that Maria Carolina mistrusted him and communicated secrets exclusively to Emma, Sir William had claimed to the government that the Queen herself had given him the letters from the King of Spain, which proved so vital to espionage in 1795. Sir William told his friends and Greville about Emma's deeds, but he inflated his role to the government (stung by gossip that Emma did all the work). He had never sent them official word that she was so much more than his 'private wife'. As a consequence, they considered her descriptions of her services as lies.

In the midst of the financial chaos, Nelson was offered the position of Commander-in-Chief of the Mediterranean Fleet. Emma had to prepare herself to cope alone. They rushed to have Horatia christened before he left. Emma wrote to Mrs Gibson to take Horatia to Marylebone Parish Church and to pay the clergyman and the clerk double fees not to mention the name of the father and mother. Horatia Nelson Thompson was recorded as born on 29 October 1800.[331] The date of her birth was put back three months to pretend that she had been born in Naples, and pursue the fiction that she was the couple's 'godchild'.[332] Emma tried to distract herself from worrying over Nelson's imminent departure by planning (and paying for) the wedding of his niece Kitty Bolton and her cousin William Bolton. Secretly, Nelson was dismayed by his family's greed and he hated the way Sarah Nelson pushed Emma to cement her friendship with the Prince of Wales in order to gain patronage for her husband, but he had no time to tell her his feelings.[333] On 18 May, the same day as the wedding, Nelson left at four in the morning for Portsmouth. Emma had been wise to keep herself busy for he hated a weepy parting and he wanted her to be affectionate but brave. She cried a little, for he sent a message from the first stage of journey:

> Cheer up, my dearest Emma, and be assured that I ever have been, and am, and ever will be, your most affectionate and faithful
>
> Nelson and Bronte

Neither of them knew it then, but she was pregnant with their second child.

45
Nelson's Lonely Mistress

*E*mma hoped Nelson might return in six months. Soon after he left in 1803, she began to suspect she was pregnant and by mid-summer she was sure. Lonely and needy, she wrote to Nelson constantly, but he did not receive any of her letters until July. She spent most of the year in mourning for Sir William, her growing bulge hidden under voluminous black robes.

Everybody clamoured to see Emma's Attitudes, but she performed them only for a select few. Even though she had declared she would never present them in London again, Elisabeth Vigée le Brun persuaded her to put on a show for two French émigré princes on their visit to London.

I placed a large frame in the centre of the room and two screens on either side of the frame. I had an enormous candle which bathed the scene in a pool of light but I placed it out of sight so that the whole might resemble a painting more. After all the invited guests had arrived, Lady Hamilton took up various poses within this frame and her expressions were indeed quite remarkable. She had brought a little girl with her who must have been about seven or eight and who resembled her greatly. I was told this was the daughter of Mme [Sarah] Nelson. She had the child pose with her and the picture reminded me of the women fleeing in Poussin's *Rape of the Sabine Women*. She passed from sorrow to joy, from joy to terror, so rapidly and so convincingly that we were all delighted.

Elisabeth adds a sly hint that Emma was performing with a daughter, but Horatia was hardly two and Emma Carew and also Charlotte Nelson were too old, so the child was more likely little Lizzy Matcham, Nelson's eight-year-old niece. Vigée le Brun spotted that Emma was pregnant, alerted by the fact that she was looking much bigger and drinking porter, which was popular with expectant women.[334]

In the summer, Emma's old friend Jane Powell begged her to visit Southend, where she was playing at the local theatre. 'Your absence is regretted by all ranks of people. Would to Heaven you were here to enliven this present dull scene.' Everyone wanted to meet her but Emma had lost interest in socialising. On 6 September, she commemorated her wedding to 'that dearest and best of men'. 'This day am I at South End forlorn & alone my Husband to a better world, Nelson our friend gone out to save his Country oh Great God protect him for all our sakes prays the hapless Comfortless Emma Hamilton.'[335]

After years in the limelight, Emma had wearied of press attention. Despite frequent bathing, she was suffering from blisters on the neck and stomach, headaches and crippling stomach upsets. The newspapers gossiped that she and Mrs Billington were singing regularly for the Duke of Queensberry at Clarges Street. She issued a disclaimer in the *Post* asserting she had been 'very unwell and does not see any company'.[336] Anxious about Nelson and feeling lost without him, she begged him to allow her to come out to live with him on ship, but he told her it was impossible.

At Christmas she packed her house with guests in a vain attempt to forget that she was without her lover. Buffeted about on the Mediterranean, Nelson was missing Emma and Horatia. 'She must be grown so much,' he wrote. 'How I long to hear her prattle.'[337] In January, his Christmas package of letters and presents finally arrived for Emma. To Horatia he sent a doting note thanking her for her letter and her present of 'a lock of your beautiful hair', and enclosing some of his own hair and £1 to buy a locket to hold it. He promised her a watch, adding, 'I am glad to hear that you are so good and mind everything that your Governess and Lady Hamilton tell you.'[338] Brimming with anticipation of being a father once more, Nelson wrote to Emma, 'Kiss dear Horatia for me, and the other.' He confessed he had 'been so uneasy for this last month, desiring, most ardently, to hear of your well doing'. 'I shall make you a Duchess; and if it pleases God that time may arrive!' he exulted. '*What changes!*' Emma had been pondering names. Nelson replied, 'Call him what you please, if a girl, Emma.'

Nelson encouraged Emma to move to Merton for her final weeks of pregnancy. He knew there had been gossip about Emma's condition and he dreaded a repetition of the press frenzy about her 'embonpoint'. 'You will live much more comfortable and much cheaper than in London,' he wrote. 'If you like to have the house altered, you can do it.'³³⁹ Although Nelson directed her to keep the architect to his estimate, he urgently expected the 'new room built, the grounds laid out neatly but not expensively, new Piccadilly gates, kitchen garden, &c'. He instructed her 'not to pay from the income', ordering her to keep account of how much she had paid for improvements, and give him the bills. He had no idea of the cost of materials and workmen. Emma lied that the alterations were cheaper than they were and paid the surplus with credit.

Soon, Emma was in no state to be thinking of home improvements. She retired to Clarges Street and by mid-January was in the final stages of a complicated pregnancy. After a difficult labour, she gave birth to a girl. She was exhausted and ill for three weeks afterward, and at least one doctor was in regular attendance. The child was also weak. Too feeble to be given to Mrs Gibson to take to Marylebone, as Emma had intended, baby Emma sickened at home. In Titchfield Street, Horatia also fell ill, possibly with smallpox. Emma believed she might lose both her daughters.

Some six weeks later, little Emma died. Emma had to ensure news of the death did not leak out, while trying to crush her grief. She could not take comfort from Nelson, the only man apart from her doctor who knew the secret.

Emma had to pay an undertaker double the usual fee to keep quiet and remove the body from Clarges Street without attracting the attention of the press. The child's burial is not recorded either in her parish of St George's Hanover Square or in the Marylebone parish of Mrs Gibson. Little Emma lay in an unmarked grave, probably outside London, for church grounds were reserved for declared parishioners. Emma usually found some consolation in expressing her emotions extravagantly, but now she had to stifle her pain and mourn in silence. She tried to focus instead on Horatia's recovery, but her daughter was too weak to visit Clarges Street. In despair, she longed for Nelson to understand and sympathise. He received a bundle of her letters in April and replied as soon as he heard.

I opened – opened – found none but December and early January. I was in such an agitation! At last, I found one without a date, which thank God! told my poor heart that you was recovering, but that dear little Emma was no more! and that Horatia had been so very ill – it all together upset me. But it was just at bed time, and I had time to reflect and be thankful to God for sparing you and our dear Horatia. I am sure the loss of one – much more both – would have drove me mad.

Nelson had his work to occupy his thoughts but Emma could not forget and nothing dulled the pain. As she confessed to Sarah Nelson, 'I have not been out these 3 weeks, so very ill I have been.' Infant mortality was high in the early nineteenth century, but few women had to endure such sorrow with almost no support from friends and family. Nelson's siblings and some of her friends knew of her loss but she downplayed her despair to them, terrified of anyone suggesting she might lose her hold on Nelson's heart because she had failed to give him the large family he so wanted. At nearly forty, she knew she was unlikely to have another child.

Always bad at being alone, Emma found it increasingly difficult to cope with the death of the baby without Nelson's passionate love or Sir William's supportive companionship. Previously, she had been less of a drinker and gambler than most high-society women. In the early months of 1804, she succumbed to binges of heavy drinking and eating, followed by days in bed, destroying her constitution with frantic dissipation. Society adored her but in private she was racked with pain and misery. Crippled by fevers, sickness, stomach ache and migraines, she took laudanum to ease the pain and to comfort her sleepless nights. She longed to be with Nelson again.

I am anxious and agitated to see him. The disappointment would kill me. I love him, I adore him, my mind and soul is now transported with the thought of that blessed ecstatic moment when I shall see him, embrace him. My love is no common love. It may be a sin to love I say it might have been a sin when I was *anothers* but I had merit then in trying to suppress it. I am *now free* and I must sin on and love him more than ever. It is a crime worth going to Hell for.[340]

46

Money is Trash

'The *thought* of seeing him again agitates me and makes me mad with joy, then fear comes across me that he may not come.' Emma had just received a bundle of Nelson's letters and she was reading fifty-four pages of news, protestations of love and advice on improving their home, veering between 'different feelings that elate and oppress me'. 'Your resemblance is never far from my mind,' he wrote in one. 'I hope very soon that I shall embrace the substantial part of you instead of the Ideal, that will I am sure give us both *real pleasure and exquisite happiness*.'[341] His romantic letters lifted her heart but others brought back the raw pain of losing her baby.

Every woman in England wanted to be Lady Hamilton, but no one understood her difficulties. She was spending heavily to try to stifle her grief. Urgently attempting to keep up appearances, all the while worrying about Nelson, she shone at the most expensive parties, and entertained a few true friends and many sycophants and hangers-on with luxur-ious dinners. Nelson worried about the 'intrigues' of the set around Lady H–, possibly Lady Hertford, intimate of the Prince of Wales, whom he termed 'as great a pimp as any of them'. Otherwise, he loved Emma's extravagance, for it seemed to him fitting to his status. 'Don't mind the expense, money is trash,' Nelson had used to fulminate to Fanny, exas-perated that she could not cut the dash he wished after the Nile.

Soon after the death of her husband, the marriage proposals began. In 1804 alone, she received one from an Earl, from the second son of a Viscount and from a relation of Sir William's. Her suitors were wealthy men – they had to be to countenance her gigantic and ever-growing debts. Emma had to dress stylishly, entertain the highest echelons of society, and maintain two houses, but her £1,200 a year from Nelson and £800 left to her by Sir William hardly covered the food bills. She still owed money to her husband's creditors. Nelson promised that he would become wealthy with prize money and would leave her rich in his will, and she borrowed more and more, eager to believe him. She comforted herself by remembering the amounts her friends owed, such as the Duchess of Devonshire who was in debt for the modern equivalent of £6 million, accrued mainly through gambling and socialising. Emma did not understand how much more vulnerable she was than such great ladies. Aristocrats like Devonshire had the assets to sustain their debt and they could always beg money from their family.

Emma's ambition was to keep in with the Prince of Wales, who she thought would protect her. She was trying to promote herself as a hostess to the glamorous Whig set, as well as attempting to win over James Perry, editor of the pro-Fox and pro-Whig and sometimes anti-Nelson *Morning Chronicle*. Bitterly disappointed in the King's treatment of her, she was convinced that the accession of the Prince of Wales would bring her and Nelson more recognition. Nelson's political loyalties wavered, so after he took his seat in the House of Lords in October 1801 the Whigs wanted him on their side.

London was fizzing with political gossip. The Whigs had been debating an alliance with Lord Grenville of the Tory party, against Henry Addington, current Prime Minister. Covert meetings mushroomed across London. James Gillray satirised the caballing in his caricature, *L'Assemblee Nationale – or Grand Co-operative Meeting*. The major Whigs discuss allying with Grenville at the house of Charles James Fox. Emma, adorned with a Nelson miniature, stands above Fox and his wife as they receive the notables. She flutters her fan and gossips with the Duchess of Devonshire. Among the luminaries in attendance are the Prince of Wales, Mrs Fitzherbert, who was still at the Prince's beck and call, despite his stream of mistresses, the Dukes of Bedford and Norfolk, the Duchess of Gordon, Lord Cholmondeley, the Duke of Clarence (future William IV) and his mistress, the actress Mrs Dora Jordan, Lord and Lady Derby and Lady Buckinghamshire. Emma was swinging with the 'in crowd'. By frantic entertaining, socialising and spending, she presented herself as the keeper of Nelson's flame and favour. The Fox set had bottomless purses – Fox once lost £32,000 at the card tables in a single night – and most owed hundreds of thousands. Emma could not afford to keep up – but she tried.

The same aristocrats were active in the 'Pic-Nics', an amateur dramatic society organised by Greville's brother Robert at Tottenham Court in London and it seems as if Emma was also a participant.[342] The press declared their weekly meetings excuses for giant orgies and extravagance. One commentator decided that if the 'uncorrupted . . . did not oppose and overthrow [private theatres], decency would abandon Britain'.[343] In *Dilettante Theatricals*, Gillray caricatured the party staging *The Rival Queens* by Nathaniel Lee, with Emma singing at the back of the party behind Mrs Billington. The gossips were wrong: the Pic-Nics' only excess was the inordinate sums expended on costumes, sets and jewels, which was money Emma could ill afford.

Like all society women, Emma was trying to establish herself as a charitable patron. She had allied herself with the fashionable London orphanage, the Foundling Hospital, by standing as 'godmother' to a child, which meant that she gave money and occasionally received updates on the child's progress. As Nelson indulged her, 'Your purse, my dear Emma, will always be empty; your heart is generous beyond your means.'[344] Otherwise, she spent her time visiting Nelson's relations, and bathing. A sharp-eyed lady spotted her in Ramsgate in the summer of 1804, lonely in the sea resort without Sir William.[345] She was endeavouring to take the waters to improve her fertility, hoping to fall pregnant quickly when her lover returned.

Emma worried that her lover 'seems to hope the rooms are done and has written a great deal about improvements'. His designs to landscape the grounds, construct a driveway and add new entertaining rooms and bedrooms were proving increasingly expensive. She was having a new entrance constructed on the north side of the house, and building stables, while planning a proper coach house. Cribb, the garden designer, had employed twenty men to turn the muddy grounds into a graceful and orderly garden. Ambitious to transform the first house that was truly her own into a handsome modern mansion, a lasting monument to Nelson's glory, and the equivalent of an aristocratic seat, she willingly paid the bills. 'What I have done has been to make comfortable the man that my soul dotes on, that I would think it little to sacrifice my life to make him happy,' she wrote. 'Nelson and Emma can have but one mind, one heart, one soul, one interest, and I can assure you that if the nation was to give my beloved Nelson a Blenheim, Merton would be the place he would live in.'

Nelson's family treated her homes like finishing schools for their adolescent children. The Boltons sent clodhopping Eliza and Anne on extended visits. Emma, who had once negotiated arguments between courtiers, now arbitrated between teenage girls. William Nelson's obstreperous son Horace stayed for his holidays from Eton and he usually needed new shoes, new clothes, and coach fare back to his parents' home, or he fell ill and required nursing with special food and expensive milky drinks. Sarah also asked if Emma could arrange a rich wife for him, even though Nelson had already claimed he hoped he would one day marry his Horatia (this was very unlikely since he would have to wait until he was at least thirty to do so). Charlotte Nelson was always at Emma's side. She was taken to hear Mrs Billington's performances, to parties and masquerades, and dinners with aristocrats, and, after many music lessons, Emma organised a private concert so that everybody could hear her sing.[346] Sarah commanded Emma subtly, 'you and I want her to be every thing that is accomplished and to marry well'.[347] How good you are to dress her so smart,' she pressured.[348] Sarah badgered her to hire dancing masters, and buy Charlotte 'Dumb-bells' and 'make her use them', and Emma treated her new 'foster daughter' to holidays by the sea and a gold watch.[349] As Sarah observed to Emma, 'you have had the bringing her up'.

The Duchess of Devonshire took notice of Charlotte, and Sarah suggested Emma might 'think of having her presented this winter? Would she not be able to go better with you into company if she was?'[350] Emma could not present Charlotte at Court, since she had never attended and her friends were apparently unable to help. Sarah deluged Emma with letters, encouraging her to turn awkward, ill-educated Charlotte into a 'Girl of Fashion, what pleasure she would have, when she walk'd across the room, to hear people say, what an elegant young woman that is . . . perseverance shall do it'. Although Nelson was often dubious about his family's greed, Sarah had hectored Emma into believing that helping her family would win his esteem. 'How often have I with pleasure seen him delighted with you & hope I shall do again.'

All the while, Emma grew more desperate for her lover's home-coming. The death of little Emma weighed on her mind and by mid-August, Nelson was so worried by her letters that he asked to return to England at the end of the year. He pressed her to keep Horatia at Merton, proposing that the country was the ideal place for their daughter to learn 'virtue, goodness, and elegance of manners . . . to fit her to move in that sphere of life she is destined to move in'. His was an impossible dream: the building work had made the house uninhabitable, covered in dust and overrun with workmen. When his return seemed imminent in the winter of 1804, Emma dropped everything and devoted herself to completing the most urgent renovations at Merton. Buried in an archive are the records of Emma's outrageous last-minute sprees on furniture to create the luxurious home he desired. In late December, she spent hundreds on rugs and mirrors from one shop alone. Nelson remained at sea, and she was left with the dozens of guests she had invited to give him a family Christmas, all of them happily eating up the lavish dinners she had ordered for him. In January 1805, again anticipating Nelson's arrival, she ran up even more bills. She bought two long mahogany chests of drawers for £7 each, five cushion covers and six chair covers for £10, a bed filled with the finest feathers for £16, and down pillows for £3, paying extra for transport. By early 1805, her debts were around £7,000 and most had been amassed since Sir William's death two years previously.

Nelson expected to soon be free to 'fly to dear Merton where all in this world which is dear to me resides'. 'I shall lose no time in coming to your dear, dear embraces,' he wrote happily. But his homecoming was continually cancelled.[351] Emma consoled herself by writing poems to him, dismissing them with ladylike modesty as 'bad Verses on my Soul's Idol'.

> I think, I have not lost my heart
> Since I, with truth, can swear,
> At every moment of my life
> I feel my Nelson there!
>
> If, from thine Emma's brest, her heart
> Were stolen or flown away;
> Where! where! should she my Nelson's love
> Record each happy day?

When Emma was not writing to Nelson, she was shopping. In summer 1805, she spent over £30 storing and transferring her existing furniture and musical instruments between Clarges Street, Brewer Street, and Merton and buying new items. Moving the pianofortes alone cost 14 guineas.[352] She bought the finest furniture: a mahogany cabriol chair with upholstered arms and seat, six scarlet and green ottoman stools, more mahogany chests of drawers, a mahogany coffee table, a

Kidderminster carpet at £14 for the master bedroom and more for chandeliers. She then paid £15 to move the furniture out so that the house could be whitewashed.

To enable Horatia to live at Merton, Nelson wrote a letter for Emma to show to curious visitors in which he explained that the child was an orphan 'left to his care and protection' in Naples. Although Nelson had found a position in the navy for Charles Connor, the son of Emma's aunt, her other Connor cousins were always demanding money. Nelson decided that the eldest girl, Cecilia, should become Horatia's governess at 'any salary you think proper'.[353] Emma paid Miss Connor a substantial wage.

Merton was beginning to correspond to Nelson's dream: a grand, spacious house full of children. But when Mrs Gibson heard that Horatia would be leaving her care, she began to demand money. Horatia was an easy, well-behaved charge, and Mrs Gibson had been paid much higher than the going rate at about £50 every two months (around £3,000). Since Emma bought the clothes, trinkets, medicines, and toys, Mrs Gibson had only to shell out for food and mending. It was not uncommon for a nurse to refuse to give up her charge until she was given a golden handshake, and Mrs Gibson saw her chance to extract a fortune from Emma. She had arranged the false baptism, knew the identity of Horatia's parentage and almost certainly knew about the second child. Emma begged Nelson to solve the impasse, and he instructed his solicitors to offer a pension to Mrs Gibson of £20 a year, on condition that she make no attempt to keep Horatia or communicate with her again.[354] Five-year-old Horatia arrived to live at Merton in May 1805.

That summer, Emma, desperate for a respite from the demands of her creditors, travelled to Southend. The fashionable resort was popular with Princess Charlotte, daughter of the Prince of Wales, and sometimes Princess Caroline, his estranged wife. A theatre was erected in 1804, and there were plentiful bathing machines, and an indoor warm bath, a billiard room and gardens. The Royal Hotel had a coffee room, a giant ballroom, music gallery, and supper and card rooms. With England at war with France, people had to holiday at home and British sea resorts were crammed. Newspapers published lists of the fashionable in attendance every day. They reported that Emma was holidaying with Charlotte Nelson, Mrs Billington, and some other 'young ladies who composed the family party', Horatia and Cecilia Connor, and possibly Emma Carew, as well as the little Matcham and

Bolton sisters. The journalists tracked her every move. On 19 August, the *Post*'s Southend correspondent filed an excited report.

Lady Hamilton suddenly quitted this place, in a chaise and four, at five o'clock this morning. She took her departure, I understand, in consequence of an express that arrived here yesterday evening.[355]

The express brought Emma the news she had waited so long to hear: the *Victory* had landed.[356] Terrified Nelson would arrive and find her absent, Emma hurried Horatia out of bed, packed some of her belongings and dashed back to Merton.

47
Relighting the Fire

On 19 August, Nelson left Portsmouth and drove through the night. He arrived at 6 a.m. to see Merton looking at its very best in the early morning sunlight. As soon as he entered the hall, he saw Emma's visions of his grandeur: busts, paintings and decorations, curtains draped in his honour, and elaborate new furnishings. 'Merton is become a perfect Paradise,' he exulted. 'The house is so entirely different, the water changed, and the grounds laid out in the most beautiful manner, and all by her taste.' They had not seen each other for two years and three months and there was so much news to exchange. 'What a day of rejoicing,' sighed Emma. She desperately wanted to fall pregnant again, frantic to wash away the pain of losing little Emma. 'She is a clever being after all,' wrote Lord Minto on the first Saturday after Nelson's arrival. 'The passion is as hot as ever.'[357]

London was wild to see him. 'He is adored as he walks the streets, thousands follow him, blessing him,' Emma gloried.[358] While Nelson visited the Admiralty and conducted business meetings, she hosted dinners for his family at Clarges Street. Nelson bought his daughter her own small fork and spoon and ordered them to be engraved with 'To my much-loved Horatia'. When they returned to Merton, guests, including the Duke of Clarence and Dora Jordan, flocked to dine, and his siblings arrived frequently with their many children. She played the graceful hostess to them all. 'What a Paradise he must think Merton, to say nothing of the Eve it contains,' flattered Mrs Bolton.[359] Minto extolled how Emma 'has improved and added to the house extremely well and without his knowing she was about it'. She appeared to be the ideal seaman's wife, managing the home, domestic life and everyday finances without bothering her man while he was away. But Emma had changed. She remained as vivacious as ever, but losing her daughter had taken away some of her intense appetite for life. In believing that Nelson's homecoming would solve her spiralling debts, allay her worries and chase away her inner pain, her expectations were impossibly high.

Nelson was nearly fifty and everybody expected he would be retired from active service after one or two more battles. Emma looked forward to turning Paradise Merton into the home of a retired hero, heavily decorated after his victories. She thought she could tell him about the expense when he returned triumphant, dripping with medals, and fabulously rich.

Emma accompanied Nelson on every visit she could and sat in on all his interviews. A young Danish journalist left entranced, gushing praise for 'elegant' Merton and the lobby packed with hundreds of Nelson paintings, objets d'art, and a bust. Although Nelson was standing at the entrance wearing a uniform emblazoned with different orders of knighthood, he only had eyes for the hostess. When 'ushered into a magnificent apartment, where Lady Hamilton sat at a window. I at first scarcely noticed his Lordship'.[360]

Nelson loved to watch his Emma, high queen of Paradise Merton, welcoming a dozen or more for dinner at his table. She was always performing. One visitor was startled when she pronounced in front of the whole table, 'I would wish with all my heart to die in two hours, so I might be your wife for one.' Nelson was similarly willing to play to his adoring audience, flirting outrageously with the ladies, cadging kisses and telling them stories. Flirtatious, amoral Bess Foster, mistress of the Duke of Devonshire, was a frequent visitor, and she simply adored Nelson. Her friends poked fun at her efforts to win him – when sharing a carriage away from Merton, another visitor, Lady Percival, declared that had Nelson kissed her goodbye but not kissed Bess, she should never 'otherwise have ventured to have got into the same carriage'. Dozens of guests joked about catfighting over him. Nelson soaked up all the adulation and Minto thought him 'remarkably well and full of spirits'.

The happy summer break was not to last. Within a fortnight of Nelson's return, Captain Blackwood arrived at the house to inform Nelson that Admiral Villeneuve and the French fleet had been detected at Cadiz. He drove to London to receive his orders from the Admiralty. He came away knowing he was to command the fleet in its assault against Villeneuve as soon as *Victory* was ready. By 10 September, Nelson knew he would be leaving three days later. 'Again he is obliged to go forth,' sighed Emma. She arranged a ceremony to celebrate their relationship, probably at Merton Church. As one witness reported, 'Nelson took Emma's hand and facing the priest, said, "Emma, I have taken the sacrament with you this day to prove to the world that our friendship is most pure and innocent, and of this I call God to witness."'[361] Emma still dreamed of more. 'I should like to say – how pretty it sounds – Emma Nelson,' she wrote wistfully.[362]

Nearly everyone who knew Nelson claimed that they saw him in the few days before he departed for Trafalgar. Most of them were lying for he was almost permanently occupied with government business. He received a last-minute invitation from the Prince of Wales to visit him in London on the 12th, and then visited Lord Castlereagh, the Secretary for War. In the waiting room, he had his first and only meeting with Arthur Wellesley, later Duke of Wellington, a youngish major general, recently arrived from India. The future conqueror of the French at Waterloo was decidedly unimpressed by the Nile hero's nervous chatter. Nelson returned home to dine with Lord Minto and some other neighbours. Emma tried hard to be happy and festive, but she could hardly eat or drink.

She knew that Nelson hated women to cry but she could not help it. On the morning of the 13th, he hurried to London for his final sailing orders and then they had the day to themselves. After dinner, the post-chaise arrived to whisk him away. He whispered a prayer beside the bed of the sleeping Horatia. Then he said his goodbyes to Emma: he promised to be true, to always love her, never to sleep off ship, and encouraged her to rally her spirits. Then he left. She could only weep hopelessly. 'I am again broken hearted,' she mourned. 'It seems as though I have had a fortnight's dream, and am awoke to the misery of this cruel separation. But what can I do? His powerful arm is of so much consequence to his country.' After not even twenty-five days with Nelson, she was alone again.

Nelson wrote in his diary on the road, 'Friday night, at half-past ten, drove from dear, dear Merton, where I left all I hold dear to this world, to go to serve my king and country.' He arrived at Portsmouth at 6 a.m. and scribbled a quick line to Emma. On board the *Victory*, he dined with George Rose, Vice President to the Board of Trade, soon to be Treasurer of the Navy, and pressed him to pursue the issue of a pension for his beloved. 'I love you beyond any Woman in this World and next our dear Ha,' he had promised. 'How I long to settle what I intend upon her and not leave her to the Mercy of any one or even to any foolish thing I may do in my old age.'[363] But he had procrastinated about arranging a settlement and Emma did not push him. Nelson believed himself invincible, and she was confident he would return. 'Cheer up', he wrote to her from the ship, 'and we will look forward to many, many happy years, and be surrounded by our children's children.'

48
Trafalgar

*A*fter Nelson's departure, Emma travelled to Canterbury with the William Nelsons. On 4 October, she wrote to him praising Horatia and forwarding a letter from Cecilia Connor who, with Mrs Cadogan, was caring for her at Merton. Cecilia had taken Horatia to London to buy shoes, stockings and a hat for her new doll and helped the little girl to make her doll a sumptuous bed with pillows and a mattress.[364] 'What a blessing for her parents to have such a child, so sweet, altho' so young, so amiable!' exulted Emma. Mrs Cadogan, she reported, 'doats on her, she says she could not live without her'.[365] Nelson wanted Horatia to be good at languages, like her mother, and Emma reported she was already picking up French and Italian.

My heart cannot bear to be without her. You will be even fonder of her when you return. She says, 'I love my dear, dear godpapa, but Mrs Gibson told me he kill'd all the people, and I was afraid.' Dearest angel she is! Oh, Nelson, how I love her, but how I do idolize you – the dearest husband of my heart, you are all in this world to your Emma. May God send you victory, and home to your *Emma, Horatia, and paradise Merton* for when you are there it will be paradise.[366]

Emma begged for details about life at sea for 'the smallest trifle that concerns you is so very interesting'. After passing on titbits of local news and Lord Douglas's request for some Turkish tobacco, she confessed she 'had begun to fret at not having letters from you'.

By far the hardest role for a navy wife or mistress was the waiting. Women scoured the newspapers and chased their friends for scraps of news in order to guess the whereabouts of the fleet, and relied on the other navy wives for emotional support. Authorities in port towns were constantly battling to suppress fortune-tellers, card readers and white witches, for sailors' wives flocked to them, desperate for any reassurance they could find. Many sailors married other seamen's daughters, girls schooled in the self-discipline needed to wait out long periods without news. Emma was not used to being left alone, and as she did not socialise with the wives of Nelson's captains, she was unable to draw on the friendship of other women waiting for their men. By mid-October, she was back at Merton, trying to keep herself busy by overseeing the renovations to the house. Little Horatia, she wrote sadly, was weeping daily for her father.

Emma received letters from Nelson on 1, 7 and 13 October. Every day she longed for his return. If he defeated the French, the government would heap him with gratitude and money (after Waterloo, Wellington was given cash sums and awarded an estate worth nearly £300,000 – somewhere in the vicinity of £18 million today). Ministers might even assist him to get a divorce. Emma believed his promise that he would win and return to her, three times a victor.

The English fleet had been preparing to tackle the French fleet throughout the autumn. When Nelson arrived, he ordered the English captains to station their vessels outside the port of Cadiz near Cape Trafalgar off the coast of southern Spain, waiting for Admiral Villeneuve and his ships to emerge. When they heard that Villeneuve's fleet of thirty-three had left port, Nelson and his twenty-seven ships prepared to attack. There was plenty of time to prepare for warships moved no faster than a stately walking pace. Now he was about to go into battle, Nelson realised that he had not made adequate provision for Emma. On the morning of Monday 21 October, Nelson wrote a codicil to his will in his pocketbook.

> I leave Emma, Lady Hamilton, therefore, a Legacy to my King and Country, that they will give her an ample provision to maintain her rank in life. I also leave to the beneficence of my Country my adopted daughter, Horatia Nelson Thompson; and I desire She will use in future the name of Nelson only. These are the only favours I ask of my King and Country at this moment when I am going to fight their Battle.[367]

Nelson had already written his final letters. He congratulated his 'dearest Angel', Horatia, that 'you are so very good a girl, and love my

Dear Lady Hamilton, who most dearly loves you, give her a kiss from me'.[368] He promised Emma he loved her 'as much as my own life; and, as my last writing before the battle will be to you, so I hope in God that I shall live to finish my letter after the Battle'. All around him, men were packing his furniture and removing the pictures from the walls. The ship was being made ready for war.

Before battle, most ordinary men removed boots, heavy coats and unnecessary jewellery and exchanged socks for silk stockings, to give the surgeon less trouble. Because snipers aimed for commanders, officers divested themselves of decorations. But Nelson was determined to wear his stars, despite the concerns of his subordinates that he was making himself a target. His officers begged him to assume the traditional position of an admiral on a ship towards the back of the fleet, ensuring relative safety and a good overall view of the battle. He refused, resolving to lead the attack from the front. Aware this was probably his last battle, he wanted to head it like a hero: swathed in glory, an inspiration to his men.

On 6 November, Emma was in bed with a skin complaint and Susanna Bolton was visiting her. When they heard the sound of gunfire from the Tower of London (a signal that a battle had been won), Susanna wondered if it was 'news from my brother'. Emma thought there could not be a result so soon and it must be a victory elsewhere. Five minutes later a carriage arrived, and Captain Whitby from the Admiralty was shown in. Emma believed he was bringing her letters. As she later told Lady Foster:

> He came in, and with a pale countenance and faint voice said, 'We have gained a great Victory'. 'Never mind your victory', I said, 'My letters – give me my letters' – Capt. Whitby was unable to speak – tears in his eyes and a deathly paleness over his face made me comprehend him. I believe I gave one scream and fell back, and for ten hours after I could neither speak nor shed a tear – days have passed on and I know not how they end or begin – nor how I am to bear my future existence.

She had to steel herself to tell little Horatia about her father's death. A week later, Lady Foster visited Emma in Clarges Street and found her weeping in bed with Nelson's letters strewn across the coverlet. 'She had the appearance of a person stunned and scarcely as yet able to comprehend the certainty of her loss. "What shall I do?" and "How can I exist?" were her first words.' Emma was eager for news about Nelson's death and Lady Foster told her what she knew, extrapolating her information from reports in the newspapers. Emma burst into further floods of tears, and when she was calmer, Bess asked her if she thought he 'had any presentiment of his fate'. Emma replied no, not until their parting, when 'he had come back four different times, and the last time he had kneeled down and holding up his hand had prayed God to bless her'. Nelson, Emma told her, 'had requested her to take the sacrament with him at Merton, "for," he said, "we both stand before our God with pure hearts and affection" '.[369]

Emma lay in bed prostrate with grief for three weeks. She told anyone and everyone about her misery. A heartfelt lament landed on the desk of Alexander Davison.

I have been very ill all Day my Heart Broken & my Head Consequently weak from the agitations I Suffer – I tell you Truly – I am gone nor do I wish to Live – He that I loved more than Life He is gone Why then shou'd I Live or wish to Live I Lived but for Him all now is a Dreary prospect before me I never lamented the Loss of a Kingdom (for I was Queen of Naples) for *seven years*, nor one Sigh ever Escaped me for the Loss I Sustained When I fell from Such a height of grateness & Happiness of Naples to misery and wretchedness – But all I lov'd have sustained with firmness but the Loss of Nelson under this Dreadfull weight of Most wretched Misery that I suffer.[370]

She received visits from Nelson's valet, William Chevailler, and Dr Alexander Scott, his secretary and chaplain, as well as Dr Beatty, his surgeon. Nelson had begged his good friend, Captain Hardy, to give Emma his personal effects and he sent, via Chevailler, Nelson's 'hair, lockets, rings, breast-pin, and all your Ladyship's pictures'. Most sorrowfully of all, she received her letters to him about Horatia and Lord Douglas's tobacco. The letters above are the only ones from Emma to Nelson that he did not burn. He never saw them.

Emma pieced together the events of the battle from the newspapers and accounts from her visitors. By twenty minutes before noon on 21 October, the French ships were firing, but the *Victory*, with Nelson standing on deck, broke through their line of ships, and attacked the French vessel *Bucentaure*. Then *Victory* met the French ship, *Redoubtable*. The French captain armed his men with guns, sent them to scale the rigging, and told them to aim for the officers. Covered in stars, walking around the main deck of a flagship, Nelson blazed through the smoke. At quarter past one, a single musket ball fired from a gun on the French ship struck his left shoulder. He was carried down to the cockpit below the waterline, now the ship's hospital, and laid on a sheet on the bare wood, painted red to disguise the blood. Nelson realised the ball was lodged in his spine and said he 'felt it break my back'. He knew he was dying.

'My sufferings are great, but they will be soon over,' he said, but he took until four o'clock to die. All around him, hundreds of men were dying while others screamed in agony as surgeons removed shrapnel, musket balls and splinters, and amputated mangled limbs. The only anaesthetic was rum or laudanum for the officers. Fifteen minutes after Nelson was hit, the *Redoubtable* surrendered. Nelson ignored his purser's promise that he would take the news of the victory home. Stripped to his shirt, his head resting on the discarded coat of a midshipman, he felt gushing in his chest and was numb in the lower half of his body. As his lungs filled with blood, he slowly drowned in his own fluids. By three o'clock, fourteen ships had surrendered. Nelson begged Captain Hardy not to throw him overboard and to 'take care of my dear Lady Hamilton, Hardy, take care of poor Lady Hamilton'. Although Hardy then heard him say 'Kiss me, Hardy,' it seems equally possible that Nelson, already on the subject of Emma, was trying to say, 'Kiss Emma for me, Hardy.'

Alexander Scott and William Beatty rubbed his chest in an attempt to dull the pain. They helped him to drink a little and fanned him until he died. In a letter written in the previous May, Nelson promised Emma she was 'my first and last thoughts'. She was his last thought. Dr Scott dashed off the news to Mrs Cadogan, 'Hasten the very moment you receive this to dear Lady Hamilton and prepare her for the greatest of misfortunes.'[371]

It was some weeks before Emma heard that Nelson's last words were of her and that he had begged the nation to care for her and Horatia. Dividing her time between London and Merton, she was overcome by grief. In the absence of William, Sarah and Charlotte Nelson, who were busy separating themselves from her, she relied on Nelson's sisters. Kitty Matcham complained to her son, George, that Merton was 'very dull; quite the reverse to what you knew it'. She wanted to leave but 'it really is cruel to mention our going to my Lady at present'.[372] Emma often took to her bed with Nelson's belongings, receiving her visitors in tears. Abraham Goldsmid, her neighbour, a wealthy Jewish banker, brought his large family to console her and found her sobbing and passing Nelson's gifts of shawls, rings and bracelets to a solemn group of fifteen, gathered theatrically at the bottom of the bed. She showed Nelson's coat with a flourish, pointing out how the bullet hole was stiff with congealed blood . . . Emma found that elaborate expression helped temper her anguish. She took Horatia to see the wax model of Nelson at Westminster Abbey and wept copiously as she rearranged the hair.

Lady Foster tried to encourage Emma to focus on practical matters. She wondered if Nelson's family had been kind. Emma praised Kitty's husband, George Matcham, who 'scarcely leaves me, but tries to make me take some food, or medicine – something to do me good – and with the greatest affection'. She was, however, surprised that William Nelson often seemed elated. Emma did not guess it, but William was exhilarated to hear that Nelson had died without changing his will. Bess thought Emma too trusting. Emma, she reported, told her that her lover had 'left her Merton, that at first she would have given it up to [William Nelson] but then she thought not. I advised her not by any means.' Emma was plagued by worries. Nelson had promised that his last breath would be 'occupied in leaving you independent of the World'. As she owed astronomical sums of money, she could only hope he had kept his word.

Nelson's will was read in November. William Nelson inherited the estate, excluding Merton, but including Bronte, and he also received Nelson's bank accounts and possessions. The government had made William an Earl and his son Horace a Viscount, the titles Nelson had so desperately desired, and now he was also Duke of Bronte. Emma received £2,000, plus Merton with all its furniture and fittings and seventy acres of land, including all the hay, and also £500 a year from the Bronte estate. She would have much less than she had when Nelson was alive.

She tried to assuage her grief for her lover by helping others. Like her, the Boltons and the Matchams had spent lavishly in expectation of Nelson's victorious return. Emma gave them money and deputised her mother to write to George Rose that Nelson died 'leaving behind his favourite Sister with a large family unprovided for'. Mrs Cadogan declared, 'Lady Hamilton who's situation is beyond description only prays that you good Sir will do all you can for this Worthy Family it will give the greatest Relief to her Mind . . . as a Mark of your true & Real attachment to our Lamented Hero.' She wrote that the Boltons 'at this Moment surround her Ladyships Bed bewailing their sad loss & miserable state'. After Nelson's death, his friends, relations and colleagues were frantic to ensure they did not miss out when the government handed out honours and money. Most demanded Emma's help.

Emma had no idea of the intrigues that swirled around her. Many ordinary people blamed the war for inflation and high taxes, and there had been an outcry at the sheer numbers of servicemen who had lost their lives. The government wanted to make Nelson's funeral into a rallying call for British patriotism. Apotheosised as the perfect hero, his love life and his personal flaws would be erased.

V. Backlash

49

Mistress of a Mourning Nation

Nelson had told Emma he wished her to sing during his funeral. They had even made plans to be buried together. The public agreed that Nelson and Emma were inseparable: print shops were full of etchings, drawings and engravings in which Emma was depicted as mourner, a Britannia figure draped in white. One popular engraving showed Emma crowning Nelson's bust with a wreath. Even James Gillray produced a sentimental caricature of Nelson taken to the sky, while Emma wept over him. The Admiralty took a quite different view. Nelson might have been Emma's in life, but now he was the property of the nation, and he would be commemorated in a service led by men.

The hero's body was preserved in a cask of spirits and shipped home, not to Fanny, not to Emma, nor even to his brother, but to the state. Emma had tried to view the body when it landed, but Captain Hardy discouraged her, knowing the sight of the swollen corpse would distress her. On 24 December, Nelson, now laid in his coffin, was transferred to an official yacht, and then taken along the Thames to Greenwich Hospital. He was placed in the Painted Hall on a platform six foot high, adorned with a black canopy spangled with gold and a wreath bearing the words 'Trafalgar'. When the doors were opened for two days on 5 January, 30,000 people scrambled past, pushed by overstressed guards. Only the Prince of Wales and the sailors from *Victory* were permitted a private viewing. Emma probably queued with the crowds to enter the Painted Hall with Horatia, swathed in the huge black veil that Vigée le Brun had seen her wear to mourn Sir William.

The funeral was one of the most lavish commemorations in British history. Emma was firmly excluded. On 8 January, Nelson's body was taken up river on a giant barge from Greenwich to the Admiralty at Whitehall, escorted by a procession of boats. Thousands gathered on the banks of the Thames to catch a glimpse of the coffin. The following morning, Nelson was driven to St Paul's Cathedral in an opulent funeral car shaped to resemble the *Victory* trailed by a procession of carriages two miles long. Hysterical crowds thronged the route, controlled by 30,000 soldiers. Inside St Paul's, 7,000 admirals, politicians and aristocrats in their finest dress coats had been shivering in the pews since early morning. Although many of them had disparaged Nelson's reckless behaviour while he was alive and mocked his lack of aristocratic pedigree, they were not about to miss out on the funeral of the century. A few fashionable ladies stole into the loft, but most had to content themselves with watching the procession in the streets. At half past five the coffin was lowered into the crypt twenty foot below the stone floor. The men of the *Victory* had been ordered to unfurl the flags of the ship over the grave. Instead, the church resonated to the sound of tearing as the forty-eight sailors ripped the largest flag apart with their bare hands, desperate to keep some small scrap of Nelson for themselves.

Emma spent the day in tears over her letters, accompanied by her mother, daughter and Nelson's female relations. The men of the Bolton and Matcham families were invited to the funeral, and Emma gave both families dinner and breakfast, accommodated the Boltons and probably also received William and Horace Nelson. A weeping female figure who looked very like Emma was carved on the coffin. Otherwise, she was absent, carefully written out of the heroic story. Nelson's body was interred in a ten feet high slab of ornately carved porphyry – a huge grave for such a diminutive man. Ever thrifty, when asked to donate in the memory of Nelson, George III sent a sarcophagus which had been hanging around in the cellars of Windsor Castle ever since Henry VIII seized it from Cardinal Wolsey. Still, as it cost only £6,300 to dedicate it to Nelson, the state saved some money. Now, Nelson's sarcophagus is the grand focus of St Paul's Crypt, brilliantly lit, outdazzling the monuments to Wellington and Florence Nightingale, proudly on show to the thousands of tourists.

The funeral cost the state £14,000. The *Morning Herald* derided the descent of Nelson's body into the crypt as a tasteless 'stage trick' and the *Morning Chronicle* disdained the 'meagre and monotonous music'.

Many judged the cost obscene, considering the dire poverty of so many injured veterans and sailors' widows and orphans.

More than anything, the funeral was an opportunity for hundreds to make a profit. Guests sold their invitations for a fortune, both before and after the event. The vergers at St Paul's earned more than £40 a day allowing visitors to have a peep before the service, and accrued £300 a day after the funeral by charging a shilling to view the catafalque. London tradesmen sold special carriages, jewellery and clothes to guests. Pie shop and tavern owners made massive takings from the crowds watching the procession. Thousands bought commemorative jewellery, prints or boxes. Nelson relics – many fake – were changing hands for ridiculous prices. Emma, however, refused to sell any of her possessions. She was determined to be the keeper of Nelson's dignity and maintain his heroic reputation for the rest of her life. It was not going to be easy.

Nelson's death and his funeral fired a spectacular market in outlandishly expensive fashions aimed at women. Embroiderers worked overtime sewing Nelson's name on to drapery for tearful fine ladies to wear while they mourned the great hero. A sumptuous fashion plate in the February 1806 edition of *Bell's Court and Fashionable Magazine* illustrated a 'Trafalgar Dress', which was another version of Emma's habitual costume: a white satin gown trimmed with gold, silver or lace along with a turban embroidered with 'Nelson' and topped with feathers. According to the March edition, the Bronte hat and muff was ideal for the 'higher order of fashionables'.[373] Trafalgar even became the name of an embroidery stitch – perhaps a cross formation – which proved so newfangled and difficult that even experienced needlewomen (including Jane Austen's sister-in-law) found it tricky. William Tassie, one of the foremost cameo makers of the day, worked feverishly to satisfy the demand for heads of Nelson for jewellers to set in rings and brooches. Shopkeepers could not stock up fast enough with black-edged, sentimental commemorative tablecloths, napkins, clocks, boxes, trunks, plant pots and door handles. Emma was the heroine of most of the items. She starred in prints as chief mourner and lockets, boxes and other decorated items were painted with her figure, a dark-haired woman, weeping and dressed in white.

Magazine stories and novels exploiting Nelson's love life poured off the presses. In them, a virginal, beautiful heroine named Amelia, Amy or Ellen was courted by a brave sea captain, Horace or Horatio, the affair often sponsored by older characters called Sir William and Lady Frances. In *A Soldier's Friendship and A Sailor's Love* (1805) by Anna Maria Porter, the lovely young musical heroine (who has a very common mother) was adopted by a Lady Frances and educated by her neighbour the aged Sir William Hereford, then courted by the handsome naval Captain. In the second half of the book, another Nelson and Emma pair appears, but the hero may only marry his beloved, Amelia, after he meets a very wealthy widow with a young son in the West Indies, because she dies and leaves her money to him; an intriguing revision of Nelson's marriage.

Eliza Parsons's *The Navy Lieutenant* (1806) was the most blatant attempt to support Horatia and extol Nelson. Parsons's Henry Thompson, the 'third son of a country curate' (Nelson was the fifth son but two elder brothers died), goes to sea at eleven, is promoted to lieutenant, but although loved by his men, he offends his superiors and is retired on half pay. When he returns to sea, he meets a young woman, Ellen, who has suffered at the hands of men and begs him to care for her baby daughter. He calls the child Fanny Thompson and gives her to a nurse. Ellen's surname is later discovered to be Thompson, and so the story is about Henry Thompson and Ellen Thompson, a piquant twist when Nelson and Emma had taken almost identical pen names. Ellen's history of exploitation by aristocrats resembles Emma's – even the ages of her seducers match those of Fetherstonhaugh and Greville at the time. The nurse becomes troublesome and demands a huge bribe to relinquish little Fanny. Parsons's novel implies that the public knew a lot about Emma's life: her previous lovers, Horatia, the Thompson letters and even about the pay-off to Mrs Gibson.[374]

As soon as Nelson was buried, the begging letters began. His former friends and colleagues believed Emma was about to become vastly rich. Some wanted mementoes of the great man but most desired money and favours. Even the King and Queen of Naples wondered if she might be able to press their cause with her influential friends. Charles Greville wanted to decorate his chapel at Milford Haven with the flagstaff of the French ship blown up at the Nile, *L'Orient*, which Nelson had once displayed in pride of place in his cabin. Only a few months after the funeral, Dr William Beatty beseeched Emma to persuade the Prince of Wales to endorse his written account of the death of Nelson, which, he declared, would outsell any biography. Then, desiring a promotion for Mr Margrath, an assistant surgeon on the *Victory*, he requested her to inform the Prime Minister of 'the high opinion Lord Nelson entertained of his conduct and Professional acquirements'.[375]

William Nelson rebuffed anyone seeking favour. He firmly informed one Captain J. Yule, 'You are in the same situation with many other Gallant officers who served with my poor Brother, & who I have no doubt would have been promoted by him had it pleased God to have preserved, – but I am truly grieved to say I have no interest whatever at the Admiralty & therefore have no power to be of the smallest service to you in furthering your wishes for employment.' He explained he had been obliged to 'give this answer to many other of my Brother's followers'.[376] Earl Nelson would not help, and Fanny declined, so everybody turned to Emma. Dr Beatty wrote, 'I shall not now, My dear Lady, enter into a long apology for this my recent intrusion.'[377] He never did thank her.

Emma spent 1806 keeping up the act. She was in demand: everyone wanted to dine with her or attend one of her parties. She continued to spend on the alterations to Merton, unfinished at Nelson's death. Nelson thought that the bequest of Merton would ensure his mistress's financial stability, but she would have been better off if he had left it to Earl Nelson. She was impoverishing herself trying to make it into a sentimental monument to him. Many goods that Nelson had ordered arrived and had to be paid for. The fine breakfast service that he had ordered from the Worcester porcelain factory while touring his adoring populace in 1802 was finally completed, and Emma had to pay for it and find space for it in her home. Other plates, pictures, ornaments and jewels of him she bought new. Every salesman knew she was a soft touch and they flocked to her, brandishing commemorative tat.

Emma attempted to pursue the subject of the codicil to Nelson's will. Everyone thought Prime Minister Pitt was 'kindly intended towards Lady Hamilton'.[378] Although he had ignored her entreaty for a pension before Nelson's death and would probably do so again, she was optimistic, but her hopes were dashed when he died unexpectedly in late January and was succeeded by Lord Grenville who was unsympathetic to her pleas. When kindly Abraham Goldsmid offered to assist her, she pushed him to pursue the claims of Nelson's sisters. In May, Lord Grenville sent the codicil to Nelson's will to William Haslewood, Nelson's solicitor, with a note saying that nothing could be done. Instead, the Boltons and the Matchams received £10,000 apiece while William Nelson was awarded £100,000 to buy an estate to be called Trafalgar, as well as £5,000 a year for life, which would also go to his descendants. Fanny received £2,000 a year. Grenville claimed the government had other families to care for. They could not set a precedent by supporting a mistress. 'I am plagued by lawyers, ill-used by the Government,' Emma despaired. 'I was very happy at Naples, but all seems gone like a dream.'

After advertising for owners of suitable estates, the government became hopelessly caught up in debating which house would best honour Nelson.[379] In the Public Record Office at Kew are dozens of heavy books full of documentation on the purchase of Earl Nelson's Trafalgar. All the while, Merton was devouring money. The popular press weighed in on Emma's side and even the morally conservative *Lady's Magazine* published an unctuous reminder that his home was Lord Nelson's greatest love. Readers were treated to a lavish depiction of Merton as a haphazard collection of towers and hexagonal buildings, as the journalist praised its 'delightful situation' and the 'equally elegant and convenient' house and tasteful grounds. The piece pointedly concludes, 'It was at this seat that the gallant admiral, before he sailed on his last expedition, took leave of his friends, among whom were some of the most worthy, and also some of the most illustrious persons in the kingdom.'[380]

Furious at the government's dismissive treatment of her, Emma threatened public vengeance. 'Let them refuse me all reward! I will go with this paper fixed to my breast and beg through the streets of London, and every barrow-woman shall say, "Nelson bequeathed her, to *us*."'[381] But the love of the ordinary people was worth nothing: the government had made its decision and it wanted Emma to disappear.

Nelson had seen many women, including his first love, Mary Moutray, refused pensions, and he knew that the government would not give Emma one for being an envoy's wife. Yet he seemed to think she would be given money for being his mistress. In the same codicil he had written, 'my relations it is needless to mention; they will of course be amply provided for'. Really, he knew in his heart how the government would distribute the honours. The situation might have been different if Horatia had been a boy for the government would have been nervous that a little Horatio Nelson would become a focus for oppositional sentiment and a force to reckon with as a future political leader. Daughters were usually disinherited for they were expected to make their fortunes by marriage. Always a dreamer, Nelson had believed that he was so great that the government would break all precedent and shower honours on his illegitimate daughter, elevating her as the inheritor of his blood.

Nelson should have predicted Emma's fate. He had left her a house, but £500 a year was not enough to maintain it, as well as a child, even if Emma had been a skilled and frugal housekeeper. A man, when he died, usually impoverished his wife and daughters by willing his property to his closest male relation, but then asked in his will that his heir care for them. Usually, the heir gave them little, an outcome scathingly laid bare by Jane Austen when she described the penurious state of the Dashwood sisters in *Sense and Sensibility*.[382] Now that he was the heir, Earl Nelson wanted every penny of Nelson's estate for his son. Nelson's vision of Emma after his death, singing at his funeral, happy with his family, bringing up Horatia in security, may have comforted him as he faced death, but it was a fantasy.

Inspired by the torrent of gossip and scandalous novels, would-be writers and biographers were demanding to read Emma's letters. Earl Nelson was the most pressing of all. Intending to commission a biography that would outsell all the others being discussed, he wanted the whole cache, even the most explicit. In between sending her cheering verses, the poet William Hayley expressly told her '*as your very sincere friend*, I should advise you to retain these Letters in your own Custody, & not suffer *even me*, your old and faithful Friend, to persuade you to impart them to the Public, except at some distant day, *as a Legacy to your Country from yourself*'.[383] Emma followed his advice, much to Earl Nelson's anger. Her relations with him quickly became strained. Sarah, now Countess, Nelson wrote to Emma demanding the bloody coat, 'in point of right there can be no doubt to whom this precious relic belongs'.[384] Emma behaved emolliently, still hoping that William Nelson might give money to Horatia. She was disappointed. He was infuriated by Nelson's provision that his estate should pay the expenses and bills at Merton for six months after his death and utterly unable to feel sympathy for the child. He accused Emma of adding on bills accrued before Trafalgar and demanded that Mrs Cadogan show him the accounts. At the same time, he failed to pay the £500 pension due her from Bronte. Believing his brother's lies that he loved Emma and Horatia, Nelson had noted in his will that Horatia might marry William Nelson's son, Horace. While his brother was alive, William enthused about the idea and encouraged him to fund his son's education. As soon as Nelson died, he forbade Horace to visit Emma and made plans for his son to marry a rich aristocrat.

In Emma's time, only the very richest woman could survive without the legal protection and financial support of a man. Emma's only chance of keeping herself and Horatia in a genteel manner was to remarry immediately. But she could not bring herself to look for another partner. Despite Grenville's refusal, she still hoped that the government would honour the codicil. She threw herself into society once more, anxious to make herself so conspicuous that she could not be overlooked.

50

Fashion on Credit

*I*n the two years after Nelson's death, Emma was the most popular guest in London. Everybody clamoured to meet the mistress of a national icon. In an attempt to numb her grief and gain support for her mission to win a pay-out from the government, Emma attended every event. From 1806 to 1808 she retained her central place in the premier society of the Prince of Wales and his chatterbox brothers Clarence and Sussex, and continued to be one of London's leading charitable patrons, as well as a cultural doyenne hosting splendid performances by singers including Madame Bianchi and Mrs Billington. She was playing a role that was impossible to sustain.

Emma received only a few thousand pounds from Nelson's will, and it was on the annual £800 left to her by Sir William (given to her net of tax by Greville) that she tried to maintain her role as the inheritrix of Nelson's glory. In December 1806, the will was published in the press. The nation read that Nelson entrusted Lady Hamilton and Horatia to the care of the government and assigned Horatia Thompson to the guardianship of Lady Hamilton, also decreeing that the infant's surname be changed to Nelson. Since women were treated as juveniles under the law, unable to retain their money and entirely subject to the will of their husbands or male relations, children were always left to the guardianship of a man, never a woman. The publication of his will made it obvious to everybody that Horatia was Emma's daughter.

Countess Sarah and Lady Charlotte Nelson moved swiftly to sever their links with Emma. 'Is it true that Lady Charlotte Nelson can be ungrateful,' marvelled Emma. About £2,000 of her debts had been accrued paying for Charlotte's education, clothes, presents, holidays and board for seven years, as well as many of Horace's expenses but, as Emma wrote resentfully, 'they have never given the dear Horatia a Frock nor a sixpence'.[385] She had cared for Charlotte in order to please Nelson and to seem respectable, but she had soon become genuinely fond of the teenager and she missed her deeply. Emma had spent hundreds of thousands supporting Nelson's bid for celebrity, but it was grasping William who benefited from it all. A letter remains in which Sarah invited Emma to dine at half past five, but communicated that the Connors and Horatia were not welcome until the other guests had left. As Sarah commanded, 'whatever young people you may have with you, we shall hope to see them at eight o'clock, as we have some other friends dine with us'. She signed herself 'S Nelson and Bronte', the title Emma so wished to possess.[386]

Charlotte's exit did not reduce Emma's expenses. The Boltons and the Matchams deposited their adolescent daughters with her to educate, clothe and introduce at parties. Incensed that Earl Nelson had refused to give them anything, they inundated her with begging letters. Emma handed over more cash she did not have and implored the government and her famous friends for money on their behalf. Susanna Bolton thought that Emma's 'affairs were drawing to a crisis' and encouraged her to focus on her own needs. 'With or without the child, if you are well provided for, she can never *want*,' she pressed. 'Depend on it she will marry *well*.'[387] But she continued to ask for favours. She shied from begging for further help from the Prince of Wales, declaring '*you must deliver the message in your own name*, we are not in the habit of sending & speaking to such great personages'. Since Nelson's will was published in the newspapers, every one of them should have realised that Emma had little to give, but it suited them to believe her act of being a wealthy woman. 'I only wish you had fortune equal to your generosity,' Susanna sighed, but by then she had helped herself to a large amount of Emma's 'fortune'.

Emma moved from Clarges Street to cheaper lodgings in 136 New Bond Street. But she could not relinquish the monument to Nelson's glory she had so lovingly created, and Merton creaked on, guzzling every penny from her purse. By February 1806, the unpaid bills had reached £1,300. Struggling to borrow and scrimp, Mrs Cadogan had no spare money for her relations and so they began to blackmail Emma. Her older brother, feckless, hard drinking William Kidd, was nearly seventy and wanted to live out the rest of his life in ease, thanks to his famous niece. He had plenty of ammunition: details about Emma's early adulthood and, most terrible of all, insinuations about the mysterious death of her father. Emma had paid him off before, but she could no longer meet his huge demands. He threatened to come and occupy Merton until she gave him the hundreds he required. Mrs Cadogan vowed to bar the door against him, staunchly declaring that she would never let him under her roof, 'never does he sleep in the house where I do'.

Ann, the youngest daughter of Mrs Cadogan's sister, Mrs Connor, was proving equally troublesome. She felt she deserved some of her aunt's riches, since Emma had adopted her elder sisters, Cecilia and later Sarah, as nursery governesses on huge salaries, and Nelson had bought her brother, Charles, a commission in the navy. Ann whipped herself up into a state of furious resentment, soon so angry with her mother for holding her back (as she saw it) that she convinced herself she was not her parents' child. In the autumn, she wrote blackmailing notes, threatening to expose Lady Hamilton as her mother and, as Emma despaired, 'persecuted me by her slander and falsehood'.[388] Emboldened to bully Emma for money because she had no male protector, her family were battering at her door. After Emma Carew came on a short summer visit in late June, Sir Harry Fetherstonhaugh sent £500 for the benefit of mother and daughter (perhaps as a bribe to ensure Emma kept his parentage a secret), but few others showed her any generosity.

By September 1806, it was clear that the government was ignoring Nelson's last request. 'It seems that those that truly loved him are to be victims to hatred, jealousy and spite,' Emma lamented. Sir William's old secretary, Francis Oliver, had solicited her help for his journalist friend, James Harrison, and his large family. She invited them to live at Merton and paid their expenses for at least six months while she employed Harrison to write a two-volume *Life of Nelson*. Published at the end of 1806, Harrison's *Life* ran rapturous on the virtuous nature of her affair with Nelson, while making it clear that Horatia was his child, and it pressed the government to honour the codicil.

Creditors were still pursuing Emma, but no one in high society suspected that Nelson's glamorous mistress was poor. When she emerged from mourning, she was once more at the helm of style. The classical look had slightly slipped out of favour, but after Nelson's death, the season's most sought-after look was once more 'petticoat white crape, a Grecian drapery elegantly drawn up' and flat slippers, just as Emma had worn for her Attitudes.[389] Everywhere she went, she took her belongings with her: the Nelson souvenirs, the relics and most dramatically his blood-spattered coat, which servants in the houses of her hosts fought to have the privilege of airing.[390] Afraid of losing her friends, Emma tried to be an exciting guest. Discussing Emma's visit to town, Lady Abercorn commanded, 'We hope you will not forget any of your shawls or things for attitudes.' Emma had previously experimented with different kinds of performance, and before Nelson's death, she had often refused to perform the Attitudes. Now, frantic to keep her place in high society, she had to recreate the old favourites she had perfected at twenty-six.

Dreary supper parties across London perked up when Lady Hamilton arrived. George Villiers Hyde, Earl of Clarendon, asked to meet her. Delighted by 'her talent and cleverness at conversation', he encouraged Emma to describe her sea voyage from Naples to Palermo in 1799.

> Her picture of the danger and horror which had surrounded her was awful almost to reality, and it was diversified by the introduction of some ludicrous incidents, which had occurred at the time, in a manner not unlike that of Shakespeare – particularly an anecdote of the pursuit of an old Duenna after her confessor, in the utmost eagerness to say a sin or two before she sank.

Since her audience seemed so interested in imitations of peasant women, Emma performed another act.

> Lady Hamilton arose from table to address herself to the supposed image of the Virgin, in the character of a young Italian peasant, who wished for permission to remarry. Her shawl was adjusted as if mantling an infant, and she supplicated her patroness with every possible intreaty . . . interrupted only by soothings and caresses of her child. The Saint being supposed to remain unmoved by her prayers, they were heightened into expostulations, and, at length, with an apparent impulse of forwardness, she arose and turned from the image – But, after having retired a few paces in disdain, she seemed to recollect herself, and again turned, her countenance and attitude changing, at once into an expression of resignation and humility so captivating that she seemed to have reserved the full effect of her genius for the conclusion of the personification, which ended in her again casting herself at the feet of the image.[391]

Emma's overblown style was perfect for an age when Sarah Siddons was acclaimed for tearing up the scenery when she played Lady Macbeth. At her writing desk, Emma scribbled begging letters, flitting between demanding the government carry out Nelson's wishes and requesting a pension for her services in Naples. Unhappy that Mrs Fox, widow of Charles James Fox and previously a courtesan, received a pension of more than £1,200 a year, she began to lie that she herself had collected the Neapolitan gold from Maria Carolina to put it on Nelson's ship, rather than receiving the convoys of luggage at the Palazzo Sessa. Still no money came. Her position was hopeless. If she had sold Merton immediately, dismissed all her servants, and retired with Horatia to a cheap rented house in Norfolk, perhaps, or by the sea, she could have managed on Sir William's legacy. But she owed about £7,000 at Nelson's death, and she had over a dozen people directly dependent on her, with many more soliciting regular payouts. She had no choice but to keep up Merton and continue wasting her money in London, the city with the highest cost of living in the world. Her life was crammed with concerts, parties and dinners with the Royal Princes, the amorous Duke of Clarence and the Duke of Sussex, and sometimes their high-rolling brother, George, Prince of Wales. She was sure they would force the government to honour her.

Emma, Horatia, Mrs Cadogan and the Boltons, Madame Bianchi and the Matcham sisters spent August at Worthing. Emma's large party rose early to bathe and then rode and walked in the balmy sun, returning to array themselves for sumptuous supper concerts featuring Emma and Madame Bianchi, to which Emma diligently invited every influential person she could meet. The press was always happy to see Lady Hamilton and her little 'god-daughter' frolicking on the sands, especially after the publication of Nelson's will had made it crystal clear to the world that Horatia was his child by her. As Emma wrote to Sarah Nelson, Horatia 'creates universal enterest alltho' Princess Charlotte is here' and 'all come to look at Nelson's angel'. Emma's residence near thirteen-year-old Princess Charlotte, the Prince of Wales's shy only daughter and the heir to the throne, was no coincidence: she wanted the press corps following the Royal party to see Horatia, and she intended to accost the Prince of Wales when he was in a receptive, relaxed mood. Instead, she was besieged by others requesting money and favour. A chaplain who had been present at the Battle of the Nile turned up, demanding money and promises of introductions to those who could help his career.

Horatia was Emma's solace.

She improves in languages, musick and accomplishments but my heart Bleeds to think how proud wou'd her glorious Father have been. *He that lived only for her . . .* 'tis dreadful to me however she is my Comfort and solace and I act as alltho' he could look down and approve and bless Emma for following up His every wish.[392]

Nelson had desired his daughter to be clever, accomplished and well educated, and Emma was determined that his dream would be fulfilled. Behind Emma's bravado, Mrs Cadogan was fighting to make ends meet and the burden was weakening her health.

Emma achieved her greatest social triumph at the end of November 1807. Eternal party boys the Dukes of Sussex and Clarence came to Merton for an extended visit and the Prince of Wales also agreed to attend. The expense finally wrecked Emma's finances. The three brothers arrived with their entourages: Dorothy Jordan and her children with Clarence, and Lady Hertford, the Prince of Wales's mistress, as well as friends, servants, horses and carriages. Rooms had to be rearranged, new furniture and decorations bought, entertainment hired, and the cellar stocked with the finest wines. Emma invited Madame Bianchi and Mrs Billington and other singers and eminent guests. Keen that everyone share her passion for Horatia, she coached the little girl in singing and dancing and the two performed Attitudes and songs together to the great pleasure of the audience. 'You delight me by saying that Horatia has so much notice taken of her,' flattered Susanna Bolton. 'I hope, when she is introduced at Windsor, George our King will fall in love with her, & give her a good pension out of his privy purse.' Convinced she had won over the Prince, Emma sent a splendid parcel of food to the Boltons. 'How favoured you have been by their Royal Highnesses passing so many days with you,' Susanna wrote. 'I do not wonder their liking Merton & *your* society.'

The Duke of Sussex so enjoyed his visit that he returned in early January with Mrs Billington. He retired to his room when young George Matcham arrived seeking money, but Emma was less skilled at dodging supplicants. Quick to capitalise on his patroness's illustrious guests, Dr Beatty wrote to her enthusing how it would be 'highly gratifying to my feelings and flattering to my reputation' if she could obtain him the position of surgeon with the Prince of Wales, a ridiculous promotion for a ship's surgeon, even if he had watched Nelson die.[393]

The Royal brothers did not give Emma money or speak to government ministers on her behalf, nor did they invite her to Court. Although the Duke of Clarence had wept copiously at Nelson's funeral and displayed a bust of the hero and a mast of the *Victory* in his dining room until he died, he was not prepared to help the admiral's struggling mistress in any way. Clarence and Sussex had no concept of financial hardship and actually thought themselves poor, while the Prince of Wales was concerned only with gratifying his many extravagant desires. He was, in the words of *The Times*, 'of all known beings the most selfish', a spoiled brat who cared only to squander money and indulge 'the most puerile caprices'.

Within three years of Nelson's death, Emma was more than £15,000 in debt. A few months after the Royal Princes left, her creditors were threatening to send officers to arrest her. Emma was in desperate straits. Merton would have to be sold.

51

Selling Nelson

*E*mma was bitterly disappointed with the surveyor's valuation.
He assessed the house and grounds as worth £10,430, with an
extra £2,500 for the effects and furniture, including the wines
and Nelson memorabilia. Although his estimate was £1,500 more than
the purchase price, Emma's projects to build new rooms, a kitchen,
landscape the gardens and drive, add stables and a tunnel, redecorate,
stock the ponds and canal with fish and build pens and coops, had cost
more than £8,000. When a reasonable estate sold for least £50,000,
and the grand estate of Standlynch near Salisbury which became Earl
Nelson's palatial Trafalgar estate, £120,000, Nelson and Emma had been
mad to attempt to turn a £9,000 ruin into a magisterial country home.

In June 1808, Merton failed to sell at auction and in July, Emma
moved out for good. The house was put on the market. Heartbroken
to leave it half-finished, she wanted the next buyer to keep it intact –
and to pay over the odds. Kitty Matcham comforted her that she would
be happier in 'constant residence' at London because 'you can enjoy
the society of your friends, without the immense expence of entertaining their servants, which you are obliged to do in the country'. She
encouraged Emma to believe that a wealthy patron would appear. 'I am
delighted to hear of your going to all these great parties.'[394] A despondent Emma consoled herself with socialising and making big donations
to the Foundling Hospital.[395] As Horatia later recalled, 'Hardly a month
passed but we used to drive to the Magdalen or the Blind School.'[396]

Aristocrats relished her dinners and applauded her dances, but they saw
her as only a pleasant diversion. Hundreds had enjoyed her generous hospitality over the years, but they fled when she begged for help. From 1800

to 1805, William Beckford praised her and expressed passionate desires to see her. In 1806, Britain's richest man would rather she left him alone. 'You are justly aware, my dear Ldy Hamilton, that I know nothing about money matters – Mr Pedlers is the Money Man and if you will send to him I dare say he will do what he can.' He tried to shunt her on to another relation of Sir William's, the eighty-four-year-old Duke of Queensberry, notorious for his colossal wealth and fond eye for the ladies. Why, he wondered, 'did you not think of old Q in the midst of those Merton Plagues? – He is wallowing in gold and a few hundreds could not be missed from his Heap – my treasury is at a very low ebb.'[397] But Emma had already turned to Queensberry and she still needed more.

Emma was losing her old friends. The Duchess of Devonshire, whom she had tried so hard to court, died in 1806 and when Bess Foster married the Duke, her position was too insecure to allow her to give her burdened friend much help. Emma's most loyal friends were actresses and singers, such as Mrs Billington, Dora Jordan and Madame Bianchi, but they could not fund her or supply government contacts. In a time when only just over one per cent of the population owned land and there were no rich foreigners to buttonhole, someone hoping for charity had only a few possible benefactors. Emma was now relying heavily on the Duke of Queensberry and her neighbour Abraham Goldsmid.

The Duke of Queensberry offered her his large villa in Richmond, then an expensive village on the Thames, for a peppercorn rent. Lavish 'Herring House' had eight bedrooms, a dressing room, a study and a bathroom, four reception rooms, a billiard room, offices, servants' quarters and ample stabling. Emma carted over the best heavy mahogany furniture from Merton, the ornate four-poster bed she had shared with Nelson, portraits, glass, china and silver plate, wine, and Sir William's treasures and library, including an original Domesday Book. She installed all her old servants, including the elderly Merton housekeeper, Dame Francis, her Sudanese maid Fatima, the highly paid Connor sisters and a troupe of footmen dressed in her own exclusive red livery. Most aristocrats cast off their staff whenever they fell into difficulties, giving them neither back pay nor a pension, just as Sir William had done to his Neapolitan valets. Emma was staunchly loyal and her large establishment drained her purse. She was similarly soft-hearted towards her hangers-on. George Matcham praised Emma's laudable 'plan of economy' but worried that it would have been better that 'the crowd of obsequeous attendance had been entirely dismissed instead of being partially diminished'.[398] Dozens of former servants, distant relatives and impoverished old friends lounged in her homes, many of them whining behind her back, others storing up rumours for future blackmail attempts. Some, like Melesina Trench, the travelling widow she had met in Dresden, visited frequently for dinners and parties while busying themselves writing bitchy accounts of her for their memoirs.

By July there was an offer on Merton of £13,000, exclusive of the valuable furniture and treasures. But there was also bad news. Mr Canning, the Foreign Secretary, had agreed to investigate the possibility of taking money from the Secret Service fund – perhaps up to £7,000 – for Emma, but he had written to George Rose that it could not be done. 'I have most anxiously and conscientiously discharged all that Lord Nelson could have expected from me if he were now alive, & I am *most sincerely grieved* that I have failed of success,' Rose wrote. He had been a true friend to Emma, but she pushed her luck too far. William Beatty rhapsodised about Emma's 'transcendent kindness' until she asked Rose to endorse his ludicrous desire to be surgeon to the Prince of Wales.[399] She felt very vulnerable to the doctor's demands. As the main witness to Nelson's final words, Dr Beatty had the power to withdraw his statement and damage her chance of help from the government.

The potential buyer of Merton pulled out, perhaps finding the kitsch decor too idiosyncratic, and aggrieved that Emma had removed the mahogany furniture and all the valuables, leaving the house stuffed with old furniture and dusty Nelson knick-knacks. The early 1800s were the worst years in decades to be selling a house. The war kept the property market sluggish and everybody dreaded a crash in the economy. There were no longer any foreign buyers and English people stayed put or rented. Emma wrote desperately to Queensberry:

you are the only hope I have in this world to assist and protect me, in this moment of unhappiness and distress. To you, therefore, I appeal. I do not wish to have more than what I have. I can live on that at Richmond, only that I may live free from fear – that every debt be paid. I think, and hope, £15,000 will do for everything, for my sake, for Nelson's sake, for the good I have done my country, purchase it; take it . . . I beseech you, my dear Duke, to imagine that I only wish for you to do this, not to lose by it; but I see that I am lost and most miserable if *you* do not help me. My mind is made up to live on what I have. If I could but be free from Merton – all paid and only one hundred pounds in my pocket, you will live to see me blessing you, my mother blessing you, Horatia blessing you. If you would not wish to keep Merton, perhaps it will sell in the spring better – only let me pass my winter without the idea of a prison. Tis true my imprudence has brought it on me, and villany and ingratitude has helped involve me, but the sin be on them. Do not let my enemies trample on me; for God's sake.

No doubt others received similar letters. Fifteen thousand pounds was more than the property was worth, and Queensberry was already juggling half a dozen houses. He knew that Emma's letter, in which she first asked for £15,000 and then an extra £100, would set off even more demands. Merton remained on the market, seldom viewed other than by curiosity seekers, still requiring to be cleaned and maintained, swallowing more money every day.

In January, Earl Nelson's son, Horace, Viscount Trafalgar, died of tuber-culosis. William and Sarah were devastated at the death of their favourite and heir. William Nelson's title and honours would now pass to the Boltons' eldest son, Thomas. Bereft of his male heir, the Earl's hatred of Emma and Horatia increased to fever pitch.

Emma claimed to Queensberry that she wanted only to keep her portraits of Sir William, Nelson, and Queen Maria Carolina. The magnifi-cent days of the *Tria Juncta in Uno* were gone forever: Sir William was buried next to his wife in Pembrokeshire, Nelson was the possession of the state in St Paul's, Maria Carolina was a virtual prisoner of Napoleon, and Emma was a struggling debtor, owing well over a million in today's money. There was no way she could survive. She would never be able to remarry: a husband was legally responsible for his wife's debts and very few men could pay off such a large amount. It seemed futile to save a few shillings when there were thousands outstanding. Only a grand gesture could save her. Emma began to despair. She fell ill with a form of jaundice in October and decided to write her will. She hoped in death to win the share of the glory that had eluded her in life.

if I can be buried in St Pauls I shou'd be very happy to be near the glorious Nelson whom I Loved & admired and as once Sir William Nelson and myself had agreed we shou'd all be burried near each other, if the King had granted him a publick funeral this would have been that 3 persons who were so much attached to each other from virtues and friendship shou'd have been laid in one grave when they quitted this ill natured slanderous world. But tis past and in Heaven I hope we shall meet.

Realistically, Emma knew that burial in the crypt was reserved for military heroes, and so she requested to be buried next to her mother, although she hoped that 'she will live, and be a mother to Nelson's child, Horatia'. Still deluded about the value of her house, Emma appeared to think that the sale of the house alone, excluding the furniture or effects, would cover her debts and leave her with enough to provide for Horatia and Mrs Cadogan.

> I beg that Merton may be sold and all Debts paid & what ever money shall be left after all Debts paid I give to my dear mother and after her death to my dear Horatia Nelson. I allso give all that I am possessed of in this world to my dear mother Mary Doggin or Cadogan for her use & after her death to Horatia Nelson I give them all my ready money, plate, linen, pictures, wearing apparel, household furniture, trinkets, wine in short every thing I have in the world to my mother during her life & after her death to my Dearest Horatia Nelson.[400]

She asked George Rose to care for her mother and Horatia, and hoped that when he died, his son would 'do me this last favour to see justice done to Nelson's Daughter'. Still cherishing fond memories of the Christmas visit, she begged 'the Prince of Wales, as he dearly loved Nelson, that his R. Highness will protect his child, and be kind to her; for this I beg of him, for there is no one that I so highly regard as his Royal Highness. Also my good friend the Duke of Queensbury, I beg of Him, as Nelson beseeched him to be kind to me, so I commend my dear mother and Horatia to his kind heart.'

Emma was clutching at straws: the Duke was nearly ninety, and the Prince, captivated by sophisticated Lady Hertford, shut his ears to depressing pleas for money. Emma made one final attempt to beg the help of the state.

> I have done my King and Country some service but as they were ungrateful enough to neglect the request of the virtuous Nelson in providing for me I do not expect they will do any thing for his child but if there should be any administration in at my death who have hearts and feelings I beg they will provide for Horatia Nelson the child who would have a father if he had not gone forth to fight his country's battles therefore she has a claim on them.

In early November, Emma was subjected to a barrage of letters and aggressive visits from hired toughs. 'Lady Hamilton has been harassed and grievously insulted by her creditors,' wrote George Matcham in shock to his parents.[401] Emma was on the brink of being arrested for debt.

52

The Friends of Lady Hamilton

'Goldsmid has been an angel to me and his bounty shall never be abused,' Emma rejoiced to Charles Greville in November. Shocked by the news that she faced arrest for debt, her neighbours had exerted themselves to save her. 'When I thought they neglected me, Goldsmid and my City friends came forward, and they have rescued me from destruction.'

On 25 November 1808, her friend, Sir John Perring, banker and former Lord Mayor of London, hosted a 'meeting of the friends of Lady Hamilton', a group of influential financiers, largely organised by Abraham Goldsmid. After advertising for all her creditors to contact him, Emma's solicitor estimated her debts stood at £8,000, with another £10,000 needed to pay off loans. The party decided to appoint trustees for the sale of Merton, judging the house and grounds to be worth £11,000. They also came up with a generous estimate of the contents at £6,500 (including £2,000 for wine), gave Emma £3,700 to pay off her most pressing creditors and pledged to form a 'Committee to follow up the claim on Government'. Emma was ebullient.

All these things and papers of my services and my ill treatment I have laid before my trustees; they are paying my debts. I live in retirement, and the citty are going to bring forward my claims; in short, I have put myself under their protection, and nothing, *no power on earth shall* make me *deviate* from my present system.[402]

Emma's promises to reform were sincerely meant but futile. Her 'Citty friends' persuaded her to sell her beloved horses, but they could do nothing about her fondness for throwing lavish parties, her determination to retain her troupe of elderly servants, and her preoccupation with using her position to help poverty-stricken old friends and distant relations of Nelson's siblings. Emma beseeched so often on behalf of others that she destroyed any chance of attracting favour for herself.

In spring 1809, the Mary Ann Clarke scandal broke. For Emma, it was an object lesson in how to make money out of a famous lover – which she had conspicuously failed to do. Clarke, a witty courtesan, captured the King's second son, the Duke of York, Commander-in-Chief of the Army. When he set her up in 1803 in a large Mayfair house, she spent thousands on exquisite furniture, china and glass, and expensive dinners. The delighted Duke had no idea that his allowance of £1,000 a year hardly covered the coal bill. Like Emma, Mary Ann lived on credit, but she added to her income by taking bribes from those seeking army commissions or trade contracts from the Duke. When the Duke abandoned her and failed to pay her an allowance, Mary Ann embarked on her revenge. Summoned to testify about whether the Duke had any knowledge of the bribes, she refused to take the blame, electrifying the stuffy lawyers with smart answers. The humiliated Duke hung his head as his love letters were read aloud and the lurid details of his domestic life were bandied around the court. Mary Ann also threatened to publish her memoirs but was bought off with an annuity of £600 a year plus a lump sum of £10,000. In such a delicate climate, the Princes would not risk pushing Emma's claims, and the government was even less sympathetic to mistresses who had fallen into debt through keeping up appearances.

Emma found great consolation in her daughter. Horatia was now nearly nine. Although she had lost her home at Merton and many of her playmates as their parents severed links with Emma, she remained an outgoing and sweet-natured child. She had proved an attentive pupil of singing and music under Mrs Billington and, proud of how the little girl lived up to Nelson's name, Emma immediately spent some of the money advanced to her by her city friends on appointing her an expensive French governess. She retained Sarah and Cecilia Connor, Horatia's nursery governesses, even though they were no longer of practical use.

The artist David Wilkie was excited to meet the 'too celebrated Lady Hamilton', but was disappointed to find that although 'lusty and tall, and of fascinating manners', all her attention was focused on her little daughter, a 'creature of great sweetness'. Emma made it clear that the child was Nelson's, but referring to her as Miss Nelson, as the will had commanded, was simply too daring for some gatherings, and she introduced her as Horatia Hamilton.

> Lady Hamilton, knowing me by name, called me and said that her daughter had the finest taste imaginable, and that she excelled in graceful attitudes. She then made her stand in the middle of the room with a piece of drapery, and throw herself into a number of those elegant postures for which her Ladyship in her prime was so distinguished. She afterwards told me of all else her daughter could do, and concluded by asking me if I did not think her very like her father.[403]

Emma was socialising with city gentlemen, sure that the government could not ignore their pleas on her behalf. To repay Abraham Goldsmid for his generosity, she persuaded the Dukes of Clarence, Sussex and Cumberland to stay with him in town and accompany him to a concert at a synagogue, to the horror of the conservative press. Meanwhile, the 'friends of Lady Hamilton' were struggling to sort out her financial affairs. One, Germain Lavie, wrote to Rose that he had an 'excellent' paper from her in which she listed her services, but he was unsure if anyone in government had ever seen it and where to take it. 'I believe I could get half the City of London to sign a commendatory Paper if it would be any help,' he flourished.[404] But the government continued to ignore her.

Addicted to spending as a way of dulling the loss of Nelson and all her other ordeals, Emma was too proud to admit to herself that she could not afford to party with London's glitterati. She also had a genius for acquiring some of England's most useless servants. The few she did manage to lose wanted money. Sir William's old secretary, Francis Oliver, upset all his successive employers and resorted to 'threatening to publish' secrets about her. One of his disgruntled ex-employers suggested she issue him with an 'action for defamation, which would fully put a stop to his nonsense'. But he knew too much about her for Nelson had trusted him to carry some of his most sexually explicit letters to her. As he had written before a torrent of risqué comments, 'I can give full Scope to my feelings for I dare say Oliver will faithfully deliver this letter.'[405] Oliver joined a growing list of blackmailers, many of them discharged servants, who had seen everything and were as interested as her creditors in the windfall from her 'Citty friends'. Her family were equally eager to share her good fortune. Thanks to them, Emma's ruin was assured.

53
Trouble with the Relations

'I am sorry to hear that you have so much trouble with your relations,' Mrs Marie Thomas sympathised. 'It is a pity that your great generosity towards them shou'd be so ill-placed.' Emma had asked her old employer to settle her troubled uncle, William Kidd, in Hawarden and to send her the bills for his clothes, lodgings and debts. Kidd sharply told Mrs Thomas 'he was not brought up to work' and demanded more money. Mrs Thomas did not give him the £5 Emma offered 'for it wou'd onely be spent in the ale house and then he gets abusive'.

Merton remained unsold until Abraham Goldsmid's brother, Asher, agreed to buy it in April 1809. At the news that Lady Hamilton had come into money, more creditors pressed forward, and the money from the sale disappeared into their pockets. In the same month, Charles Greville died at his home in Paddington Green, just a few weeks short of his sixtieth birthday, beaten down after a year of sickness. On his walls were the Romney portraits he had inherited from Sir William, the sophisticated *Emma Hart in Morning Dress* and the glamorous *Bacchante* in which Emma is draped in pink and gauze. After devoting his life to becoming Sir William's heir, he had never married or had children, and ended his days in the place where he had been young and happy with Emma, so many years before.

Emma mourned Greville deeply. The estate went to his brother, Robert, who refused to pay her annuity until he had sorted out his brother's affairs. The Duke of Queensberry gave Emma money through Goldsmid to bridge the gap, but on condition that she was not 'informed of his interference on this occasion', guessing that Emma was ashamed of the demands she made on her friends. A few months later, Greville's belongings were put up to auction. Sir William's fabulous library went on sale at Christie's on 8 and 9 June and raised over £1,000. On 10 June, all the paintings of Emma were sold, including Romney's *St Cecilia* and *Cassandra*, a *Thais*, and Angelica Kauffman's wedding portrait of her as the *Comic Muse*.[406]

Meanwhile, the Connors were fully occupied doing what they excelled at: making trouble. In her will of 1808, Emma complained, 'I have the mother and six children to keep, all of them, except two, having turned out bad . . . This family having by their extravagance almost ruined me, I have nothing to leave them.' When Emma heard they had been spreading rumours that she had been miserly, she responded by making Mrs Connor sign a document acknowledging that 'she and her children have been generously supported for many years by the bounty of Lady Hamilton, who has expended on her account, as she believes, little less than Two Thousand pounds', as well as benefiting from Mrs Cadogan's generous assistance.[407]

Weakened by the catalogue of deaths and debts, Mrs Cadogan became very ill in 1809. She managed to feebly struggle through Christmas, but died on 14 January 1810. Emma had lost an invaluable friend and essential support. Many had dismissed Mrs Cadogan as no better than a servant or a brothel madam, but few women had a mother as strong as Emma's. Only in her early forties when she arrived in Naples, she contentedly took a backseat, intent on helping her daughter to shine. She nursed the Royal Family as they travelled to Sicily and withstood the exhausting journey to England. Her loyalty may have stemmed from her guilt at abandoning Emma as a child, but she soon became her daughter's greatest defender and staunchest ally.

'I have lost the best of Mothers,' Emma grieved. 'My wounded Heart, my Comfort all buried with her. I can now not feel any pleasure but that of thinking and speaking of her.' She buried her at the church on Paddington Green six days after her death, possibly in one of the vaults that held many coffins below the church floor. Presumably she chose the area because Mrs Cadogan had once lived there happily with Emma. Greville, Sir William, Nelson, and most of those who had loved Mrs Cadogan were dead and so it was a small funeral. Since the register notes her residence as in the parish of St George's, Hanover Square, Mary had probably died in Emma's Bond Street apartment and it would have cost substantially more for her to be buried in the church near her old home. The funeral expenses inflated Emma's debts. Mary's death was also a practical disaster for her. Emma no longer knew what groceries or lodgings should cost. She moved to a hotel in Stratford Place and then to an apartment at 76 Piccadilly to save money.

Emma had paid the Blackburns and then her aunt, Mrs Connor, to look after her daughter, Emma Carew, but she could no longer afford to do so. Miss Carew realised she had no choice but to go into service as a governess or companion. She wrote to her mother begging her for sympathy, asking for the identity of her father, in the hope that he might intervene to save her. 'My memory traces back circumstances which have taught me too much, yet not quite all I could have wished to have known – with you that resides, and ample reasons, no doubt, you have for not imparting them to me. Had you felt yourself at liberty so to have done, I might have become reconciled to my former situation and have been relieved from the painful employment I now pursue.' Emma never told her daughter that Sir Harry was her father. She was keeping an old promise to her ex-lover, but she also dreaded that her daughter would be caused even more pain if she found her father was alive and did not want her. Fetherstonhaugh was so unpredictably volatile that he might cut Emma off for good if she confirmed the secret – and she needed every friend she could get.

Ill and fighting off her creditors, there was nothing Emma could do to save her daughter. Miss Carew's chance of marriage was much higher as a governess than as a relation of Lady Hamilton. She sailed away alone. The rest of her life remains a mystery. Since her lungs were weak when she was only in her early twenties, she probably died young.

In early July, twenty-two-year-old Charlotte Nelson married Samuel Hood, Baron Bridport, grandson of Nelson's old superior, Lord Hood. When Emma had introduced them at Merton, Samuel had been fascinated by Charlotte. Then, Sam 'seemed to devour her with his eyes. That would be a good match,' Emma had reported in delight to Sarah Nelson. Although Emma had tried to encourage the relationship, neither she nor Horatia were invited to the wedding or a reception. To rub salt into the wound, the ceremony took place at St Marylebone, where Emma had married Sir William. The new Baroness Bridport paid a bridal visit to Fanny, Viscountess Nelson.

Emma's debts were still not public knowledge. Gossip columns reported on her parties and fashion commentators continued to promote the Grecian look her Attitudes had perpetuated.[408] Out of the public eye, she shot off begging letters. Relaxing amidst commemorative bronzes of the Battle of the Nile, Sir Harry Fetherstonhaugh replied, 'No one better deserves to be happy,' but he would only send her baskets of game.[409] In debt himself, he later tried to coerce the nation into buying Uppark for the Duke of Wellington, and he may have strengthened bonds with Emma after 1805 in case she could have encouraged the government to choose Uppark as the Trafalgar Estate.

The Duke of Queensberry advanced £2,500 to Abraham Goldsmid to pay Emma's debts and instructed that 'Lady Hamilton herself is to have no control over or to have any interference with any part' of the sum, for it must be devoted to payment of 'abovementioned debts & for that purpose only'.[410] But Goldsmid let the news slip, and Emma seems to have wangled £800 of the money. It was the last of Abraham's many kind acts to Emma. He had battled depression since the suicide of his brother in 1808. In September, he suffered two massive losses on the stock market, and he was left owing £350,000 to the East India Company, as well as being partly responsible for a £13 million loan. On the morning of 28 September, the day his payment to the East India Company was due, instead of hopping into his coach and setting off to his office in the City, Abraham walked into the grounds of his house and shot himself. The coachman found him dying, the pistol still clutched in his hand.

In December, Queensberry died. Emma had hoped for a legacy. William Beckford calculated he could be bled of '5 or 600,000'.[411] Susanna Bolton, looking forward to lots of presents when Emma got her half a million, was quivering with anticipation, declaring her husband wanted to place a bet on the sum, 'Anne dances; Tom says he is as nervous as my Lady to hear the contents . . . we are full of hopes'. But Queensberry died in a bed strewn with begging letters from famous beauties, and he had already been more than generous to Emma. He left her only £500 a year. His family immediately contested his will and she never received a shilling.

After attacks of sickness and stomach pain, Emma was losing weight. 'I should be sorry to see you grow any thinner than you were when I last saw you in Town,' worried Susanna Bolton. Under increasing pressure, Emma had begun to pledge future payments of her annuity in return for amounts of ready cash. Everyone was trying to extract money before they made the final break with her. Susanna besieged Emma with letters, on behalf of herself, 'invalids' in her family, and distant relations, such as Bob Nelson who needed £100. Dr Beatty still hoped to become surgeon to the Prince of Wales. 'I am all anxiety for the result of your friendly exertions on my behalf, which alone can bring me near you, and my prayers are offered up daily, even hourly, for the speedy success of your endeavours.'[412]

Since her credit was bad, Emma had to pay huge interest rates for loans and high prices for even basic goods and services. Sarah Connor was shocked to find her cousin had paid a landlady astronomical sums for accommodation and food, even when she hardly occupied the rooms.[413] By 1810, there was no money to pay the bread bill, let alone two expensive governesses for Horatia. An argument over a foreign visitor – possibly Melesina Trench – who declared Mrs Cadogan had been a prostitute was finally an excuse to let Sarah go. Begging Emma to change her mind, Sarah wrote she had been the 'happiest Girl in the World in living with you', and promised 'everything in my power to serve and please you', claiming she would love her 'until the last hour of my existance'.[414] It was no good. Soon afterward Emma asked Cecilia to leave. She could no longer afford her high salary. Emma also tried to dismiss Fatima, but her old maid was unemployable and had to be boarded at a workhouse for ten shillings a week. There she suffered a breakdown and had to be taken by Cribb the gardener to St Luke's madhouse.

Emma was drifting between cheap lodgings in Piccadilly and Bond Street. Although she was squandering her money, it was impossible for her to flee to the country to live in quiet retirement. With Queensberry and Goldsmid dead, she had realised she needed a protector for herself and Horatia – and she was trying to encourage herself to hunt for a rich husband. Emma's love for Nelson ruined her twice over: she ran up debts improving his house and supporting his relations, and she was too faithful to his memory to find another husband within a few years of his death. Unless they were elderly or very rich, all women began hunting for a second husband soon after the death of the first. In trying to live independently Emma made a fatal mistake.

An eager reply from one of the men she tried to fascinate survives. Her tempting letter set Sir Richard Puleston chomping at the bit to pay tribute to her:

Many thousand thanks for your kind invitation to your *fairy palace* in Bond Street, where I shall be most happy to pay my earliest respects when I get to town . . . How soon do you return there?

How delighted I shall be next year to escort you & ramble with you over your almost native mountains, & to tell you, which is true, that *we have met before.*

Daringly she invited Sir Richard to come to her home alone. Her 'fairy palace' would have been expensive: lovely decorations, candles, food and wines. Desperate to make him her protector, she even offered to accompany him on a tour to Sicily.

Beckford expressed his pleasure that 'you are recovering a little of those charming spirits which vivify and animate every object around you'.[415] Her social standing was still formidable. The Countess of Banbury felt she had arrived when she was invited to a party where Lady Hamilton and Mrs Billington sang a duet.[416] At the close of 1810, Emma had more reason to feel hopeful. The King's mental state had deteriorated rapidly and the Whig factions in Parliament were demanding that his son assume the reins of power. When the Prince of Wales was finally appointed Regent in early 1811, Emma thought her troubles were over.

54

Afflicting Circumstances

*L*ondon society had been waiting for decades for the Prince of Wales to become Regent. Everyone was disappointed. Declaring that he was only representing the King, he dismissed any requests he found tiresome and concentrated on wrangling with his estranged wife. For years, Emma had staved off her creditors with the promise that the Prince would help her. When he refused her, she was lost.

Emma spent most of 1811 and 1812 in fear of being arrested. Ill and anxious, she went into hiding at the comfortable Fulham home of Mrs Billington, although she kept her apartment at 150 Bond Street and sometimes emerged for dinners and parties. When the author Thomas De Quincey met her with Samuel Taylor Coleridge at a supper party, he was smitten by 'Lord Nelson's Lady Hamilton – the beautiful, the accomplished, the enchantress!', declaring that she had 'Medea's beauty and Medea's powers of enchantment'. After seeing her perform the sleepwalking scene from *Macbeth*, a favourite of Mrs Siddons, twenty-seven-year-old De Quincey decided her 'magnificent' and 'the most effectively brilliant woman he ever saw'. Coleridge had long wanted to meet her, after spending a hot summer in Malta in 1804 hearing about Lady Hamilton and her efforts to help the starving people. Equally bewitched, he 'admired her, as who would not have done, prodigiously', while she appeared equally fascinated by him.[417] She worked hard to dazzle and enchant, determined not to disappoint.

Not long after meeting Coleridge, Emma sparkled at the gala party for the Prince of Wales's birthday. In the midst of crippling debt, she had bought a magnificent new dress, still refusing to believe that he would never help her. By the end of the year, however, no money had arrived. Emma's bravado seeped away. The government had finally compensated Sir William's estate for his outlay in Naples, to the tune of nearly £8,300 – but it all went to Robert Greville who was not about to hand out more money to his aunt.[418] Nervous and tense, her petitions hopeless, her annuity from Sir William pledged to creditors, she fell into a profound depression. This was not how she imagined herself, Nelson's Britannia, to be living less than ten years after his death.

In December, Emma was so afraid of arrest that she resorted to desperate measures. She actually chose to commit herself to prison, lodging herself voluntarily in the area of the King's Bench Prison in St George's Fields in Southwark. The general view is that Emma was actually convicted; however, her name does not appear in the King's Bench record books and there is no documentation of her appearance before the magistrate or any record of her discharge. Genteel prisoners of the King's Bench – usually debtors – could escape the squalor of the cells by buying the right to live and move 'within the Rules', a three-square-mile area around the prison walls where dozens of shops, taverns, brothels, gaming dens, and cafés served the prison population. Once in prison or 'within the Rules', no debtor or criminal could be arrested again and many on the brink of capture sought refuge there. Guards stood on the street corners to prevent prisoners escaping, but they had no mandate to prevent the hundreds who had not been convicted from creeping into the Rules in order to avoid arrest. Emma hired a discreet carriage and sent Dame Francis, a long-standing house-keeper, along with four or five maids or footmen on ahead. Then, in the middle of the night so her creditors did not see, she and Horatia hurried into a carriage and drove at full speed to the Rules.

Emma had recently thrown herself on the goodness of Joshua Smith, leader of Southwark Borough Council, and he gave her the money to rent an expensive home, 12 Temple Place, in the Rules, a terraced house on the east side of Blackfriars Road where it joins what is now St George's Circus. Out of her front window, she could see the Magdalen House, the home for penitent prostitutes, but she no longer had the money to visit as a fine patroness – or the inclination to imitate the impecunious girls as she once had. 'I am so truly unhappy & wretched,' she wrote despairingly to James Perry, the editor of the *Morning Chronicle* who would be one of her most faithful visitors. Years earlier, she had roamed Blackfriars, a maid dreaming of stardom. Now she was bereft and confined, unable to think of a way out of her terrible predicament.

Emma adorned her new home with her fine mahogany furniture from Merton and the exquisite china, for when her well-connected friends deigned to call. The pictures, the bust of Nelson, a few books, her jewels, and some gorgeous dresses, the remnants of her old glory, now decorated rooms that bore the traces of dirt left by the many debtors before her. The new decoration did little to lift Horatia's spirits. She had grown up petted by doting adults, followed by the press, and indulged by her grandmother, and she was utterly miserable in the Rules. She had only seen Blackfriars from the comfort of a carriage when visiting the Magdalen House, and the sights and smells of her new home sickened her. Gutters ran with blood from the nearby slaughterhouses and fetid smoke from the factories hung in the air. Children sold gin, prostitutes solicited openly, and beggars and stray dogs lingered in alleyways and courtyards. Since about a hundred families were living in houses in the Rules, most of them unlucky debtors, there were many respectable playmates for her, but she tended to stay indoors. Emma hired a piano, paid for singing and music lessons, bought the best meat and fish, and threw a big party for Horatia's birthday in January.

Although Emma could not go outside the Rules, she could order in food, clothes, medicines and books as well as receive visits from friends, family, merchants and doctors. Even the Duke of Sussex was a frequent visitor. But the prison was a profit-making institution and living within the Rules was disastrously expensive, with accommodation and services such as washing costing around five times more than they did outside. Joshua Smith covered the bills.[419]

The New Year prompted Emma to gather her energies. She wrote to Perry in January 1813, 'My friends come to town to-morrow for the season, when I must see what can be done, so that I shall not remain here.' She fired off petitions to the government and the Prince of Wales, and sent begging letters to her friends. Melodramatically, she declared, 'I will appeal to a generous public, who will not let a woman who has served her country with the zeal I have, be left to starve and insult.'[420] When the newspapers published details about Lady Hamilton's efforts, men in high places were even more annoyed. As she flustered, probably to Lord Sidmouth, 'this unexpected publication made me pause as a continuance in that manner wou'd appear absurd'. But she could not think of another way to help herself and she ended passionately that, 'Nelson loved you, & I am alone and feil folorn in the world and his Spirit if it cou'd look down wou'd bless you for your kindness & attention to his last wishes in the moment of Death & Victory.'[421] All her petitions failed. Joshua Smith coughed up £400 for the contents of the Richmond house (including Nelson's bloody uniform). He and James Perry somehow persuaded other creditors that petitions to the Prince would succeed. Within a few weeks, the most importunate of the creditors were paid off and Emma was able to return to 150 Bond Street.[422]

Although the Matchams begged her to allow them to take Horatia, Emma was afraid that if she gave up her daughter even for a short period, she would lose her for good. But Horatia was becoming a teenager and the strain of living together was showing. Resentful over the loss of their home and terrified that they might have to return to the Rules, she grew angry with her mother. Emma saw any demonstration of independence as an insult.

> Listen to a kind, good mother, who has ever been to you affectionate, truly kind, and has spared no pains to make you the most amiable and most accomplish'd of your sex . . . I have weathered many a storm for your sake, but these frequent blows have kill'd me . . . I lament to see the increasing strength of your turbulent passions.[423]

Emma promised Horatia that their lives would soon be more secure, but she was slowly realising that she would never get her pension. The Prince Regent passed her pleas to the Prime Minister, Lord Liverpool, who communicated through Lord Sidmouth that he could not help as he had received 'representations of difficulty and distress, in many other quarters'. In June three creditors threatened to have Emma arrested. Agitated and afraid, she advertised the sale of 'The Property of a Lady of Distinction'. She sold dozens of her belongings, including the diamond star, the gold box, and the four poster bed she had shared with Nelson, a Domesday book, portraits of Nelson, French chintz curtains, heavy Grecian-style mahogany furniture from Merton and fine commemorative services of china, including a fifty-piece white and gold tea set, as well as goose-feather beds, chintz hangings and a piano. She also auctioned her copy of Rehberg's *Lady Hamilton's Attitudes*, Hayley's *Life of Romney*, and another book that owed much to her, Thomas Baxter's illustrated book of *Ancient Costume*. In other boxes were magazines and fashionable novels, including *The Memoirs of Miss Sidney Biddulph* and her beloved *The Wife and the Mistress*.[424] Emma had clung to her most treasured possessions, rather than leave them to be sold with Merton, and now they went for a pittance. One lucky lady snapped up six dining chairs, cases, earrings, bracelets, a miniature and a reading chair as well as other items for £22. Joshua Smith kindly took many of the Nelson relics, but even then the auction did not raise enough.

On 28 June, for a debt of £400, Emma was publicly seized by officers of the court and bundled into a carriage.* She was taken first to an officer's house, and then to appear before the court. Still proud, she was arrested as Lady Hamilton, and demanded when she made her appearance in court to be called by her grandest title, Dame Emma.[425] She still had her gold and diamond Maltese Cross. Sentenced to imprisonment until she could pay, Emma chose to live once more at 12 Temple Place, taking Horatia with her. In the autumn, she fell ill and her spirits were crushed when Susanna Bolton died and she was not permitted to attend the funeral. In a letter to Sir Richard Puleston, she was almost incoherent with distress about 'the scenes of plunder, Robery & villainy which has been practised on my unsuspicious Heart & pocket', still holding fast to the delusion that the Prince Regent was trying to win ministers to her cause.

Emma wrote that she was determined to 'act with firmness, Fortitude, Honor, and Prudence'. But prison sapped her strength and soon she was describing herself as 'broken . . . with grief and ill health'. She became so weak that the authorities permitted her to take some fresh air in a carriage outside the Rules. Terrified that her daughter might desert her, she was unable to handle Horatia's bouts of anger. 'Your cruel treatment of me is such that I cannot live under these afflicting circumstances; my poor heart is broken,' she protested. Always grasping after the dramatic, she described an imaginary scenario in which she would defend herself against Horatia's accusations before a tribunal of their servants and friends.

Horatia was dismayed by her mother's feverish efforts to entertain possible patrons and old admirers, including the Royal Princes. Mrs Billington and the Duke of Clarence celebrated Horatia's 'false' birthday in October and the anniversary of the Battle of the Nile was another excuse for a big celebration. Emma's house was full to bursting every Sunday, as fashionable visitors who had watched the girls at the Magdalen Chapel popped in for refreshments at Lady Hamilton's. In her desperation, she was spending more than Joshua Smith could give her, and

* Debtors were arrested in public and the officers chose a place the accused frequented regularly, usually church.

she had turned to the extortionate rates of the King's Rules money-lenders.

Emma invited everyone she could think of to dinner. One guest, Sir William Dillon, an admiral who had known Nelson, remarked afterwards that he had not seen her for three years, but it did not strike him that she needed his help. He was amazed to find that his fellow guest was the Duke of Sussex with his mistress, 'Mrs Buggin' (Lady Cecilia Letitia Buggin, daughter of the Earl of Arran and later his second wife), and startled by the rich silver dishes on the table and the luxurious food. Dillon gaped at the main course, a giant goose – without a servant to carve it. Emma had no knife, and she pressed him to pull it apart with his fingers, which he did, doling out the portions between the illustrious guests, to much hilarity. Dillon trotted home, full of good food and satisfied 'after a very sociable and agreeable entertainment'. In the midst of despair, Emma could still retrieve her old vivaciousness to charm her guests. But, despite her efforts, she spent the freezing winter as she had the previous one, in Temple Place. Still, as she knew, most of her friends were indignant on her behalf and she had the sympathy of the public. All that was about to change.

55

Reading the Herald

'To my great surprise', Emma wrote to James Perry on 22 April 1814, 'I saw yesterday in the *Herald* that Lord Nelson's letters to me were published. I have not seen the book, but I give you my honour that I know nothing of these letters. I have been now nine months in Temple Place, & allmost all the time I have been very ill with a bilious complaint, brought on by fretting and anxiety, & lately I have kept my bed for nearly twelve weeks.' Perry believed her protestations of innocence, but few others were so generous. The most sensational book to be published in decades, the *Letters of Lord Nelson to Lady Hamilton* scandalised the nation.

The publishers chose the perfect time. Ten days before, the war with France had been declared over. London lit up in celebration at the news that Napoleon had abdicated and retreated to exile on the island of Elba. Fireworks exploded every night. Central London was so crowded that the St James cows dashed in a panic out of Green Park. The city was crammed with visitors with money to burn – and everybody was reading the *Letters of Lord Nelson to Lady Hamilton*.

Nelson's adoring populace lapped up the book, shocked by his complaints about the Admiralty, greedily appalled by his jealousy of the Prince of Wales, and outraged that he had wanted to dally with Emma rather than fulfil his duty at sea. Almost overnight, the image of Emma in the public imagination as the adoring mistress of Nelson and mother of his child was shattered. If she had ever had any chance of a pension, the book crushed it for good. The Prince – even though he had sold the King's fraught letters to him to three newspapers in 1803 – seized the excuse to reject her petitions. The government followed suit.

The Royal brothers and Nelson's family welcomed the opportunity to turn their backs on her.

Emma implored James Perry to defend her, declaring she had once left her papers in a case with a friend she thought she 'cou'd depend on'. Emma and Horatia believed the culprit was James Harrison, who had stayed in her house while working on his *Life of Nelson*. She had allowed him to look at her papers, and he could easily have found other letters and transcribed them with the help of his blackmailing ex-secretary friend, Francis Oliver. Emma had always been dogged by former acquaintances and staff who wanted to spill the details about life at Merton to the newspapers, but Oliver had the biggest hold of all, for he had delivered Nelson's most explicit letters to her.

Emma had not helped herself by being chronically disorganised through the chaos of moving between homes and taking frequent holidays. She was a compulsive hoarder and, by 1810, having lost her mother and more reliable maids, she was drowning in a confusion of memorabilia and belongings. In 1811, Dr Beatty was entreating her to return a letter from Nelson to a friend he had sent her in 1806, but she never found it.[426] She had failed to keep track of her letters – and now she was paying the penalty.

The sale of Nelson's letters would have brought her a sizeable injection of cash, but her finances only declined from 1805. If she had wanted to sell them, it would have made sense to do the deal via James Perry, but he was ignorant of the affair and the *Herald*, his rival paper, had the scoop. Unlike certain mistresses who had extorted money from aristocrats by threatening to publish their letters, Emma had never contemplated her love letters as some kind of pension. She expected the government would recompense her for her services.

As her last friends turned their backs on her and the newspapers feasted on the remnants of her reputation, she frantically beseeched Earl Nelson for the £500 a year pension from Bronte that Nelson had left her.[427] When he reluctantly paid over £200, it was a drop in the ocean. Emma's health had taken a turn for the worse for she was in terrible stomach pain and she was so weak, dizzy and sick that she could not leave her bed. She believed she was dying and she begged her friends not to leave her to live out her last days in prison. But if they bailed her out, she would only be arrested once more on the demand of another creditor. Loyal James Perry and Joshua Smith hatched a plan. As they told her, she could not be arrested in a foreign country and now that the war was over, travellers could visit France.

Smith and Perry sold her remaining valuables, including silver dishes that had pleased Sir William Dillon, and raised further cash from other friends. Smith put up bail on 22 June and the next day, after a year living under the Rules of the King's Bench, Emma was free. Perry and Smith arranged for her and Horatia to escape. Emma's discharge certificate is still in a box in the Public Record Office, along with those for hundreds of other debtors released in the same month. For the clerk writing out paper after paper, the poignant decline of Nelson's mistress was just one story of self-delusion and bad luck among many.

Emma was anxious to leave the country immediately, but she risked being arrested again if she travelled on a normal cross-channel ferry. To put her creditors off the scent, she and Horatia hid in England for a week as Perry and Smith worked frantically to arrange her escape. On 1 July, Emma and her daughter boarded a small private boat from London Bridge, bound for Calais, on France's northern coast. She was exhilarated to be free but had only £50 in her purse.

56

A Chance I May Live

After a miserable 'three days sickeness at sea', Emma was relieved to be on dry land. 'I managed so well with Horatia alone that I was at Calais before any new writs could be issued out against me,' she reported in delight.[428] With Napoleon in exile on Elba, Calais was retrieving its pre-war swing as one of the most fashionable – and expensive – resorts in Europe, crowded with pleasure seekers on their way to Paris or nearby spas. Emma hoped to prevail on some of those who had enjoyed her hospitality in the past and to regain her old glitter.

Emma knew only one way of raising her profile: to spend money. She took apartments in the expensive Dessein's Hotel, the only place for travelling luminaries. Aristocrats supped on boiled turtle in the exquisitely decorated restaurant and swapped fashion tips in the glamorous lounge. The Duke of Clarence had been rather fond of the town when he had visited and Emma hoped he might return. She still cut a grand enough dash to fool the Calais moneylenders into giving her credit and, flush with bundles of new notes, she threw splendid dinner parties and hired a harp and piano for Horatia as well as music teachers, insisting 'I would sooner starve than her fine and beautiful mind should not be cultivated.' Radiating optimism and new hopes, Emma wrote to George Rose on 4 July,

> I feel so much better, from change of climate, food, air, large rooms and *liberty*, that there is a chance I may live to see Horatia brought up. I am looking out for a lodging. I have an excellent Frenchwoman who is good at everything; for Horatia and myself, and my old dame,

who is coming, will be my establishment. Near me is an English lady, who has resided here for twenty-five years, who has a day school, but not for eating and sleeping. At eight in the morning, I take Horatia; fetch her at one; at three, we dine, and then in the evening we walk. She learns everything – piano, harp, languages grammatically. She knows French and Italian well, but she will improve. Not any girls, but those of the first families go there. Last evening we walked two miles to a fête champetre pour les bourgeois. Everybody is pleased with Horatia . . . our little world of happiness is in ourselves.

Emma was proud that Horatia was becoming a fine young lady proficient in French and Italian, as well as speaking a little German and Spanish. She was also making progress in music, mathematics, geography, and English and classical history. As Horatia later asserted of her mother, 'through *all her* difficulties she *invariably* till the last few months, expended on my education etc., the whole of the *interest* of the sum left me by Lord Nelson, and which was left entirely in her control'.[429] Emma implored Rose to petition Lord Sidmouth for money for Horatia's education and clothes, declaring that she was 'the victim of artful mercenary wretches, and my too great liberality and open heart has been the dupe of villains'.

After a few months, the Calais lenders and shopkeepers began to question Emma's grande dame act, and she began the old game of hiding from them and fobbing them off. At the same time, she was increasingly dispirited by the hopeless watch for the mail, and her health began to suffer. Her long-standing stomach complaint had returned with a vengeance and she was plagued by agonising pain in her bowels, as well as sickness, dizziness and headaches. Fretting about money, Emma moved into a large farmhouse in the village of St Pierre, two miles from Calais, so out of the way that she did not trust her post to arrive and she asked friends to send mail to Dessein's Hotel. The rent in the country was cheaper and she thought that the air might alleviate her sickness. She hoped that moving away would help her to hide her illness, for the Calais creditors would start pressing in earnest the minute they knew she was seriously unwell. She also aimed to keep her poor health out of the newspapers: she had a chance of a pension to care for Nelson's daughter only if she looked to live a long time.

Emma and Horatia were not dirt poor. They felt destitute because they had recently lived so stylishly but they were never without food. Emma's old housekeeper, Dame Francis, came to run the household and she hired other servants such as one Mary Cornish, to do her cooking, cleaning and washing and serve her guests. Emma sent her maids to buy nourishing food at prices much cheaper than in London. In one letter, she described how they bought the best meat at 5d a pound and two big turkeys for 4s, a large turbot for a half a crown, partridges and excellent Bordeaux. She was anxious that Horatia live as normally as possible, taking her to parties and dances, delighting when her daughter's graceful dancing and fluent French made her the pet of the company.

By the end of September, the Calais tradesmen were demanding repayment. Her annuity from Sir William had been pledged away. She begged Robert Greville, executor of Sir William's will, for an advance of £100, but he was still fending off her creditors and had no money to spare. Her attempt to hide her illness was working too well – the gossip columns in England reported on Lady Hamilton living it up in Calais, exaggerating her spending, which did not help persuade Robert Greville or the government to send her money. Emma protested angrily that she was living quietly and contested the revelations of the *Letters of Lord Nelson to Lady Hamilton*, declaring to the *Morning Herald* that she, Sir William and Nelson were all 'too much attached to his Royal Highness ever to speak or think ill of him', but her quest to win sympathy was doomed.[430]

Convinced that she would be rescued, Emma kept up the show to the end. She continued to solicit assistance by hosting grand parties but for most of the English in Calais, a drive out to Nelson's flamboyant mistress simply meant a free dinner and a good story to tell their friends. In October, she beseeched the government that she had not a shilling, pleading 'if there is Humanity still left in British Hearts they will not suffer us to die in famine in a foreign Country for God's sake'.[431] Money failed to appear, and her health worsened. She began to seek the solace of religion, attending the local Catholic church and finding a sympathetic friend in the local priest. The behaviour of Earl Nelson, erstwhile clergyman, perhaps convinced her to embrace a faith in which priests seemed less worldly. Her reasons for turning to Catholicism were also pragmatic – in the St Pierre congregation, she was free of the prying eyes of the English at the Anglican church in Calais, a gossipy little social club for expats and travellers.

Religion gave her optimism, but her body was unable to keep up. Emma's long-term problems with sickness, diarrhoea and stomach pain were the result of amoebic dysentery, probably picked up in Naples since Sir William had suffered from the same complaint. At some point while she was living in the Rules, it developed into an abscess in her liver and by Calais it was killing her. Although her love of rich food and fine wines did not help, her health was ruined not by gluttony, as is commonly argued, but by a parasite caught in the city that made her famous. She was growing sicker every day, sometimes so faint and nauseous that she could hardly get out of bed.

By November, Emma was unable to afford the farm and too ill to live in the country, for she needed daily access to doctors and chemists. She, Horatia, Dame Francis, Mary and the other maids moved to a cheap flat in 27 rue Française in Calais, rented from a Monsieur Damas. Emma had one room, Horatia lived next door, and the servants were crammed into another. The move exhausted her last shreds of energy, and within a week of arriving, she took to her bed. She wrote no more letters. In an attempt to dull the pain, she drank spirits and took heavy doses of laudanum, which, mercifully, was freely available and cheaper than alcohol. She was dying.

Shivering and struggling to breathe, Emma passed her final weeks in a blur of pain. Initially, her hands and feet began to swell, then her legs filled with fluid as the abscess drained into the lungs, stomach and chest. Eventually, as her kidneys failed and her body became saturated, she suffered severe shooting pains, coughing and vomiting. Horatia believed she had 'water on the chest' or tuberculosis, which suggests she was coughing blood and unable to drink or eat solids. Doctors commonly treated stomach and liver complaints with doses of mercury, so her sufferings would have been intensified by even more vomiting.

Dame Francis, Mary and possibly a hired nurse tended Emma, but there was little they could do to make her comfortable. The British consul, Henry Cadogan (coincidentally named but no relation), gave them money and covered the outstanding bills. Emma gave him some jewellery and a lock of Nelson's hair in gratitude. The last of her dresses and trinkets went to the pawnbrokers.

When the effects of the laudanum wore off, Emma had little to cheer her. She knew that Nelson's child would be left a penniless orphan. Thirteen-year-old Horatia bravely tried to keep Emma company. Washing and trying to feed her mother was beyond her, but she was determined to help. Earl Nelson refused to give them their instalment of the Bronte allowance before it was due in spring. Horatia begged him for an advance of £10 on the interest due on the sum Nelson left for her, and beseeched a loan of £20 from a friend, probably James Perry or

Joshua Smith. She also attempted to give her mother some comfort by writing to the Matchams to ask if she could live with them after her mother's death. The flat resounded to Emma's coughing and sickness, and it was difficult to sleep. As Horatia later confessed, the period of her mother's decline was 'too indelibly stamped on my memory ever to forget'.[432]

Nelson had died in glory in an afternoon, but Emma gasped out her life in long terrible weeks, drifting in and out of consciousness. Toward the end, she asked for her priest, but she was soon too delirious to speak. 'Latterly she was scarcely sensible,' Horatia recalled.[433] On 15 January 1815, at one in the afternoon, she breathed her last.

Emma had wished to be buried in England, in the vault next to her mother in Paddington Green, but there was no money to transport her body back home. Henry Cadogan planned a modest funeral in the Roman Catholic church: £28 compared to Nelson's £14,000. Emma's faithful friend, Joshua Smith, reimbursed Cadogan for both the funeral costs and the price of an oak coffin. England's mistress was buried on 21 January in the land of her lover's enemies, in the public ground outside town. The *Gentleman's Magazine* reported that 'all the English Gentlemen in Calais' attended her funeral. It was said that the captains and masters of the many vessels in the harbour also joined the procession behind her coffin to the grave, out of respect for Nelson's Emma. Journalists across Europe fought to be first to announce her death.

57

Horatia Alone

enry Cadogan cared for Horatia in the aftermath of Emma's death. Presumably, he bought her a mourning dress and paid to liberate the trinkets that her mother had pawned. After persuading Emma's creditors in Calais to allow Horatia to leave, he gave her the money to travel as far as Dover. The deeply traumatised teenager had a miserable fourteenth birthday under his protection at Calais, and then, accompanied by Dame Francis and probably Mary Cornish, set off home on 28 January 1815. It was just in time: hostilities resumed with France at the end of February and the gay tourists who had danced in the ballroom at Dessein's Hotel were stranded in Calais. Emma's creditors had insured her life, and they were paid off (solicitors pursued Mary Cornish for an affidavit to prove Emma had actually died). Horatia was now free of debt, but she had inherited nothing from her mother. Mr Matcham met Horatia at Dover and took her to their home.

At the Matchams', after a week or two of pampering, she took up her new life. No longer the benefactress's daughter, she was a dependent relation and had to earn her keep by caring for the younger children, eleven-year-old Horace, nine-year-old Charles and four-year-old Nelson. Horatia tried to fit in with her new family and their demands, quelling her grief for her mother and trying to forget the misery of her final days in Calais. She had to work hard to maintain her composure when Mr Matcham decided to take the whole family to Calais for a holiday in July 1815 and again the following year. After Emma's careful tutoring, she could speak five languages and sing and play well, but she had little chance to practise her gifts while working as a glorified upper servant.

No longer able to enjoy so much fine meat or perform for the Prince of Wales, she became a voracious reader and, unlike her mother, an excellent needlewoman.

Two years later, at the age of sixteen, she was sent off to live with the Boltons, deemed old enough to act as housekeeper for her uncle Bolton whose wife, Susanna, had died in 1813. Anxious to escape her position as poor relation, she married her neighbour, the Reverend Philip Ward, at the age of twenty-one. With her husband, she found a happiness she had not experienced since childhood. The mother of eight (one son died in infancy) and the grandmother of many more, Horatia became what Emma had desired to be: the matriarch of a big family.

Emma's daughter was never rich. Even when her mother's old friend, the Duke of Clarence, became King, there was no money for her. She battled to raise her family on a clergyman's income. But she had Emma's natural style. A photograph of her in old age shows her wearing a rich crinoline dress of dark purplish silk, one of Emma's favourite colours, with ruffled sleeves and a full skirt. In a miniature of her aged thirty-six she looks captivating in a blue off-the-shoulder dress. She is slender and her face is beautifully regular, with Emma's limpid eyes and Nelson's straight nose. Thanks to her mother's efforts, Horatia became a lovely, graceful and accomplished woman, and her health was not impaired by her experience of misery during her teenage years.

One of the few possessions of Emma's that Horatia brought back with her from Calais was a dress of green and pink embroidered silk. The dress was altered many times, and ended up in the dressing-up box of Horatia's great-great-great-granddaughter, but, even years later, the material is still thick and opulent, the embroidery delicate. Although she sold most of her fine clothes and lost others, Emma was still, in her last days, trying to keep up some of the style and beauty that had once set Europe alight.

Emma's obituaries were generally salacious. The *Morning Post* reported:

> The origin of this Lady was very humble, and she had experienced all those vicissitudes in early life which too generally attend those females whose beauty has betrayed them into vice, and which un-happily proves the chief means of subsistence. Few women, who have attracted the notice of the world at large have led a life of more freedom. When, however, she became such an object of admiration as to attract the attention of Painters, she formed connections which, if she had conducted herself with prudence, might have raised her

into independence, if not affluence. ROMNEY, who evidently felt a stronger admiration for her than what he might be supposed to entertain merely as an Artist, made her the frequent subject of his pencil. His admiration remained till the close of his life in undiminished ardour. The late CHAS GREVILLE, well known for his refined taste in VIRTU, and who was a prominent character in the world of gallantry, was the PROTECTOR, to use the well-bred language of the polite circles, of Lady Hamilton, for some years; and when his uncle, the late Sir William Hamilton wanted to take abroad with him a chère amie, he recommended the LADY with so good a character that Sir William took her with him and having a reliance on her fidelity, married her.

The journalist dwelt on the '*friendship* between Lady Hamilton and our great Naval Hero', criticising her for being 'intoxicated with the flattery and admiration which attended her in a rank of life so different from the obscure condition in her early days', but still admitted that in 'private life, she was a humane and generous woman . . . obliging to all whom she had any opportunity of serving by her influence'.[434]

Emma died just short of fifty but she outlived many of her friends and contemporaries. A few remained: Sir Harry was bluff and dim-witted until the end, a living testament to the health-giving properties of killing foxes every day. At the age of eighty he married his young dairymaid and packed her off to Paris to be refined. Earl Nelson was so determined to have an heir that he married a twenty-eight-year-old at the age of seventy, his wife, Sarah, hardly cold in her grave, but he died without a son. William, Sarah and their son, Horace, were buried near Nelson in the crypt of St Paul's Cathedral – even in death, the hero couldn't escape his officious brother and his family. Fanny Nelson outlived everybody. She lived comfortably near Exmouth until her death in 1832 at the age of seventy-six. Her beloved Josiah became a successful merchant and married happily. She saw Emma die poor and lonely, Horatia grow up in obscurity and Earl Nelson squander his money and the goodwill of the country.

In 1994, a group of faithful supporters erected a plaque in Emma's honour in the Parc Richelieu in Calais. But many of her other friends, relations and lovers have no monument. An owner of Slebech Castle demolished Sir William's grave and his final resting place is unmarked.

The graves of Mrs Cadogan and Greville in Paddington Green are also lost. Only Nelson's magnificent tomb remains.

Britain was at war throughout most of Emma's life. Four million Frenchmen, and hundreds of thousands of Russians, Austrians, Italians and English were slaughtered, with 650 English sailors killed at Trafalgar alone. Emma died just months before the end of the wars that had made her famous, missing the days of celebration that greeted Lord Wellington's cataclysmic win at the Battle of Waterloo on 18 June 1815.

After 1815, public sympathies about England's most notorious love triangle began to fall with Fanny. Jane Austen's dearest brother, Frank, was one of Nelson's favoured captains and his ship even took a despatch to Nelson while he was living at Palermo with Emma and Sir William. In her novel *Emma*, the brazen, obsessively matchmaking Emma Woodhouse is taught a lesson: she must behave more like restrained Jane Fairfax, a second Fanny. In *Mansfield Park*, quiet Fanny – whose brother brings her a cross from Italy in the fashion of Emma's Maltese Cross – wins Edmund from Mary Crawford, an excellent actress who makes a scandalous joke in public about admirals and their fondness for 'Rears and Vices', just as Emma would have done. Another character worries that visitor numbers at his guesthouse have dropped because he called it Trafalgar and 'Waterloo is more the thing now'.

Soon Emma and all she stood for was out of fashion, replaced by Victorian piety. The time when a girl from nowhere could rise to become the most famous woman in England was over. Glamour was gone and mistresses were kept tucked away, not paraded around fashionable London. After the death of Emma's friends, the Prince of Wales and the Duke of Clarence, who became George IV and William III respectively, Queen Victoria ascended the throne, and a new age of dynamic industry and public professions of virtue began.[435]

Emma could have only achieved her success in the last years of the eighteenth century. She was a woman of her period. But her natural abilities and her ambitions cried out for a different time, when there were more options available to a woman than marriage, motherhood or the life of a courtesan.

Myths dominate our view of Emma. She has been castigated as fat, drunk, extravagant, promiscuous, a prostitute. And yet she was slimmer than most women of her class and her drinking, gambling and spending were, although reckless, nothing unusual. Most of her debts were incurred in an effort to improve Merton and make herself the glamorous, generous hostess Nelson so craved. If she was a courtesan, she was in good company: many female aristocrats had once been *demi-mondaines* and at least one in eight women had worked as prostitutes at some period in their lives. She was a good wife to Sir William, a faithful mistress to Nelson and her relationship with Horatia was only spoilt by the pressure of debt and illness. She cannot be held responsible for breaking Nelson's marriage; for he had long fallen out of love with his unhappy wife and resented her inability to have children. Nor was Emma a distraction from his duty. His pursuit of glory was in part motivated by his desire to win money and fame for his daughter and 'wife in the face of heaven'.

This is a story about ambition and heartbreak, beauty and pain. My aim has been to shake off the old myths about Emma, and find out the truth, good and bad, by using the hundreds of documents, letters, reports and diaries, untouched over the years. While writing, I discovered that everybody knew about Nelson and his battles, but not so many about Emma, and those who did were often dubious about her. A pensioner at a family wedding told me she must have been a 'fantastic fuck'. Another guest said, 'That's what happens to you when you don't live a good life.' It is still Nelson's mistress – not Nelson – who is judged and must suffer for the affair.

Although Emma Hamilton has been disparaged, I have been startled by the hundreds of people who claim to be her descendants. Most were people I simply happened to meet, such as an estate agent or a friend of a friend, others contacted me directly after seeing me speak on television programmes. Surfing on the internet revealed many more and it seems that thousands of people around the world believe themselves to be descended from Nelson and Emma, based on perceived physical resemblances and family myth. Nearly everyone whose male ancestor passed within a mile of Emma (and some female relations too) claims he had a torrid affair with her, and often that she bore his child. Nelson and Emma are probably the most cited ancestors in British history. Historians may condemn the pair, but enchanted by the glory and tragedy of their lives, scores of us wish to be related to them.

Even more of us wish we owned some of their belongings. I have been shown hundreds of items that dealers and owners assert originally belonged to her, including shoes, dresses, musical instruments, and furniture, and nude pictures that families say she gave to Nelson's captains. Very few of these items date from the early 1800s – and most were made later in the nineteenth century. Almost all of her belongings were sold and those she gave away were lost or even destroyed, for the belongings of most of her friends were also destroyed after their death. The Prince of Wales did keep his mementoes of Emma, in a bizarre, secret collection. After George IV died, his executor, the Duke of Wellington, was shocked to find a stash of 'a prodigious quantity of hair – women's hair – of all colours and lengths, *gages d'amour*', or love tokens.[436] Stuffy Wellington reeled at the 'Volumes of love letters . . . trinkets of all sorts, quantities of women's gloves', even pocket handkerchiefs which he had used to wrap up old 'faded nosegays . . . in short, such a collection of trash as he had never seen before'. He decided the best thing would be to burn the whole lot.[437] Locks of Emma's chestnut hair, her gloves and letters, were tied up in these bundles, along with those of other society beauties such as Maria Fitzherbert, Mary Robinson, Elizabeth Billington, Lady Jersey, and Lady Hertford.

Emma's life was intense, dazzling, and soon over. She fought for her fame by constantly recreating herself and directing her image. Emma refused to be beaten but she was destroyed by her mix of overconfidence and a wish to please, desires that made her vulnerable in a society that had no place for a woman like her. She was always tormented by what she had achieved and what she had sacrificed to achieve her aims. Despite all her charisma, intelligence and charm, Emma had to rely on what she could win from men – and when men would not give it her, she had nothing. Glamorous, open-minded, optimistic and showy but also undisciplined, unaccustomed to compromise and overreaching, she epitomised the high Georgian age. At the same time, her life showed its limitations, as she struggled and failed to forge her own destiny, ignore social prejudice, and survive without a protector. Today when women have more opportunities than ever before to realise their ambitions, but still feel terrible compunction about doing so, her story has even more resonance than it ever had. A woman who both embodied and transcended her age, she was, truly, England's mistress.

Source Notes

This book is based on the original documents of letters by Emma, as well as letters, diaries and reports by those who knew her. These are contained in archives across the world: in the Houghton Library, Harvard University; the Beinecke Library, Yale University; Huntington Library, San Marino, California; the British Library in London; the National Maritime Museum in Greenwich; the Nelson Museum in Monmouth; the Bodleian Library, Oxford and the Fitzwilliam Library, Cambridge, as well as records offices across the country, and also in private collections.

If a letter has been cited but not footnoted, this is because it is in a private collection, seen by the very kind courtesy of the owner, or printed in *The Collection of Letters and Historical Documents formed by Alfred Morrison, the Hamilton and Nelson Papers*, edited by Alfred Morrison, two volumes (privately printed, 1893–4) or the *Dispatches and Letters of Vice-Admiral Lord Nelson* by Sir Nicolas Harris Nicolas, seven volumes (London, 1844–46), and the originals have been lost.

Abbreviations are:

BL: British Library Manuscript Room. Hundreds of Emma documents are contained in the sixteen Egerton volumes of correspondence between Maria Carolina and Emma, as well as the Egerton collection of Nelson's letters to Emma, and there are hundreds more, chiefly in the ninety bound volumes of Additional MSS, 34902–34992, between Nelson and his wife, and within the Nelson family, and also the Additional MS collection of William Hamilton correspondence, as well as the papers of St Vincent and the Althorp MS papers of the Spencer family.

NMM: National Maritime Museum Greenwich. More than 2,000 Emma documents are contained in the Nelson-Ward (NWD), Bridport (BRP),

Trafalgar (TRA), Davison (DAV), Keith (KEI), Girdlestone (GIR), and Matcham (MAM) collections, as well as in the Letterbooks (LBK).

PRO: Public Record Office, Kew. The letters from William Hamilton to the Foreign Office, and also to Charles Greville, contained in the 13 volumes, FO 70, 1-13, covering the period 1780 to 1800, have proved an invaluable source, along with the prison record books, PRIS.

Monmouth: The Nelson Museum, Monmouth, have more than eight hundred letters and documents, most unpublished and many throwing much new light on Emma.

Bodleian: Bodleian Library, Oxford.

Fitzwilliam: Fitzwilliam Library, Cambridge.

Wellcome, Wellcome Library for the History of Science and Medicine, London.

Beinecke: Beinecke Rare Book and Manuscript Library, Yale University.

Houghton: Rare Book and Manuscript Library, Harvard University.

Huntington, Huntington Library, San Marino, California.

Notes

1. William Mortimer, *History of the Hundred of Wirral* (Manchester, 1972), p. 65.
2. Nathaniel Spencer, *The Complete English Traveller* (London, 1771), p. 412.
3. National Library of Wales, PA 1605–1630. See also Flintshire Record Office, D/HA/ 312, 599, 601.
4. Dr Thomas was buried in 1805 at the age of seventy-six.
5. Samuel and Sarah Adams, *The Complete Servant* (London, 1825), p. 258.
6. It is said that the family used her as a model for their drawings – although there is no evidence for this – and if so, perhaps she had become too friendly with her new employers.
7. *Carlton House Magazine*, April 1793.
8. At this date, London was just bigger than the other world cities: Peking and Edo, modern-day Tokyo.
9. Sophie Von La Roche, 'Diary for 1786', in *Sophie in London*, ed. Clare Williams (London, 1933), p. 141.
10. Johann Wilhelm von Archenholz, *A Picture of England* (London, 1791), 2 vols, I, 191.
11. Henry Fielding, *An Enquiry into the Causes of the Late Increase of Robbers* (London, 1751), p. 10.
12. Pierre Grosley, *A Tour to London* (London, 1772), 2 vols, I, 75.
13. Anon, *A Present for Servants from their Ministers, Masters or other Friends*, the eighth edition (London, 1768), p. 17.
14. As Emma's later portraits by Romney show exquisitely pale hands, one has to question how hard she scrubbed the hearths and saucepans at Chatham Place.
15. *Town and Country Magazine*, April 1777, p. 186.

16. Fielding, *Late Increase of Robbers*, p. 76.
17. Anon, *Authentic Memoirs of the Green Room* (London, 1801), pp. 184–5.
18. Anon, *The Secret History of the Green Room* (London, 1793), p. 185.
19. See Philip H. Highfill, *A Biographical Dictionary of Actors, Actresses . . . in London, 1660–1800* (Carbondale and Edwardsville, 1973), pp. 65–6.
20. Grosley, *Tour to London*, I, 49.
21. Fielding, *Late Increase of Robbers*, p. 6.
22. John B. Morritt, *Letters and Journeys, 1794–96, A Grand Tour*, ed. G.E. Marindin (London, 1985), p. 215.
23. Melesina Trench, 'The Recollections of Melesina Trench', Hampshire Record Office, 23 m/93 2/1.
24. Elizabeth Steele, *Memoirs of Mrs Sophia Baddeley* (London, 1787), 6 vols, II, 114.
25. See *The London Stage 1660–1800*, ed. William van Lennep, Emmet L. Avery, A.H. Scouten, G.W. Stone Jr and C.B. Hogan, 12 vols (Carbondale, Illinois, 1965–1979), V, 104.
26. *Secret History of the Green Room*, p. 155.
27. *Secret History of the Green Room*, p. 69.
28. Grosley, *Tour to London*, I, 160.
29. Henry Angelo, *Reminiscences of Henry Angelo* (London, 1828), 2 vols, II, 21.
30. Sir John Fielding, *A Plan for a Preservatory and Reformatory for the Benefit of Deserted Girls* (London, 1758), p. 10.
31. One of Sir William's colleagues, James Bland Burges, declared Emma 'set out as a common prostitute in Hedge Lane', before being 'engaged by the Committee of the Royal Academy to exhibit herself naked as a model for the young Designers'. James Bland Burges, 1791, Fitzwilliam Museum, Percival Bequest MSS.
32. William Hickey, *Memoirs* (1809), ed. Roger Hudson (London, 1995), p. 276; James Northcote, *Memoirs of Sir Joshua Reynolds* (London, 1813), p. 280; *World*, September 1781.
33. Joseph Farington, *The Farington Diaries*, ed. Kathryn Cave, Kenneth Garlick and Angus McIntyre (New Haven, 1978–84), 16 vols, XIII, 247.
34. See *Sir Joshua Reynolds: A Complete Catalogue of his Paintings*, ed. David Mannings (New Haven and London, 2000), p. 556.
35. Nicholas Penny, ed., *Joshua Reynolds* (London, 1986), p. 295.
36. Thomas Rowlandson implied she modelled for the Academy in his caricature, *Lady H-'s Attitudes*.
37. Northcote, *Memoirs*, p. 103.
38. Emma to Romney, 20 December 1791, Houghton Library, MS Eng 156.

39. See Elisabeth Vigée le Brun, *Memoirs*, trans. Siân Evans (London, 1989), p. 101.

40. *Town and Country Magazine*, 1778, p. 177. The newspapers also made sly hints on her work in the 'Nunnery' and many of those who knew Emma commented on her experiences at Kelly's. Nelson's contemporaries suggested she had been employed by a St James madam.

41. Archenholz, *A Picture of England*, I, 179.

42. *The Whore's Rhetorick* (1690), p. 70.

43. Archenholz, *A Picture of England*, I, 192.

44. The way in which both Charles Greville and Sir Harry refer to her stay at Uppark makes it clear that she was a member of the party in the house.

45. *Morning Post*, 4 October 1780.

46. Uppark Papers 228, West Sussex Record Office.

47. John George Sutherland Campbell, 9th Duke of Argyll, ed., *Intimate Society Letters of the Eighteenth Century* (London, 1910), 2 vols, II, 415.

48. In 1784–5, Sir Harry entertained the Prince to a raucous extended visit.

49. Uppark Papers, 227.

50. Uppark Papers, 227.

51. See Uppark Account Books, 227, unpaginated 1780–1781.

52. *Morning Post*, 8 April 1780.

53. Emma to Charles Greville, January 1782, NMM, LBK/6.

54. Greville to Emma, 10 January 1782, NMM LBK/6.

55. Westminster, Marylebone and Hawarden parish registers.

56. It has been argued that the Cadogans owned Broad Lane Hall but there is no possibility that the owners of Broad Lane Hall before Sir John were the Cadogans.

57. Greville to Emma, 10 January 1782, NMM LBK/6.

58. Emma to Greville, 3 July 1784, NMM LBK/6.

59. Emma to Greville, 12 June 1784, NMM LBK/6.

60. *European Magazine*, July 1782, p. 16.

61. *European Magazine*, May 1784, p. 400.

62. Ibid.

63. In letters from Naples, Emma asked Greville to send on her dresses and hats.

64. Sir William later purchased *Sensibility* from Greville.

65. William Hayley to Emma, 17 May 1804, Beinecke Library, Osborn MSS File 16927.

66. William Hayley to Emma, 7 June 1806, Beinecke Library, Osborn MSS File 16927.

67. Romney's Victorian descendants claimed he had visited her in Edgware Row, even though it would have been impossible for him to transport all his materials and props to Paddington.
68. See Francis Cotes's *Portrait of Lady Hare, c.* 1760.
69. *European Magazine*, July 1785, p. 24.
70. Although ostensibly based on a more simple style, the dress, like the pastel suit for men, served the purpose of elite fashion: a long white dress in flimsy material was impractical and showed off the wearer as someone who did not have to work and could travel by carriage.
71. Von la Roche, *Diary*, ed. Williams, p. 82.
72. His salary as Envoy Plenipotentiary (confirmed 1766) was handsome, at £3,000 a year, but not enough to keep up with the Court.
73. Charles Greville, 'Memorandum', BL Add MSS 42071, f. 40.
74. John Hervey, *Memoirs of the Reign of George III* (London, 1884), 3 vols, II, 475.
75. *European Magazine*, April 1784.
76. Mary Hamilton, *Letters and Diaries of Mary Hamilton*, ed. Elizabeth and Florence Anson (London, 1925), pp. 174–5.
77. Charles Burney, *A General History of Music* (London, 1776–89), 4 vols, IV, 45.
78. *Chester Chronicle*, 1782.
79. Emma to Greville, 22 June, NMM LBK/6.
80. Emma to Greville, 27 June, NMM LBK/6.
81. *Morning Post*, 5 July 1777.
82. Elizabeth, Lady Craven, *The Beautiful Lady Craven: The Original Memoirs of Elizabeth, Baroness Craven*, ed. A.M. Broadley and L. Melville (London, 1914), 2 vols, II, 150.
83. William Hamilton to Greville, February 1785, BL Add MSS 42071, f. 2. (Sir William confessed his feelings to Greville some time after the proposal.)
84. *European Magazine*, July 1785, p. 251.
85. Sir William to Greville, 1 June 1785, BL Add MSS 42071, f. 4v.
86. Anne Miller, *Letters from Italy* (London, 1776), pp. 209–10.
87. Hester Thrale, *Observations and Reflections made in the Course of a Journey through France, Italy and Germany* (London, 1789), p. 223.
88. Since Emma had given her letters to the servant to seal and put in the postbag, Sir William would have opened them and read them.
89. Hamilton, *Letters and Diaries*, ed. Anson, p. 305.
90. Thomas Martyn, *A Gentleman's Guide to his Tour Through Italy* (London, 1787), p. 264.

91. Thrale, *Observations*, p. 231.
92. Martyn, *Gentleman's Guide*, p. 286.
93. William Beckford, *Italy, with Sketches of Spain and Portugal* (London, 1834), p. 200.
94. Sir William to Marquis of Camarthen, 20 November 1786, PRO FO 70/3, 306.
95. Thomas Watkins, *Travels through Swisserland, Italy, Sicily* (London, 1792), 2 vols, I, 425.
96. Miller, *Letters from Italy*, pp. 248–9.
97. James Boswell, *Boswell on the Grand Tour*, ed. F.A. Pottle (London, 1953), 2 vols, I, 111.
98. Stendhal (Marie Henri Beyle), *Rome, Naples and Florence*, ed. Henri Martineau (Paris, 1927), p. 350.
99. Sir William to Camarthen, April 11 1786, PRO FO 70/3, 267.
100. Watkins, *Travels*, p. 50.
101. Miller, *Letters*, p. 60.
102. Thrale, *Observations*, p. 260.
103. *Boswell on the Grand Tour*, ed. Pottle, pp. 62, 111. Even those who relished visiting the churches, buildings and museums felt, like Goethe, uncomfortable admiring Catholic art.
104. Charles Mercier Dupaty, *Travels through Italy* (London, 1789), p. 303.
105. Johann Wolfgang von Goethe, *Italian Journey*, ed. W.H. Auden and Elizabeth Mayer (Harmondsworth, 1970), p. 216.
106. James Edward Smith, *A Sketch of a Tour on the Continent in the years 1786 and 1787* (London, 1793), 3 vols, II, 91–2.
107. Sir William to Camarthen, 20 November 1786, FO 70/3, 305.
108. Sir William to Camarthen, 2 January 1787, FO 70/3, 322.
109. Miller, *Letters*, p. 383.
110. Dupaty, *Travels*, p. 337.
111. Sir William to Camarthen, 25 July 1786, FO 70/3, 290.
112. Sir William to Banks, Autumn 1786, BL Add MSS 34049, f. 33.
113. Emma to Sir William, 26 December 1787, Houghton, MS Eng 195.5, 55.
114. Emma to Sir William, 8 January 1787, Houghton, MS Eng 196.5, 56.
115. Sir William to Camarthen, 20 November 1786, FO 70/3, 305.
116. Goethe, *Italian Journey*, ed. Auden and Mayer, p. 205, Thrale, *Observations*, pp. 263–4, Watkins, *Travels*, p. 422, Smith, *Sketch of a Tour*, pp. 127–8.
117. Sir William to Camarthen, 20 June 1786, FO 70/3, 281.
118. Sir William to Camarthen, 17 November 1786, FO 70/3, 203.
119. Sir William to Greville, BL Add MSS 34048, ff. 2–3.

120. Dr Alexander Drummond to Catherine Hamilton, 19 April 1791, BL Add MSS 40714 f. 193.

121. Vigée le Brun, *Memoirs*, ed. Evans, p. 106.

122. Watkins, *Travels*, pp. 401–2. Samuel Sharp, *Letters from Italy* (London, 1767), p. 78; Martyn, *Gentleman's Guide*, p. 282.

123. Friedrich Stolberg, *Travels through Germany, Switzerland, Italy and Sicily* (London, 1796), pp. 124–5.

124. Martyn, *Gentleman's Guide*, p. 300.

125. *Boswell on the Grand Tour*, ed. Pottle, p. 58.

126. Miller, *Letters*, p. 222.

127. Goethe, *Italian Journey*, ed. Auden and Mayer, p. 208.

128. *Memoirs of the Comtesse de Boigne*, trans. Sylvia de Morsier-Kotthaus (London, 1956), p. 65.

129. Sir William never declared he tutored Emma in the Attitudes, although he always claimed the credit for her improved singing voice and polished manners.

130. Smith, *Sketch of a Tour*, pp. 119–23.

131. Carlo Gastone, *Opere del Cavaliere Carlo Gastone*, ed. and trans. F. Machetti (1819), pp. 247–8.

132. Joseph Thomas d'Espinchal, *Journal d'Emigration*, ed. Ernest D'Hauterie (Paris, 1912), pp. 88–9.

133. Sir William to Camarthen, 19 May 1789, FO 70/4, 122.

134. Sir William to Joseph Banks, 20 October 1789, BL Add MSS 34048, f. 58.

135. Sir William to Camarthen, 7 August 1789, FO 70/4, 144.

136. Sir William to Camarthen, 27 October 1789, FO 70/4, 158, 27.

137. Sir William to Banks, 6 April 1790, BL Add MSS 34048, ff. 61–2.

138. Catherine Hamilton had refused to receive women of ill repute, even after they had married into the aristocracy.

139. Sir William to Banks, 6 April 1790, BL Add MSS 34048, f. 61.

140. *Town and Country Magazine*, September 1790, p. 483.

141. Hamilton, *Letters and Diaries*, ed. Anson, p. 308.

142. *European Magazine*, 29 July 1791. Emma made an expensive painting: he later had to pay £300 for both canvases.

143. Sir Thomas Lawrence to Daniel Lysons, *The Life and Correspondence of Sir Thomas Lawrence*, ed. D.E. Williams (London, 1831), 2 vols I, 103; *Sir Thomas Lawrence's Letter Bag*, ed. G.S. Layard, (London, 1906), p. 29.

144. Hamilton, *Letters and Diaries*, ed. Anson, p. 316.

145. Hamilton, *Letters and Diaries*, ed. Anson, p. 309.

146. Sir William to the Archbishop of Canterbury, 22 August 1791, BL Add MSS 46491, ff. 129–30.

147. William Beckford to Sir William, 1791, Bodleian, MS Beckford, c. 31, f. 120.
148. Elizabeth Foster, 'Journal' in *Dearest Bess: The Life and Times of Lady Elizabeth Foster*, ed. Dorothy Stuart (London, 1955), p. 59.
149. Horace Walpole, *Correspondence*, ed. W.S. Lewis (New Haven, 1955–80), 42 vols, XI, 340.
150. Sir William to the Countess of Spencer, 17 August 1795. BL Althorp Collection. The Countess drafted a stern reply, still in the Althorp Collection, but eventually sent only an understanding note.
151. Dickenson to Mary, 29 August 1791, in Mary Hamilton, *Letters and Diaries*, ed. Anson, p. 312.
152. James Bland Burges, 1791, Fitzwilliam Museum, Percival Bequest, MSS.
153. *Gentleman's Magazine*, September 1791, p. 872.
154. *New Lady's Magazine*, September 1791.
155. *The Times*, 14 September 1791.
156. Emma to Mary Dickenson, in Mary Hamilton, *Letters and Diaries*, ed. Anson, p. 312.
157. John Romney, *Memoirs of the Life and Works of George Romney* (London, 1830), p. 218.
158. Sir William to Camarthen, 5 November 1791, FO 70/4, 48.
159. Letters of Lord Palmerston, in *Portrait of a Whig Peer*, ed. Brian Connell (London, 1957), p. 250.
160. See Emma's description of her meeting with Marie Antoinette, Houghton MS Eng 196.5, 72.
161. Sir William to Camarthen, 5 November 1791, FO 70/4, 48.
162. Lord James Wright to Earl of Ailesbury (who he hoped would pass on the information to Lord Grenville), 29 January 1792, Wiltshire and Swindon Record Office, 9/35/278.
163. Ibid.
164. Sir William to Banks, March 1792, BL Add MSS 34048, f. 66.
165. Hamilton, *Letters and Diaries*, ed. Anson, p. 320.
166. Emma to Romney, 20 December 1791, Houghton MS Eng 156.
167. Sir William to Camarthen, 20 November 1786, FO 70/3, 306.
168. As a scandalous account of the Court later claimed, 'She [the Queen] machinated hard to push Hamilton out of the King's favour, but she failed, conquered by the love of hunting that kept the two men firmly bonded' (Giuseppe Gorani, *Mémoires Sécrets et critiques des cours de gouvernmens et des moeurs des principaux états d'Italie* (Paris, 1793), 2 vols, I, 99).
169. Sir William to Camarthen, 29 May 1792, FO 70/4, 101, 22 September 1792 and 11 December 1792, FO 70/4, 136 and 155.

170. Emma to the Prince of Wales, [n. d.], Houghton Joseph Husband Collection, letter 72.
171. *Memoirs of the Comtesse de Boigne*, trans. Morsier-Kotthaus, p. 66.
172. Even demure Catherine Hamilton had needed £400 worth of diamonds for one attendance. See BL Egerton MSS, 2634, f. 409.
173. *Lady's Magazine*, January 1792, p. 330.
174. *Lady's Magazine*, October 1792, p. 592.
175. *The Times*, 3 May 1793.
176. Brand to Ailesbury, 20 November 1792, Wiltshire and Swindon Record Office, 1300/3846.
177. Emma to Countess of Plymouth, n.d., Warwickshire Record Office, CR 1998/SS/5/7.
178. Lady Spencer to Sir William, 6 November 1794, BL Althorp Papers, FIII.
179. Letters of Lady Palmerston, in *Portrait of a Whig Peer*, ed. Connell, pp. 276–7, 208–10.
180. Morritt, *Letters and Journeys*, ed. Merindin, p. 215.
181. Maria Carolina to Emma, BL Egerton MSS 1615.
182. The Sardinian man-of-war was essentially a false alarm and Nelson soon returned to cruising the Mediterranean.
183. *Bon Ton Magazine*, June 1794.
184. When a young sailor told him that he had been sent to sea at the age of eleven, Nelson remarked wistfully, 'Much too young.'
185. Syphilis and gonorrhoea, two of the most common diseases of the time, usually produced severe insanity in the months before death, and any doctor who recorded madness as a cause of death (and Nisbet's did so) implied that the patient had suffered a venereal disease.
186. John Rymer, *A Description of the Island of Nevis* (London, 1775), p. 15.
187. Nelson decided Nisbet 'very rich' and rhapsodised that his 'income is immense'.
188. Sir William to Grenville, 12 November 1793, FO 70/6, 277.
189. Gorani, *Mémoires* I, 23, 35, 60.
190. Brand to Ailesbury, 20 November 1792, Wiltshire and Swindon Record Office, 1300/3846.
191. Eighteenth-century revolutions needed leaders from the upper or genteel classes, and the doctors, lawyers, bankers and intellectuals of Naples were disgruntled that the only way that any power could be gained was through accessing Ferdinand by hunting or attending balls, to which they were not invited because they were not noble.
192. *Lady's Magazine*, April 1796, p. 185.

193. Elizabeth, Lady Holland, *Journal of Lady Holland*, ed. the Earl of Ilchester (London, 1909), 2 vols, I, 243.

194. Morritt, *Letters and Journeys*, ed. Marindin, p. 215.

195. Sir William to Grenville, 4 February 1793, FO 70/6, 32.

196. Lady Palmerston, in *Portrait of a Whig Peer*, ed. Connell, p. 230.

197. Holland, *Journal*, ed. Ilchester, I, 242, 219.

198. *Ackerman's Repository of the Arts*, 3 (1809), 171.

199. *Lady's Magazine,* May 1796, p. 265.

200. *Lady's Magazine,* April 1795, p. 181.

201. *Lady's Magazine,* January 1796, March 1796,

202. Sir William to Grenville, 19 April 1793, FO 70/7, 80.

203. Sir William to Grenville, 1 September 1795, FO 70/8, 348.

204. St Vincent to Emma, 22 May 1798, BL Add MSS 31,166 f. 64.

205. Emma to Nelson, n.d., BL Add MSS 34989, f. 3.

206. Nelson to Emma, BL Egerton, 1614, f. 1.

207. *The Lady's Monthly Museum*, July 1799.

208. Emma to Nelson, 8 September 1798, BL Add MSS 34989, ff. 4–7.

209. Malta was desirable thanks to its strategic importance in the Mediterranean, south of Sicily and east of North Africa, for Napoleon wanted it in order to pursue his aim to invade Egypt.

210. Nelson to Sir William, Houghton Library MS Eng, 196.5, 14.

211. Sir William to Nelson, BL Add MSS 34907.

212. Cornelia Knight, *Autobiography*, ed. Sir J.W. Kaye (London, 1861), 2 vols, II, 55.

213. Fanny to Alexander Davison, 11 April 1799, NMM DAV/2/7.

214. Fanny to Josiah Nisbet, 1798, BL Add MSS 34988, f. 302.

215. See Fanny to Nelson, BL Add MSS 34908, ff. 601–2.

216. Emma to Nelson, 26 October 1798, BL Add MSS 34989.

217. Sir William to Grenville, January 1799, FO 70/12, 9.

218. Maria Carolina to Emma, 20 December 1798, BL Egerton 1615.

219. Maria Carolina to Emma, 21 December 1798, BL Egerton 1615.

220. Sir William to Grenville, 6 March 1799, FO 70/12, 130.

221. Sir William to Greville, 19 July 1799, FO 70/12, 224.

222. Pryse Lockhart Gordon, *Personal Memoirs* (London, 1830), 2 vols, I, 201, II, 385, 210–11.

223. Lord Bristol to Emma, 28 March 1799, Suffolk Record Office, 941/51/6.

224. Lockhart Gordon, *Personal Memoirs*, II, 211.

225. Lord Keith to Mary Elphinstone, 10 April 1799, NMM KEI.

226. Sir William to Grenville, 30 December 1799, FO 70/12, 370.

227. Sir William to Grenville, 14 July, FO 70/12, 194.

228. Maria Carolina to Emma, 25 June 1799, BL Egerton 1616.

229. Sir William to Grenville, 14 July 1799, FO 70/12, 203.

230. Sir William to Grenville, 16 August 1799, FO 70/12, 230.

231. See BL Egerton 1621.

232. Nelson to Mrs Cadogan, 17 July 1799, Monmouth Museum, E448.

233. 'List of Jacobins', 1799, NMM Girdlestone Papers/3a.

234. Maria Carolina to Emma, 2 July 1799, BL Egerton 1616. When Helen Maria Williams's pro-Republican *Sketches of the State of Manners and Opinions in the French Republic* was published in 1801, he and Emma bought a copy and annotated it with vigorous defences of their actions. BL Add MSS 34, 991.

235. Sir William to Grenville, 14 July 1799, FO 12, 200.

236. Sir William to Greville, 4 August 1799, FO 12, 230.

237. Sir William to Greville, 19 July 1799, FO 70/12, 224.

238. Nelson to Mrs William Suckling, 22 August 1799. See Christie's Catalogue for 'The Age of Nelson, Wellington and Napoleon', 18 October 2005, p. 36.

239. Sir William to Grenville, 6 March 1799, FO 70/12, 74.

240. Sir William to Greville, 4 August 1799, FO 70/12, 223.

241. Sir William to Greville, 22 September 1799, FO 70/12, 224–6.

242. Sir William to Greville, 4 August 1799, FO 70/12, 223.

243. Sir William to Greville, 22 September 1799, FO 70/12, 224–6.

244. Henry Aston Barker, 'Journal', National Library of Scotland, MSS 9647.

245. *The Times*, 14 November 1799.

246. *The Times*, 28 November 1799.

247. Mary Elgin, *The Letters of Mary, Countess Elgin*, ed. Nisbet Hamilton Grant (London, 1926), pp. 17, 22, 24.

248. M. Eyre Matcham, *The Nelsons of Burnham Thorpe* (London, 1911), p. 230.

249. The supplies sent by Emma finally arrived in April 1799.

250. Lord Dalkeith to Arthur Paget, 1799, Sir Augustus Paget, ed., *The Paget Papers* (London, 1896), 2 vols, I, 206.

251. *Grätzer Zeitung*, 18 August 1800.

252. *Der wiederaufgelebte Eipeldauer*, 1799, I (p. 47).

253. *Eipeldauer Briefe*, 1800.

254. Countess of Minto, ed., *Life and Letters of Sir Gilbert Elliot* (London, 1874), 3 vols, III, 147.

255. *Morning Post*, 15 September 1800.

256. *Magyar Hirmondo*, 10 September 1800.

257. Greville to Banks, 1 September 1800, Houghton MS Eng 196.5, 97.

258. Melesina Trench, 'Journal for 1800', Hampshire Record Office, 23

M93/2/1. In Cornelia Knight – whose acid comments on Nelson and Emma would later be much quoted – she immediately saw another poor woman hanging on to the shirttails of the rich, and hated her on sight for fawning over Emma and Nelson and everyone else (except her).

259. *Morning Herald*, 20 November 1800.
260. *Morning Post*, 21 November 1800.
261. *Morning Herald*, 20 November 1800.
262. *Lady's Magazine* June 1801, 226–7, and May 1800, 305.
263. Elizabeth and Florence Anson, eds., *Mary Hamilton* (London, 1957), pp. 325–7.
264. *Morning Herald*, 19 November 1800.
265. *Morning Post*, 21 November 1800.
266. *The Times*, 18 November 1800.
267. *Morning Herald*, 25 November 1800.
268. *Morning Herald*, 25 November 1800.
269. William Beckford to Emma, November 1800, Bodleian Beckford MSS, c 4, f. 55.
270. *Gentleman's Magazine*, April 1801, p. 258.
271. Beckford to Emma, 24 November 1800, Bodleian Beckford MSS, c 5, f. 58.
272. Louis Dutens to Emma, 20 December 1800, Wellcome Library MS 7362/6.
273. *Morning Post*, 1 December 1800.
274. See, for example, the *Morning Chronicle*, 20 January 1801.
275. Nelson to Fanny, cited by Fanny in a letter to Alexander Davison, 24 February 1801, NMM DAV/2/30.
276. Nelson to Emma, [n.d., February 1801], BL Egerton 1614, f. 22.
277. Nelson to Emma, 29 July 1801, Monmouth Museum, E95.
278. Nelson to Emma, 28 January 1801, Monmouth Museum, E91.
279. Nelson to Emma, 2 March 1801, Houghton Library MS Eng 196.5, 22.
280. She later put out a disclaimer declaring that she did not attend. See *Morning Herald*, 7 February 1801.
281. In 1787, Maria Fitzherbert had been *Dido Forsaken* and Gillray also recalls Joshua Reynolds's *The Death of Dido*, for which Emma probably modelled in her youth.
282. Nelson to Emma, 29 January 1801, BL Egerton 1614, f. 16.
283. Nelson to Emma, 20 February 1801, Huntington Library, HM 34044.
284. Foster, *Dearest Bess*, ed. Stuart, p. 166.
285. Nelson to Emma, 2 March 1801, Houghton MS Eng 196.5, 22.

286. Nelson to Emma, 1 March 1801. See Christie's Catalogue *The Age of Nelson, Wellington and Napoleon*, p. 40.

287. Fanny to Davison, 20 February 1801, NMM DAV/50.

288. Beckford to Emma, 24 November 1800, Beckford MSS, c. 4, f. 55.

289. Emma to Mrs Gibson, 11 February 1801, NMM/NWD/9594/9.

290. Abraham Gibbs to Sir William, 13 July 1802, BM Add MS, ff. 221–2.

291. *Morning Herald*, 12 April 1801.

292. Nelson to Emma, 1 March 1801, Houghton FMS Lowell, 10.

293. Nelson to Emma, 17 March 1801, NMM/MON/1/19.

294. Sir Nathaniel Wraxall, *Historical Memoirs of my own Time* (London, 1904), p. 141.

295. Nelson to Emma, 25 April 1801, BL Egerton 1614, f. 46.

296. Nelson to Emma, 8 June 1801, BL Egerton 1614, f. 63.

297. *The Times*, 4 August 1801.

298. Nelson to William Haslewood, 27 August 1801, Monmouth Museum, E96 and E98.

299. Nelson to Haslewood, 4 September 1801, Monmouth Museum, E100.

300. Nelson to Emma, 2 October 1801, Houghton, FMS Lowell 10.

301. The paintings probably included the Schmidt pastel, a Romney portrait and also Vigée le Brun's *Bacchante*.

302. See Houghton Library MS Eng 196.5, 25.

303. Thomas Bennett to Nelson, 30 August 1805, Monmouth Museum, E401.

304. Minto, ed., *Life and Letters*, III, 242.

305. Samuel Ragland to Sir William, 6 April 1802, BL Add MSS 41200, f. 214.

306. Sarah Nelson to Emma, October 1801, Beinecke Library, General MSS, 4: 12, ALS, 3.

307. Ibid

308. Sarah Nelson to Emma, 1801, Beinecke Library, General MSS, 4: 12, ALS 4 and 5.

309. Sarah Nelson to Charlotte Nelson, October 1802, NMM BRP/1.

310. Fanny to Nelson, 18 December 1801, Monmouth Museum, E979.

311. Emma to Mrs Gibson, 14 December 1801, NMM/NWD/9594/9.

312. 'Favourite Sultana', Monmouth Museum, E206.

313. Emma to Captain Bedford, 13 February 1802, BM Add MSS 34902, f. 6.

314. Merton Church Registers, April 1802.

315. *Morning Post*, 25 August 1802.

316. *Coventry Mercury*, 6 September 1802.

317. Emma to Kitty Matcham, 1802, NMM/MAM 23.

318. *Morning Post*, 31 August 1802.

319. *Lady's Magazine*, January 1803, p. 44.

320. *Morning Herald*, 14 September 1802.

321. Emma to Mrs Gibson, September 1802, NMM/NWD/9594/1 and 9.

322. Emma to Sir William, 1803, MS Eng 196.5, 64. Sir William wrote his reply on Emma's letter.

323. *Morning Herald*, 19 October 1802.

324. Merton Accounts, 4–11 October 1802, Houghton Library MS Eng 196.5, 27.

325. *Oracle and Daily Advertiser*, 18 March 1802.

326. Emma to Kitty Matcham, 23 December 1802, NMM/MAM 23.

327. Mary Eyre Matcham, *The Nelsons of Burnham Thorpe* (London, 1911), p. 204.

328. *Morning Post*, 31 January 1803.

329. Emma to John Parrott, 14 May 1803, private collection.

330. *Morning Herald*, 19 April 1803.

331. Mrs Gibson to Emma, 'Copy of Horatia's Baptism', 13 May 1803, NMM/NWD/9594/9.

332. Friday 13 May 1803, St Marylebone Church Registers, LMU.

333. See Sarah Nelson to Emma, Monmouth Museum, E538.

334. Vigée le Brun, *Memoirs*, ed. Evans, p. 154.

335. See Christie's Catalogue, *The Calvin Bullock Collection*, (London, 1985), p. 102.

336. *Morning Post*, 21 December 1803.

337. Nelson to Emma, 7 December 1803, NMM/MAM 28.

338. Nelson to Horatia, 13 January 1804, NMM/NWD/9594/16.

339. Nelson to Emma, 13 January 1804, NMM/NWD/9594/16.

340. Emma to Davison, October 1804, private collection, citation taken from Martyn Downer, *Nelson's Purse* (London, 2005), p. 276.

341. Nelson to Emma, 16 March 1805, NMM/TRA/13.

342. See Gillray's *Dilletante Theatricals* and also *The Pic-Nic Orchestra* and *Blowing up the Pic-Nics*.

343. John Corry, *A Satirical View of London* (London, 1801), pp. 71–4.

344. Nelson to Emma, 26 August 1803, NMM Phillips, 34. See also Nelson to Emma 5 October 1804, BL Egerton 1614, f. 108.

345. Elizabeth Stanhope to Dr Vaughan, Ramsgate, 17 August 1804, Leicester Record Office.

346. NMM BRP/9292/1.

347. Sarah Nelson to Emma, 11 September 1804, Beinecke, General MSS, 4: 12, ALS 8.

348. Sarah Nelson to Emma, 27 February 1805, Beinecke, General MSS, 4: 12, ALS 13.

349. Sarah Nelson to Emma, c. 1803, Beinecke, General MSS, 4: 12, ALS 14. Watch is in BRP/NMM/9292/4.

350. Sarah Nelson to Emma, 6 November 1804, Beinecke, General MSS, 4: 12, ALS 11.

351. Nelson to Emma, 9 September 1805, BL Egerton 1614, f. 106.

352. Nelson to Emma, 10 September 1805, Monmouth Museum, E400.

353. Nelson to Emma, 16 May 1805, NMM/TRA/9421.

354. Nelson to Haslewood, 16 May 1805, NMM/TRA/9421.

355. *Morning Post*, 21 August 1805 (report filed on 19 August).

356. William Marsden, Secretary to the Admiralty, had sent an express to Merton. See NMM/CRK 9/5.

357. Minto to Lady Minto, 26 August 1805, Minto, III, 363.

358. Emma to Mrs Lutwidge, 3 September 1805, NMM/PST 39.

359. Susanna Bolton to Emma, 1805, NMM/NWD/9594/7.

360. J.A. Andersen (pseud. for A. Feldborg), *A Dane's Excursions in Britain* (London, 1809), 2 vols, II, 94–5.

361. *Diary of Frances, Lady Shelley*, ed. Richard Edgcumbe (London, 1912), 2 vols, I, 79.

362. Emma to Mrs Lutwidge, 3 September 1805, NMM/PST/39.

363. Nelson to Emma, 4 April 1805, Monmouth Museum, E445.

364. Cecilia Connor to Charlotte Nelson, 4 October 1805, NMM/NWD/9594.

365. Emma to Nelson, 4 October 1805, NMM/NWD/9594.

366. Emma to Nelson, 8 October 1805, NMM/NWD/9594.

367. Nelson, 21 October 1805, NMM/JOD/14.

368. Nelson to Horatia, 19 October 1805, BL Add MSS 44584, f. 32.

369. Foster, *Dearest Bess*, ed. Stuart, pp. 127–8.

370. Emma to Davison, 1805, Sotheby's Catalogue of the Sale of the Alexander Davison Collection, 2004, p. 175.

371. Rev A.J. Scott to Mrs Cadogan, 27 October 1805, BL Egerton 3782, f. 1.

372. Eyre-Matcham, *The Nelsons of Burnham Thorpe*, p. 238.

373. *Bell's Court and Fashionable Magazine*, February and March 1806.

374. For more on novels about Nelson and Emma, before and after his death, see my 'Nelson and Women: Marketing, Representations and the Female Consumer', in *Admiral Lord Nelson, Context and Legacy*, ed. David Cannadine (Basingstoke, 2005), pp. 67–89.

375. William Beatty to Emma, Spring 1806, Wellcome MS 6242/1.

376. Earl Nelson to Captain J. Yule, c. 1806–7, Wellcome MS 7262/3.

377. William Beatty to Emma, 15 October 1806, Wellcome MS 6242/2.

378. *The Diaries and Correspondence of the Rt. Hon. George Rose*, ed. Leveson Vernon Harcourt (London, 1860), 2 vols, II, 255.

379. See PRO, TS 317–35.

380. 'Lord Nelson's Seat at Merton', *Lady's Magazine*, July 1806, p. 60.

381. *Dearest Bess*, ed. Stuart, p. 133.

382. In *Sense and Sensibility*, Austen's Dashwood leaves his substantial estate to his son by his first marriage, John, and asks him to care for his second wife and their three daughters. After some debate, John decides his father meant him to help them move their furniture and the women are left with nothing.

383. William Hayley to Emma, 31 January 1806, Beinecke Library Osborn MSS 16927.

384. Sarah Nelson to Emma, 1806, BL Add MSS 34992. When the coat was acquired for the nation nearly a hundred years later, the later Earl Nelson used this same letter to argue that the coat was his possession and should be attributed as his gift when on display. See Earl Nelson, 'Deposition', 1898, PRO Adm/69/221.

385. Emma to Sir William Scott, Autumn 1814, NMM/NWD/9595/34.

386. Sarah Nelson to Emma, c. 1806, transcripts in a private collection.

387. Susanna Bolton to Emma, December 1806, NMM/NWD/954/10–11.

388. Emma Hamilton, Draft of Last Will, 16 October 1806, Houghton MS Eng 196.5, f. 167.

389. *Lady's Magazine*, June 1806.

390. Reminiscences of a servant at Bradenham Hall cited in William M.R. Haggard, Letter (not sent) to *The Times*, 16 March 1801. Norfolk Record Office, HAG175 602.

391. Memoir of George Villiers Hyde, Fifth Earl of Clarendon, in Jeremy Jepson Ripley, 'Recollections of the late Thomas Ripley by his Son' (manuscript, c. 1814), Beinecke Library, Osborn D29.

392. Emma to Sarah Nelson, 27 August 1807, NMM/BRP/4.

393. William Beatty to Emma, 2 February 1808, Wellcome MS 6242/4.

394. Kitty Matcham to Emma, March 1808, NMM/NWD/9594/7/A.

395. See Horatia to Sir Harris Nicolas, 7 November 1844, NMM/NWD/9594/13–24.

396. See NMM/NWD/9594/13–24.

397. William Beckford to Emma, 1806, Bodleian Beckford MSS, c. 30, f. 99. c. 16, ff. 52–5, 58, and c. 31, ff. 92–100 (see also MS Beckford, c. 16, 40–1, 31, ff., 90, 107–26).

398. Eyre-Matcham, *The Nelsons of Burnham Thorpe*, p. 267.

399. William Beatty to Emma, 31 January 1809, Wellcome MS 6242/3.

400. Emma Hamilton, 'Draft of Last Will', 16 October 1806, Houghton MS Eng 196.5, f. 167.

401. Eyre-Matcham, *The Nelsons of Burnham Thorpe*, p. 267.

402. Emma to Greville, Houghton Library MS Eng, 196.5, 68.

403. David Wilkie's Journal, in *The Life of David Wilkie*, ed. Allan Cunningham (London, 1843), 3 vols, I, 220.

404. Germain Lavie to George Rose, 1 April 1809, Birmingham University Special Collections, MS21/2/70.

405. Nelson to Emma, 1 March 1801, Houghton MS Eng, 22.

406. Catalogues in Christie's archives.

407. Mrs Sarah Connor, 29 December 1808, NMM/NWD/9594. 1808.

408. One suggested that the English lady should follow her look, appearing one day 'as the Egyptian Cleopatra, then a Grecian Helen, next morning the Roman Cornelia; or if these styles be too august for her taste, there are sylphs, goddesses, nymphs of every region, in earth or in air, to lend her their wardrobe'. *The Mirror of the Graces, or the English Lady's Costume* (London, 1811), pp. 59–60.

409. On Sir Harry's possessions, see West Sussex Record Office, Uppark MSS 658–697.

410. Duke of Queensberry to Abraham Goldsmid, 9 July 1801, Coutts Archives, Doc 123.

411. Beckford to Emma, 18 October 1810, Bod MSS Beckford, 30, f. 99.

412. Beatty to Emma, 30 August 1811, Wellcome MS 6242/5.

413. Sarah Connor to Emma, 10 September 1810, NMM/NWD/9594/A.

414. Sarah Connor to Emma, 19 December 1810, Monmouth Museum, E543.

415. William Beckford to Emma, 18 October 1810, Bod MSS Beckford, 30, f. 99.

416. Countess of Banbury to sisters-in-law, 17 December 1811, Hampshire Record Office, 1M 44/138/6.

417. *The Collected Works of Thomas de Quincey*, ed. Grevel Lindop (London: Pickering and Chatto), 21 vols, II, 209.

418. See PRO AO/1/850/5, 3 September 1811.

419. NMM/NWD/9594/34.

420. *Letters and Diaries of George Rose*, I, 270.

421. Emma to Lord Sidmouth, 7 February 1813, Monmouth Museum, E242.

422. See King's Bench Record Book, 1813, PRO, PRIS 7/32.

423. Emma to Horatia, 18 April 1813, Houghton FMS Lowell, 10.

424. 'Sale of Household Furniture The Property of a Lady of Distinction', 8 July. NMM/NWD/9594/13–14.

425. King's Bench Record Book, 1813, PRO, PRIS 4/26/128.

426. William Beatty to Emma, 22 October 1811, 30 August 1811, Wellcome MS 6242/5, 8.

427. Emma to Earl Nelson, 29 April 1814, BL Add MSS 34992.

428. Emma to George Rose, 4 July 1814, *Letters and Diaries of George Rose*, II, 272–3.

429. Horatia to Sir Harris Nicolas, April 1846, NMM/NWD/ 9594/13–14.

430. Emma Hamilton, Draft, 14 September, BL Add MSS 34992.

431. Emma Hamilton, 7 October 1814, NMM/NWD/9594/34.

432. Horatia to Mr Paget, 8 November 1874, NMM/NWD/9594/2.

433. Horatia to Sir Harris Nicholas, April 1846, NMM/NWD/9594/ 13–14.

434. *Morning Post*, 26 January 1815.

435. Just after Nelson's column was erected in Trafalgar Square in 1845, William Thackeray published *Vanity Fair*, in which Becky Sharp, a second Emma, comes to a sticky end. Becky, a dancer and artist's model, flirts with the Prince of Wales, exploits her connections to aristocratic men, and distracts soldiers from their duty. She even performs Attitudes at parties, playing the role of Clytemnestra, armed with a dagger to stab Aegisthus, dressed in white as 'her tawny hair floats down her shoulder'. Thackeray's Lady Crawley raves to Becky on 'the most beautiful part of dear Lord Nelson's character', extolling how he 'went to the deuce for a woman. There *must* be good in a man who will do that.' But Lady Crawley is out of touch – the society she lives in reviles any man for going to the 'deuce' for a woman. Thackeray's world had no place for a strong-minded woman who refused to accept her place at the bottom of society.

436. Robert Fulke Greville, *The Greville Memoirs*, ed. Lytton Strachey and Roger Fulford (London, 1938), 7 vols, III, 160.

437. Harriet Arbuthnot, *Journal of Mrs Arbuthnot, 1820–1832*, ed. Francis Bamford and the Duke of Wellington (London, 1950), 2 vols, I, 65.

Bibliography

In the course of my four years of research, I have read over 3,000 books. To list all would be too cumbersome for the reader, and not help those readers looking for more about certain areas. Therefore, in the following pages, I list those I have found most useful and enjoyable. A fuller list of works used for the book will be posted on my website, www.kate-williams.com.

Newspapers and Magazines

Belle Assemblée
Dell's Court and Fashionable Magazine
Carlton House Magazine
Coventry Mercury
Covent Garden Journal
European Magazine
Gentleman's Magazine
Lady's Magazine
Oracle and Daily Advertiser
Morning Herald
The Morning Post and Gazeteer
Morning Post
Morning Chronicle
The Naval Chronicle
The Sun
The Times
Town and Country Magazine
The Carlton House Magazine
Bon Ton Magazine

Manuscript Sources

I have been fortunate enough to find many previously unused manuscripts, including eight hundred unpublished letters in the Monmouth archives, many in the over one hundred and fifty volumes in the British Library and volumes in the National Maritime Museum. I also found hundreds in collections in the United States, many in the Wellcome Library, and in archives across the country, and in private collections all over the world.

Beinecke Rare Book and Manuscript Library, Yale University
Osborn MSS, William Hayley to Emma Hamilton and Sarah Nelson to Emma. Emma Hamilton's songbooks
Bodleian Library
Beckford MSS
Hamilton Notebooks (MSS Eng. hist g. 3-16).
British Library
Egerton:
1617-1620, Queen of Naples to Lady Hamilton
1614-23, Hamilton-Nelson papers
2240-41, will and dying request
2634-37, Hamilton's Letters to Secretaries of State, 1764–1781
2641, Letters to Sir William Hamilton
Additional:
38361, Works at Milford
40714-15, Hamilton-Greville Papers
41197-41200, Sir Williams's Correspondence and Papers, 1761–1803
42069-71, Sir William's Correspondence and Papers, 1764–1803
59031, Sir William and from Lord Grenville, 1796–1802
31166, St Vincent Papers
34902-34992, Nelson Papers, in particular:
    34933-6, Official Correspondence 1781–1799
    34938-40, St Vincent to Nelson,
    34966-8, Private Journals, 1803–5
    34988, Nelson Family Correspondence
35194, Bridport Papers,
3782, John Scott to Lady Hamilton and Mrs Cadogan
34724, Miscellaneous letters
44584, ff. 31, 32, Nelson to Horatia
34989, ff 1, 3, 4, 12–32, et al, Nelson to Emma
34988, ff 123–376, Letters to Nelson from his wife
Althorp Papers

Foster MSS, Add MSS 4159, Journal of Lady Elizabeth Foster
Coutts Archives
Queensberry Papers
Flintshire Record Office
Hawarden Papers, John Glynne Papers
Hampshire Record Office
Melesina Trench to Richard Trench, 1808–1809, 23M93/28/63, 23M93/28/88,
23M93/28/105, Journal of Melesina Trench
Houghton Library, Harvard University
Joseph Husband Collection of Nelson and Hamilton Papers pf MS Eng 196.5
Lowell Collection, fmS Lowell 10
Huntington Library, San Merino, California
Nelson Papers
Hamilton-Greville Papers
Leicester Record Office
Elizabeth Stanhope to Dr Vaughan, Ramsgate, 17 August 1804, Leicester Record
Office.
London Metropolitan Archives
Foundling Hospital Records, Letter from Emma
National Library of Wales
John Glynne Papers, papers relating to Catherine Hamilton's Estate
National Library of Scotland
Henry Aston Barker, MSS 9647
National Maritime Museum, Greenwich
Bridport Papers (BRP)
Alexander Davison Collection (DAV)
Gilbert Elliot papers (ELL)
Girdlestone Papers (GIR)
William Hamilton Papers (HML)
John Jervis (JER)
Keith Papers (KEI)
Matcham Papers (MAM)
Nelson-Ward Papers (NWD)
Phillips-Croker Collection (PHL and CRK)
Trafalgar House Collection (TRA)
Xerox of Spiro Collection of Nelson Letters (XAGC)
Nelson Museum Monmouth
Nelson Manuscripts (E series)
Norfolk Record Office
Bradenham Papers

Parish Registers
Marylebone Parish Church
St Mary the Virgin, Merton
Registers of the Diocese of Chester
Registers of the Diocese of Ness
Hawarden Church

Public Record Office, London
Foreign Office 70/1-13, Sir William Hamilton to Secretaries of State, 1780–1800
State Papers, TS 317-335
Records of the King's Bench Prison
Earl Nelson Deposition

St Bartholomew's Hospital, London
Records and Register

University of Birmingham Special Collections
Germain Lavie to George Rose, 1 April 1809, MS21/2/70.

Victoria and Albert Museum, London
Romney Papers

Warwickshire Record Office
Plymouth Papers

Wellcome Library for the History of Medicine, London
Beatty and Hamilton Manuscripts

Westminster Archive, London
Broadley Collection

West Sussex Record Office
Uppark MSS and record books

Wiltshire and Swindon Record Office:
Ailesbury Papers

Secondary Works
This is a very select secondary bibliography. For a fuller list, see www.kate-williams.com.

Acton, Harold, *The Bourbons of Naples* (London: Methuen, 1957)
Adams, Samuel and Sarah, *The Complete Servant* (London: Knight and Lacey, 1825)
Angelo, Henry, *Reminiscences of Henry Angelo*, 2 vols (London: Kegan Paul, 1828)
Anson, Florence and Elizabeth, *Mary Hamilton, Afterwards Mrs John Dickenson, at Court and at Home, from Letters and Diaries, 1756–1816* (London: John Murray, 1925)
A Present for Servants from their Ministers, Masters or other Friends, eighth edition (London: John Rivington, 1768)

Bibliography

Archenholz, Johann Wilhelm von, *A Picture of England*, 2 vols, (London: Edward Jeffrey, 1791)

Aspinall, A. ed., *The Correspondence of George, Prince of Wales, 1770–1812*, 8 vols (London: Cassell, 1963–71)

Beatty, Sir William, *Authentic Narrative of the Death of Lord Nelson* (London: T. Cadell, 1807)

Beckford, William, *Italy with Sketches of Spain and Portugal* (London: R. Bentley, 1834)

Black, Jeremy, *The British Abroad: The Grand Tour in the Eighteenth Century* (Stroud: Sutton, 1999)

Boigne, Adelaide d'Osmond, Comtesse de, *Memoirs of the Comtesse de Boigne*, trans. Sylvia de Morsier-Kotthaus (London: Museum Press, 1956)

Boswell, James, *Boswell on the Grand Tour*, ed. F. A. Pottle, 2 vols (London: Heinemann, 1953)

Brewer, John, *The Pleasures of the Imagination: English Culture in the Eighteenth Century* (London: HarperCollins, 1997)

Campbell, John George Sutherland, 9th Duke of Argyll, ed. *Intimate Society Letters of the Eighteenth Century*, 2 vols (London: S. Paul, 1910)

Clarke, James Stanier, and M'Arthur, John, *The Life of Admiral Lord Nelson, from his Lordship's Manuscripts*, 3 vols (London: T. Cadell and W. Davies, 1809)

Coleman, Terry, *Nelson: the Man and the Legend* (London: Bloomsbury, 2001)

Coleridge, Ernest Hartley, *The Life of Thomas Coutts, Banker* (London: John Lane, 1920)

Colley, Linda, *Britons: Forging the Nation 1707–1837* (New Haven and London: Yale University Press, 1992)

Colvin, Sidney and Lionel Cust, *History of the Society of Dilettanti* (London: Macmillan, 1898)

Connel, Brian, *Portrait of a Whig Peer, Compiled from the Papers of the Second Viscount Palmerston, 1739–1802* (London: Andre Deutsch, 1957)

Constantine, David, *Fields of Fire: A Life of Sir William Hamilton* (London: Weidenfeld and Nicholson, 2001)

Constantine, David, 'Goethe and the Hamiltons', in *Oxford German Studies*, 26 (1997), pp. 101–31

Craven, Lady Elizabeth, *The Beautiful Lady Craven: The Original Memoirs of Elizabeth, Baroness Craven*, ed. A. M. Broadley and L. Melville, 2 vols (London: John Lane, 1914)

Downer, Martyn, *Nelson's Purse* (London: Bantam Press, 2004)

Dupaty, Charles Mercier, *Travels through Italy, in a series of letters written in 1785* (London: G. G. J. and J. Robinson, 1788)

393

Dutens, Louis, *Memoirs of a Traveller, now in Retirement*, 5 vols (London: Richard Philips, 1806)

Elgin, Mary, *The Letters of Mary Nisbet of Dirleton, Countess Elgin*, ed. Nisbet Hamilton Grant (London: John Murray, 1926)

d'Espinchal, Joseph Thomas, *Journal d'Emigration,* ed. Ernest D'Hauterive (Paris: Perrin, 1912)

Eyre Matcham, Mary, ed. *The Nelsons of Burnham Thorpe* (London: John Lane, 1911)

Farington, Joseph, *The Diary of Joseph Farington*, 16 vols, ed. Kathryn Cave, Kenneth Garlick, and Angus McIntyre, 16 vols (New Haven and London: Yale University Press, 1978–84).

Fielding, Henry, *An Enquiry into the Causes of the Late Increase of Robbers* (London: A. Millar, 1751)

Fielding, Sir John, *A Plan for a Preservatory and Reformatory for the Benefit of Deserted Girls and Penitent Prostitutes* (London: R. Francklin, 1758)

Foreman, Amanda, *Georgiana, Duchess of Devonshire* (London: Harper Collins, 1998)

Foster, Elizabeth, "Journal", in *Dearest Bess: The Life and Times of Lady Elizabeth Foster*, ed. Dorothy Stuart (London: Metheun, 1955)

Fothergill, Brian, *Sir William Hamilton, Envoy Extraordinary* (London: Faber and Faber, 1969)

Fraser, Antonia, *Marie Antoinette* (London: Weidenfeld and Nicholson, 2001)

Fraser, Flora, *Beloved Emma* (London: Weidenfeld and Nicholson, 1986)

Gastone, Carlo, *Opere del Cavaliere Carlo Gastone*, ed. and trans F Mochetti (Rome: Como, 1819)

George, M. Dorothy, *Catalogue of Personal and Political Satires Preserved in the Department of Prints and Drawings in the British Museum* (London: British Museum, 1935–54)

Gerin, Winifred, *Horatia Nelson* (Oxford: Clarendon Press, 1970)

Giglioli, Constance, *Naples in 1799* (London: John Murray, 1903)

Goadby, M, *Nocturnal Revels, or the History of King's Place*, 2 vols (London: M. Goadby, 1779)

Godfrey, Richard T., *James Gillray: The Art of Caricature* (London: Tate Publishing, 2001)

Goethe, Johann Wolfgang von, *Italian Journey*, ed. W. H. Auden and Elizabeth Mayer (Harmondsworth: Penguin, 1970)

Goodden, Angelica, *The Sweetness of Life: A Biography of Elisabeth Louise Vigée Le Brun* (London: Andre Deutsch, 1997)

Gorani, Giuseppe, *Mémoires Sécrets et critiques des cours de Gouvernements et des Moeurs des principaux États d'Italie*, 3 vols (Paris: printed for the author, 1793)

Bibliography

Gordon, Major Pryse Lockhart, *Personal Memoirs*, 2 vols (London: H.Colburn and R. Bentley, 1830)

Graham, James, *Address to the Public in General* (handbill)

—, *The General State of Medical and Chirugical Practice Exhibited* (London: Almon, 1779)

—, *Lecture on the Generation, Increase and Improvement of the Species* (London: printed for the author, 1780)

—, *A New and Curious Treatise* (London and Bath: Cruttwell, 1780)

—, *A Sketch, or Short Description of Dr Graham's Medical Apparatus* (London: Almon, 1780)

—, *A Discourse Delivered in Edinburgh* (Hull: Briggs, 1787)

—, *A Short Treatise on the All Cleansing Earth* (Newcastle: Hall, 1790)

Grosley, Pierre, *A Tour to London*, 2 vols (London: Lockyer Davis, 1772).

d'Hancarville, Baron Pierre François Hugues, *Collection of Etruscan, Greek and Roman Antiquities from the Cabinet of the Honble Wm. Hamilton His Britannick Majesty's Envoy Extraordinary at the Court of Naples, 4 vols* (Naples: printed for the author, 1766–67, actually 1767–76)

Hardwicke, Mollie, *Emma, Lady Hamilton* (London: Cassell, 1969)

Harrison, James, *Life of Horatio Lord Nelson*, 2 vols (London: C. Chappell, 1806)

Harris's List of Covent Garden Ladies

Haslewood, Joseph et al [Published anonymously], *The Secret History of the Green Room* (London: H. D. Symonds, 1793)

Hecht, J. Jean, *The Domestic Servant in Eighteenth Century England* (London: Routledge and Kegan Paul, 1980)

Herbert, Lord, *The Pembroke Papers*, 2 vols (London: Cape, 1939)

Hervey, Baron John, *Memoirs of the Reign of George III*, 3 vols (London: Bickers & Son, 1884)

Hickey, William, *Memoirs* (1809), ed. Roger Hudson (London: Folio Society, 1995)

Hicks, Carola, *Improper Pursuits: the Scandalous Life of Lady Di Beauclerk* (London: Macmillan, 2001)

Highfill, Philip H., *A Biographical Dictionary of Actors, Actresses... in London, 1660–1800*, 16 vols (Carbondale and Edwardsville: South Illinois University Press, 1973)

Hill, Bridget, *Servants: English Domestics in the Eighteenth Century* (Oxford: Clarendon Press, 1986)

Holland, Lady Elizabeth, *Journal of Elizabeth Lady Holland*, 2 vols, ed. Earl of Ilchester (London: Longmans, 1909)

Hölmstrom, Kirsten G, *Monodrama, Attitudes, Tableaux Vivants* (Stockholm: Almqvist & Wiksell, 1967)

Hooton Hall, Chester. Catalogue of the whole of the Magnificent Contents (London: W. Clowes & Sons, 1875)

Hubbard, Vincent K., *Swords, Ships and Sugar: History of Nevis to 1900* (Oregon: Premiere Editions, 1996)

Ingamells, John, *A Dictionary of British and Irish Travellers in Italy 1701–1800* (New Haven and London: Yale University Press, 1997)

Jaffé, Patricia, *Lady Hamilton in Relation to the Art of her Time, Exhibition Catalogue* (London: Iveagh Bequest, 1972)

Jenkins, Ian and Sloan, Kim, *Vases and Volcanoes: Sir William Hamilton and his Collection* (London: British Museum Press, 1996)

Knight, Carlo, *Hamilton a`Napoli* (Naples: Electa, 2003)

—, *Il Giardino Inglese di Caserta* (Naples: Eklund, 1986)

Kidson, Alex, *George Romney, 1734–1802* (London: National Portrait Gallery, 2002)

Knight, Cornelia, *Autobiography*, ed. Sir J. W. Kaye, 2 vols (London: W. H. Allen, 1861)

Knight, Richard Payne, *An Acccount of the Remains of the Worship of Priapus, Lately Existing at Isernia, in the Kingdom of Naples* (London: T. Spilsbury, 1786)

Lennep, William van, Emmet L. Avery, A. H. Scouten, G. W. Stone Jr. and C. B. Hogan, eds. *The London Stage 1660–1800*, 5 vols (Carbondale: Southern Illinois Press, 1960-1968)

Lewis, Judith Schneid, *In the Family Way: Child-bearing in the British Aristocracy, 1760–1860* (New Brunswick, NJ: Rutgers University Press, 1986)

The Letters of Lord Nelson to Lady Hamilton, 2 vols (London: T. Lovewell, 1814)

Lincoln, Margarette, ed. *Nelson and Napoléon* (London: Maritime Museum, 2005)

Mannings, David, ed.. *Sir Joshua Reynolds: A Complete Catalogue of his Paintings,* (New Haven and London: Yale University Press, 2000)

McLaren, Angus, *Reproductive Rituals: the perception of fertility in England from the sixteenth century to the nineteenth century* (London: Methuen, 1984)

Martyn, Thomas, *The Gentleman's Guide in his Tour Through Italy* (London: G. Kearsley, 1787)

Matcham, Mary Eyre, *The Nelsons of Burnham Thorpe* (London: John Lane, 1911)

Memoirs of Lady Hamilton (London: Henry Colburn, 1815)

Memoirs of Mrs Billington (London: J Ridgway, 1792)

Miller, Lady Anne, *Letters from Italy*, 3 vols (London: James Ridgway, 1776)

Minto, Countess of (ed.), *Life and Letters of Sir Gilbert Elliot*, 3 vols (London: Longmans, 1874)

Mortimer, William, *History of the Hundred of Wirral* (Manchester: E. J. Morton, 1972)

Morrison, Alfred, *The Hamilton and Nelson Papers*, 2 vols (London: privately printed, 1893–94)

Morritt, John B., *Letters and Journeys, 1794–96, A Grand Tour*, ed. G. E. Marindin (London: Century, 1985)

Naish, G. B., ed. *Nelson's Letters to His Wife* (London: Routledge and Kegan Paul, 1958)

Nicolas, Sir Nicholas Harris, *The Dispatches and Letters of Lord Nelson*, 7 vols (London: Henry Colburn, 1845–1846)

Northcote, James, *Memoirs of Sir Joshua Reynolds* (London: Henry Colburn, 1813)

Oman, Carola, *Nelson* (London: Hodder and Stoughton, 1947)

Penny, Nicholas, ed., *Reynolds* (London: Weidenfeld and Nicholson, 1986)

Pottle, Martin, ed. *Joshua Reynolds: The Creation of Celebrity* (London: Tate Publishing, 2005)

Pettigrew, T. J., *Memoirs of the Life of Nelson*, 2 vols (London: Boane, 1849)

Pocock, Tom, *Horatio Nelson* (London: Bodley Head, 1987)

Porter, Roy, *Quacks* (London: Tempus, 2000)

Prentice, Rina, *The Authentic Nelson* (London: National Maritime Museum, 2005)

Prentice, Rina, *A Celebration of the Sea* (London: HMSO, 1994)

Rehberg, Freidrich, *Drawings Faithfully Copied from Nature at Naples* (Rome: Niccola de Antonj, 1794)

Roach, J. et al [Published anonymously], *Authentic Memoirs of the Green Room* (London: J. Roach, 1796, reprinted 1801)

Roche, Sophie von la, "Diary for 1786", in *Sophie in London,* ed. Clare Williams (London: Cape, 1933)

Romney, John, *Memoirs of the Life and Works of George Romney* (London: Baldwin and Cradock, 1830)

Rose, George, *The Diaries and Correspondence of the Rt Hon George Rose*, ed. Rev. Leveson Vernon Harcourt, 2 vols (London: R. Bentley, 1860).

Russell, Jack, *Nelson and the Hamiltons* (London: Blond, 1969)

Rymer, John, *A Description of the Island of Nevis* (London: T. Evans, 1775)

Scott, A. J., *Recollections of the life of the Rev A. J. Scott* (London: Saunders and Otley, 1842)

Sharp, Samuel, *Letters from Italy in the Years 1765 and 1766* (London: R. Cave, 1767)

Sichel, Walter, *Emma Lady Hamilton* (London: Constable, 1905)

Smith, James Edward, *A Sketch of a Tour on the Continent in the years 1786 and 1787*, 3 vols (London: B. & J. White, 1793)

Southey, Robert, *The Life of Nelson*, 2 vols (London: John Murray, 1813)

Spencer, Nathaniel [pseud. for Robert Sanders], *The Complete English Traveller* (London: J. Cooke, 1771)

Steele, Elizabeth, *Memoirs of Mrs Sophia Baddeley*, 6 vols (London: printed for the author, 1787)

Stendhal (Marie Henri Beyle), *Rome, Naples and Florence*, ed. Henri Martineau (Paris: Le Divan, 1927)

Swinburne, Henry, *Travels in the Two Sicilies*, 4 vols (London: T. Cadell and P. Elmsly, 1783)

Testar, Carmel, *The French in Malta 1798–1800* (Valetta, Malta: Midsea Books, 1997)

Thrale, Hester, *Observations and Reflections made in the Course of a Journey through France, Italy and Germany* (London: A. Strahan and T. Cadell, 1789)

Tillyard, Stella, *Aristocrats* (London: Chatto and Windus, 1994)

Vickery, Amanda, *The Gentleman's Daughter: Women's Lives in Georgian England* (New Haven and London: Yale University Press, 1998)

Vigée-Lebrun, Elisabeth, *Memoirs*, translated by Siân Evans (Bloomington: Indiana University Press, 1989)

Watkins, Thomas, *Travels through Swisserland, Italy, Sicily*, 2 vols (London: T. Cadell, 1792)

White, Colin, *The Nelson Encyclopaedia* (London: Chatham, 2002)

White, Colin, ed., *Nelson: The New Letters* (Stroud: Sutton, 2005)

Wilkie, David, 'Journal', in *The Life of Sir David Wilkie*, 3 vols, ed. Allan Cunningham (London: John Murray, 1843)

Williams, Kate, "Nelson and Women: Marketing Representations and the Female Consumer", in *Admiral Lord Nelson: Context and Legacy*, ed. David Cannadine (Basingstoke: Macmillan, 2005), pp. 67–89.

Wraxall, Sir Nathaniel, *Historical Memoirs of my own Time* (London: 1904)

Index